A Century
and Beyond

John Purdue, 1802–1876

A Century

and Beyond

The History of Purdue University

by Robert W. Topping

Purdue University Press
West Lafayette, Indiana

Book and jacket design by Donald K. Carter

Photographs and other illustrations in this volume are from a variety of Purdue University sources unless otherwise noted.

The woodcut of early Purdue University campus used on endsheets is from University Libraries Special Collections.

Published in 1988
Printed in the United States of America

Library of Congress Cataloging-in-Publication Data

Topping, Robert W.
    A Century and Beyond: The History of Purdue University / by
Robert W. Topping.
        p.   cm.
    Bibliography: p.
    Includes index.
    ISBN 0-911198-95-4
    1. Purdue University—History. I. Title.
LD4673.T67 1988
378.722'95—dc19   88-5921
                                                             CIP

For all those who love Purdue:
>Who have taken from it freely
>Who have given to it freely
>Who have shared its glories
>Who have shared its sorrows
>Who have done its work
>Who have been challenged by it
>>or sheltered by it
>And who have learned the great lessons
>>to be found within it.

—R. W. T.

Contents

Foreword

This is the story of the prototype of the land-grant university: Purdue. In his wildest imaginings, Vermont Senator Justin Morrill could never have envisioned an institution which, throughout its history, has carried out so fully the mandate of his famous law:

> At least one college where the leading object shall be, without excluding other specific and classical studies, and including military tactics, to teach such branches of learning as are related to agriculture and mechanic arts . . . in order to promote the liberal and practical education of the industrial classes in several pursuits and professions of life.

It is the story of the long battle in the Indiana General Assembly concerning where to locate the new institution and of how John Purdue finally resolved the issue by gifts of money, land, and his own name. It recounts the halting, difficult early years. It relates how President Emerson E. White set the real direction of the university because of his deep commitment to the true "land-grant" philosophy, before he succumbed to the Sigma Chi fraternity—and his own stubborness. And it tells the tale of how Presidents Smart, Stone, Elliott, Hovde, and Hansen, each the right man for his time, developed Purdue to its current world-class status.

The last and only comprehensive history of the university was published in 1925, just after Elliott assumed office. Another volume is long overdue. In 1982, when I was acting president, I commissioned Bob Topping to undertake this work. After reading the manuscript, I am delighted that I did.

As he demonstrated in *The Hovde Years,* Bob is a most readable author. In this history, after chronicling the early years and John Purdue, he devotes a chapter to each president from White through Hansen to Steve Beering's appointment. While some may argue that such an approach attributes too much to the influence of the president, it is a logical manner in which to chart the history of the institution. And certainly at Purdue, presidents have exerted a very large influence over the course of the university's development.

Perhaps the most fascinating and heartening aspect of Purdue's history, well reflected in this volume, is that it is a university still on the way up. This becomes particularly clear in the last chapter and in Steve Beering's brief closing in which he enumerates Purdue's current status and his expectations for the remainder of the twentieth century.

Reading this history will, I believe, help to explain why Purdue has become such a fine university, undoubtedly the best of the "separated" land-grant institutions and certainly one of the ten finest state universities in the nation. Among the reasons for this distinction are:

- The single-mindedness of purpose of Purdue. It has clung tenaciously to its original mission, rather than attempting to be all things to all people
- Dedication to serving the people of the state and nation in all appropriate ways, rather than snobbishly serving only the most influential
- The tradition of the trustees—developed after an initial few years of meddling—of choosing a strong and able president and letting him operate the institution, rather than trying to do it themselves
- Another trustee tradition: to insist upon impeccable financial management and to select outstanding chief business officers to supply this management
- The wisdom of the Indiana General Assembly in giving its state universities a high degree of operational freedom and freedom from partisan political influences
- The policy of fiscal responsibility of the State of Indiana which, while it may have prevented occasional huge appropriation increases enjoyed in some states, has also prevented the huge reductions suffered in the same states
- The excellence of the greater Lafayette community as a location for a university
- The steadfast loyalty of alumni and supporters, and the competence and dedication of the faculty who make Purdue the excellent institution it is.

It is fascinating to speculate on where the university would be located and what its name would be had it not been for John Purdue. Would it have been Indiana Agricultural College at Battleground? Would it have been the Indiana A&M in Indianapolis? Or would it be part of Indiana University at Bloomington? What then of the Old Oaken Bucket?

But old John did exist, and through his grace and that of the General Assembly, everything turned out for the best. Thanks for the memories, Bob Topping. Hail Purdue!

John W. Hicks
Senior Vice President Emeritus
Purdue University

Preface

I well remember the day in 1978 that John Hicks ambled into my broom-closet-size office on the third floor of Hovde Hall to return a copy of an early draft of *The Hovde Years* manuscript. He complimented me on it—at a time in that project when I needed a compliment. John always seemed to know about such things.

We chatted briefly; he sat down, casually hung one leg over the arm of a chair, and proposed, "You ought to think about writing the history of the university. The last time it was done was in 1925, and we really need a new one. Think about it."

"John," I replied wearily, "would you mind if I thought about it after I get Fred Hovde's book finished?"

While John was acting president in 1982 and 1983, I began to think seriously about his idea for a new Purdue history and went to him to talk about it again. The upshot was that I wrote a proposal, he approved it, and that was how this project got started.

There is this about it: readers will find themselves well into the second chapter before they read much specifically about Purdue University. I believed it was necessary to define, insofar as possible, what higher education is all about—the beginnings even as early as medieval times. I think a history of Purdue would not have been complete without asking about the attitude of a pioneer populace toward education. What about the struggles, political and economic, in the Congress, in the Indiana General Assembly, in the board of trustees? What about the events that led eventually to the passage of Justin Morrill's land-grant act, especially at a time in history when the republic appeared about to tear itself to shreds? What about the political infighting in the Indiana legislature that failed to produce any support at all for agricultural education, much less anything as progressive as the federal act of 1862 establishing land-grant colleges, or more accurately, the concept thereof? What about the addled schemes that would have squandered land-grant receipts in Indiana on almost everything but the endowment of a college to teach the mechanic arts and agricultural sciences? What about such ideas as a state-funded professorship for each private college in Indiana, or a soldiers home?

The events that produced Purdue University were little more than a series of fights—several in Congress over the preposterous idea of land granting; as many as four in Indiana over where the new college would be located; several in Tippecanoe County among members of the first board of trustees as to the campus location; and finally—once the campus site was selected and purchased—countless arguments over siting the buildings.

Strangely, little if any fuss was raised about who was to be hired to run it, or about what was to be taught, or about who was to teach it.

All of these preliminaries are important to note because both the concept and the reality of a separate land-grant university in Indiana endured the obstacles, the fussing, the ineptness—a classic case of the phenomena of survival.

Several years ago, someone asked me whether there would be any "great surprises" in the book, a question I deftly parried with a casual, palms-up shrug. Later, as the work went on, it occurred to me that in the historical sense, the most surprising thing about Purdue is that it exists at all. It came within a hair's breadth of not even happening. It came within a whisker of becoming a part of Indiana University. It was a close shave.

After it was established in its own right, Purdue did not, could not, open its door for five years, and in that relatively short span in its history, it had two presidents. One was a hopeless dreamer, an Indiana University geology professor who was forced to quit before he arrived. The other was a capable but frail educator virtually hijacked by the Indiana governor from the superintendency of the Indianapolis public school system to get Purdue's doors open by the fall of 1874.

There was no headlong rush to enroll. Those who did were mostly kids from Lafayette and the surrounding countryside. Few were prepared for the academic rigor of college, so a preparatory academy was started—producing a situation where the president of the university found himself teaching spelling and arithmetic.

The forlorn little school's detractors were busy, of course, gleefully predicting that at most Purdue would last two, maybe three, years. By then, they believed, that little folly would dry up and blow away for lack of interest and be quickly forgotten. But that has always been the way of anti-intellectualism.

Even at the first commencement, the squabblings among the trustees surfaced in John Purdue's astonishing and candid address. It was not an encouraging start. Not in their most fanciful musings could the university's founders have envisioned the Purdue of today—without doubt one of the best state universities in the nation and one of the most respected institutions of its kind in the world. They could not begin to imagine its magnitude nor its impact on the state and nation. They would have been hard put, indeed, to remember a time when Purdue was not under the excruciating pain of public ridicule.

From that inauspicious start to this day is Purdue's triumph. It is a story of remarkable progress, certainly, but what makes that story fascinating is not so much the achievements as the achieving and the people who made things happen—of courage, and loyalty, and vision, and dreams, and determination, and uncanny resourcefulness. And human foibles. That explains in part why this volume attempts to trace the university's development by way of each of the nine presidents. Traditionally, the Purdue presidency has been a powerful force. With the power to appoint, the power to appropriate, and the support of the board of trustees, the president can in a real way control the destiny of the university.

And that is how it all happened, in my view.

In a large sense, this volume borrows from many others— the 1925 Purdue history written as a part of the fiftieth anniversary commemoration by Louis M. Sears and William M. Hepburn; *Edward C. Elliott, Educator,* by Frank K. Burrin; *David Ross, Modern Pioneer,* by Fred C. Kelly; *The Dean,* Robert B. Eckles's biography of A. A. Potter; *The Dean,* the biography of Stanley Coulter, by his brother John; *The Story of Purdue Engineering* by H. B. Knoll; *R. B. Stewart and Purdue University,* by Ruth Freehafer; and *The Hovde Years,* the biography of Frederick L. Hovde that I wrote. Of course, much other material was scrutinized: books, articles, brochures, collections, minutes, photos, reports, newspaper clippings, and so on. A selected list comprises the bibliography.

As I so quickly learned when I wrote Fred Hovde's biography in 1980, only the author's name goes under the title, but many others have had their hands in it. I must acknowledge some, with the wish that space could be found to mention all of those who have been interested, who have offered suggestions and information, who were supportive when at one point, for personal reasons, I was not sure I cared to go on with it. To those who helped in so many ways in the making of this book, thank you.

First, of course, I must note John Hicks, now retired, the man who, had he had the time, might well have written this book himself; he not only had the interest but also most of the knowledge. He made it possible for me to write this book and lent me his time, interest, and moral support. President Steven C. Beering also must be credited for following through with great interest in the project and making certain it was properly underwritten.

I dare say, I might not have gotten through the four years (on a part-time basis, I hasten to add) that this work took without the constant advice, support, and yes, push, of William J. Whalen, a good friend and boss. And my gratitude, too, to Verna Emery and Anita Ashendel, the editors on this project. They have a way with manuscripts that makes authors look better than they probably are.

I also appreciated the critical reading of the manuscript by Professor Oakah L. Jones of the Department of History.

Of inestimable help also was Tom Schmenk, director of facilities planning and construction, who made available much information about early physical facilities at the West Lafayette campus. Before his death in 1987, Frank Burrin, a longtime friend and Edward C. Elliott's biographer, was always helpful with advice and information, as was Charles H. Lawshe, especially on the regional campuses. Arthur G. Hansen, the only living ex-president of Purdue, and his lovely wife, Nancy, invited me to their home at Zionsville where we spent many pleasant fruitful hours talking about the Hansen years at Purdue. Nancy Weirich, Sally Cooke, and all of the gracious and helpful members of the Tippecanoe County Historical Association research staff generously gave of their time to find answers to a number of questions I posed, especially about John Purdue's days as a Lafayette merchant and civic leader.

The photographs in this book come from a great variety of sources—the files of the Office of Publications and University News Service; the Tippecanoe County Historical Association Archives; the Special Collections section of University Libraries; the J. C. Allen collection; and a collection of remarkable pictures of campus buildings taken by the late Wallace Gamble and given to the university after his death by his granddaughter, Mrs. Valeria Gamble Downey of Milwaukee, Wisconsin. The willing work of Julie Oesterle of the Office of Publications and University News Service staffs in helping to unscramble and make sense from a mind-boggling mass of pictures was absolutely essential. Her work in searching and recopying many of our finds was a marvelous help. Thanks also to Professor Leslie A. Geddes for his generosity in the search for photographs.

I cannot express fully my appreciation to Keith Dowden, the retired University Libraries director of Special Collections, and his successor, Helen Schroyer, for their assistance in pulling together much of the research material I consulted. And my special thanks— for myself and on behalf of the entire university—for the gift by Mrs. Robert F. Munro of the prodigious amount of material about John Purdue and the early years of Purdue written by her late father-in-law, Professor George W. Munro, who came as close to being a university "historian" as anyone. That material, by the way, is to go permanently to the University Libraries Special Collections.

Judy Clinton, executive director of University Relations at Indiana University-Purdue in Fort Wayne, was of great assistance on the history and important dates at that campus.

A special thanks to Roseanna Behringer, office secretary, and Doris Pearson, secretary of the Purdue University Board of Trustees, for their cheerful labors in checking old trustee records for me to answer what must have seemed an endless number of irrelevant questions.

Nor will I forget the generosity of James R. Mitchell, for providing me with a copy of his well-documented history of the Purdue Department of Education from whence he retired in 1966.

There were many others and I hope I have not forgotten anyone, though I probably have, and undoubtedly I will hear from them. Yet, there are two people who were absolutely essential to the completion of this project, Joyce Provo and Sharon Wiggins, compositors and my colleagues in the Office of Publications, who went beyond the call in "keyboarding" the Purdue history manuscript on the word processor and preparing it for computerized typesetting. Not once did either express—at least not in my presence—what certainly must have been their astonishment at one who has hinged an entire writing career of nearly forty years on the ability to type with only two, sometimes three, fingers, and at that not very well. They are convinced there is no way I will ever fully master the electric typewriter or any of the other electronic gadgets now used to transmit human thought via the printed word. They may be right.

Bob Topping

"Resolved: That in the judgement of this Board the legitimate and proper work of Purdue University, is to furnish instruction of the highest order *in those branches of science which pertain to any profession or industrial pursuit in life in preference to those branches pursued in the High School, Academy or College."*

Minutes of the Board of Trustees
Purdue University
Twenty-third meeting, December 1, 1870
Lahr House
Lafayette, Indiana

Introduction

The Setting

For an eon the American tribes belonged to the land—gently rolling, fertile land—interrupted only by the glacial caprice of a meandering stream they called Wah-ba-shik-a, meaning "water flowing over white stone." The name was corrupted to Ouabache by the French and to Wabash by the English. Along its banks and tributaries stood great forests of oak, poplar, locust, hickory and other hardwoods, spilling out over the valley ridges, then coming to an abrupt halt; yonder to the western horizons were the endless, riffling waves of the prairie's mixed grasses.

Here, Indians tended small plots of melons, corn, and pumpkins; they hunted their primeval haunts and fished the plentiful streams; they traded with their brothers. They knew how to live at peace and in harmony with themselves and the gifts of their surroundings.

But eventually it became the land of the whites who tore it from aboriginal grasp and domesticated it, cultivated it, and often defiled it. Until the whites intruded, the various tribes occupied this place later called, for the obvious reason, Indiana. A part of the land where Wah-ba-shik-a meandered southward from its general westward flowage ultimately became known as Tippecanoe, from Keth-tip-pe-ca-nunk, the name the Indians gave to a major tributary.

On a great plain that seemed to spread endlessly to the south and west, the Wea of the Miami nation lived in their villages. The Pottawatomie dwelled to the north along the Tippecanoe River. The Shawnee occupied a southern corner of what is now

1

Tippecanoe County; around what is today called Shawnee Mound, as many as sixteen thousand of that tribe lived at one time. The Kickapoo had a village about where today the Indiana Veterans Home sits atop a prominent bluff overlooking Wah-ba-shik-a. The Purdue University campus at West Lafayette covers what was part of the Kickapoo hunting grounds. The Winnebago lived northeast along the River Poucepichoux, or Wildcat Creek, in its scenic valley east and beyond, and down to its mouth where it empties into the Wabash.

On a day in 1717, a French ensign, Sieur de Ballestre, with four French soldiers and four French civil servants drew up canoes on the sandy west shore of the Wabash and, from under the giant cottonwoods that lined the bank, gazed out across the heavily populated Wea plain. He had been ordered to establish a trading post among the Wea and did so, ending a journey of several months' paddling and portaging from French Canada. Thus was established the first white settlement in Indiana. Three years later a Jesuit priest, Père Guimoneau, arrived to bring Christianity to the Indians—and help strengthen the lonely fur-trading outpost against British aggression. The site became Fort Ouiatenon, one of the most important and the strongest outposts of the French in the Midwest region—a military establishment against British claims. As a trading post, it was surrounded by Indian villages and altogether had a red and white population of several thousand. Eventually the fort fell into British hands as a part of the English booty won in the French and Indian War and thence was discarded when it fell into American hands following the American Revolution. Abandoned, the fort became the launching place for Indian attacks on white settlers, and General Washington sent a force in the late eighteenth century with orders to destroy the fort. It did.

Less than two decades later, an Indian confederation dedicated to retaking the lands invaded by the white settlers developed near the juncture of Wah-ba-shik-a and Keth-tip-pe-ca-nunk. General William Henry Harrison and a troop of volunteers and militia slogged through swampy ground and over prairie between the outpost at Vincennes and the Indian village white men called Prophetstown. A short distance west, on November 7, 1811, American troops fought the Indians in the Battle of Tippecanoe, forever settling the question of whether red or white would dominate the North American continent east of the Mississippi River. Red men died, white men died, and Harrison later got elected president.

White domestication of the area grew. As a part of trade and economic growth, the Wabash and Erie Canal was dug to help transport the rich treasures of the Wabash Valley and its nearby regions. The canal snuggled against the banks of the Wabash River. After it had been dug through Lafayette, people began to take the town seriously. What had been a "miserable huddle of shanties along the river bank" began to take on new importance. The derision of "Lay-flat" and "Laugh-at" was silenced, and Lafayette's commerical river-rivals at Americus upstream and Granville downstream could not keep up. Riverboats came from major cities throughout the country and moved the vast store of Wabash Valley agricultural riches from the town's wharf to a hungry, growing young nation. William Digby, the town founder, would probably have been proud had he not been too busy playing cards and fighting with his cronies to notice.

The canal was the key that opened the valley; commerce and agriculture brought in more and more people. People brought in more "things" and they wanted more "things." Altogether, that is change. Some call it progress. But no matter. An Ohio merchant named John Purdue and his business partner, Moses Fowler, were so impressed they gave up their mercantile business and cast their lots with the new town as early as 1839. Both won.

The canal was too expensive to operate; it may have done wonders for Lafayette prosperity, but it impoverished the state treasury so badly the Indiana constitution had to be rewritten. The canal began its demise; the railroads were its coup de grace. Today, the Wabash and Erie is nearly obliterated.

As a new culture grew, the means for the growth of pioneer minds became as necessary to human sustenance as the fall harvest itself. In 1869, Purdue University was established on ground where the Kickapoo once stalked his food.

Thus four events mark the historical meander of this minute corner of the world:

- The rise and demise of the French outpost Fort Ouiatenon
- The outcome of the Battle of Tippecanoe, ending forever the Indians' ageless claim to a land with which they had always lived at peace
- The construction and eventual destruction of the Wabash and Erie Canal which so significantly changed the economic face of the area

- The establishment of Purdue University and the struggles that made it one among many American achievements.

Three are little more than vestiges of a past—admired, respected, to be learned from—historical curios strewn along a colorful path leading willy-nilly toward some vague notion of human progress. The fourth, Purdue University, alone remains as a vital creation of men and women unafraid to dream. It has an exciting past, a dynamic present, and a promising future, assured as long as human curiosity continues to kindle our pervasive dissatisfactions with the status quo.

This is Purdue's story—its heritage, its character, its people, its symbiosis with a world changed and ever changing.

Chapter I

Early Education and the Land-Grant Act of 1862

American higher education comes closer than any other institution of society in narrowing the gap between human hopes and human results. For the American people, higher education more than either politics or religion puts into clear focus their deepest aspirations and ideals. Education was seen by the frontiersman, as it is seen today by mainstream Americans, as the best hope of fulfilling in their children those dreams they were denied by caprice, rigor of time, or manifest inequality.

Liberal higher education—education at any level for that matter, whether technical or classical—should have to do with freedom and civilization. If so, it therefore has to do with power; most often it has to do with attaining the means to control one's own destiny. The major test of a free society is whether human attainment is limited solely by the extent of each individual's competence, ability, and motivation.

Nineteenth-century America was a developing civilization, a part of an experiment in freedom and self-governance. Its people, instinctively or consciously, then as now, persistently sought the wells of knowledge, though the types of information and instruction they called for varied with need, time, place, and social nuance. Short-term demands that certain varieties of subjects be taught have always been in tension with traditional scholarship, none more ludicrous, for example, than the good-hearted offer of early Puritan colonists to teach Latin to the American Indians.

The roots and traditions of higher education as it evolved in the United States derive from the early institutions of medieval Europe. The chief object of that period was to reconcile the traditions of the church with the growing demands of philosophy and learning. Latin was the church's language; logic was its means of explaining its theology. The ideas of Plato and Aristotle were deemed to elucidate the problems of faith. Although the medieval church may have been authoritarian, medieval higher education enjoyed a comparatively high degree of independence (i.e., academic freedom) not known by any other social institution of that time.

Evolved from the ancient monasteries and convents, the great universities of Europe and England looked to Paris, in medieval times the "first city" of teaching. The ecclesiastical origin of higher education did not anticipate that the universities and colleges would become the chief testing grounds for untested ideas. Yet, Oxford University in England, for example, had its greatest growth after A.D. 1170 and became a stormy battlefield of incipient reform and various cultural movements. It even became a political sanctuary and played a great role in the struggles of church and state; it survived the ecclesiastical revolution. In fact, at the time, students (scholars) were known as clerks or clercs, a corruption of *cleric.* The universities, in short, existed to educate the clergy—education which was an avenue to priestly, even papal, powers "before which even princes trembled" (as Sears and Hepburn put it in their 1925 history, *Purdue University—Fifty Years of Progress*).

Within religious education lay the key to power and influence, and nearly two centuries of Puritan New England higher education were colored by that tradition. (Hence, the need to teach Latin to the "heathen" Indian as the beginning of his "civilizing.") Despite its original tie to religion, higher education became increasingly secularized; in seventeenth- and eighteenth-century Europe, English political concepts, reinterpreted and clarified by French philosophers, began to reduce the emphasis on religion as the basis for the education and training of the young. The American founding fathers, many of them educated in the classical English tradition, were Deists; their influence stressed the classical basis of education rather than the traditional religious rationale.

Still, higher education in America, even at the close of the eighteenth century, was not entirely consistent with the demands of a new democratic ideal—quite likely because most of the then existing American colleges and universities were private, church-based schools, the classic educational ground of a monied aristocracy.

As the nineteenth century dawned, however, the stage was being set for profound modifications in traditional higher education that rank among the most important American cultural contributions to the history of human social order.

•   •   •

The development and expansion of the United States as an economic and political power began in earnest in the first third of the nineteenth century with the growth of the industrial factory system in the East and Middle Atlantic regions and the pioneer agrarian sprawl of the new nation westward and south. Together, the two separate and distinct movements created a previously unidentified demand for industrial and agricultural knowledge and enlightenment. The demand was not entirely utilitarian, however; in that same period the American people began to respond also to a wave of social reform which originated in western Europe and England and spread to America via a relatively small group of radicals. Though they were widely separated philosophically, the Brook Farm experiment in New England and the New Harmony adventure of Robert Owen along the lower Wabash River in southern Indiana were expressions of a common zeal for cultural fulfillment.

New Harmony was Indiana's link with a growing world altruism that originated as a reaction to the abuses of the industrial revolution in England and Europe. Owen had practical knowledge and experience as a factory manager and an immense desire to abate its horrendous toll on human lives, especially those of children. Owen's sons, Robert Dale and Richard, carried on their father's humanitarianism. Richard became a widely known geologist, scientist, soldier, university professor—and the first president of Purdue University. Robert Dale devoted his energies to practical reform such as the creation of a system of state-aided township public libraries in Indiana. He is also credited with several other legislative enactments of a humanitarian nature, and in general he fostered programs that directed Indiana towards Thomas Jefferson's views.

The new land was aflame with the ideal of Jeffersonian democracy in the first decades of the nineteenth century. Jefferson, the great agrarian democrat in attendance at the birth of the nation, believed without reservation that the nation would not long withstand despotism without an enlightened citizenry. In a letter to a Colonel Yancey in 1816, he penned the words that continue to echo wherever and whenever the price of liberty is pondered, "If a nation expects to be ignorant and free, in a state of civilization, it expects what never was and never will be."

As any youngster should know, Jefferson's immortality derives, of course, from his role as a framer of the Declaration of Independence, as the third United States president, and as founder of the University of Virginia. There he not only organized the administration but also planned the curriculum and was the architect of the buildings and the campus. For all of that, in none of his many accomplishments throughout his life was his enthusiasm as broadly manifest as in the proposed ordinance he drafted in 1784 for governing the Northwest Territory north of the Ohio River. That particular document did not pass, but the Ordinance of 1787—though modified from Jefferson's original—did.

Among other things, the ordinance bestowed on the territory north of the Ohio River a fundamental guarantee of education for all of the people. In Ohio, Indiana, and Illinois, the provision of the ordinance for free soil (immunity from slavery or involuntary servitude) has at one time or other been severely strained. The other part of the ordinance—"religion, morality, and knowledge being necessary to good government and the happiness of mankind, schools and the means of education shall be forever encouraged"—has been fervently protected.

On that foundation, a structure was needed. In 1800, the United States Congress established the Indiana Territory; in its first five years, it included not only the area of the present state but also Michigan and, for four years more, both Wisconsin and Illinois. While the Indiana Territory was at its maximum geographic size, the 1804 Congress passed an act reserving a sixteenth section of every township within the territory for the support of local schools and an entire township in each of its three major districts for the use of an institute of higher education. The township for such use in Indiana was selected in Gibson County and constituted a provision for Vincennes University; though it did not flourish, the university maintained its claim on the endowment and involved Indiana in years of long and tedious litigation.

December 11, 1816, the date of Indiana's admission as a state, was also an important milestone for Indiana's education, for in Indiana's new constitution further provision was made for public education. Congress, in admitting Indiana, had also made provision for setting aside an additional township for a "seminary of learning." Additionally, the new state constitution reserved in perpetuity all funds accruing from school lands. These funds were to be used for educational purposes. It further empowered the Indiana General Assembly to provide for a general system of education, ascending from township schools to a state university, "wherein tuition shall be *gratis* and equally open to all." The framers of the first Indiana Constitution were years ahead of their time.

The establishment of free public schools so wisely embodied by the document's framers did not materialize until after 1850, the year the present Indiana Constitution was reframed and readopted. Common free schools were *permitted,* not compulsory; local taxation that would support such schools was long withheld. Oddly enough, Indiana for a great many years was better served with private secondary and college-level schools than with elementary and primary ones.

Indiana University was first called into existence by legislative fiat in 1820 at Bloomington. In 1828, it became Indiana College and a decade later was organized as Indiana University. But the churches, lest Indiana higher education become too secularized, were busy. The two decades preceding 1850 were times in which church and privately supported colleges and/or academies blossomed throughout the Hoosier state. Many of these still contribute strength and vitality to Indiana educational life and remain essential to meeting contemporary demands for higher education. They include, among others, DePauw, Earlham, Evansville, Franklin, Hanover, Notre Dame, and Wabash.

In the days before the development of the common school system, a movement for local seminaries had begun; usually they provided training for teachers. The pioneer was the Union County Seminary at Liberty, founded in 1825. Others followed, sometimes under church auspices, sometimes under public sponsorship. Their purpose was useful; they provided not only a source of teacher training in Indiana but also raised educational standards and tended to bring otherwise elusive formal education within the reach of the people.

An important name in the history of early educational development in Indiana is that of Professor Caleb Mills of Wabash College who for more than forty years worked in behalf of free schools. In the half dozen years prior to 1852, Mills bombarded the Indiana legislature with arguments for a compulsory system of free public schools. A favorable statewide referendum on the question in 1848 and subsequent school laws in 1849 and 1852 reflected Mills's hard work and influence. Thereafter Indiana moved, albeit painfully, toward a system of free public schools. Even so, the 1852 act was declared unconstitutional; by 1867, court appeals and new legislation had answered the question of the constitutionality of local taxation for schools.

•   •   •

Against such a background, a people fueled by Jeffersonian "currents of idealism" (as Hepburn and Sears put it) sought to join the imponderable influences of education to the then imprecise intangibles of a developing American society. The effort of the time brought about the convergence of a triad of identifiable forces which ultimately produced the land-grant concept that made the establishment of Purdue University (and its sister schools) possible, namely:

- The strong burst of agricultural activity following the American Revolution when better ways were sought to feed a growing populace
- The American importation of the European Industrial Revolution, requiring liberalization of the so-called mechanic arts, especially in New England and the Middle Atlantic states
- The less well-defined and intuitive need to bring a system of altruistic values to a newly emerging American society—the continuous development of intellect and heart that gives societies the culture, the heritage, and the permanence by which they have the possibility of becoming civilizations.

Agricultural education did not, of course, have its birth in the land-grant idea. The agitation for that particular activity began in the late eighteenth century, manifested as agricultural societies where members presented books and papers about agriculture. Chemistry as applied to agriculture got attention first at Columbia College as early as 1792 and soon afterward, curiously, at such a classic school as Yale and other traditionalist schools. The natural development in agricultural education next called for institutes of college rank. Schools of agriculture were sought after in New England and the Atlantic states. One was opened as early as 1853 in New York with Ezra Cornell, significantly, as a trustee. The Civil War took a toll in staff, faculty, and students, and its existence was brief. Similar demands for such schools were made in Massachusetts; the attempts were by and large abortive except in Maryland and Pennsylvania. Nearer Indiana, enthusiasm for agricultural education was manifest in Iowa, Michigan, and Illinois. As early as 1858, Iowa established an agricultural school and farm and was thus in a position to take early advantage of the 1862 Morrill Act.

In Michigan, the state legislature, after vainly seeking a grant of public land, established without federal largess the Michigan Agricultural College with an appropriation of $50,000. It opened its doors in May 1857, thereby becoming the first college of its type in the United States.

As early as 1829, Indiana statutes established awards and exhibitions in agriculture. In 1835, without even considering the possibility of agricultural education, the General Assembly established a State Board of Agriculture which functioned rather indifferently over the years. Its annual reports alluded to statewide education in "the science of agriculture." But the board itself could do very little; it existed on a fifty-dollar-a-year appropriation. County agricultural societies grew in numbers and size during the 1850s, and their meetings invariably ended in written recommendations (presumably to the legislature) for scientific education in agriculture in Indiana. Although such societies were no doubt useful, they had little if any political clout. Little evidence exists to show that Indiana educators of the time held any sort of consensus for an agricultural-industrial college or university. Most of the attention of the 1850s and early 1860s was on the development of common schools; educators wanted normal schools for teacher training. A resolution recommending an agricultural school for Indiana, introduced in the State Board of Agriculture in 1852, was tabled for two years. When the board in 1854 adopted resolutions favoring statewide agricultural education, they were virtually without substance. One raised the question of whether a prize might not be offered by the legislature for the best essay written on the subject of establishing an agricultural college in Indiana.

The resolutions did recognize an 1852 act which called for reorganization of the state university (Indiana University) and the inclusion of both a normal and an agricultural department. So far as Indiana University was concerned, the act was farcical. While calling for the new programs, nowhere in the statute, or elsewhere, was provision made for their financial support. But the state university, to abide by the letter of the law, established agricultural courses on paper—but did not offer them. The 1852–53 catalog contained the prospectus for an unusually elaborate department to offer agricultural education, but it remained only that—a prospectus. It was an empty gesture not worthy of Indiana University and a discredit to the Indiana General Assembly, evidence that the forces of anti-intellectualism were very much alive in the Hoosier state. A half dozen years later, none of the listed courses in agriculture was actually offered, no teachers were employed or assigned to them, and the Indiana University administration still complained that no funds were forthcoming in the state appropriation to support them.

Equally a myth was Indiana University's claim to a "School of Theoretical and Practical Engineering." A contemporary of the nonexistent agriculture courses, the "school" was listed in the catalogues through 1858. Some of the courses listed were offered, but they duplicated courses already offered elsewhere in the university's academic departments. So far as is known, no other courses were offered, and engineering had the same status, and fate, as agriculture at Bloomington. After 1858, none of the state university catalogs mentioned either agriculture or engineering.

The State Board of Agriculture in 1856 tried once again and in January of that year appointed a special committee to investigate the practicability of founding a separate school for agriculture/industrial instruction. It took the committee only one day to report, concluding that the need for such a school was far greater than it was obtainable, given the Indiana history for such proposals. The report sketched what would be ideal for such a school—that falling far short, of course, of what ultimately became the reality of Purdue University.

The committee's report also wisely pointed out that the school would meet a present need while establishing a base for future growth. Instructor salaries would be defrayed by student fees. It was a good plan, well thought out. Yet, nothing came of it, and the State Board of Agriculture, smarting from having burned its hands on the issue at least twice before, thereafter confined itself chiefly to supervising state and county fairs, gathering agricultural and commercial statistics, and maintaining some contact with newer developments in farm implements, methods, and machinery.

Its final word before the advent of the 1862 Morrill Act was advocacy by the board's officers in 1856 for legislative establishment of both an agricultural college and a model farm. That recommendation reflected a widespread consensus from all parts of the state's agricultural constituency. It was carried forward by the momentum generated three years earlier by such men as Horace Greeley, who, in a Lafayette appearance, challenged the Hoosier state to a friendly rivalry with New York in the establishment of what Greeley described as a "people's college." Other widely known citizens supported the college proposal, not the least of whom was Richard Owen, faculty member at the state university, state geologist, and eventually the second choice for the first presidency of Purdue University.

Still, despite grass-roots fervor, the Indiana General Assembly did not act favorably for more than a decade. Indeed, with its attention diverted to Indiana's role in the Civil War, not until seven years after the passage and signing of the Morrill Act did it act favorably.

The idea of granting land to the states for educational purposes was not new; such grants for the support of education were common as early as the passage of the Northwest Ordinance of 1787. Every state had used such benefits to aid in the development of common schools and universities. Yet the concept of granting federal lands to the states for higher education met resistance even when there seemed to be, on the surface at least, ample political lip service paid to it. The idea of "people's universities," simple enough to understand and truly imaginative in scope, was still politically revolutionary.

Some of the friends of agricultural education, as well as those of the so-called mechanic arts, envisioned a single college analogous to the naval and military academies at Annapolis, Maryland, and West Point, New York. That seemed to be, at least, the intent of a petition from Massachusetts citizens sent to Congress in 1852.

Four years later on February 28, 1856, Representative J. S. Morrill, the Vermont Republican who ultimately authored the definitive legislation on the subject of land-grant colleges and universities, arose on the floor of the House to offer his resolution calling upon the Committee on Agriculture to inquire into the feasibility of one or more national agricultural schools. Morrill's 1856 document held the seed of the idea which matured into the 1862 act which carries his name, though it agrees with earlier concepts for national schools, not state ones:

> That the Committee on Agriculture be and they are hereby requested to inquire into the expediency of establishing a Board of Agriculture under the direction of the Secretary of the Interior; and also of establishing one or more national agricultural schools upon the basis of the naval and military schools, in order that one scholar from each Congressional district, and two from each State at large, may receive a scientific and practical education at the public expense.

Given the times and the instability of the political climate of nineteenth-century America, the great wonder is that a bill establishing land-grant colleges was ever introduced, much less passed. The path to its signing in 1862 by President Lincoln was a rocky one that took five to six years of frustrating political and parliamentary maneuvering to travel.

Antebellum America was electric with change. The new nation was imbued with energy. Social experiments of all kinds were ventured in countless directions, new forces in politics began to appear, and in religion a great liberalizing movement stirred. Much was still to be done to change a colony into a sovereign nation. A western frontier of hostile and primeval majesty awaited the human struggle to harness it. Above the entire nation hung the bleak possibility of a Union about to self-destruct over the issue of black slavery.

Into such ubiquitous political upheaval was thrust an imposing six-foot Vermonter, Justin Smith Morrill, son of a blacksmith, born and reared in the tiny, pastoral village of Strafford, nestled in a valley among modest eastern Vermont hills, cut through by a river with the resounding name Ompompanoosuc. Morrill, wrote his biographer William B. Parker (*The Life and Public Services of Justin Smith Morrill*), was "a New Englander of New Englanders."

Morrill grew up in Strafford and knew hard manual labor as a youngster. He was, he once said, "brought up on a farm and I know how to plant corn, to pull flax, and to dig potatoes." The eldest of ten children, five of whom died in infancy or early childhood, Morrill and his surviving three brothers and a sister all lived to ripe old ages. Justin himself died in 1898 of pneumonia at age eighty-eight, still a senator from Vermont. He had a combined service of forty-four years in the United States Congress, the first thirteen years in the House of Representatives, the balance in the Senate. At the time of his death and for many years after, he held the distinction of having served in Congress longer than anyone in United States history.

Amid the Washington tumult of the times, Morrill was a pillar of patience, a brilliant though inexperienced parliamentary strategist who early in his first term in the House of Representatives in 1855 mastered the procedural maze ideas must run before they become laws. Yet, he never made claim to any distinctive ability as a speaker or grand orator, although Daniel Webster had been his idol. (Morrill once described Webster as "not a man diminished when you came close to him.") Nor was Morrill a great writer. Later writers, however, have been inclined to credit him with prophetic vision, preternatural patience, and extraordinary intelligence. His career in Congress was probably most impressive for his consistency and for the tenacity with which he maintained his interest and sustained his championship for the causes he espoused and supported. It would be less than truthful to say that his public service was always grandly absent of self-interest.

Yet Morrill's was the voice of reconciliation, hardly ever that of the provocative adversary. He seemed to stand alone as the civilized voice of reason at a period in congressional history when many congressmen carried pistols concealed beneath coats or, as in the case of some of the militant, rough-and-tumble representatives from frontier regions, Bowie knives—usually used more for idle whittling during dull floor speeches than anything else.

As a striking example, the fight, literally, over the election of the Speaker of the House in Morrill's first session in 1855 was a legislative battle that lasted from December 3, 1855, to February 2, 1856, through 133 ballots and a floor brawl that involved nearly every member of the House of Representatives. It began when sharp words, then blows, were exchanged between Lawrence Keitt, Democrat from South Carolina, and Galusha Grow, a Pennsylvania Republican. It spread quickly so that all but a few congressmen, Morrill obviously among the few, were involved in either throwing or ducking wildly swung blows or avoiding brandished brass cuspidors. Fortunately, no pistols or knives were drawn. Years later Morrill recalled with his dry Vermont wit that at the height of what he described as a "hurly-burly," Speaker J. S. Orr desperately rapped his gavel while screaming for order. Then he turned resignedly to the unarmed sergeant-at-arms and shouted, "Arrest all those making this disorder!"—one man against a sea of nearly 240 flailing, irate bodies. Courageous, if not foolhardy, the sergeant-at-arms waded onto the floor armed only with the symbolic mace and American eagle of his office. Seeing it, the brawlers quickly cooled into chagrined dishevelment.

The rival candidates for Speaker of the House were William Aiken, a South Carolina Democrat, and N. P. Banks, a Republican from Massachusetts. The contest drew a clear North-South line: every vote for Banks was a free-state vote; every vote (but one) for Aiken was a slave-state vote. The session was described by Morrill as "the first gust, the large pelting drops that preceded the storm of 1861."

First to last, Morrill was a moderate, although expressing a profound revulsion of slavery—universal among Republicans of that era. Yet, despite his hatred of slavery, he refused to be led into condemnation of the South in any language that could be labeled provocative.

He preferred reconciliation, and his primary concern, like President Lincoln's, was holding the Union together. Morrill's talent was most valuable in the organization of the new Republican party's apparatus in Vermont from what was left of the Whigs, Free-Soilers, and anti-slave Democrats. He played the key role as conciliator among various wrangling factions, and the new party's state organization in Vermont came on the scene amicably as a result of Morrill's work.

Morrill had never anticipated a life of politics. It was the furthest thing from his mind. As a lad, after serving an apprenticeship in the mercantile business (it paid him forty-five dollars the first year; seventy-five dollars the second), he settled into storekeeping at Strafford, retiring at the age of thirty-eight to tend a small farm, improve his orchard, care for his small flock of sheep, and read. Almost imperceptibly he began to be drawn into the political life of the community, then the region, then the state, and eventually to stand for Congress from Vermont's Second District. He won wide respect for his views, his moderation, and his reconciliatory attitude. He was also a rock-ribbed New England conservative. Through such successes, Morrill throughout his life painfully regretted the fact that his formal schooling had consisted of the one-room school in his own community and two terms at two academies in nearby communities. It had ended when he was fifteen.

Biographer Parker believes that Morrill's intense interest in higher education and his subsequent authorship of the land-grant college bill were not so much an altruistic tribute to higher education's intrinsic values, but rather a "nationalizing" of the unrealized educational needs of his own youth. Likewise, his support of wool tariffs had strictly to do with the fact that it was a major Vermont industry that produced more than 3.4 million pounds of wool annually.

If he was ever vituperative in his speeches, it was in those having to do with polygamy, which crept onto the American scene temporarily with the establishment of Mormonism. He saw polygamy as an abhorrent evil; but even in condemning it, he avoided outright attacks on the church itself, save for one presentation in the Senate. In one of his early floor speeches in the House of Representatives in favor of legislation outlawing polygamy, he declared that "there is no purpose to interfere with the most absolute freedom of religion, nor to intermeddle with the rights of conscience, but the sole design [of the bill] is to

Justin S. Morrill, the Vermont representative in Congress who doggedly
fought for his bill that finally became
the Land-Grant Act of 1862.

Martin L. Peirce, Lafayette businessman
and banker, probably talked John
Purdue into making a gift of $150,000
to locate the new university in Tippecanoe County. Peirce later became the
first treasurer of the board of trustees
and the only man to serve the board
as secretary-treasurer.

John A. Stein, state senator from
Lafayette, was responsible for guiding
the bill containing John Purdue's pro-
posal through the roiled waters of the
Indiana's legislature's special session in
May 1869.

Gov. Conrad Baker in 1869 called the
Indiana General Assembly into a
special session to act on the land-grant
college question in Indiana.

Richard Owen was Purdue's first president, 1872–74, but never occupied an office on the campus, never received a paycheck from the University or served when classes were in session.

Prof. John S. Hougham was Purdue's first faculty member and served as a campus "handyman" for the trustees who appointed him acting president between the administrations of Shortridge and White. He resigned not long after White was appointed.

Emerson E. White came to Purdue in 1876 and steered Purdue on a course from which it has deviated little. He found himself in trouble in a controversy over barring fraternities at Purdue and resigned in 1883.

Abraham C. Shortridge, already distinguished as superintendent of Indianapolis schools, was recruited as the second president. He resigned in 1875 after two years.

This photo is believed to be the first ever taken of the Purdue University campus about the time classes opened in September 1874. University Hall was not yet built, although an excavation for it had begun. (Tippecanoe County Historical Association Archives)

University Hall was completed in 1877 and was the central building of the seven then existing on the Purdue campus. An example of early campus architecture, it is the only remaining building of the original campus. It cost $35,000 when built; it was restored for more than $600,000 in 1959 and 1960. (Tippecanoe Historical Association Archives)

A winter view of the campus in 1877. Buildings from left are Boarding Hall, Science Hall, the power plant, University Hall and the Library, the Men's Dormitory, and Military Hall and Gymnasium.

The Science Building was called Building No. 2 when it was eventually torn down in the early 1950s. A replica of a similarly used building at Brown University, the building was the birthplace of chemistry, engineering, physics, and pharmacy at Purdue. It was located just north of Matthews Hall, along University Street.

The Boarding Hall, best known later as Ladies Hall, housed the university faculty and their families and women students from 1875, and had the campus's only dining room. Science Hall and Ladies Hall were among the six original buildings. (Tippecanoe County Historical Association Archives)

Also among the original buildings were the Dormitory (above) and in the background, right, the Military Hall and Gymnasium, and in the other photo (below) the original power plant. In the roof tower of the power plant is the bell now used as the Victory Bell rung after football victories in Big Ten games. The Dormitory became Purdue Hall, a classroom building, and was approximately on the site of the present Mathematical Sciences Building. The power plant was just south of the Dormitory. (Dormitory photo from Tippecanoe County Historical Association Archives)

Michael Golden, who earned his education in practical mechanics in a two-year program at Massachusetts Institute of Technology by being a sparring partner in Boston's boxing parlors, gained a reputation at Purdue as a tough, quick-tempered combative—but much loved—teacher and department head. He was immortalized when the Michael Golden Shops were named for him. He is also pictured with his sisters, Helen and Katherine both Purdue graduates and instructors, Helen in practical mechanics and Katherine in biology. As Katherine Bitting, she returned to Purdue in 1935 to receive an honorary degree. The three posed either in a house at 128 South Grant Street he shared with Helen or in an apartment occupied by Katherine at 132 State Street.

Harvey Washington Wiley was a member of the original faculty and one of the most outstanding persons on campus. He was first state chemist, first professor of chemistry, first ROTC instructor, first baseball coach, and—to the disdain of the board of trustees—rode a bicycle to work.

Henry A. Huston, a protégé of Wiley, was a versatile Purdue professor who served both in engineering and agriculture. He had a long career at the university, although he had once turned down an invitation to study at Purdue, replying, "Who'd want a degree from that dump?"

William Freeman Myrick Goss was the first dean of engineering who, with the help of President James H. Smart, enthusiastically pushed staff and students forward in an effort to make Purdue University a top engineering institution.

punish gross offenses whether in secular or ecclesiastical garb; to prevent practices which outrage the moral sense of the civilized world, and to reach even those 'who steal the livery of the Court of Heaven to serve the Devil in.'"

•   •   •

Morrill's immortality as a statesman will always be associated with the federal act of 1862 which he introduced on December 17, 1857. Andrew D. White, for many years United States minister to Germany, but prior to that the venerated president of Cornell University, ranked Morrill's work on behalf of the land-grant college legislation as having the historical importance of Hamilton's advocacy of the federal Constitution, Jefferson's acquisition of the Louisiana Territory, and Clay's gift of a truly American foreign policy.

Before he authored the land-grant bill, Morrill had discussed the idea with many of his legislative colleagues; nearly all of them favored the idea and thought that such was needed, but not one ever expressed any belief that such a progressive idea had the slightest chance of approval.

Morrill's bill was motivated mostly by the success he observed in the Western European agricultural schools. But he cited five conditions unique to the United States which he believed his proposed legislation would correct: the dissipation of the most valuable land largely for private benefit; the existence, because the land was cheap, of bad farming practices (the wasting of soil which then required scientific farming methods); the absence of opportunities for mechanics education at the college level for offspring of the working class (of whom he was one); the dominance in major universities and colleges of "classic" education which led almost exclusively to the "learned" professions; and the inequalities in existing schools, both common and higher, from state to state—and the likelihood that the deficient states would remain so without the financial aid of land grants.

Over Morrill's objections, his first bill was referred to the House Committee on Public Lands, known to be hostile to the measure. Morrill's initial floor battle to have it referred to the House Committee on Agriculture had failed. The bill nearly died in committee; and Morrill worked hard to muster support for it both in the House itself and among the bill's lobbyists. He also had the perplexing job of prying it out of committee and back onto the House floor. When it arrived back from committee in

April 1858, its opponents and proponents lined up almost solely along North-South lines. But Morrill's work began to pay off.
Finally through cloakroom strategy, the bill was passed 105 to
100 and went to the Senate, into committee, and eventually back
to the Senate floor with a recommendation to pass. Delays and
debate in the Senate postponed final action until February 9,
1859, when it finally passed, 25 to 22. After minor revisions with
which Morrill himself concurred, the bill returned to the House
and was finally approved on February 16, now needing only
President James Buchanan's signature to become law.

Fearing Buchanan's veto and believing that an override of
that veto would be impossible, some of Morrill's friends hastened
to the White House to appeal to Buchanan. But the opponents
had been there earlier; before the day was over, Buchanan's veto
was a fact, and the Morrill land-grant college bill was, at least
temporarily, becalmed.

Hope for the land-grant college concept revived in 1860
after the election of Abraham Lincoln. Morrill reintroduced his
bill on December 16, 1861, amid a throng of urgent subjects
then pressing on the wartime Congress. Once again, Morrill was
disappointed to see the bill referred to the House Committee
on Public Lands—and a predictable recommendation "that it do
not pass." As a hedge against that possibility, he had given a
copy of the measure to his friend "Old Ben" Wade, the Ohio
senator who had introduced it on May 2, 1861. Numerous delay-
ing tactics and postponements stalled final action until June 10,
1862, when it passed in the Senate by a surprisingly large
majority, 32 to 7. On June 17, the Senate version was introduced in the House, and Morrill and his friends managed to
thwart a large number of stalling tactics, mostly by members
of the Committee on Public Lands. The House finally concurred, 90 to 25, and the bill was signed into law by Lincoln
on July 2, 1862.

The Northern states promptly accepted the grants—30,000
acres of United States lands for each representative and senator.
The Southern states were included in the terms of the act when
they returned to the Union. Eventually, all of them took advantage of the act following the end of the war.

The persistent opposition to Morrill's bill was to a great extent an honest difference of opinion over its possible long-range
effect, that it would deplete federal lands to a dangerously low
level and create rampant and uncontrolled land speculation.
However, most of the opposition was motivated along North-
South factional lines. The bill was sponsored by Morrill; Morrill

and his land-grant friends were Yankees; a loyal Southerner voted against all Yankee bills regardless of what they might be.

Another aspect of the genesis of the Morrill Act must be mentioned: Morrill's first work on behalf of the land-grant college was his 1856 resolution memorializing Congress to establish one or more agricultural and mechanical arts colleges along the lines of the military academies at West Point and Annapolis. His 1857 bill called for land grants to each state to finance endowments for its own schools, a concept entirely different from the one proposed by his resolution of a year earlier.

Morrill's name will undoubtedly always be attached to the land-grant act, but since its success in 1862, others have come forward to claim the bill's authorship, chief among them Professor Jonathan Baldwin Turner of Illinois College at Jacksonville, a precursor of the University of Illinois. Turner, a native of Massachusetts, was an educator, farmer, and lecturer. He had studied at Salem Academy and Yale and in 1833 went to Illinois as an energetic apostle of education for the masses of people, enthusing over new ideas and teaching methods. He was devoted to the idea of the industrial university which he had devised and urged its acceptance with great zeal.

Turner had little use for the concept of classic education in America of the nineteenth century and spoke of it contemptuously:

> A classical teacher who has no original, spontaneous power of thought and knows nothing but Latin and Greek, however perfectly, is enough to stultify a whole generation of boys and make them all pedantic fools like himself. . . . It may do for the man of books to plunge at once amid the catacombs of buried nations and languages, to soar to Greece, or Rome, or Nova-Zembla, Kamschatka and the fixed stars, before he knows how to plant his own beans, or harness his own horse, or can tell whether the functions of his own body are performed by a heart, stomach, and lungs, or with a gizzard and gills. But for the man of work thus to bolt away at once from himself and all his pursuits in afterlife contravenes the plainest principles of nature and common sense.

The claim that it was Turner who authored Morrill's bill was not put forward until more than a decade after Morrill's and Turner's deaths. A 1910 paper authored by then University of Illinois President Edmund J. James contends that the documents supporting the land-grants-to-the-states idea were all given to Morrill by Turner and his colleagues and points to the language of the act as being similar, or in places identical, to Turner's.

The subject of authorship had been broached to Morrill in 1894 while he served in the Senate, four years before his death. He did not deny that he had talked to Turner in Washington and even admitted to a vague recollection of a conversation with a professor who came to him when the bill was before Congress to heartily support the idea. "It may," Morrill once admitted, "have been Turner. It is so long since, I have forgotten his name." He pointed out that during the development of the bill he visited with dozens of college professors, some for it, some against. James contended in his paper, and attempted to prove, that Turner was the real "father" of the act; that he was the first to formulate it; and that he began and continued the agitation that made its passage in Congress possible. Parker, Morrill's biographer, disagrees, pointing out that much of the evidence James used was based on the recollections of Turner's elderly daughter of conversations she had had with her father when he was ninety-three. Parker dismisses as preposterous a further claim that Turner actually selected Morrill to introduce and guide the bill through the legislative maze.

That is not, however, to denigrate Turner. He was among a vanguard of educators and others who fought, agitated, wrote, and spoke alongside Morrill in favor of the land-grant college bill that, though it ranks as one of the most imaginative and profound pieces of federal legislation in American history, required such painful labor in its birthing. Ultimately, it gave the American people and their nation power and strength through higher education, research, and service of a magnitude unprecedented in all of human experience.

Chapter II

The Political Struggle in Indiana

Although many states moved swiftly to take advantage of the federal land grants made available under the Morrill Act, a dozen years ensued between the signing of the legislation by President Lincoln in 1862 and its fruition in Indiana with the opening of Purdue University's first classes on September 16, 1874.

Indiana was not different from most states in its zeal and apparent desire to provide agricultural education; the State Board of Agriculture had repeatedly pushed for facilities or programs in agriculture for Indiana's rural youth. Agitation for the state to move ahead in agricultural education was almost universal among farm leaders and Hoosier educators; indeed, considerable grass roots sentiment existed for it.

Yet the halls of the state capitol were permeated with rampant political inertia. Whereas a half dozen states already had founded and opened colleges of agriculture before the passage of the Morrill Act, Indiana still fumbled about through the years that the federal legislation was aborning.

On January 7, 1858, the State Board of Agriculture sent to the floor of the Indiana General Assembly a resolution to support congressional passage of the Morrill Bill. It went nowhere. The board sent a second, similar resolution to the legislature almost exactly a year later and followed it up the next day with a lengthy report from the board's secretary, R. T. Brown, pointing out the state's need for agricultural education, while warning that Indiana lagged behind its sister states Michigan and Ohio.

Still, there was no legislative interest. A motion to send Brown's report to the committee "with instructions to recommend some plan of giving agricultural education to the young farmers of the state" brought resounding silence and the motion died on the floor without a second.

The agricultural movement in Indiana may have bubbled to some extent, but it certainly did not boil as it had elsewhere. Meanwhile, outside the legislature, an industrial ingredient was added to the lukewarm cauldron if only to see whether it might heat up. The idea was that the mythical students in the still mythical agricultural college could, in part, be rendered more self-supporting by means of manual labor performed for the college (had one existed).

More popular interest in an Indiana college or university that would provide both agricultural and mechanical arts training was aroused by the *Indiana Farmer*, a newspaper established in 1851 at Richmond, Indiana, by David P. Holloway of Wayne County and W. T. Dennis. Holloway, who served Indiana in Congress from 1855 to 1857, was a staunch supporter of the land-grant idea and the concept of agricultural-mechanical arts education. He was a chairman of the House Committee on Agriculture and was instrumental in early work to establish a Department of Agriculture as a cabinet-level agency.

The *Indiana Farmer* insisted editorially that the day of the agricultural college was at hand, if given a reasonable opportunity to demonstrate its usefulness to Indiana agriculture specifically and the state's economy generally, as had occurred in other states. The newspaper became allied in the cause of the agricultural-industrial college after carrying an article on Professor J. B. Turner's ideas for reserving public lands to finance industrial universities. Of course, Holloway became a staunch supporter of the Morrill Bill after it was first introduced in 1857 (although he no longer served in Congress) and was perhaps the bill's leading proponent in Indiana.

But Holloway and his newspaper moved quickly against a halfway measure that proposed to turn the old statehouse into an agricultural college for Indiana. He protested against "such iniquity," declaring that Indiana farmers did not want or need the old statehouse "slimed all over as it is with corruption and scarred with a thousand perjuries." What Hoosier farmers wanted and needed was "a real farmer's college, a great big farm where boys can learn to work and work to learn."

Downtown Indianapolis as the site of an agricultural college seems extraordinarily illogical today, but using the old statehouse as its site seemed logical enough in the mid-1800s. In January 1857, a resolution was introduced in the Indiana House of Representatives that would have used the old statehouse space "for a place of deposit for all agricultural implements and records belonging to the State Agricultural Society" and eventually to the establishment of a university for "the education of the young men of the State of Indiana in mechanical and agricultural science."

Despite the grassroots support such a proposal—or any agricultural education proposal for that matter—might have had, it evidently did not impress members of the house. The resolution did not carry.

Still, though nothing seemed to get done toward establishing an "A&M" in Indiana, the effort continued to arouse interest and sustain it. However much grassroots Hoosiers may have wanted the school, Indiana's delegation to the Congress seemed either unaware of, or indifferent to, constituent sentiment. Politics could not solve the problem of moving the project off dead-center because politics *was* the problem.

When the first Morrill Bill came up for vote in the United States House of Representatives in April 1858, all eleven members of the Indiana delegation were present, five Democrats voting against it and five Republicans and one Democrat for it. When the bill came to a vote in the Senate the next February, the votes of the two Indiana senators, Jesse D. Bright and Graham N. Fitch, were not recorded: Fitch was absent from the session, and Bright was "paired." (Pairing was an arrangement between two legislators who had opposing views on any proposed bill. Since their votes would cancel one another, they agreed not to vote at all. The practice then was permitted in Congress, but the rules of the Indiana General Assembly prohibited it.)

The second version of the Morrill Bill came to the Senate floor for final passage on June 10, 1862. Again, the Indiana senators did not support it. Senator Henry S. Lane, the Republican, managed to be absent; Senator Joseph A. Wright, a Democrat, actively opposed it and a few days earlier had made a long speech of disapproval. He objected to the possibility that large amounts of land might fall into the hands of nonresident speculators, saw menace in a large school fund that would likely reduce the local interest in educational maintenance, and believed the act would interfere with the operations of the Homestead Act. And, he added, if large land grants were to be made on behalf of education, they should be made on behalf of the education of women.

Wright's opinion in the Senate was the only one expressed, for or against, on the final passage of the Morrill Act. In the House of Representatives, an early vote was forced with slight opportunity for debate. At the time, although Republicans in the Indiana delegation to the House now outnumbered Democrats, seven to four, no one arose to counter the adverse opinions expressed by Wright in the Senate.

Only one Indiana congressman, Republican Albert S. White of Stockwell, even voted for the bill—a historical twist, a cause for satisfaction inasmuch as the Indiana institution which resulted from the Morrill Act was eventually put in his home county and his former hometown, Lafayette.

•   •   •

Although the need for a land-grant institution in Indiana seemed great and the federal legislative machinery was in place to permit it to happen, its establishment was not easily insured. The Civil War, of course, delayed action, as it did in other states. A bigger problem was bewilderment on the part of the Indiana General Assembly because of divided sentiment among the chief supporters as to what should be done. The friends of education were at loggerheads. The decision was made doubly difficult because of the rival claims of Indiana University at Bloomington and the various sectarian colleges and universities in Indiana (though it is doubtful that the Morrill Act had ever contemplated use of land-grant funds under sectarian sponsorship).

Greater peril to the land scrip fund, certain to be meager at best, were the forces which would have scattered it among various competitors, thus losing whatever efficacy it would otherwise have had.

The "agricultural college," as it was popularly called, finally made its debut in the Indiana General Assembly of 1863 when it began a frustrating six-year legislative journey rivaling even that of the Morrill Act itself through Congress. The early bills regarding it had to do with establishing a commissioner or board to receive and sell the scrip allotted to Indiana on the basis of its thirteen members of the Congress. A more detailed bill, endorsed by the state superintendent of public instruction and "other friends of education," called for a separate college with a normal school (i.e., teacher training institute) attached. Still another proposal advanced the claims of Northwestern Christian University (now Butler University) as the place to establish a new college or department to comply with the Morrill Act provisions. Butler and Indiana universities remained strong as contestants for the land-grant monies until the end, mostly because they had entered the controversy quite early.

Indiana's great Civil War governor, Oliver Perry Morton, did not offer any clear solution in his 1864 message to the legislature. Morton was ambivalent, hesitating between a potentially disastrous proposal to divide the fund among the existing colleges of the state and a plan—dependent upon the amount received from land-grant scrip—to establish a separate educational institution with free tuition for the sons of soldiers who died in the war. Amid all of these suggestions, the legislative session closed with no agreement and no decision. Though it would be two years before the legislature could do anything further, the interim gave the several contenders time to fortify their positions.

In 1865, plans were offered in the Indiana legislature that proposed the diversion of the land-grant funds to uses not even hinted at nor intended in the Morrill Act. One proposed the endowment and support for a soldiers home; another sought to divert the fund for common school uses.

Indiana University's proposal to use the funds to expand along the lines suggested by the act were more in keeping with the state's interests. That university's claim was a strong one, held at political bay only by the hostility to it of the denominational colleges and universities and Indianapolis interests.

Yet, the efforts to divide and dilute the fund remained insistent. The easiest solution would have been to yield to them, but wiser heads prevailed at the capitol. One bill provided for a research division at Indianapolis with no more than two professorships to be established in each of not less than five existing public and private colleges and universities in Indiana. Another divisionist proposal would establish twelve colleges, one at Bloomington and one in each of the eleven congressional districts. The issue finally narrowed to a single college, in itself a sufficiently serious political problem. By 1865, the number of localities seeking the college had grown substantially, thereby adding to the possibility of a long and tedious struggle merely to solve the sticky issue of a site for a single campus. It took four more years.

Each of the interested locales offered its own inducements. One of these was Tippecanoe County where the Stockwell Collegiate Institute offered its buildings and 160 acres. Battle Ground Institute in the same county offered a considerably higher bid: a total in land and buildings of $100,000.

The Bloomington-Indiana University offer came nearest to being accepted by the General Assembly, which arrived independently at a decision set forth in the Dunning Bill, a senate measure passed on December 20. A bill of similar scope received sympathy in the house of representatives, but the session closed without further action on either bill; Bloomington's efforts to gain the land-grant college came no nearer to success.

Still, the proposed agricultural college was not without some success in the 1865 legislature. By formally accepting the federal grant and incorporating the "Trustees of the Indiana Agricultural College," the 1865 session went further than any previous ones in making progress toward widened higher educational opportunities for the state's citizens. A further decision to establish a state normal school at Terre Haute simplified an educational question that more than likely would have confronted future sessions of the legislature.

•   •   •

Despite the one small step for an agricultural college, the leap toward a full-fledged land-grant institution was still two sessions of the Indiana General Assembly away. The question was simple: where would Indiana put its new college? Arriving at the answer was still excruciatingly political. In the 1867 and 1869 General Assembly sessions, Tippecanoe County had an able champion in John A. Stein, state senator from Lafayette, who spoke for the Battle Ground site. A bill to that effect emerged from a joint session of the Indiana Senate committees on education and agriculture and came to a test vote on the senate floor on February 22, 1867. Twenty-six votes were needed for passage and in early balloting were greatly scattered. As the issue narrowed, Battle Ground and Indianapolis became sole contenders. The final vote was twenty for Battle Ground, eighteen for Indianapolis with no prospect of any change. So with no decision possible, the senate bill was indefinitely postponed, and a similar fate confronted like bills before the house of representatives. In a way, the situation was fortunate. The divisionists had been busily at work and would have scattered the resources among Battle Ground, Indianapolis, and Bloomington. Agreement in 1867 seemed more remote than two years earlier. Nor was the prospect simplified by the appearance of a new and serious contender for the land-grant college—Greenfield, a community east of Indianapolis, and Hancock County, jointly proposing an offer of $125,000 in land and buildings.

At this point, Indiana University, whose choice had seemed so logical and which came so near success two years previously, forfeited any chance it may have had by getting into a fight over ownership of University Square, north of the federal building in Indianapolis. The dispute cost it many powerful legislative friends. Title to the land was clouded. Besides the state university, the state government and the City of Indianapolis claimed it. The issue was acute in 1867 and eventually proved injurious to the state university's primary interest in gaining the land-grant school as a part of its bailiwick.

The delay in finding a location for the land-grant college was beginning to take on the proportion of a scandal. In the 1869 session, as a move to harmonize conflicting claims, an omnibus bill was introduced that awarded the coveted new college location to Battle Ground, reconciled the ownership of the University Square in downtown Indianapolis to Indiana University, and increased support for the proposed normal school at Terre Haute. Other bills confusing the issue followed, and neither the house nor the senate could agree.

After five legislative sessions in six years, the issue of the new agricultural college had been debated with increasing acrimony and maddening reiteration. Although the solution seemed far away, the problem had unquestionably focussed; instead of the original six counties, there were now only three— Monroe, Marion, and Tippecanoe. For the others the bidding had become too high.

The drama was heightened by the addition to the Monroe County offer of the Dunn farm, the Owen scientific cabinet, and $50,000 in county bonds. Marion County expanded its original offer of the facilities of Northwestern Christian University with the addition of twenty-seven adjoining acres from the Fletcher heirs, plus $100,000 in county bonds, and at the last minute added another bond pledge of $75,000 to the original.

The Tippecanoe County offer likewise went up. The offer of the Stockwell Institute properties, supplemented by the Battle Ground facilities, was substantially increased by 320 acres at Shawnee Mound (in the county's southwest corner), a promise of $50,000 from others in the neighborhood, and a pledge of $50,000 in county bonds in the event any site within Tippecanoe County was accepted.

The three offers, thus nearly equally balanced, created an embarrassing dilemma for a legislative body that had debated the issue ad nauseam. It proved to be a deadlock. Any combination of two of the offers could defeat the third. Only some unexpected weight could tip the scale—some personal factor. John Purdue was that factor.

Legend more than historical fact has it that Martin L. Peirce, one of Purdue's most trusted friends in Lafayette, suggested that Purdue use his largess for the new land-grant college and that it might bear Purdue's name. Peirce was another of Lafayette's wealthy—a businessman and founder and president of Spears, Peirce and Company which became the Commercial Bank of Lafayette, a forerunner of Lafayette National Bank. Both Peirce and Purdue were generous with their money; once they teamed to buy and ship 1,000 bushels of corn gratis to help alleviate the suffering of the Irish famine of 1847.

The apocryphal story is that Purdue and Peirce, driving past a local cemetery, noted a prominent grave marker that had cost $36,000; both agreed that it was a woeful waste of money. At that point, Peirce made the suggestion to Purdue that a more suitable, lasting, and useful monument would be a college bearing Purdue's name.

Somewhere between the cemetery and the floor of the Indiana General Assembly, somewhere between legend and history, Purdue agreed to make his immortal gift.

On March 3, 1869, as the session neared its scheduled close, Senator Stein read to the state senate a letter from Purdue that offered $100,000 "out of his own purse" (in addition to tenders already made in behalf of the Tippecanoe County location) subject to two provisos: the college should be located at Battle Ground, and it should "by law have his surname identified with the corporate name of the college."

Purdue's offer came at a bad time. It ran headlong into a totally unrelated and unanticipated political reality that involved a great, collective lack of courage of a majority of members of the General Assembly. One of the items on its 1869 agenda was consideration of a proposed joint resolution to approve the proposed "black suffrage" amendment, the fifteenth, to the United States Constitution. (Proclaimed as the law of the land about a year later, the amendment guarantees that the right to vote shall not be denied or abridged by the United States government or by any state on account of race, color, or condition of previous servitude.)

The problem was that the Fifteenth Amendment proposal, for various reasons, evoked controversy throughout all of Hoosierland. To avoid voting on it altogether, fifty-four members of the assembly simply resigned and went home. (Thirty-seven were representatives, seventeen were senators.) Without a quorum to conduct business, other members soon followed. The 1869 Indiana legislature thus quietly dissolved with no formal adjournment and, of course, no action on the offer Purdue made to the state by way of Senator Stein.

Less than a month later, Governor Conrad Baker called a special session; the no-quorum tactic failed when Baker ruled that for the purpose of the session a quorum consisted of a majority of the then existing members, not counting vacancies due to resignations.

The special session was called for April 8, 1869. At 2 A.M. on April 2, Stein was awakened by a messenger from John Purdue who relayed some changes he wanted made from his original offer. He continued his provision that the university be named for him in perpetuity, but he dropped another that it be located at Battle Ground, proposing only that it be located at a site within Tippecanoe County as determined by the board of trustees. More importantly, he raised his original gift proposal by $50,000. He added a new condition that was to make him either a full-fledged trustee for life, or at least an "advisory member" with "visitatorial power over the University during my lifetime."

Stein's 2 A.M. awakening turned out to be an unnecessary nuisance inasmuch as Purdue outlined the same stipulations in a letter to Governor Baker less than two weeks later. Five days after that, the governor conveyed Purdue's letter to members of both houses:

> To His Excellency Conrad Baker, Governor of Indiana;
> Sir—
> As the General Assembly, at its present session, will doubtless be called upon to consider the questions relating to the establishment and location of the Agricultural College, contemplated by the act of Congress of July 2, 1862, I desire to avail myself of the opportunity to render a testimonial to the county in which I have spent thirty years of the ripeness of my life, and also to manifest my interest in the cause of collegiate education, by offering (as I now do) through your Excellency to the State of Indiana, to donate the sum of one hundred and fifty thousand dollars for the use of such college, provided the General Assembly will, by law, secure me in the following conditions:
> First. Locate the said college at such point in Tippecanoe County as may be decided upon by a majority of the present Board of Trustees of the Indiana Agricultural College, to whom I be added as a member.
> Second. Name the Institution by an irrepealable law "Purdue University".

Third. Provide that I be a member of the Board of Trustees having control of said institution, and should I cease to be such, I be retained as a advisory member thereof, and have visitorial power over the University during my lifetime.

Upon these conditions I offer this donation, which I agree to pay in yearly installments of $15,000 until the full sum of $150,000 is paid; and I am prepared to render my obligations accordingly as may be required.

I will thank you to present my offer to the Houses of the General Assembly for their consideration.

Very respectfully yours,
John Purdue
April 15, 1869

Further details of the legislative discussion included a prospect for 100 acres for campus and farm and a possibility that Purdue's $150,000 cash gift could be included in the endowment. Some legislators thought Purdue's rich New York friends could be persuaded to put up the money for buildings.

Apparently the members of the General Assembly were pleasantly impressed by the Purdue munificence and the prospect that perhaps if they handed over the land-grant college to a wealthy individual, the state would be relieved of most of its responsibility. Though that was a dream never realized, it lasted long enough to guide Stein's bill safely through the political waters which had been roiled for so many years. Four test ballots were needed in the house to bring about the final result, and the Tippecanoe County bid won in all four.

The friends of Indianapolis, Bloomington, and Greenfield fell back to take their last refuge in the senate from the Tippecanoe County avalanche. Senator Stein assembled with such great skill the arguments against the site claims of Indianapolis and Bloomington that the triangle collapsed, and in desperation the Indianapolis-Bloomington-Greenfield forces began to resort to personalities, attacking the vanity of John Purdue in seeking to tag his name to the new college of which he was to be chief benefactor.

Stein's defense of Purdue's alleged vanity was also an eloquent defense of educational philanthropy—and still may be considered as such today:

I am surprised to find this feature of the offer the subject of censurious criticism on this floor. It has been stigmatized as selfish vanity for Mr. Purdue to ask that the institution be named "Purdue University."

Sir, it strikes me as a vanity worthy of all honor and imitation. It is the vanity of all the genuine philanthropists of our race.

It is the honorable and praiseworthy vanity which associates itself with the cause of education and public morals. We can look with contempt upon the selfish vanity of the Egyptian monarch who sought his immortality in the everlasting worthless pyramid, but he who seeks his fame in the advancement of his fellowmen, in the dedication of his fortune and his efforts to mental enlightenment and public virtue appeals to every sentiment of admiration and respect which can animate the human mind. To call this a selfish vanity is to misname things. May the kind Providence who has ever kept the destinies of our commonwealth in friendly keeping, shower down such selfish vanity bountifully upon our people. As a legislator I shall always be delighted to assist and encourage it.

Stein was one of Lafayette's leading citizens as well as a skilled politician, orator, and lawyer. Like Purdue, he was a Pennsylvanian by birth who at fourteen was employed in a military supply store in Philadelphia. At seventeen, he entered a law office at Lebanon, Pennsylvania, to begin studying law and came to Lafayette to finish his work with his uncle, Godlove S. Orth (who opposed Purdue in the 1868 congressional election). Orth was not only a leading Lafayette attorney but also a colorful individual noted for his poetry and short stories.

Stein probably had as much to do with winning the new agricultural college for Tippecanoe County as anyone besides Purdue himself, although neither the university nor the Lafayette community has ever seen fit to memorialize his name in some appropriate way. Not only did Stein present the Purdue offer to the Indiana Senate, but he was its imposing oratorical defender as well. More important, however, was his calm, steadying influence during the infighting and political dealing that occurred in the legislative hallways and cloakrooms.

The opposition finally capitulated to Purdue's offer on May 4, 1869, when it was accepted by a thirty-two-to-ten vote in the senate, and two days later, May 6, by a seventy-six-to-nineteen vote in the house of representatives. Thus, May 6, 1869, came to be known as the university's founding date. It was also the date when a bitter contest that had gone on for the greater part of seven years terminated to the relief, if not satisfaction, of nearly everyone in Indiana.

Five more years elapsed before the tiny new school opened its doors. But the struggle in Indiana not only kept pace with a similar one in the Ohio legislature, it actually passed it by one year. The Ohio legislature fought over location until 1870, though school opened in 1873, in contrast to Purdue in 1874.

For whatever such statistics are worth, Indiana was the twenty-first state to accept the Morrill Act, the twenty-fourth to locate the campus, and the thirtieth to open. None of these was a permanent handicap inasmuch as Purdue soon passed many of its land-grant counterparts in numbers and resources.

During the last four years of the Indiana legislative fight over the site for the new college, the trustees, already appointed under the 1865 Indiana act, prepared for the sale of scrip. Under the Morrill Act of 1862, each state was entitled to 30,000 acres of federal land for each senator and representative in Congress under an apportionment based on the 1860 census. States with insufficient lands within their borders to meet this grant could get from the secretary of the interior scrip (or land certificates) that allowed the land to be located wherever the purchasers of the scrip desired.

The funds so collected then constituted an endowment for the college but were not to be used to purchase land or buildings. Indiana did not have sufficient federal lands to fulfill the maximum grant and sold scrip, eventually the equivalent of 609 sections or 390,000 acres. On April 9, 1867, the bids for Indiana scrip were opened with prices ranging from forty to sixty-two and a half cents per acre, netting for the college the land-grant endowment fund of $212,238.50—not a bad price overall considering that the land market was then glutted.

The trustees immediately invested the funds in United States bonds and took no further action. Interest accumulated meanwhile, and on May 25, 1869, the day John Purdue was sworn in as a life member of the trustee board, a treasurer's report showed an endowment fund then worth $232,963.90.

•   •   •

Though the story of Purdue University from a dream to a reality seems excruciatingly slow, progress was fairly rapid; progress of any kind often seems feeble in latter-day perspective. Yet, the foundation for the new university had been well laid. Although many steps remained before the institution actually began to function in the fall of 1874, the vision of Jefferson, Morrill, John Purdue and others like him, reinforced by public sentiment for higher education, had borne rich fruit and found articulate expression.

Chapter III

John Purdue

The nineteenth century dawned on a freshly foaled America thrashing awkwardly to gain its sovereign feet, to take its first difficult but brave steps toward nationhood. The times were fluid and uncertain, yet they produced men and women of certainty—individuals who knew what had to be done, then did it.

One of them was John Purdue, the only son among the nine children of Charles and Mary Short Purdue (who are believed to have been married about 1790 in Maryland). He was born in the Purdues' sturdy log cabin, eighteen by twenty feet, on the eastern lower slope of Black Log Mountain on October 31, 1802, in an area called Germany Valley not far from Shirleysburg, Huntingdon County, Pennsylvania.

Few men are so blessed by the accident of birth as to be reared alongside a unique experiment—the beginnings of a new nation dedicated, in spirit if not always in fact, to the sanctity of individual freedom. John Purdue was one so blessed, born less than two decades after the signing of the Treaty of Paris which established the new country as a nation; his arrival was only fourteen years after the new United States Constitution became the law of a land previously governed by the law of royal caprice, or not governed at all.

Eli Whitney had filed his first patent for the cotton gin only nine years prior to John Purdue's birth. The Whitney invention had so profound a social effect on the new nation that many of the problems resulting from its creation and use still exist.

A mere two years before Purdue's birth in the Pennsylvania mountains, John and Abigail Adams first occupied the newly built presidential manse in Washington, D.C. At about that same time, the United States Congress arrived to move into the unfinished capitol in the same city—then not yet a city, much less a federal capital.

John Purdue was not a year old when young America paid France $15 million in cash for the Louisiana Territory, a purchase of a vast stretch of interior North America that doubled the young country's area, giving it its heartland and breadbasket, though straining its pocketbook.

Purdue turned nine years old a week before William Henry Harrison and 920 militia regulars and Hoosier volunteer troops from the government's Vincennes outpost, some on horseback, some afoot, arrived at a spot a short distance downstream from the confluence of the Tippecanoe and Wabash rivers. There on a small flat-topped rise along Burnett's Creek (once called Dead Gulch Creek) they fought an obscure but smart little skirmish with a swarm of peevish braves led by a Shawnee mystic, a thirty-six-year-old, one-eyed rogue named the Prophet, also known as Laulawasikaw, (some authors spell it "Laulewasika"), literally, "loud mouth."

The area was a forlorn, often-flooded wilderness of malarial swamps, mosquitoes, copperheads, rattlesnakes, a variety of varmints in great number and varying degrees of ferocity, a hellish tangle of vines and undergrowth, and other capricious vegetation pervasive on the lonely, dark edge of the Great Prairie. Yet, men seemed willing enough to kill or maim one another over it. In the predawn hours of November 7, 1811, they did so—200 casualties in all. It became known as the Battle of Tippecanoe, the precursor some theorize of the War of 1812, although that may be quite likely an undeserved historical approbation. Not incidentally, the battle was won by the higher moral persuasion of the white man's rifle balls which, Laulawasikaw had been able to convince his naive young braves, would turn magically to sand at the muzzles and fall harmlessly. That they did not raised some serious doubts and caused no little consternation (not to mention bloodshed) among the Prophet's braves about the credibility of his leadership. Eventually, he was driven in disgrace and dishonor from among his own, who included, ironically, his highly respected brother, the great Chief Tecumseh.

As a nine-year-old schoolboy, John Purdue at best could have been only slightly aware of the momentous events taking place on the wilderness frontier several hundred miles west of his central Pennsylvania world. How could he really care about such things happening along the Wabash and Tippecanoe rivers when the fishing was so good along Aughwich Creek that meandered through one of the many valleys between the Allegheny ridges? How could he imagine—especially one who at age twelve "hired out"—that one day he would make a mercantile fortune, immortalize his name, and live out his years only a relatively few steps from that historic battleground.

Growing up in those times, Purdue and his contemporaries took on as personal qualities many of the same traits that eventually gave dimension to the character of the new, evolving nation. He was steady, independent, and persistent to the point of being downright mule-headed at times. But he was also endowed with a penchant for hard work, undoubtedly acquired from a boyhood dominated by it, and, as the Purdue mythology would surely have it, an unimpeachable integrity. He was the equivalent of his surroundings.

Along the way, John Purdue also acquired a trader's acumen. With that and whatever other qualities and combination of resources he mustered, he became one of that fraternity of select nineteenth-century farmer-trader-merchants who came to learn the fine and rare art of winnowing profit from the vaguest hint of commercial opportunity, to learn to stay just far enough behind the leading edge of America's westward-moving frontier to make their fortunes from it.

•   •   •

Most of the details of John Purdue's early life in Pennsylvania were either not recorded or are lost. We know virtually nothing about his father, Charles, and mother, Mary, or why they came to choose a mountain wilderness as home for their nine children. We can surmise that the father could earn the family living there. John was halfway down the family skein. He had four older sisters, Catherine, Nancy, Sarah, and Eliza. Margaret, Susan, Mary (Polly), and Hannah were younger. Another sister, name today unknown, died in infancy.

One's birth and rearing in a log cabin does not necessarily imply a childhood of poverty and dire need. In John Purdue's case, the evidence appears to be strong that, although the family had to work hard, it was well fed and comfortably housed, and had a modest savings. Father Charles worked at several jobs but was primarily a charcoalburner at a nearby iron smelter. That may account for the fact that the frugal Purdue family had enough money to make the difficult and expensive trip west to Adelphi and later to Worthington, Ohio, in 1823 when John was twenty or twenty-one.

• • •

The surname Purdue is considered to be English, existing in England long before the era of the French Huguenots from the late sixteenth to the early eighteenth centuries. Nevertheless, the name is subject to several theories as to its derivation. Perhaps it was French in origin and that it was originally Perdue, but only Purdue in its rarer forms. Even on the early Pennsylvania frontier, John's family name often was spelled Perdue; early census takers even spelled it that way. Regardless, one theory has it that the name had its origin in the Latin *per deum*, through the French, *par Dieu*—the battle cry of the Norman knight, or possibly the motto emblazoned on his pennon, surplice, and shield, or often a name given to those who used it as an oath. Another theory suggests that the name derives from the French *perdu*, meaning "lost," a word used to describe a foundling, or a soldier on outpost duty cut off from his troops by an enemy.

John Purdue's lineage may go back to William Purdue of Closworth, Somersetshire, England, head of a fairly widely known family of bellfounders who were also established in Ireland. In fact, William himself was buried in Limerick Cathedral and a favorite epitaph chiseled on his tombstone in this couplet:

Here lies a bellfounder honest and true,
Till the Resurrection, named Purdue.

Though most sources indicate that the Purdue family was English (albeit established in Ireland as well), Charles Purdue is believed to have come to America from Scotland. Other sources indicate he may have been born either in Maryland or Virginia about 1765 and migrated as a young man to central Pennsylvania. The correct family name is not altogether clear; Charles is identified in the 1800 census of Shirley Township in Huntingdon County as "Charles Purdin" and in the 1810 census as "C. Purdoo." Even as a young man in Ohio, John may have occasionally signed his last name as "Perdue" or "Perdoo." The evidence that suggests it, however, may simply be a case of an incorrect deciphering of his handwriting.

An early and pervasive belief that the Purdue origins were in Germany, possibly because of some vague, assumed connection with the Pennsylvania home in Germany Valley, has long been discounted. The only safe conclusion one may draw from the available information about the Purdue ancestry is that today it seems rife with confusion.

•　　•　　•

At the age of eight, John Purdue was sent to the Pennsylvania community's one-room school, down a rough and rocky road near the foot of Black Log Mountain not far from the Purdue cabin. What formal education Purdue had, he obtained there. He was good in school, especially in "the English branches of study," and for several years in Ohio, he eked out an existence as a schoolteacher in the same kind of classroom where he had been taught.

The westward trek of the Purdue family to Ohio took most of the summer of 1823, an arduous and tragic journey. Nancy, one of John's older sisters, died en route; his father died not long after the family arrived in Ross County, Ohio, at the town of Adelphi. The route of that trip is not known today. The family probably crossed over the ridge and traveled south fifty miles through the Aughwich Creek valley, a much traveled trail used by both Indians and pioneers between the Susquehanna and the Ohio country that brought them to the National Road. A principal east-west artery between Cumberland, Maryland, and (at that time) Wheeling, Virginia, the road bore outbound settlers westward and the products of early pioneer farms eastward.

At Wheeling, the Purdues very likely boarded a flatboat to Portsmouth, Ohio, thence traveled overland north up the Scioto River valley to Adelphi, a tiny community tucked away in the northeast corner of Ross County in south central Ohio. It is a region with quaint place names such as Tar Hollow, Rattlesnake Knob, Yellow Bud, and Kinnickkinnick. Not long after John's father died, Mary Short Purdue and her daughters packed off for Worthington, Ohio, a settlement about twenty miles north of Columbus. Worthington was a "road's end" community at the edge of a frontier from whence the courageous, intrepid, and/or foolhardy left civilization at its fringe and plunged headlong into a primeval wilderness.

As the American frontier crept westward, the greatest supply of eligible bachelors seemed to move with it; thus, Worthington was a likely spot where Mary Purdue could help her daughters find husbands—a necessity in those days, especially in a family with seven marriageables. In due course, the Purdue family at Worthington enlarged by six sons-in-law. Eliza never married.

John, then about twenty-one, struck out on his own. The exact sequence of events that comprised his Ohio years is hazy. We do know that he taught in Pickaway County in a select (i.e., private) school. He was successful at it but also nearly poverty-stricken since he was paid the handsome stipend of $10 per month—a sum so "handsome," in fact, that he was "warned out" of one township for fear he would become an indigent charge. Yet, in retrospect, Purdue recalled his periods as a schoolteacher as "the happiest days of my life." One of his pupils from those days was Moses Fowler, a farm lad born near Circleville, Ohio, who was Purdue's junior by thirteen years. They later became business partners in Adelphi and Lafayette.

Fowler later married Eliza Hawkins of Hamilton, Ohio. Purdue, the lone son among the nine Purdue children, never married, and it was often observed, even in later years, that although he was always a gentleman he was also always extremely shy in the company of women.

A preponderance of evidence indicates that John Purdue probably taught in Ohio schools from about 1826 to 1830. One account says that he was recommended by the president of Athens University (now Ohio University at Athens) for a schoolteaching job in 1831 at Little Prairie, south of Decatur, VanBuren County, Michigan, and taught there for a part of that year.

Purdue had put together enough capital by 1831 to purchase 160 acres in Marion County, Ohio, for $900. He paid $450 down, with the balance to be paid when convenient and without interest. He farmed the land for about a year and sold it for $1,200 in 1832. That sale with its $300 profit to himself was an early and classic example of the entrepreneurship that typified Purdue's business style. During the year he farmed, his reputation for shrewd but honest dealing brought his neighbors to him with a request that he market their hogs for them. It was a new experience for Purdue, but he took 400 animals to market, probably at Cincinnati, paying the farmers a fair price, and collecting a $300 commission for himself.

From that exhilarating adventure, Purdue, astride his horse, developed a profitable farm products brokerage, covering as much as a fifty-mile radius in and around Adelphi, Worthington, and Columbus. As word spread, Purdue's reputation for fair dealing spread also; he became popular among the residents of the area who, until then, had no convenient market for their foodstuffs. Purdue created one; in fact, he became their market. Ohio was being domesticated; the state had embarked upon an ambitious public works program to build a network of canals and to extend the National Road from Wheeling, across Ohio to Richmond, Indiana. Work camps east of Columbus needed food; farmers needed markets. Purdue satisfied both needs. On that basic economic axis turns the world of capitalism.

•   •   •

In 1833, in partnership with Fowler, Purdue opened a general mercantile business in Adelphi. He was then thirty-one; Fowler was eighteen and a journeyman tanner. Although they were young and relatively inexperienced in mercantile trade, their business prospered. So what motivated them to take the risks inherent in moving it to an obscure, depressing little river settlement with an uncertain future in west central Indiana?

Conventional wisdom states that John Purdue first saw Lafayette in 1837, two years before he and Fowler moved their business to that community. Rather convincing evidence suggests that Purdue was aware of the western Indiana possibilities as early as 1834. He first passed through the city either by stagecoach or on horseback as early as the late fall of 1836 on a business trip to Galena, a northwestern Illinois community near the Mississippi River, where Purdue and Fowler seemed to have conducted an extraordinary amount of business by mail.

The 1834 evidence includes a land transaction in Adelphi in which Jesse Spencer conveyed to John Purdue 240 acres in Tippecanoe County on December 9 of that year. Spencer bought it through the federal land office in Crawfordsville for $850. The parcel lies in Fairfield Township at the northeast corner of Creasy and McCarty lanes east of Lafayette. One assumption is that the Spencer conveyance was in trade for goods purchased at the Purdue-Fowler store in Adelphi and that the agreed-upon price was that paid at the original government purchase. Quite likely, Purdue first inspected the land on his western trip in 1836. Purdue retained ownership for twenty-three years, adding parcels, buildings, and other improvements, then sold the farm in 1857 to William McCarty for $10,000.

Did John Purdue move to Lafayette in 1839 (again, as is generally believed)? Or perhaps earlier? While still in Ohio, he was in a dispute with an Illinois man over a tax matter involved in the purchase and sale of an unspecified parcel of land near Prophetstown, Illinois, northeast of Moline on the Rock River. In a letter to his antagonist dated August 5, 1837, Purdue wrote that "I have closed my business in Ohio and am nearly ready to leave the state for good," adding that he should write to him next at Lafayette, Indiana, "where I expect to be located permanently again next spring and where I expect to spend some time this fall."

Whether 1837, 1838, or 1839, the date is important only as a date; when Purdue and Fowler arrived to reestablish their Adelphi business, Caleb Scudder, first white child born in Lafayette, was a ten-year-old tad. Purdue was thirty-six or thirty-seven, Fowler twenty-three or twenty-four. What they found was a settlement of mostly saloons, a brawling river village where pigs freely rooted in dirt streets or cooled themselves in the frequent mud wallows, where, undoubtedly, a tanyard, a foundry, cabinet shop, and other appropriate rivertown industries throve along the Wabash. There were several churches; Purdue arrived for good the same year, 1839, as the town's first church bell, founded for the tower of Saint John's Episcopal Church.

A visitor from Massachusetts in the 1830s described Lafayette as "like all the rest of the Western villages we have seen, filled with stumps, hogs, horses, cattle, and Indians." Lafayette survived the vituperation, having been blessed, apparently, with people blithely indifferent to the opinions of outlanders. The populace had been toughened by the earlier scorn and derision of its older neighbor, Crawfordsville, where wags referred to the town as "Lay-flat," "Laugh-at," or similar distortions of language.

Over land, Lafayette was not easily accessible except by bone-jarring wagon or buggy ride through rutted mud paths or over plank roads—or by horseback. Lafayette's almost total economic orientation was to the river, without which Lafayette had no raison d'être.

The town was founded by William Digby, the son of a veteran of the War of 1812, a tall and handsome ne'er-do-well cardplayer. At age twenty-two, he poled up and down the upper Wabash either by keel boat or dugout, carrying items for his itinerant trading business with the Indians. His familiarity and knowledge of this stretch of the Wabash led him to attend a government sale at the federal land office in Crawfordsville on Christmas Eve 1824. Digby knew that commercial vessels could navigate the Wabash as far upstream as the present site of the city and probably no further—even when the current was high in the spring.

No doubt Digby was also aware of the site of an abandoned Indian trading post built along the Wabash at Lafayette by

James Wyman. Wyman thought the site was an ideal location, especially from the standpoint of the river's seasonal levels. He erected a post building and one or two others for his residence but abandoned it to the undergrowth and overgrowth after most of the Indians withdrew from the region in 1819 and 1820. Wyman remained in this area but never claimed ownership, and it thus became a part of the land eventually offered for sale at the United States land office at Crawfordsville years later.

In 1821, Tippecanoe County was believed devoid of white men except for Peter Longlois, the French trader who, with his Indian wife and two children, occupied a trading post at the mouth of Wildcat Creek northeast of what is now Lafayette. But only three years later, Digby and others bid frantically for purchase of Wabash valley lands as white settlers began to move westward and northward.

At the 1824 land sale, Digby dug deep and bid bravely against a man named Major Whitlock for 84.23 acres on the east side of the river and finally acquired them for $231.63. He hoped to establish a trading post, albeit in an area tangled with hazel and plum brush vines and trees of every description. In the spring of 1825, he and a bartender friend, Robert Johnson, who was also a surveyor, surveyed the rough site—a difficult chore because of the nearly impenetrable underbrush—and divided 50 acres of it into 140 lots. On May 25, 1825, inspired by the triumphant return to this land of the Revolutionary hero General Marquis de LaFayette (who had made a stop at Jeffersonville on the Ohio River), Digby named his little plat "LaFayette" in the Frenchman's honor. Two days later, he filed the plat at the Crawfordsville land office. It covered the area bounded by the river and the present Lafayette streets of Sixth, South, and North.

Not known for his reliability or astuteness, the improvident Digby sold most of his plat to Samuel Sargent for $240—$1.71 per lot—or a gross profit to Digby of $8.37. Within a month, he sold the balance for a paltry $60 dollars.

Digby first operated a general store, then bought a ferryboat which he operated across the Wabash River for many years, ferrying pioneer farmers and their goods to the Lafayette markets. Eventually, Lafayette became the head of Wabash navigation and an important commercial hub. But over the years, Digby engaged mostly in drinking, card-playing, and the brawling that usually resulted therefrom. As Digby's prestige as the founder of the town diminished, his notoriety as a public nuisance grew. He died at age sixty-two in 1864, "in reduced circumstances" his death notice called it, apparently unaware that had he retained just one-tenth of his original purchase, he would have been a wealthy man. As it turned out, he was a virtually penniless railroad bridge watchman in Attica when he died.

William Digby never knew that "his" Lafayette, Indiana, is perhaps the only town ever founded by the town drunk.

•   •   •

There was this itinerant who wandered through Tippecanoe County on his way to nowhere in 1827. Lafayette was only two years old at the time. You can read about him and the problem they were having with itinerants in those days in the minutes of the seventh meeting of the Lafayette Board of Justices. This itinerant was different. His name was John Chapman and they called him "Johnny Appleseed." Downstream on the Wabash, near West Point, Johnny accidentally killed a rattlesnake while clearing space for a seedling apple nursery, and they say he suffered acute remorse for the rest of his life because he had carelessly killed a living thing.

•   •   •

What impressions John Purdue may have absorbed on his first visit we do not know. Descriptions of the time spoke of a dreary, unkempt settlement of log cabins and frame buildings. What was it about this surly little settlement on the Wabash floodplain that held such attraction? John Purdue was a trader, an entrepreneur, a capitalist. He would give something for anything and take something for anything. The successful traders of the world are those with a clear focus on the future. Purdue was far more interested in what Lafayette could be than how it might have appeared at the moment. For example, he could not have overlooked the coming of the Wabash and Erie Canal to Lafayette, a part of a vast system of "improvements" that in a spate of financial lunacy Indiana had decided to undertake. As a businessman, he had to be aware that the advent of the canal had raised the price of wheat from forty-five cents to one dollar a bushel while dropping the price of salt from nine dollars a barrel to four.

Such were the intimations for a growing and healthy commerce in Indiana, although intimations created at the expense of the state's solvency. It was the kind of prosperity which tended to camouflage the bankrupt condition of the public treasury: a state debt of $10 million which carried a $479,000 annual interest charge, far more than the revenues from the mismanaged canal system could satisfy.

Yet, the plain fact was that a rich land was coming to commercial maturity; river towns such as Lafayette, though nondescript, dreary little huddles, were on the make; the fact of public insolvency seemed to matter little or was dismissed outright as a temporary political trauma. Life near the frontier's edge pulsated. Make the area more easily accessible and the opportunities to exploit its richness seemed endless.

Considering the high cost of its construction, the canal itself prospered relatively briefly, sputtering along for little more than three decades but destined for an ignominious death in the 1870s. Notwithstanding, the area's long-range possibilities seemed undeniably clear to Purdue and, collectively, were undoubtedly the principal factors that influenced his decision to tie his wagon to the Lafayette star, despite a thriving business and a solid, statewide reputation in Ohio.

Purdue and Moses Fowler displayed superb timing. They arrived in Lafayette four years before the canal, moving their dry goods and grocery business from Ohio. They made the then squalid Wabash River town in western Indiana their lifelong home, contributing mightily along the way to its eventual civility and domestication. Their firm's first advertisement appeared in an early Lafayette newspaper, the *Free Press*, and hawked "200 bbls. of sweet cider—just received and for sale cheap." Purdue and Fowler, before they ended their partnership in 1844, were known to sell any merchandisable goods.

Lafayette—the star city on the Wabash—may have had (as the late Paul Fatout so colorfully observed in his 1972 book, *Indiana Canals)* "a bucolic air of caliker and butternut jeans." But in business dealings, its citizens were far more astute than the small-town jaspers they may have appeared to be. The atmosphere virtually reeked with an all-consuming need to make a dollar. Growers, shippers, and merchandisers, Purdue and Fowler included, pursued the Wabash Valley's riches, benefitting from the then booming canal and river shipping business which could move products northeastward via Toledo and the Great Lakes to the east coast or southward via the Ohio and Mississippi rivers. By 1851, in the shipping season, as many as thirty-one steamboats bound to or from Evansville, twenty-five from or to Cincinnati, and twenty to or from Pittsburgh tied up at the Lafayette docks; others were out of Louisville, St. Louis, and New Orleans. Later, the Wabash and Erie Canal was extended south to Evansville, increasing the volume of stuffs shipped from, to, or through Lafayette via canal packet or steamboat. The last commercial riverboat at Lafayette steamed away in 1861.

But at one period during the short-lived canal's heyday, Lafayette annually exported more than forty thousand barrels of flour and pork, well above one million bushels of corn, and more than four million pounds of bacon and lard, in addition to huge quantities of wheat, oats, butter, soap, cheese, potash, hides, and tanbark. The town had a drydock for canal packet boats. It had commission houses (Purdue's was considered one of the largest and finest west of New York City), livery stables, and even a boatmen's infirmary.

Fowler quit his partnership with Purdue in 1844 to pursue other business interests in commerce, banking, the railroads, and Benton County farmland northwest of Lafayette. Eventually he came to be known as Indiana's richest man. In the ensuing years, Purdue continued his business interests with other partners— usually men much younger than himself—men on the way up whom Purdue chose to give a helping hand. As early as 1844, Purdue purchased the downtown Lafayette real estate needed for the Purdue Block. In 1847, the block was completed and in 1848, he founded the company known as Purdue, Stacey and Company, which included wholesaling as well as retailing. He also had partnerships with Samuel Curtis and Oliver H. P. McCormick and had formed, with L. (for Lazarus) Maxwell Brown, Purdue, Brown and Company which occupied a major portion of the Purdue Block bounded by First and Second, and Columbia and South streets.

Whether John Purdue made the correct decision in moving to Lafayette was never in question. As he once said in reference to his business career, "I never made a mistake in my life."

•   •   •

The land around about was full of copperheads and rattlers and you watched where you stepped, but the Wabash River and the creeks that fed it were full of fish—bass, trout, pike, and sauger. What roads existed were mostly mud in winter and dust in summer, but you could haul a wagonload of corn into Lafayette for three cents or less from the Wea country where yields went anywhere from forty to ninety bushels an acre. That was in 1848.

In 1849, you did not go into Lafayette too often. The roads were a fright and there was a cholera epidemic—two or three deaths for every four or five cases; what doctors there were worked nearly to exhaustion. They used up the town's supply of dry flannel and red pepper mustard and salt they rubbed on those who came down sick. More than half the population had gone in all directions out to the country, intending to return only when the cholera abated, if it did. Country folk were shy about going into town.

The new railroad was going in at about eight rods a day, and by 1852, Lafayette had five rail and three plank roads to it, good houses, fine churches, and blocks of neat, brick store buildings. And the Wabash and Erie Canal throve. So did the saloons. So did the Democrats with Franklin Pierce and William Rufus King, who got elected the country's president and vice president, and who left no vestige of Whigging in all of Indiana.

•   •   •

The 1849 cholera epidemic was one of the darkest moments in the young town's brief history. It lasted about six weeks. Thousands fled the city in panic, many of them camping along Wea Creek south of the city. In one brief period at the outset, only a handful of untrained nurses, their helpers, and one local doctor, Elizhur H. Deming, a member of the faculty of the Indiana Medical College at LaPorte, were available to treat the sick. They worked day and night, seemingly in vain; eight hundred died, about fifteen of every one hundred citizens. Those who stayed in town reported later the eerie sensation of living in a city of deadly silence—broken only by the occasional sound of wagon wheels creaking over the town's gravel streets as they carried coffins to Greenbush Cemetery. Three Lafayette prostitutes had fled to a rural cabin where they fell ill with the disease. Those who discovered them there immediately torched the cabin, immolating the sick women inside.

Business and commerce slowed and nearly stopped. Many merchants closed their shops and businesses as they fled; many never reopened. John Purdue survived the catastrophe, seemingly none the worse off financially or physically.

If there was a darker moment than the summer of 1849, it may have been the summer of 1854 when the second cholera epidemic broke out, most likely because of a failure to correct the conditions that were the source of the first. Six hundred citizens, mostly adults, died in the 1854 miasma. Several movements to clean up the heaps of garbage in alleyways and along city streets had been started as a result of the 1849 epidemic, but nothing seemed to get done. Such efforts broke down in political squabbles, despite the fact that Lafayette had prided itself on being an early (1833) Indiana city to establish a board of health, a development that grew out of citizen complaints that too many people were urinating in the Wabash River.

John Purdue must have been deeply moved and concerned by the 1849 event, but his particular interest, besides making money, was in education, engendered partly from his own school-teaching years in Ohio, partly from a lifelong regret he often alluded to that he had not had more opportunity for formal education himself.

When Indiana rewrote its constitution in 1851, provision was made for free schools. Quickly the following year, the Indiana General Assembly adopted legislation empowering common councils in Hoosier communities to appoint boards of education empowered, in turn, to levy school taxes. The Lafayette Common Council in 1852 appointed the city's first school board. John Purdue, Israel Spencer, William P. Heath, Jacob Casad, and Samuel Hoover were its first appointees. Purdue was a member of that first board's first committee to seek school building sites—the first being the Southern School at Fountain and Third streets. It was later replaced at the same site by the Tippecanoe School which was razed in recent years to make way for a community center.

An 1854 Indiana Supreme Court decision found the taxing portion of the new free school statute flawed and therefore unconstitutional. A year later, Indiana free schools found themselves without operating funds. Across Indiana the public schools closed—all but in Lafayette where, thanks to the personal largess of John Purdue, they remained open. Indiana public schools opened again in February 1856, but not until 1860 was the law finally corrected to the satisfaction of the Indiana Supreme Court.

Purdue served a term on the Lafayette Common Council in addition to his appointment to the school board. But he preferred to commit most of his community stewardship and resources to other matters. His life as a leading citizen, businessman, and budding philanthropist was interrupted in 1855 when he formed a new company in New York with John S. Ward, then twenty-five, an employee of an eastern pork packer named J. B. Thompson. Their New York commission house, known as Purdue and Ward, did a spectacular Civil War business as a chief supplier of pork and pork products to the Union armies. Purdue became a rich man. Presumably, so did Ward. Purdue also became a tower of financial stability and integrity in New York and was known among his colleagues in trade as the "King of Produce" and/or "Mr. Pork." Still, he retained his residency in Lafayette and his interest in his Lafayette businesses and the community at large.

Purdue made his first trip to New York as a Lafayette businessman in 1847. (He may have made a trip to the eastern seaboard while an Adelphi businessman.) The purpose of his 1847 trip was to dispose of $100,000 in pork products he and his partner Brown had shipped to New York and to purchase goods for wholesale and retail business in Lafayette. He left Lafayette in August and returned in October. New York visits became more frequent for Purdue. But he was getting older; trips to the East from Lafayette were long and arduous. He began to spend more time in New York and less in Lafayette; in 1855, after establishing Purdue and Ward, he lived there most of the time for a decade.

Purdue returned to Lafayette in 1865, his fortune in war profits intact. He was then sixty-three, and in most of his remaining eleven years until his death in 1876, he did those things which stamped his name forever on the age. They were years that gave him the public attention he secretly loved and whetted his deep interest in educational matters but left his fortune in a shambles, an executor's nightmare.

Purdue's widely known munificence and his comparatively large fortune brought him a plethora of suggestions from the well-meaning as well as from the misguided as to how and to whom he should dispose of his wealth. He was as busy in his later years making sure it was disposed of properly as he had been in earlier times acquiring it. It was a tough job; he waded through a great number of suggestions, investigated each of them himself, and made up his own mind. He tried to make his money work to the advantage of the entire community. Obviously, his primary interest was in doing the things that would improve education. That interest was described in George W. Munro's writings as "pocket deep" and went back many years before the gift that brought him immortality as the university's chief benefactor.

Generous though he was, Purdue had a vanity as wide as the Wabash River and, as a member of the first faculty, Harvey Washington Wiley, put it in his own memoirs, a vanity "as innocent as that of a child. He was certain that any opinion he had was the only correct one on any subject."

Wiley recalled that although Purdue was not a member of any church in Lafayette, he often gave generous sums for religious and philanthropic causes and had given $1,000 toward the construction of the Second Presbyterian Church. When it was completed, he was invited to the dedicatory service. He entered the sanctuary just as the members of the congregation rose to sing the first hymn. Purdue thought it was a gesture in his honor and said in a voice heard throughout the sanctuary, "Keep your seats, ladies and gentlemen; don't mind me."

When Purdue played Santa Claus, the gifts he loved to give the most were those with his own name on them. Thus, when a "Purdue Institute" in downtown Lafayette was suggested shortly after his return to Lafayette, he agreed to bankroll one-third of its cost, $25,000. The institute was to be an all-inclusive facility combining public library, reading rooms, lecture hall, and art gallery. One of the letters to him urging his contribution to a facility that was to bear his name may have been too pretentious, and he probably lost his enthusiasm. Signed by a gentleman named "I. Rice," the letter read in part, "It would be a child of whom any man living might feel honored in being called its father, while his heart should throb with the leap of quicker pulsations, as he saw unfolding the future, ever-growing promise of its ripe manhood."

As 1866 dawned, Purdue felt obliged to enter politics, probably the biggest mistake he ever made, in spite of his own self-encomium that he had never made one.

His calling to the political wars was based primarily on his view that federal policy with respect to post-Civil War Reconstruction should be less harsh and more compassionate. He became an independent candidate for Congress and faced a strong and popular Republican incumbent, a famed Lafayette attorney and poet named Godlove S. Orth, who sought a third term as a representative from Indiana's eighth district. To further his campaign, Purdue bought the Lafayette *Journal* from James P. Luse for $30,000 and became its editor—a decision which compounded his original error. The Chicago *Tribune*, referring to Purdue as "John G. Purdue of Lafayette, Ind.,"[*] came out strongly for the reelection of Orth, opining that since Purdue's purchase of the *Journal*, "its editorial columns have been almost exclusively devoted to proving that the Convention system is all wrong. His platform is short, ambitious, and, if it means anything at all, it means bread-and-butter."

Running as an independent was literally true for Purdue; he did things his own way. Some of his methods were no more virtuous than those of his opponents, some of them worse. He knew nothing of political acuity, nor much about editing a newspaper. In one notable example of illogic, referring to his refusal

---

[*] The reference to "John G. Purdue" is the only instance this writer has ever seen of John Purdue's name used with a middle initial. Whether he had a middle name—and if he did, what it was—could not be documented.

One of the earliest buildings was the first U.S. Agricultural Experiment Station, built in 1882. Totally inadequate, it was replaced in 1908 by the present building at Marsteller and State streets. (Tippecanoe County Historical Association Archives)

Twenty-six years after it opened with five buildings and a workshed, Purdue University campus looked like this in a 1900 panoramic view that shows, from left, the Agricultural Experiment Station, the tower of Ladies Hall, University Hall, the Dormitory, the first Electrical Engineering Building, and Heavilon Hall, then considered the Midwest's showpiece in engineering education.

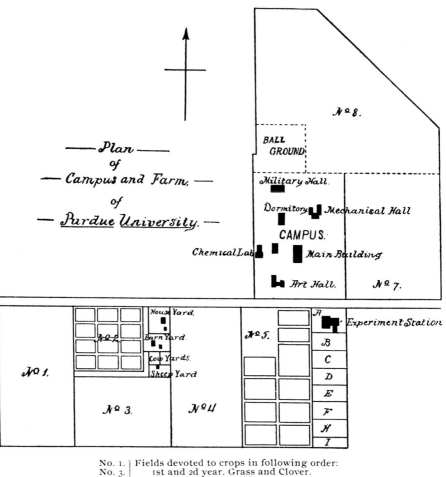

—— Plan ——
of
— Campus and Farm, —
of
— Purdue University. —

No. 1. ⎫ Fields devoted to crops in following order:
No. 3. ⎪   1st and 2d year. Grass and Clover.
No. 4. ⎬   3d year, Corn.
No. 7. ⎪   4th year, Oats.
No. 8. ⎭   5th year, Wheat.
No. 2.   Horticultural Plats.
No. 5.   New Permanent Experiment Plats.
B-I.   Old Experiment Plats.

From an agricultural bulletin, a
schematic map of the campus in 1891
details experimental farm plots which
nearly surrounded the campus.

James Henry Smart, who once dropped out of high school, became Purdue's fourth president in 1883 and brought Purdue University to greatness in engineering by his own enthusiasm and chancy decisions.

Stanley Coulter, while fishing in northern Indiana, received his invitation from President Smart to join the Purdue staff. He became one of the university's stalwarts, serving simultaneously as dean of men, dean of the School of Science, and as chairman of the faculty.

Reginald Aubrey Fessenden was the first Purdue faculty to hold the title of professor of electrical engineering. He was at Purdue in 1892–93, then later near Washington, D.C., conducted the first transmission of the human voice by wireless telephony.

The Heavilon Hall saga began with construction of the famed landmark and symbol of pride. . .

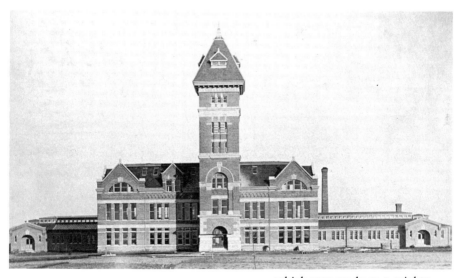

. . .which was ready as a mighty engineering laboratory with the name of its principal benefactor, Amos Heavilon. Four days after it was dedicated on January 19, 1894, disaster struck. . .

. . .and before the sun arose on January 24, Heavilon Hall was the victim of a gas explosion and fire that left it a forlorn, charred hulk. At chapel that day. . .

. . .President Smart spoke softly, then with determination declared, ". . . but I tell you, young men, that tower shall go up one brick higher!—a speech that echoes down the years as Purdue's rallying cry.

The first football team played one game in the fall of 1887, losing to Butler, 48-6. Jacob M. Sholl, front row right with his hand on the football, scored the first points ever in a Purdue football game. The team trained, wrote George Ade, '87, "on pie and donuts."

Probably the forerunner of Purdue University Bands, this group was pictured about 1886 near what later became known as Purdue Hall. Players are unidentified, including baritone player at far right in mufti.

"The Village"—downtown West Lafayette—in the formative years of Purdue University. The town and the university grew together. Scene above looks eastward at the intersection of State, South, and Vine (now Northwestern Avenue) streets. The lower view is at the same site, looking westward. Trolleys were the chief mode of transportation, except for occasional horse-drawn vehicles. (Trolley scene from Tippecanoe County Historical Association Archives)

The *Schenectady No. 2* was nearly the same kind of engineering education showpiece that Heavilon Hall was in Smart's administration. Smart gambled on the locomotive as one way of putting Purdue on the map as one of the nation's leading engineering schools. He won. Purdue was the only engineering school at the time that did serious locomotive testing.

to print a letter from a reader who wanted to use a false name, Purdue wrote editorially, "I don't like these underhanded licks, anyway. Whenever I write an anonymous communication I always sign my name to it."

An opposition editorial in the Lafayette *Daily Courier* read:

> Daily we have evidences of that wonderful intellect which in colossal grandeur o'ertops the small statesmen of the day. Mr. Purdue says himself, and he surely wouldn't lie about a little matter of that kind, that as he grows older his brain expands, and he takes "enlarged views," not visible to the clouded comprehension of weaker minds. The expansion of his brain is such that in filling an order for a campaign hat the other day the hatter took the measure of the Court House Dome and it fit him exactly. Besides, he understands the great "commercial interests." He can tell the weight of a hog by sight and recite its pedigree by the curl of its tail.

Orth defeated Purdue by 118 votes. He was beaten, the Indianapolis *Daily Sentinel* editorialized in Purdue's obituary a decade later, "through the base treachery of men who had been pledged to his support." It is quite likely also true that Purdue, as a politician, was his own worst enemy. He not only lost the election, but many friends and immense popularity. The adventure hurt him as well as the university of which he became the chief sponsor three years after his ill-fated congressional campaign. He was left with a residue of hard feeling, a newspaper he no longer wanted, and a pile of campaign debts that, though he did not know it at the time, he could ill-afford.

Despite the setback, Purdue seemed undeterred by the experience and managed to retain not only his good nature but his interest in civic and educational matters. He continued his membership as a trustee of the Tippecanoe Battle Ground Institute as well as an interest in the Alamo Academy in Montgomery County and the Stockwell Institute, to which he is known to have made contributions of "scientific and philosophical apparatus." His interest in higher education extended beyond Purdue University; while working to get the doors open at the new campus a mile or so west of the courthouse, he agreed to provide $1,000 as a deferred gift, payable upon his death, to Buchtel College, now the University of Akron, Ohio.

Another enterprise, apparently a product of Purdue's generosity, was the Purdue Rifles, a company of Lafayette-area men whom he equipped for the Civil War—a group that, legend has it, helped drive the rebel Morgan Raiders out of southern Indiana.

Probably it is more accurate that the Purdue Rifles served on border patrol along the Ohio River. Later, the same military group was supposedly active in "chasing Copperheads out of northern Indiana and Illinois." (Copperheads were Northerners who sympathized with the South.)

There is also a record of a "Purdue Silver Mine" in which Purdue had an interest. At various times throughout his adult years, Purdue loaned money or paid delinquent taxes to help friends or colleagues about to lose all. Such charity left him with such absurdities as unneeded canal dockage, warehouses, a paper mill, two hotels, and uncounted parcels of real estate scattered hither and yon and of which he was (Munro wrote in later years) "not overly fond."

As a bachelor, Purdue never gave a thought to the money he spent on his own rather simple needs and wants. He lived most of his life in well-furnished rooms at the Lahr House in downtown Lafayette. He had an ample personal library of about three hundred volumes, many of them religious or biblical references. He dressed well and was considered by the eligible women of the city as a rather handsome gentleman, though he never had, so says Munro, "an affair of the heart."

Toward women and womanhood, Purdue held a strange and starchy attitude that today would mark him as rather an odd Victorian eccentric. To Purdue, women were apparently unapproachable, fragile personae of moral porcelain to be placed upon high pedestals surrounded by chastity moats. But such was the generally accepted nature of morals and mores of mid-nineteenth-century America.

A rare glimpse of Purdue's views on the subject of women and the courtship thereof is contained in the only personal letter among the aggregate of his papers in the Purdue University Special Collections; the rest are either business or legal documents.

Dated December 29, 1836, the letter Purdue wrote was to a Miss Ann Knauere as he waited in Columbus, Ohio, for a break in wintry weather to make what is presumed to have been his first journey to Lafayette. Purdue was then thirty-four. Just exactly who Miss Knauere was is a mystery, but Purdue called himself her "sincere friend," though even in his letter he was stiffly formal, addressing her in the salutation as "Madam." Very possibly she was a daughter of the merchant under whom Purdue apprenticed. The letter was, peculiarly, mostly a rather lengthy essay on "the impropriety of young ladies keeping the company of gentlemen at night."

He wrote:

Not having much to do at present but read, write, talk, etc., concluded I would scribble a few lines for your amusement. I did expect when I left old Delphi [Adelphi] two weeks ago I should likely be at Lafayette, Indiana, ere this. A part of the time the weather was so extremely cold that I could not form a resolution to face the coldness of the west winds, therefore I am still here in Columbus and its vicinity: amusing myself sometimes in the busy crowd about the taverns at Columbus, at other times in smaller circles in the country disposing of time as cheap as possible and with as much ease as convenient. Columbus is really very pleasant at this time but much crowded. Some of the hotels are full to running over, there are a great many visitors in from different parts of the state, the Supreme Court in session and the Legislature including all makes a very crowded city. Mr. Havens was married on yesterday to a Miss Squires, a very pretty young girl. This was disposing of another bachelor in the right way: The way that I should like to see a few more go: right into the arms of a fair young lady. . . .

I have reflected considerable since I saw you on the impropriety of young ladies keeping the company of gentlemen at night after the family retired to bed and I have come to the conclusion that it is a habit that ought to be abandoned by every young lady that has any claim to respectable society. The practice is never attended with any good results but frequently with very serious and lamentable consequences to the character of young ladies, and I believe it has the attendance in some degree to cast a shade of some consideration upon everyone that practice it: it has certainly the effect of depreciating that pure and unspotted character of real moral worth that ladies should possess. Recollect few men are what they profess to be. Whenever a gentleman calls to spend the evening with you and inclines to tarry after the family retires you have then cause to suspect his motives. Few men have any regards strictly speaking for the reputation of young ladies and it is in the dark houses of night when all evil men carry their designs into effect. The night is the highway robber's time to plunder his neighbor's property. The adulteror waiteth for the night and baser than the vilian on the highway betrays the honor of his bosom friend. Deep layed crimes hide their odious heads in day and haunt the seats of Society at night when they think all is safe that no eye sees. When night is the selected time to execute all the accursed evils in the land. Some other time, then, I think might be chosen for young ladies to make their marriage contracts than in the darkness of night as the object of private company between young ladies and gentlemen is to form a social acquaintance: But of which matrimonial contracts are to be formed and upon those contracts measurably depend all the future happiness or misery of our time on earth. It being a subject of more seriousness than almost any other specially so far as earthly happiness is concerned it being a subject of so much importance to everyone that is concerned in it therefore every step that has the least reference to it cannot be observed with too much caution and prudence in every particular. In regard to keeping night company in private apartments I have frequently been astonished at mothers who permitted their daughters to receive almost any company that would call. Mothers should never in my opinion permit a daughter to keep the company of any after they retire to bed—there is one certain fact that is the gentleman that is seeking a wife would make a choice of one who had never kept night company with any man. The reverse is also true, the gentleman that seeks the company of a young lady to enjoy her society at night is not seeking a wife.

While I am on the subject there is another fact that I will notice: Every fallen monument of female reputation I believe had its origin in keeping night company. And every one that has wept and mourned over their own sad misfortune and ruined characters will tell you the ill misspent time of keeping night company was the only cause of [their] wretchedness and misery today. I have written you or rather scribbled a long string on this one subject. If it does not meet your appreciation excuse my pen, but I think it certainly will and it would give me much pleasure if you would adopt my opinions as given. There is another important fact that ladies and gentlemen both neglect too much that is reading. Reading good authors on such subjects as is calculated to instruct the mind and to aid in forming correct principles is highly necessary and it is the duty of every one to attend to it as much as lies in their power. There is nothing that appears so beautiful in a young lady as to have a mind well based on correct principles and have some knowledge of the different leading topics that pertain thereto. Every one has not perhaps time to read as much as he should like to, but everyone has time to read more I think than they do. I presume you're getting tired trying to read my scribbling. I will therefore begin to wind up and close. My trunk has never arrived. As soon as it comes or very soon afterwards I will move for the west without the weather should be very bad. I think very long to get west and I presume I shall think as long to get back. If I can return against the first of March I will. My respects to any of my friends that enquire of me and you see proper to give. My health is reasonable good. My friends are well. You must write to me direct to Lafayette, Indiana.

Receive my best wishes to your self and others

Your sincere friend,
John Purdue

Miss Ann Knauere
Columbus O. Dec. 29, 1836

• • •

Purdue was once described as a "valiant trencherman," enjoying with great relish such goodies as walnut pickles, brandied peaches, and mince pie—especially those prepared by the mother of his partner, Mack Brown, at whose home he spent a great many convivial evenings. He was especially fond of oysters; in season, he and Brown would have a barrel shipped from the East Coast for a stag dinner lasting "unto the wee hours of the morning." Though Purdue did not drink, even he, in the spirit of such affairs, was known to have taken a snort from a demijohn of rare old whiskey kept in the Brown basement. Purdue's portly figure in later years seemed to bear out his penchant for rich foods.

If he had any real extravagance, it was travel. He was known to leave his home in the Lahr House for months on end as whim or occasion dictated. Especially did he enjoy train travel and used visits to his sixteen-hundred-acre Walnut Grove farm near West Lebanon as an excuse for a train ride. Eventually, Purdue invested in an early, narrow-gauge railroad, the Lafayette, Muncie, and Bloomington (Illinois), which later became a part of the Lake Erie and Western, which became the Nickel Plate and is today a part of the Norfolk and Western system. The line was begun by Lafayette investors and Purdue's love of railroad travel made his financial interest in it inevitable. He even contracted to build the Lafayette-Tipton section. Purdue was also a heavy—in fact, the principal—investor in the Lafayette Agricultural Works late in his career. The firm manufactured farm implements of a variety, one writer later said, "in which the farmers seemed not at all interested." Both investments, plows and railroads, later proved to be drains not only on his fortune but his personal health.

Beyond his letter to Ann Knauere in 1836, there exists little that tells us about the Purdue psyche. His existing personal correspondence was rare, and even that deals primarily with business matters—the ordering of stock for his business establishments and so on. He devoted his entire life to tangibles, although the intangibles and the abstract were not beyond him. But he was not considered an erudite individual who could have perhaps easily defined a personal philosophy beyond simple Christian belief. He is known by his deeds much more than by his words, although that does not mean he was inarticulate. To speculate, he was simply a quiet, self-assured man who seemed to yearn for the formal education, perhaps in the classics, he was never able to have beyond the readings in his own personal library.

These must have been treasured moments of solitude for the "good old man" as he began to approach the biblical three score and ten.

If he was overly self-conscious about his lack of capital "C" culture because of his lack of early schooling, it may have been because of his inability to throw into English conversations the well-turned Latin or French phrase that his educated friends knew. But his own reading in history, politics, philosophy, and theology served him well. It is correct to say that he was lacking in formal, institutionalized education but absolutely inaccurate to say he was uneducated.

One of Purdue's hallmarks, despite his bachelorhood and a mercantile life spent mostly in the company and presence of adults, was his love of children. Many a Lafayette boy remembered him as the donor of his first pocketknife. Early summers invariably produced a John Purdue ritual. He would ask Mrs. Jane Clark Harvey, a prominent Lafayette woman who was the daughter of Dr. O. L. Clark, a pioneering physician in Tippecanoe County, to "collect a carriage full of girls" for an all-day outing—Purdue holding the carriage reins—that always ended with a visit to the confectioners where ice cream, cake, and candy were consumed, seemingly inexhaustibly.

"In these excursions, the merriest, happiest person in the crowd was Mr. Purdue," Mrs. Harvey reminisced in later years He once confided to her that the great mistake of his life was in not getting married—a surprising admission from a man who once believed he had never made a mistake. Yet, he remained a social creature, certainly, and the holidays always found him making the neighborly calls which fulfilled the custom of his day. He liked to be around people and to play an occasional game of cards, usually whist, a forerunner of bridge. He was a gracious host and an appreciative guest. And though he began to suffer the infirmities of old age, had business worries, and was involved deeply in supervising the construction of the first buildings on the campus west of the river, he complained little about his own physical problems. There was little to signal that his long and fruitful life was in its last refrain.

During the summer of 1876, having differed with President Abraham C. Shortridge over the administration of the new college which bore his name and having faced the financial problems of two business ventures, the agricultural works and the railroad, John Purdue began to suffer health problems. He complained of "nervous chills" and suffered attacks of vertigo that eventually made him decide to move temporarily from his comfortable quarters in the Lahr House to the Hygienic Institute, a "water-cure" establishment in the southeast part of the city. (The address of the Hygienic Institute in 1875 was listed as 306 South Seventeenth Street, a location at or near today's intersection of Kossuth and Eighteenth streets.)

He took with him his personal library and was prepared for a lengthy stay. After several weeks of careful diet, medicated baths, and undisturbed rest, he seemed visibly improved, though the financial complications of his unpaid university pledge, the railroad debts, and the liabilities of the Lafayette Agricultural Works weighed heavily—as well they might.

Two months after Purdue's death, the executors of his estate were appalled to discover that he had incurred debts of $300,000—later it became apparent it was much nearer $500,000—by signing notes indiscriminately in the last year of his life in a desperate move to raise money for the railroad. He also owed four installments of $15,000 each, as well as an unaudited account of $5,000, on his original $150,000 pledge to the university. The final payment on the original pledge, $27,281.94, was received by the university in January 1880, more than three years after his death.

•   •   •

September 12, 1876, was one of those rich, fall days that occasionally presage the Hoosier autumn, and John Purdue, then seventy-three, felt well enough for a day's outing. By carriage, he first visited the agricultural works, then crossed over the Wabash through the three-span, covered Main Street bridge, up the long State Street hill, and west the short distance to the new campus, then still being built.

September 12 was the opening day of classes for the infant university's third academic year. Emerson E. White was the new president; the problems the old man had encountered with President Shortridge seemed in the past.

"It was a proud day for the good old man," wrote the Lafayette *Daily Courier* a day later:

> He was feeling quite well and, shaking off the burdens of his cares, visited the university, chatting pleasantly with the professors and the students on the campus. He inspected progress of the work on the new college structure [University Hall] and, after a walk through the grounds, drove to the Lahr House. He sat down in the public room for awhile and, complaining of chilling sensations, was induced by Mr. O. K. Weakly, [proprietor of the Lahr House] who had watched over him and waited on him

tenderly for years, to lie down for a rest. He [was] evidently [suffering] in a nervous chill. A fire was made and with proper applications he became quite comfortable and asked for oyster stew which was prepared for him. He ate heartily and [Weakly] left him, thinking he might sleep. [Weakly] returned thirty minutes later and found Mr. Purdue had disappeared.

Purdue had dressed, and Thomas Park, his nephew, had come with a buggy and driven his uncle back to the Hygienic Institute where he had tea with the Park family, chatted briefly, got up to walk among the flowers on the grounds, then went to his room. Several minutes later, two attendants came to his room to see whether he needed anything. The time was 5 P.M. Purdue was face down on the floor just inside the door. He had apparently tried to call for help. The attendants turned him over on his back. John Purdue gasped feebly and died.

A messenger was immediately dispatched to the downtown area, and his closest friends and business colleagues—Weakly, John Sample, Brown, and other cherished friends—were summoned to plan his funeral.

Purdue's body was placed in a suitable casket, taken to the James Spears mansion at the southeast corner of Fifth and South streets, and placed in the center of its spacious east drawing room. Spears, Purdue's longtime friend and fellow businessman, was a wealthy grain dealer and capitalist who agreed to have the funeral held at his home. (In 1901, the mansion became the second home of the city's public library.) A student guard of honor, selected by President White, took charge and watched through the night. Another guard of honor from the Lafayette Guards, of which Purdue had been an honorary member, was also on duty. A large photograph of Purdue was placed on a nearby mantel and draped in black mourning cloth. Vases filled with a variety of flowers crowded the room, and at the head of the casket, supported by an alabaster column, was a large crown of tuberoses. A floral arrangement combining the cross, an anchor, and a heart—apparently representing faith, hope, and charity—lay on the casket. A monument with pedestal and column and a large cross, done in white flowers by Dorner, a local florist, "completed the decorations," as the Lafayette *Daily Journal* put it. The board of trustees minutes of February 8, 1877, show approval of a twenty-five-dollar payment to Dr. A. M. Moore of Lafayette for making John Purdue's death mask, kept by the trustees in the vault of the First National Bank of Lafayette for many years. (It is now in custody of the University Libraries.)

Because none of the embalming and preservation techniques usually associated with funerals had been performed, "the condition of the remains did not warrant the full programme of exercises as contemplated yesterday [September 14] and at 2 o'clock precisely the funeral cortege with Laird's Military Band, the Lafayette Guards, and citizens in carriages moved to Purdue University where the last sad honors to one whose name is honorably associated with the institution, were paid," the *Journal* explained.

Purdue had often expressed a desire to be buried on the campus. Thus a committee of John Stein, secretary of the Purdue Board of Trustees and a Lafayette legislator who guided the Purdue bill through the Indiana General Assembly in 1869; John Coffroth, a Lafayette attorney who was board president; and President White selected the site a few feet east of the unfinished main building, now University Hall, on what is now Memorial Mall. There, White delivered Purdue's funeral oration, comparing his immortal gift with those of John Harvard (a mere $4,000), Elihu Yale, Ephraim Brown, Ezra Cornell, George Peabody, and Commodore Vanderbilt.

"The long life of the deceased," White said of Purdue, "was filled with beneficient activity; and his business enterprise will be long felt in Lafayette, but the one act that crowned his life and makes the name of John Purdue immortal, was his magnificent donation to this University." White's eulogy continued:

> That one act will never fade out; it will grow brighter as the years pass, and generations to come will rise up and call him blessed. In looking over the noble patrons of learning, the fact is noticeable that their great acts of benevolence are remembered while all their other acts have been forgotten. . . .
>
> The gift of our friend of one hundred and fifty thousand dollars to aid in the establishment of this institution will make the name of John Purdue live just as long as learning lives and this people keep their civilization. The lesson taught by this fact is that those similarly blessed with wealth will do well to imitate John Purdue's noble example, instead of leaving their possessions to spoil their children or to be lost in conflict. . . .
>
> This institution will be a perpetual monument to his memory while it was the joy of his life. On the morning of his death he visited the institution with a good word for all whom he met. There was a joy in his heart, and he expressed a desire to a student to be young again and [to] come here to study, adding that if he could do this they would find him a hard-working student. . . .

These buildings shall crumble to dust, the very ground on which we stand may be a wilderness and the owls hoot in the branches above this place, but every truth and good impulse given here will never die, but live forever in the hearts of the students here instructed . . . . We may engrave upon brass and rear temples, but they will crumble into dust: but he who writes upon the tablet of the human soul does that which no time can efface—which will grow brighter throughout the age of eternity.

Chapter IV

The First Five Years

By contrast with the seven years of foot-dragging that ensued between the passage of the 1862 Morrill Act and the 1869 Indiana act establishing Purdue University, the haste and fervent activity that followed were striking.

Only four days after the May 6, 1869, passage, Governor Conrad Baker, who signed the act almost immediately, called a meeting of the board of trustees for May 25, 1869, to be held at the Lahr House in Lafayette, its first as trustees of "Purdue University." The first order of business was to swear in John Purdue as a life member of the trustee board. The second was to set up the machinery to select a precise site for the new campus within Tippecanoe County. The board met twice in June 1869, once at Lafayette, once at the state capitol. The result of both meetings was to reject earlier claims of Stockwell, Battleground, and Shawnee Mound for the new campus site.

When the trustees met July 21 in Indianapolis on the final siting of the campus, Stockwell's bid never came to the table; Smith Vawter's motion to build it at Battle Ground was also rejected, as was that of Henry Taylor for Shawnee Mound. Purdue's motion that the campus be at Lafayette was approved, as was a following motion by Vawter that the campus be located within two and a half miles of the county court house.

Members of the board of trustees at that time were Lewis A. Burke, Richmond; Isaac Jenkinson, Fort Wayne and Richmond; Henry Taylor, Lafayette; Smith Vawter, Jennings County; Governor Baker, Evansville; and John Purdue, Lafayette.

Purdue and Taylor, a close friend of Purdue's and a local lumberman, had been appointed as a committee to determine the campus's more precise location. The two swiftly recommended a site across the Wabash River and west of the new town of Chauncey, atop the glacial alluvial shelf that dominates Lafayette's west horizon. It was land not long domesticated, unfettered by the trappings of urban civilization—an area largely of woods, pasture, or cultivated fields.

Two covered toll bridges, the first at Brown Street, the second at Main Street, made the "west side" of the Wabash River readily accessible and undoubtedly encouraged faster development of that area. The bridges were originally built by corporations established for the purpose but were eventually bought by Tippecanoe County and made free bridges.

There was one natural hindrance, a large outcropping of cemented glacial aggregate jutting out at about the intersection of Salisbury Street that made the so-called State Road a crooked, twisted path up the side of what is now known as State Street hill. The rock was correctly named Rattlesnake Rock—and avoided for that obvious reason. It was later removed in the straightening of State Street.

At the top of the hill, the area's first platted town was known as Kingston (from 1855), a two-block area bounded by Vine, Salisbury, North, and South streets. The town of Chauncey was the second and much larger platting, covering the area bounded by the Wabash River's west bank on the east, the present railroad tracks on the south, an east-west line between Grant Street and near the intersection of Happy Hollow and North River roads on the north, and Grant and Marsteller streets on the west. That plat covered a scattered community of 197 souls, 48 of them registered voters.

West of, and contiguous to, the western boundaries of the Chauncey town plat were the original purchases of acreage for the new university—a relatively small piece of prairie, devoid of trees, that soon became the symbol of hope and promise for a handful of dreamers—a dream that went far, far beyond even their wildest imaginings.

•   •   •

Dreams do not come true with the wave of a magic wand but through struggle and hard work; the next step, of course, was the purchase of the land. Purdue and Taylor received from Rachel and Hiram Russell a gift of ten acres which at the time formed the western edge of the campus on a north-south line running just west of the present intersection of State and Russell streets. From John Opp and Nicholas Marsteller by purchase at one-half the appraised value, and from Silas Steely under similar terms, the trustees were able to acquire two parcels of 51.25 acres and 38.75 acres extending eastward from the Russell land to what is now Marsteller Street. Together these three tracts met John Purdue's pledge of 100 acres to go with his monetary gift. The deeds were turned over to the trustees and accepted by them on December 22, 1869, at a meeting in the governor's office in Indianapolis, thereby forever committing Purdue University to its present locale. The state accepted the land on December 29, 1869, just two days before the legal deadline.

John Purdue was then named as a committee of one to consider campus planning and specifications for a building program. Meanwhile, a petition was filed with the board of trustees by the contributors to the fund used to buy the 100 acres. Although a complete list of the contributors was apparently never preserved, the petition—requesting the first buildings to be located at the east end of the tract as conveniently as possible to Chauncey and Lafayette—included the names of some of the major donors: John Opp, Daniel Royce, J. H. Pender, Nicholas Marsteller, Hiram Russell, Silas Steely, Peckham and Smith, and, through their local attorney, the heirs of H. L. Ellsworth and the heirs of N. C. Chauncey.

The Chaunceys were the owners of much of the land occupied by what is now West Lafayette, although they were Philadelphians and never lived in Indiana. Ellsworth owned much of the timberland which lay north of Chauncey; Peckham and Smith was a real estate firm credited with acting for Purdue in the purchase of the original 100 acres; Pender and Royce were active in Chauncey's development; the others on the list either gave or sold the land to Purdue.

The trustees, having approved the purchase of the 100 acres south of State Street, believed the land north of State and somewhat closer to Lafayette and Chauncey, (the farm of Jesse B. Lutz) also ought to be purchased—up to 200 acres of it at least. Accordingly, the board authorized Purdue to purchase no more than 200 acres, the payment for which was to be credited against the last two installments of his original gift. When the proposed purchase became known, however, the land prices became so exorbitant that the board gave serious consideration to abandoning the land already purchased and moving to another site. Finally, Purdue filed with the board a deed for eighty-four acres and received a credit against his gift of $24,000—a price of nearly $287 per acre.

Purchase of the original campus acreage now seemed to be complete. But the question remained as to the location of the buildings on the site—an issue as intense as the long struggle to narrow the site from several throughout the state to the then bleak cornfield and pasture west of the Tippecanoe County courthouse.

Purdue and Lafayette architect W. H. Brown traveled to the east not long after the land acquisitions to look at college buildings at Cornell and Brown universities and Vassar College. Brown was highly respected and experienced as a school architect and had designed Lafayette's Eastern School, later renamed Ford School. It had an imposing tower and sat on the edge of a high bluff at the crest of South Street hill overlooking the city.

Not long after they returned, Brown went to Purdue's Lahr House quarters to present a "ground plan" of a proposed campus building, 108 by 50 feet. There was need for expediency. The statute establishing the university required the first building to be erected on or before July 1, 1871. Yet, it was not until August 9, 1871, that ground was broken. It was one of those by now obscure but yet important milestone days in Purdue University's history. M. L. Peirce turned the first shovel. The site was approximately the same as that of the present Smith Hall. Shortly after the building's foundation was in, it was abandoned, and the first three buildings were started north of State Street.

The first groundbreaking did not, however, help to improve John Purdue's disposition. Things were not going his way. Eight months earlier, Governor Baker had asked the General Assembly to amend the statute governing the board of trustees to relieve the governor of his ex-officio duties as a member of the board and to add one new member to replace him. The legislature, however, added three new members, bringing the total to nine. Purdue was furious. From his perspective, Purdue believed the Baker amendment diluted his power on the board from one-sixth to one-ninth.

Purdue was still miffed eight months later and refused to attend the groundbreaking ceremony. Of course, at that time John Purdue was mad at everybody about almost everything that was happening at the new school. He found it almost impossible to reconcile his belief that it was *his* university (since he had literally bought and paid for it) with the fact that the university—

his contribution notwithstanding—belonged to the State of Indiana and its citizens.

Though his health began to decline, Purdue was still in charge of construction. He was a committee of one, and his stubbornness won out as one building committee after another brought revised plans and reports of disagreements. The board had twenty-three meetings before coming to any conclusion about siting the first building. The only person who still disagreed was Purdue. Eventually, the situation reached a point where building locations seemed to require only the recommendation of one man, John Purdue. In one resolution of exasperation, the trustees on January 4, 1871, rescinded all previous actions with regards to building locations and "resolved, that John Purdue is authorized to deliver the materials for the college buildings on any part of the grounds he pleases."

Purdue eventually agreed with the board's action to locate the first buildings on the newly purchased land, presumably closer to the town of Chauncey and downtown Lafayette. Such action reserved the lands south of State Street for other uses.

Regardless, he went ahead with the construction of a brick residence and a barn, using stone from the abandoned first building site. The farmhouse was initially occupied by the first faculty member employed by the trustees, Professor John S. Hougham (pronounced Huff'-um), who later was the university's first acting president and jack-of-all-professions.

The principal building program included the Boarding Hall (Ladies Hall), a design based on an Amherst building, partly on and partly west of the site of present Stone Hall; a dormitory for men (Purdue Hall), designed by architect Edwin May but also patterned after a structure at Amherst, approximately on the site of the present Mathematical Sciences Building; and the Science Building (later the Pharmacy Building), located between today's Matthews Hall and the Education Building.

Of these, Boarding Hall was the most expensive at a cost of $40,000. It not only housed the college dining room but also the living quarters for new faculty and their families.

The Science Building was a replica of that at Brown University and resulted from an eastern visit by Professor Hougham and Trustee Martin L. Peirce to Brown, Amherst, and the Massachusetts Institute of Technology to inspect science facilities. Their return to Lafayette was the signal to start construction on the Brown replica which began on August 13, 1872, the same day the board appointed Richard Owen Purdue's first president.

Financial outlay was generous for those days: $32,000 for the men's dormitory (Purdue Hall) and $15,000 for Science Hall.

The minutes of the board of trustees do not begin to convey the consternation inevitably created when members learned that the new $15,000 Science Hall had been built on land Purdue did not own. The building invaded property of a minor of the Stockton family. Lutz was his guardian. The parcel was along the west boundary of the 84-acre purchase made by John Purdue from the Lutz farm. The board was forced to negotiate for a 2.5 acre purchase from Lutz—and had to pay $1,000 per acre for the mistake. It was a major error that goes a long way toward explaining why university buildings along University Street are so close to the right-of-way. In later years, topographical considerations dictated construction of a retaining wall along the east side of University Street, a part of which came from scorched foundation stones from the rubble of the fire which destroyed the original Heavilon Hall in 1894.

The trustees ran into another embarrassing situation. In building Science Hall, they had used the plans from Brown University. Later, the trustees were informed that A. C. Morse, a Providence, Rhode Island, architect, had placed a bill for the plans in the hands of his attorneys for collection from Purdue. It was simply further evidence that the original Purdue building program was without experienced leadership.

There was still another problem. Architect Brown believed he had been retained as the university's architect, but the board denied that assumption, paid him off (though Brown protested vehemently), and hired James K. Wilson, a widely known Cincinnati architect, to design what is now University Hall.

Meanwhile, John Purdue believed the Wilson plan for a building 135 feet by 54 feet was too large, but he finally agreed to it when it was proposed he contract the building himself and superintend the work. University Hall did not get under way until after the first six buildings were completed and in use. Construction was not yet complete when Purdue died in 1876.

The board authorized more building early in 1874, including a military hall and gymnasium costing $6,500 and, in March of the same year, a boiler and gas house with its necessary equipment costing $25,000. It included a class bell now known as the Victory Bell which today, mounted on a carriage pulled by students, signals Purdue's Big Ten football victories. When the university opened September 16, 1874, all of these buildings were either completed or under construction. In addition were the farm structures Purdue built south of State Street and a small

Emma Montgomery McRae (in black) was matron of Ladies Hall and professor of English literature. With her on the east side of Ladies Hall are "her" women students. Time is in the 1890s. She counseled women students on every conceivable subject, but never had the title of dean of women. Inevitably, among her students, she was known simply as "Mother."

Typical of engineering education before the turn of the century is this scene of students in a Purdue forge shop learning the hands-on art of the practical.

Students in an early engineering laboratory class in Heavilon Hall with another of Purdue's prides of the time: a Corliss engine. Adding such facilities, revolutionary as they may have seemed, would encourage more good students to attend Purdue, Smart believed.

Mechanics Hall was the first engineering building constructed at Purdue. Previously, Purdue engineering students worked mostly in a laboratory built personally by W. F. M. Goss in the basement of Science Hall. Erected in 1885, this structure soon became obsolete as engineering enrollments burgeoned. It was on the site of present Stanley Coulter Hall.

Another campus view with trolley now traversing State Street. Shown are the twin towers of Ladies Hall, Science Hall, the chimney of the power plant, University Hall, the Dormitory, Mechanics Hall, and the Electrical Engineering Building, constructed in 1889, a year after the School of Electrical Engineering was founded.

A later view of the Electrical Engineering Building also shows the university's second power plant, added to keep up with an expanding campus.

The drawing room of the Practical Mechanics Building held a near-capacity class of engineering drawing students not long after it opened in 1910.

Commencement processions on the Memorial Mall were traditional at Purdue at the turn of the century, but a suitable assembly hall was needed. Eventually, a generous gift from Eliza Fowler provided a hall named for her. It was razed in the late 1950s for the construction of Stewart Center.

Winthrop E. Stone was president from 1900 to 1921 when he was killed in the Canadian Rockies in a mountain-climbing accident.

An early test of Stone's presidential capabilities was his handling of the devastation caused by the 1903 train wreck that killed seventeen players and Purdue boosters on their way to the Indiana-Purdue football game in Indianapolis.

The tragic 1903 train wreck in
Indianapolis figured in newspaper
headlines for several days.

Harry G. Leslie captained the 1902 football team and managed it in 1903 when almost all of the team were injured or killed in a train wreck near Indianapolis on October 31. Severely injured, Leslie at first was believed to be dead. He recuperated and went on to become governor of Indiana from 1929 to 1933.

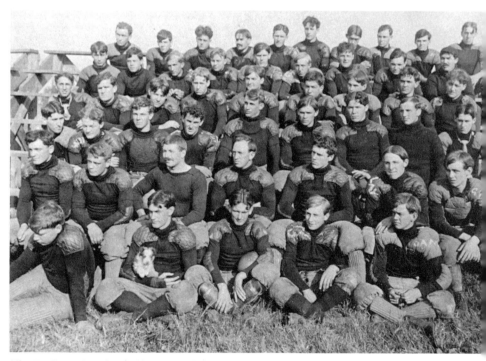

The Boilermaker football squad of which ten died and many were severely injured in the Indianapolis train wreck on October 31, 1903.

workshop built north of Science Hall. By October 31, 1874, John Purdue's seventy-second birthday, the university had made expenditures of more than $200,000, including land, buildings, furnishings, scientific apparatus, books, farm implements, livestock, and landscaping.

To Trustee Peirce must go the credit for the early work toward creating a campus environment out of a treeless stretch of farmland. For years, he donated his entire $600-a-year salary as treasurer of the board of trustees, as well as his tireless personal attention, to the campus landscape. His generosity permitted the establishment of a nursery of 10,000 trees and shrubs; he personally laid out hedges of arbor vitae, cedar, and hemlock. Assisting him were Major Luke A. Burke, an early trustee who resigned from the board to become the university's first farm superintendent, and Professor John Hussey, the first Purdue faculty member in natural science.

Some sources credit Burke as the man who laid out the original campus. Other sources say it was done by Esekial Merrill Talbot, chief engineer of the Lafayette, Muncie, and Bloomington Railroad, the narrow-gauge line of which John Purdue was a chief stockholder. It is probably accurate to say that Burke laid out the landscaping plan and that Talbot did a topographical map of the campus site. There is no record that the board of trustees ever ordered such a survey, but Talbot was paid $117 for it. Regardless, John Purdue undoubtedly had things his way from the beginning.

Another individual deeply involved in the initial campus construction was the builder himself, Joshua Chew. Born in Virginia in 1830, He migrated westward, first to Ohio, then to Iowa, and eventually landed in Lafayette in 1857 at age twenty-seven. He had learned brick and stone masonry from his father in Virginia. In Lafayette, he worked first as a bricklayer, then with a partner started a brick kiln on the banks of the Wabash and Erie Canal. In 1871, as the Purdue construction program was about to open, he went into business as a brick contractor.

Chew was well-known to Purdue; years earlier, Purdue contracted with him to fire all of the bricks for his Purdue Block in downtown Lafayette. Chew then worked under Purdue's supervision on the construction of the university's first six buildings—only one of which remains, University Hall.

• • •

The original land purchase made, their building program underway, the trustees next turned their attention to finding the leadership the new university would need to carry forward its educational program. How unfortunate it was that the trustees placed the search for the university's first president third in their list of priorities. The right leadership in the university presidency at the outset could have saved much wasted motion over the beginning of the construction program, the siting of the first buildings, and at least the beginnings and thrust of the first curriculum and educational program.

While the divisions within the board of trustees were not easily discernible, they were there, made obvious by the early mistakes in the building program. The problem was partly the fault of the state. Although it had passed the legislation and accepted John Purdue's gift, the state had not yet exercised its ownership of Purdue University by assuming its obligations and paying its running expenses. Until it did so, Purdue was fairly certain to control the university's policies and dominate board actions under the trite, old rule that he who has paid the fiddler gets to call the dance. As a result, board meetings were disagreeable because they were so futile.

As it was, the university nearly foundered, not so much because of its choice of a president, but because the choice became embroiled in unfortunate circumstances that ought have never occurred, and a penchant of the trustees to dabble in the affairs of new presidents once they were appointed. Hence, the university's first president never received a Purdue paycheck (although he was paid expenses for four trips to Lafayette), never occupied an office on the campus, and resigned before the first classes ever opened. The second president found himself at full-time odds with John Purdue and stayed a year and a half, although he must be credited with enrolling the first students and opening the university for its first classes in September 1874.

On April 23, 1872, the board of trustees, feeling perhaps the need of expert leadership in faculty selection and curriculum development but more immediately for the building program, offered the first presidency to William S. Clark, then president of Massachusetts Agricultural College. Clark had been a professor of botany and horticulture at Amherst College until his election in 1867 as the third president of the agricultural school. Outside of Massachusetts, Clark is best known in Japan where he went in 1886 to help found Sappora Agricultural College, now known as the University of Hokkaido, on the northernmost island of the Japanese island chain. The Purdue offer carried a $5,000-per-year salary (then considered very liberal) as an inducement. He seriously considered the westward move to the infant school but eventually decided against it.

Astonished and disappointed, the trustees looked at possible presidential candidates from Indiana colleges and universities and finally selected Professor Richard Owen of Indiana University, an avowed candidate for the Purdue presidency after Clark rejected it. Owen had already distinguished himself as a geologist, had made a notable military contribution, and had also had an enviable career in chemistry and medicine. He was the youngest of the four sons and three daughters of Robert Owen, the founder of the second New Harmony community, who purchased the town from the originating Rappites for $150,000.

Richard Owen had first been assistant state geologist, then succeeded to state geologist at the death of his brother, David Dale Owen, an equally distinguished scientist. Together, they had conducted Indiana's first statewide geologic survey as well as an earlier, comprehensive geologic study in Minnesota, extending along the southern shore of Lake Superior near what is now Duluth northwestward to the Lake of the Woods.

On August 13, 1872, the board of trustees offered Owen the Purdue presidency at a salary of $3,500 a year, a salary that included bringing Owen's considerable fossil and mineral collection to Purdue. He promptly accepted and returned to Bloomington and his teaching duties, awaiting his call to office.

Meanwhile, John Purdue, who had begun to suffer ill health, could not attend a trustees meeting scheduled for November 12, 1872, so he wrote the board a letter in which he deplored a proposed statute that would have placed all of the state universities and colleges under a single board of regents.

"I respectfully submit," Purdue wrote, "that the law regulating the Purdue University and all laws of similar character hereafter to be enacted, should be so shaped as to allow any person, corporation, or municipality giving aid to any institution of learning in any form, control over such institution in proportion to the aid given."

Purdue also warned the trustees to go slow in appointing additional professors. "I respectfully suggest that it would only be a manifest and profligate waste of the public money, but also an act of useless folly. In no event does the university need any professors until it is ready to be put into active operation."

While he did say he approved boring an artesian well on the campus, it had to be done without "trenching upon the present funds of the university." Purdue, however, saw no reason to ask the legislature for "aid for the university." His reason was, he said, "that we have an abundant fund on hand to answer all our wants for the next two years. Economy, not waste, is our duty. Agricultural colleges are yet in their infancy, and, as yet, we scarcely know what is needed, and there is greater danger in making too much haste than too little. I think I hazard nothing in reminding the Board that we are better informed now than we were two years ago; and that decisive action then would have resulted in very bad mistakes."

Historically, from the standpoint of his appointment as Purdue's first president, Owen deserved far better than fate gave him. Though it may be futile to speculate, the evidence suggests that, given the right circumstance, Owen probably would have served Purdue long and well. As it was, he never got the chance. Perhaps the most extraordinary fact of the matter was that—in the words of Sears and Hepburn in their 1925 Purdue history—"face-to-face with what should have been the prize of his career, he so completely failed to grasp it."

Owen was an unusual individual from an unusual family. His father, Robert, was one of Europe's celebrated radical humanitarians who fought tenaciously against many of the industrial abuses of the time—such as child labor, including the actual chaining of six-year-olds to factory machines to prevent their running away from the depredations of twelve-hour work days (fourteen hours for nine-year-olds).

Richard was born in 1810 in Scotland. His early childhood education was by a tutor at the Owen home, Braxfield, on the Clyde River at New Lanark. The environment was cheerful and wholesome, and his early learning was by way of the Pestolozzian principles of which his father was a devotee. Pestolozzi, the Swiss educational reformer of the late eighteenth and early-nineteenth centuries, advocated a "natural order" of intellectual development encouraging tactile, concrete experiences and replacing memorization and harsh discipline with love and understanding of the child's world. He believed that education should be moral as well as academic.

Owen's early education at home was followed by his schooling at New Lanark's manual training and grammar schools, then at the educational institute of Emmanuel Fellenberg at Hofwyl in Switzerland where he spent most of his time studying the natural sciences, specializing in chemistry. He also took gymnastics, military drill, French, and German. Three years later he returned to Scotland to study chemistry and physics under Professor Andrew Ure at the Andersonian Institution of Glasgow.

Owen was only eighteen when he came to America and New Harmony with his father and two older brothers in 1828. For all of his private schooling, Richard's father, Robert, had the greatest influence on the development of his personal philosophy and his direction toward a life of the mind. Robert's successes in America as humanitarian-educator were even greater than in Europe. He established America's first kindergarten, its first free school, its first coeducational school, its first industrial school, and the first school to prohibit the use of liquor among pupils and students by administrative decree. Richard's mother was a woman of equally high idealism, unusual charm, and great devotion to her family. She did not accompany her husband to America because of failing health and died in 1831 in Scotland.

At New Harmony, Richard became a teacher and engaged in long horseback rides in the wilderness territory around New Harmony. He was stung by needling from others in the community over such supposed idleness and finally left New Harmony for Lancaster County, Pennsylvania, for several years. Not satisfied with that life, he floated down the Ohio River and spent three years working in a Cincinnati brewery. But eventually he was drawn back to New Harmony where he owned land. He farmed and taught school for seven years until the outbreak of the Mexican War in 1846.

As absorbing as farming and teaching at New Harmony were, he forsook both to accept a captaincy in the Sixteenth United States Infantry Regiment under General Zachary Taylor in 1847. After service at Monterrey, Owen returned to civilian life and joined his older brother, David Dale, in the Minnesota geologic survey where as artist as well as scientist, he made illustrative sketches and diagrams and recorded barometric pressures.

Still, Owen found teaching more attractive and took a position as a professor in natural science at the Western Military Institute at Drennen Springs, Kentucky. Not only did he teach the natural sciences, but also found himself teaching classes in French, German, Spanish, the military sciences, and even fencing. He taught at the military school for nine years, and during the last three, he also studied at the University of Nashville, Tennessee, and received the M.D. degree in 1858. Owen's outlook, especially regarding slavery, was wholly out of harmony with that of the Tennessee area, and in 1861, at his brother's death, he returned to the North to succeed him as Indiana state geologist.

When the Civil War began, Owen was immediately offered a lieutenant colonelcy in the Fifteenth Indiana Volunteers. Later, he found himself in the fighting in West Virginia, first in the battles of Rich Mountain and Green Briers, then in a confrontation with General Robert E. Lee at Cheat Mountain. He was called home by Governor Oliver P. Morton to raise and organize the Sixtieth Indiana Volunteers. Governor Morton promoted Owen to full colonel and placed him in command of the new regiment.

His most significant service in the Civil War, however, was probably his compassionate leadership as commanding officer of the Confederate prisoner stockade at Indianapolis—Camp Morton—in the spring of 1862. His administration there undoubtedly prevented the camp from being a Northern version of Andersonville, the notorious Southern prison camp where so many Union soldiers died of disease and neglect. Owen's treatment and care of Southern prisoners was humane—so much so that at war's end, those Confederate soldiers who had been captive there presented the State of Indiana with a bust of Owen in appreciation. It still resides in the Indiana capitol.

After Camp Morton, Owen returned to the front with his Sixtieth Indiana Volunteers and was captured at Munfordville, Kentucky, by Confederate troops under General Bragg. As an officer, he was paroled and returned to Indiana, reassigned to the Union Army of Tennessee, and detailed to the Arkansas region. Later, Owen fought with Grant at Vicksburg and with Sherman in the capture of Jackson, Mississippi. Near the end of the war, Owen resigned his commission and at fifty-four became a professor of geology at Indiana University, retaining his professorship there through his brief "presidency" at Purdue until 1879. He was deeply respected and revered in Bloomington for his mastery of geology and his talent as a teacher.

After his retirement, he traveled through Europe and the Middle East collecting geologic samples, visited his family haunts in Scotland and Switzerland, and spent much of his time as a Sunday school teacher in the Bloomington Presbyterian Church.

He finally returned to New Harmony to spend the remaining years of his life. His death March 25, 1890, was a result of a horrible and unfortunate accident. He mistakenly drank from a bottle of embalming fluid sold to him in error by his local grocer from whom Owen regularly purchased mineral water for the "indispositions of aging." The cases of mineral water had been stacked near a supply of embalming fluid ordered by the grocer for a neighboring mortician.

The epitaph on his gravestone explained in one brief sentence the guiding philosophy of life: "His first desire was to be virtuous, his second to be wise."

Though Owen in his time could be described as a "Renaissance man," his strange passion for excruciating detail made him seem at least somewhat peculiar if not downright eccentric. For example, Owen faithfully and systematically recorded in his diary week by week the number of socks, handkerchiefs, shirts, and underwear he sent to the laundry, and the weddings he solemnized or funeral orations he delivered, but there is scarcely a word anywhere in it about his appointment as Purdue's first president.

Neither he nor, for that matter, the board of trustees took any aggressive measures to organize the university (beyond the acquisition of land and buildings) after his 1872 appointment until May 6, 1873, when the trustees summoned him to Lafayette and requested that he draft a plan of university organization. Three-and-a-half months later on August 26, 1873, he returned to Lafayette to deliver his preliminary report. It was, indeed, an unmitigated disaster, compounded when the board ordered one hundred copies made without first reading it.

Owen's "A Scheme of Education Appropriate for the University," was a masterfully detailed exercise in irrelevancy and minutiae, punctuated by occasional bursts of trivia. It was obviously written in very general and oblique terms, outlining in three divisions such matters as physical and moral training while suggesting a student government and speculating about types of occupations for which students might be suited upon graduation. While clouded by vague and peripheral generalities, the report also ignored almost totally the intellectual requirements of a university, virtually omitted the academic and administrative organization of departments and schools, and was inadequate from the standpoint of any long-term or overall financial plan or outline. Conspicuously absent was any articulation or definition of goals for the institution; goals were, in fact, not a part of the report.

Owen's downfall stemmed not, however, from what his report omitted but from what it included—a fanciful, riotous jumble of extraordinary details covering such nonacademic, nonscholarly matters as fire protection, heating, lighting, ventilation, management of the boarding hall, sewage and sanitation, water supply, the living quarters for the faculty, and even diet. In one spate of insignificancy, Owen even suggested that napkin rings in the dining hall be numbered and assigned to each student.

Before his report delved into matters of academic organization, Owen made clear that he believed cleanliness (of students) was perhaps more important than godliness, or even academic organization: "If immediate arrangements for baths can not be made, there should be means of access, at all times, to an abundance of cold and hot water for the purpose of a tepid sponge bath when the weather is cold."

Not until the third section of his report did he outline the seven departments he envisioned for Purdue University, to include an educational department "under the faculty"; agricultural department "under the management of farm superintendent"; horticultural department, "under management of Professor of Botany, Head Gardener, and students"; a boarding-house, "to be superintended by a House Superintendent, Steward, and the necessary numbers of waiters"; a laundry, "under direction of a matron and head laundress"; a lodging house or dormitory, "under charge of the House Superintendent, for male students; a separate building if ladies are admitted, to be under charge of the matron"; and the department of accounts, "to be under the management of the Accountant (who may, if thought best, be also House Superintendent)."

Owen next proceeded to detail how accounts should be collected and when "hands" (presumably, he meant farm hands) should be paid. Then he launched into the details of a campus system of drainage "carried out under supervision of the Mathematical Department, aided by students."

Next from the Owen mind came his system of fire protection for campus buildings, including how many hooks, ladders, pickaxes, and such would be needed. The Owen obsession with detail perhaps hit its high point in discussing dietary arrangements—ideas that certainly must have at least raised the eyebrows if not the blood pressure of old John Purdue, whose fortune, gained largely as a pork packer, gave him the wherewithal which made possible his gift to the university. Wrote Owen, in part:

> A dietary should be adopted which should at the same time give sufficient variety from day to day, and be of not the most expensive kind, yet nutritious, palatable and wholesome, avoiding the free use of pork, meats fried in grease, rich pastry and the like, as being highly injurious to those having more work of the brain than of the muscles. It is further recommended to give animal food only once a day, and to use largely of corn meal and unbolted flour for bread and mush, in order to avoid the great evils incident on a sedentary life, constipation, and hemorrhoids. It is also recommended that to all who will abstain from tea and coffee a somewhat reduced rate of weekly board should be given, also the various farinaceous puddings and the like be substituted most of the time for the rich pastry too commonly used as a

dessert. For the sake of health, the meals, if three are taken each day, should be at least six hours apart, and served with great punctuality at the appointed hour.

Owen's report was nothing less than a mass of housekeeping trivia; he seemed oblivious to the relevant business at hand—the organization of a new institution of higher education for which land had been purchased and buildings were under construction.

He had managed to discuss, ad tedium, such matters as what kind of chemicals he thought worked best in the earth closets (i.e., outhouse pits) and which stoves, described down to the model numbers, would best serve the campus kitchen—even the fact that a supplier of unbolted flour had moved from Canada to Rockford, Illinois—but little or nothing about the purpose of the university.

In the last sentence of his report, Owen described his vision of a campus where students did not merely walk to class, but somehow strolled in introspective reverie in an environment of sylvan beauty:

> As far as practicable, extensive gravel walks through the campus, garden, etc., should afford dry walking, even after rains, and plats in all directions, with shrubbery and flowers chiefly perennial, should enliven the students' home, so that homesickness would be unheard of, especially when to these attractive surroundings would be added the sympathizing kindness which professors, employees, older students, in fact all, should be urged to extend to new comers, until they felt themselves indeed at home, and until they could realize the fact that their student life readily could be one of attractiveness, happiness, and preparation for a future of usefulness to themselves and others, and as calculated to prepare them to fulfill the commands and responsibilities assigned [to] them by their Divine Creator.

Although the report may have revealed Owen's human compassion and a certain obsession with meticulous detail, its absurdities overshadowed all else, subjecting him to a withering barrage of public ridicule and scorn. One article, written anonymously and signed "Humbug," appeared in the *Indiana Farmer.* Reprinted in the Lafayette *Journal,* it did nothing to assuage the great disappointment of the trustees and Owen's friends. The *Indiana Farmer* writer found nothing at all worthy in the report and began his verbal fusillade, "When I read this report of the President—which is as good as law—I must say I was much disappointed—not to say disgusted."

Owen's first reaction to the widespread criticism was that the report had been prepared not as a plan for the university as much as a starting point for discussion with the trustees. It was, he said, a confidential report not intended for public consumption. He also conceded that there were items in his report that should have been changed or omitted, and it seemed a mystery to Owen and others that the report somehow got out of the hands of the trustees and was published.

Given a better turn of luck, Owen undoubtedly would have been a good first president of the university, but the criticism mounted steadily and quickly. Noteworthy was the broadside in the *Educationist* edited by Abraham C. Shortridge, who had been the popular, highly respected superintendent of Indianapolis schools and who was to become Owen's successor in the Purdue presidency. The selection of Owen was, Shortridge wrote in his January 1874 issue, "a mistake" and insisted that "his immediate resignation is a necessity." But he refused to deprecate Owen further and rather enumerated the qualities which a president of a university ought to have, such as a spirit that "should direct him and inspire the work of each department. He should be a man of broad views, liberal culture, practical common sense, having the power to organize and generalize."

Nor, Shortridge implied, should the university stint by paying such a man less than $10,000 per year, for "one ten-thousand-dollar-a-year man was better than ten one-thousand-dollar-a-year men in any position where an unlimited amount of brainpower is needed."

Owen's detractors took great pains to point out that their criticism in no way took away from his great competencies as a scientist or his varied cultural accomplishments. Indeed, it was a form of damnation by faint praise; Owen's considerable scholarly and humanistic talents demonstrated, his critics implied, his impracticality as an administrator.

There were other problems. He disagreed with the trustees over fundamental policies; he insisted, for example, on a greater emphasis on agriculture than the trustees had in mind. He also disagreed over details. Trustee Peirce did not like Owen's view of a campus where students "sauntered about in sylvan beauty." Peirce himself had already spent much of his energy, time, and money on campus landscaping. Thus, the disagreements accumulated, and on March 1, 1874, a day before Professor Hougham taught a special class to meet a legislative deadline for first classes to begin, Owen submitted his letter of resignation. Not allowing rancor to mar his obviously bruised feelings, Owen expressed hope that the trustees would find someone "who will more fully carry out your views of the new institution" and expressed a hope for the new school's success.

The board had already paid Owen travel expenses of $39 for his first trip to Lafayette in April 1873 and $36 for his second in August. Six months after his resignation, the board authorized payment of $976.60 covering the fossil and mineral collection, its labeling, and scientific books Owen had agreed to sell to the new, yet-to-open university. The books, appraised at $180, became the nucleus of the first university library, housed in the southwest corner of the first floor of the men's dormitory (later Purdue Hall). That room served as the library until the completion of University Hall in 1877. The library then occupied the east half of the central portion of that building until the library building itself was built in 1911 with a $100,000 appropriation from the state legislature.

The first library, which included Owen's scientific collection, grew with donations from Lafayette citizens, notably Godlove S. Orth—the Lafayette attorney and Indiana congressman who won re-election in running against John Purdue in 1866. Jesse Harvey Blair, a senior student, was appointed the first librarian. He served one year until the appointment in 1878 of Eulora J. Miller, the first woman graduate of the university.

Another factor entered in Owen's resignation: Indiana University was not happy to see one of its most talented scholars and professors leave for the Purdue presidency and not only gave him an opportunity to retain his professorship in geology but also offered him the post of curator of that university's new museum. He preferred the tranquility of the academic life and was far more interested in wrestling with complicated scientific problems and seeking new knowledge than he was in wrestling with prima donna temperaments among faculty and trustees and pursuing appropriations from recalcitrant, tightfisted legislators. But, tenuous as Owen's relationship with the university was, Purdue was honored to have had an association with him.

•   •   •

With its first buildings under construction and an urgent need to get the institution open for classes, Purdue now found itself in dire need of academic leadership—and was virtually without it.

The board, consulting with the presidents of Cornell University and the Universities of Wisconsin and Minnesota, made some progress toward curriculum by deciding on seven professorships with these teaching duties: the president: rhetoric and logic, history, constitutional law, political economy, moral philosophy; professor of mathematics: algebra, geometry, trigonometry, surveying, civil engineering; professor of natural sciences: chemistry, natural philosophy, natural history, physiology, geology; military professor: military tactics, architecture, landscape gardening, rural architecture; assistant professor of natural sciences: botany, zoology of domestic animals; professor of veterinary science and surgery and of practical agriculture and horticulture: to be in charge of the university farm; and a teacher of bookkeeping, arithmetic, geography, and English grammar.

Though a new president was not yet appointed, whoever it was to be would arrive with half of a new faculty already appointed for him. The board proceeded, starting, restarting, and deviating from its own faculty scheme. Hougham had already been appointed, at the age of fifty, as Purdue's first faculty member—presumably to guide the building program—and had performed sundry duties for the trustees since May 1, 1872. He had had a brilliant career at Franklin College and Kansas State Agricultural College. The second faculty member, appointed May 5, 1874, was William B. Morgan of Indianapolis, as professor of mathematics; on June 3, John Hussey of Lockland, Ohio, (the only member of the first faculty with a Ph.D.) arrived to teach botany, horticulture, "and kindred subjects." Finally, on June 12, 1874—only a relatively short time before the university was to open for classes that fall—the trustees appointed Abraham C. Shortridge of Indianapolis as the university's second president.

Shortridge had, said H. B. Knoll in his 1963 book, *The Story of Purdue Engineering,* "the misfortune to be Owen's successor." But his appointment was almost a matter of sheer desperation, and Governor Thomas A. Hendricks "more or less conscripted him" (Knoll said) although Shortridge's health was questionable and he was almost blind. In the spring, despite his doctor's warning that for him to stay in education would surely kill him, Shortridge, then forty, nonetheless succumbed to the governor's entreaties and that fall began the arduous job of trying to steer the university on its maiden voyage through waters that were tempestuous and dark.

Not many doubted that Shortridge would succeed. A native Hoosier, he was born October 22, 1833, in Henry County. When he was eighteen, Shortridge took a year off from his farm labors to learn printing but returned to the farm a year later and never practiced the trade. He immediately sold a colt he had raised and used the proceeds to attend Fairview Academy in Rush County and later attended Greenmount College near Richmond. He taught in Indiana county schools and at the age of twenty-one became a teacher of mathematics. Nine years later, his career took him to Indianapolis. He came to the superintendency of the Indianapolis public school system when he was thirty and the system owned two books (a dictionary and an account book) and had 900 pupils, not one of whom was qualified to enter high school. Two years later, Shortridge had more than thirty pupils in high school preparatory training, and during his administration, enrollment rose to 10,000. His leadership was commemorated in the name given to Shortridge High School. (The school was closed in 1981 and reopened in the fall of 1984 as Shortridge Junior High School.)

While he was not as widely known in Indiana as Richard Owen, nor as colorful, Shortridge was a real power in Indiana public education and had assisted in organizing the Indiana State Teachers Association in 1854. After eleven years as superintendent of Indianapolis public schools, Shortridge continued his distinguished career as editor successively of various educational journals published in Indianapolis in the 1860s and 1870s. He became known as a champion of industrial education, although his conception of its function was narrowly utilitarian.

He, like Owen, had championed the cause of the land-grant philosophy when it had been an issue before Congress. Though he may have been less gifted as a scholar than Owen (in fact, Shortridge had no college degrees), he was certainly a much better educational administrator; he gave much greater promise for constructive service to Purdue than his predecessor. In fact, he must be credited with getting its doors open, thereby saving the university from possible collapse at the outset.

Having found Shortridge, the trustees in the following month approved the appointment of a new faculty member of scarcely less significance to the new university: Harvey Washington Wiley, already a distinguished food chemist, physician, and member of the faculty of Northwestern Christian University (now Butler University), and not incidentally, an admirer of Shortridge. Wiley stands out as one of the most colorful of all faculty members in Purdue history; his accomplishments as chief food chemist for the United States Department of Agriculture after he left the university brought him the renown as the "father of the pure food and drug act."

Prior to the expected opening of the university on September 16, 1874, the trustees rounded out a faculty of six with the appointment of Professor Eli F. Brown, Richmond, Indiana, to the chairs of English literature and drawing. He quickly developed a singular unpopularity among students.

Though the university had hoped for an earlier start, it was not practical for a great number of reasons. A nominal session was held from March to June 1874 by Professor Hougham to meet a legal requirement of the Indiana law, but the official start was scheduled for the September date. The first student admitted to the so-called "presession" in March was Charles Howard Peirce of Lafayette, the son of Martin L. Peirce, the treasurer of the board of trustees and a local businessman-banker. As such—from the historical perspective at least—Peirce may lay legitimate claim to being the first student admitted to Purdue University. Peirce also was first to enroll for the beginning of the regular semester on September 16, 1874, by enrolling on September 9.

The other "first" enrollees were John Bradford Harper, the chemistry junior transfer from Northwestern Christian University who came to Purdue with Wiley, and Daniel Webster Noble, a freshman from Indianapolis, both as regular, nonacademy students. Harper was nineteen; Noble, seventeen and a half.

The 1874 presession from March 1 through June was conducted by Professor Hougham merely to meet a statutory requirement. That and the fact that Peirce was the first enrollee are, beyond historical trivia, hardly worth noting. What is significant is the fact that eight young women were denied admission solely because of their sex. Nancy Baldridge, twenty, and Flora Steely, nineteen, both of Lafayette, were the first to be denied admission—(a dubious brush with historical greatness). Others denied admission in 1874 because of their sex were Ruth Davis, Lulu Opp, Mary Magovern, Katie Slayback, Ruth Weaver, and Harriet Cadwallader, all of the Lafayette area.

The stricture on female admission was lifted in 1875, and thereafter women were admitted to Purdue ostensibly on the same basis as men.

Although there seemed no basis for predicting, the university fully expected two hundred or more students to gather for the official fall opening of the university in 1874. Instead, thirty-nine students, all male, almost all from Tippecanoe County—most of these from the old Lafayette High School—showed up for the hastily prepared entrance examinations, and only thirteen of that number were found to be at all prepared for college-level studies. No tuition was levied.

That initial response to the new institution was one of extreme disappointment. There was an impasse at that point—

but one which President Shortridge recommended be overcome by plunging ahead with the institution and establishing an academy of preparatory classes for the unprepared. Thus some highly paid (for that era) professors of considerable distinction suddenly found themselves teaching such subjects as arithmetic and geography. Shortridge himself taught spelling—a subject still the headache of nearly the entire community of pedagogy.

· · ·

The time was 4 P.M., September 16, 1874, and Purdue University had been open exactly eight hours. President Shortridge sauntered south across the new campus to his office in Boarding Hall.

He had been at what became known as "the settling" and watched with the same interest as any of several other spectators as more than twenty young men—boys actually—settled in their new quarters in the dormitory. The four-story, barn-like building later became the classroom building known as Purdue Hall.

Settling was an exciting time for the newcomers to a new university with new buildings. It was fairly simple, consisting mainly of taking a fresh bed-tick (i.e., mattress cover) to the horse barn south of State Street, filling it with fresh oat straw, making up your bed with some care, and hoping that your new roommate was going to like you. Perhaps you pinned a large picture of your (and every youth's) hero on the freshly-cured plaster wall—Ulysses S. Grant, his feet of clay out of sight somewhere below the bottom margin of his portrait.

The dormitory Shortridge had just left was the *ne plus ultra* of college dormitories in 1874. It cost $32,000, was of red brick, and accommodated 120 male students. It had a bathroom at each end of the hall—eight bathrooms under one roof. Each bath had a zinc-lined tub you could lie down in at full length and never touch either end—and hot water without limit. To prevent overcrowding, they allowed only two young men to each three-room suite—two bedrooms and a large study room—each furnished save for towels and bedding.

The new dormitory also had gas light, and as he walked south toward his office, Shortridge made a mental note that he must return to the dorm immediately after supper and make sure everyone understood that gas lights are *turned* out, never *blown* out.

Shortridge paused at the new laboratory building, first known as Science Hall and in its latter years by the most unglamorous of titles, Building No. Two. He unlocked the door. Here, he mused, was ample space for both teaching and research in the sciences. The fact that the rooms were vacant, with no laboratory equipment, not even tables or chairs, did not phase him. The choices of equipment would be made by whoever was going to teach the sciences.

Glancing to his left, the nearly blind Shortridge squinted intensely to view the preliminary excavation work already done to ready the site for construction of the university's main building, University Hall.

He permitted himself the brief indulgence of wondering whether a more suitable name might be suggested for the Boarding House. He believed it to be a truly magnificent structure with its ornate twin towers and spacious dimensions. Shortridge's attention was diverted momentarily to the clear sound and vague outline of a flock of thirty to forty English sparrows—imported birds known also as Weaver finches—that John Stein, the Lafayette lawyer, Indiana legislator, and now secretary of the trustee board, had managed to acquire for only one dollar each the previous year. Shortridge swelled with pride.

Then he thought about the distinguished faculty he had helped recruit and was filled with an even greater sense of satisfaction: Morgan in mathematics and engineering; Hussey in horticulture and botany; Wiley, chemistry; Brown, English literature and drawing. Indeed, with Professor Hougham who was hired two years earlier to help plan the college, it was a distinguished company.

Shortridge could also contemplate a $350,000 endowment safely invested at six percent and guaranteed against loss by the State of Indiana; $75,000 in annual installments still to come from Mr. Purdue; a $50,000 contribution from Tippecanoe County to meet its original pledge; a 100-acre farm bought by popular subscription, plus $60,000 already spent from state appropriations for the new buildings; $1,000 in cash; and 10,000 tree seedlings from Mr. Peirce.

"Judge" Purdue came to mind: generous, but cantankerous and argumentative. He argues too much about matters he knows little about, Shortridge reflected. He and I do not get along at all. But then no one gets along with John Purdue except his downtown cronies. No matter; the path ahead looks smooth and firm—for the time being at least. Purdue University—a perfect plant, a distinguished faculty, eager new students about to take entrance examinations the next day—an assured future.

Well, perhaps every college president is entitled to at least *one* perfect day. . . .

•   •   •

In his first report to the trustees in November, Shortridge outlined what had been done to get classes started, the work of the preparatory academy, and what was planned. He leveled a devastating observation about the dearth of industrial education in this region of the nation, explaining that scrutiny of the manufacturing facilities in the United States revealed that positions calling for the greatest, most sophisticated skills were not filled by those born in this nation but by people from other lands or, if born here, had been sent abroad for their technical educations.

"It is assumed, therefore," Shortridge wrote, "that young men who desire to fit themselves technically to become leaders in these industrial pursuits should no longer be compelled to go elsewhere for their educations."

The university then bravely announced four-year courses for civil engineering, physics, and mechanical engineering—although it was nearly ten years before such courses could flourish.

Shortridge earned a share of Purdue immortality because he, despite ill health and near blindness, came to Purdue at a time when the trustees were caught in the dilemma of having begun the physical facilities for the new institution while appearing incapable of getting its dynamics developed. He came as president only weeks before Purdue was to open its doors and almost alone got the school organized so that it could accept its first students.

Still, the struggle for survival as a university had only begun, and it was several years before Purdue began to find the direction and develop the academic stamina it needed to be an effective instrument of higher education.

Even though Shortridge deserves credit for getting the doors opened, he managed to antagonize not only John Purdue but also some faculty, some trustees, and most of the students. Eventually, they prepared a written protest against him for his failure to investigate their claims of "insulting" and otherwise shabby treatment by Professor Brown who had to enforce the hated but inviolate rule that no students were permitted in Lafayette or Chauncey after sunset.

History must show that Shortridge weathered a severe storm in his relatively brief presidency at Purdue—a storm not of his own making. Yet, he did his best, and Purdue owes him at least historical credit as the midwife in attendance at its difficult birth.

Chapter V

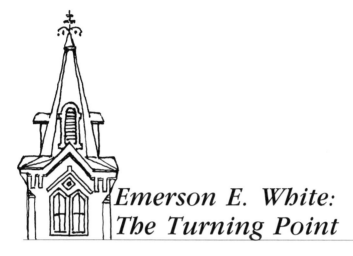

Emerson E. White:
The Turning Point

Abraham C. Shortridge was relatively young but in bad health and nearly blind when the governor virtually conscripted him for the Purdue presidency. Ironically, he accepted a $3,000-a-year salary for a position he had once stated was worth at least $10,000.

He tussled constantly with a faculty each paid $2,000 a year (save the professor of English and drawing who had to be content with $1,500). The minutes of the faculty meetings and the board of trustees do not reveal the stormy sessions that sometimes ensued. Rather (as Sears and Hepburn put it) "they [the minutes] were normal to the point of banality." Yet, the Shortridge administration, brief as it was, was hectic—the storm center most of the time being John Purdue, who managed to disagree with almost everyone about almost everything that happened on the new campus.

Shortridge's accomplishments in quickly developing a curriculum, getting the doors opened, and starting classes (even spelling and arithmetic were taught in the preparatory academy) were doubly heroic because of the great dissatisfaction that surrounded him, coming virtually from all elements of the faculty and the trustees. Among the drawbacks with which Shortridge struggled was the fact that the immediate families of the six faculty members were expected to reside in the dormitory in a continuous state of harmony. It was an experiment in communism "exposed" in a hostile article in the *Indiana School Journal* which blamed "the unpleasant state of affairs that exists at Purdue University" primarily on the fact that "all members of the faculty live in the same house." As skilled an administrator as he was, Shortridge could not long cope with the frustrating problems that situation must have created.

Too, in those years, faculty control of university affairs was undoubtedly much closer, more personal, than in the complex organization of a university today. Faculty meetings in the first years of the institution were far more animated than at a later time. (Sears and Hepburn, both Purdue professors, called faculty meetings circa 1925 "the dreariest of human gatherings.")

For all of that, Purdue somehow stumbled through its first academic year and, despite the problems, grew from the initial thirty-nine enrolled in September 1874 to forty-six by November of the same year. At the first year's end, attendance had risen to sixty-five; of these, only thirteen were in regular college classes, two were in special or advanced courses, one was considered a graduate student, and the remaining forty-nine were in the preparatory academy work.

It was an inauspicious start, but it *was* a start—marked at the end of the first year by the university's first commencement in May 1875, an event equally as inauspicious. There was only one graduate, John Bradford Harper, a transfer student in chemistry from Northwestern Christian University in Indianapolis, who was one of the first students admitted a year earlier. He had followed his close friend and instructor, Professor Harvey W. Wiley, to the tiny new school out in a west central Indiana prairie pasture. For the first commencement, there gathered only a small crowd, in it many skeptics who gave the institution two, maybe three, years before it fell flat on its face and closed.

The ceremony was held in Military Hall. John Purdue, then seventy-three, rugged, plainspoken, and practical—"very much of the old school," George Ade later wrote of him—was on hand to witness "this small beginning of his pet enterprise and to offer some fatherly advice." His speech was impromptu.

Purdue stood up and first dwelt on the advantages of higher education, allowing that some day or other, Purdue University would become "one of the most useful high schools in Indiana." He obviously had high hopes for this rather lonesome set of homely buildings in an Indiana farm field "exactly one mile and forty feet" from a rather raucous county seat and rivertown. (The campus was surveyed as being "exactly 120 feet above the Wabash River.")

Purdue expressed confidence that the university would meet the expectations of the authors of the Morrill Act, and he generally praised their foresight. He had looked the country over, he said, and decided that no place he had yet found needed education worse than this one. Young Harper must have listened with some discomfort, if not downright consternation, inasmuch as the commencement was supposed to honor him.

Purdue then allowed his talk to degenerate into a confession of his spat with President Shortridge and most of the trustees. Things, he said, had been done too hurriedly, including the hiring of faculty. He said he looked to a bright future when the men who made all the blunders in the first year would be gone and a new set of men would give the university a new look by removing all of the evils.

It was a painful appraisal from the man who had really provided the means for starting the new institution which bore his name. It was evident that he was not happy with the way things were going. He finally concluded his speech, either overcome by his emotions or intending to quit anyway, saying, "We don't get along very nicely" and sat down.

Though history does not record Harper's feelings about the affair, certainly they must have been mixed, for he was awarded the first bachelor of science degree in Purdue's history at a ceremony where the university's founder decided to air some dirty laundry. It would be interesting to know, too, what his reaction was to the three-deck headline in the next day's *Daily Courier* over the story on that first commencement:

"Of All Horned Cattle, Deliver Me From a College Graduate"
Another Addition to the Herd to Which Horace Greeley Refers
John B. Harper Turned Loose with the Title "Bachelor of Science"

Harper, despite the lugubrious turn his commencement ceremony had taken, remained a Purdue booster and was, logically, the first president of what was then called the General Alumni Association, founded three years after his graduation.

•   •   •

The rules for student conduct at the university's outset were starchy and, to students, seemed to cover every move they made, every thought they had. The easiest thing a student could do was get into trouble with the administration and/or the faculty. Any hint of youthful resourcefulness usually brought faculty frowns or a new imposition of what seemed to students some unreasonable rule.

Some conduct was regarded so immoral that despite how well a guilty student performed academically, his grades were dropped by faculty fiat. Grades were lowered when students were caught using profane language, intoxicating liquor, or tobacco. Even talking about alcohol (except in chemistry class) could get a student in trouble. The shortest route to academic oblivion was even the faintest hint a student cheated. It was easy to get caught; there were fewer than sixty students in the university. Other misde-meanors that brought faculty-administrative wrath: whispering in class and assuming an "unseemly posture."

The rule that students had to have official permission to visit Chauncey or Lafayette after dark was based on some fairly substan-tial evidence. Pool halls and saloons were absolutely taboo and, as most faculty believed, that was about all that the River City offered—that and the street temptations offered by the town's sullied women.

The carrying of firearms, especially to class, was banned. But, though it was discouraged, students then could spit on the floor without fear of faculty retribution.

Virtually forced by the trustees to do so, Shortridge an-nounced his resignation in the fall of 1875, effective the last day of that year. He was a broken man, and lived in boarding- house quarters of a college with which he was to be no longer connected. Though John Purdue had been his chief antagonist, characteristical-ly Purdue came to his rescue with an unsecured personal loan of $2,000, a well-kept secret until disclosed the following fall after Purdue died.

Shortridge retired to his Hancock County farm, moving later to a smaller country place near Irvington, east of Indianapolis. He was honored in 1897 by the city of Indianapolis which re-named Indianapolis High School as Shortridge High School to memorialize his work in establishing a modern public school system in that city. In 1906, Shortridge attempted one day to board an interurban car near his home and accidentally stepped into the path of the car and lost a leg. A month later, bravely talking of an artificial limb, he left the hospital on crutches.

The Indianapolis black community was instrumental in stag-ing a benefit program for him in appreciation of his efforts to open the doors of Indianapolis public schools to black children—doors that had been traditionally closed to them.

Shortridge lived with a son in Indianapolis and died there October 8, 1919, at age eighty-six.

His shabby treatment as Purdue president had raised the ire of Indiana schoolmen who were highly critical of John Purdue, especially at the time of Shortridge's resignation. The *Indiana School Journal* said of Purdue in direct terms not so far from the truth: "Mr. Purdue, who has given the institution a great deal of money, is a very peculiar man and knows but little of school matters, and yet he assumes to direct and control everything."

Certainly, Purdue still held the fort. Yet, Shortridge may claim credit for having gotten the university off the ground with a solid foundation for his successor, Emerson Elbridge White, who was elected president on February 17 and who arrived May 1, 1876. White wasted little time in letting the world know which direction and what thrust he believed the infant university should take.

Meanwhile, Professor John Hougham, the first faculty member appointed by the trustees and the "old reliable" upon whom the trustees seemed to depend even when they could not depend upon their appointed president, was named Purdue's first "official" acting president, serving until White's arrival. Hougham could well have served as the university president in his own right.

Hougham was born on a farm in Fayette County near Connersville, Indiana, and graduated in 1846 from Wabash College. Two years later, he accepted a professorship in mathematics and natural philosophy at Franklin College. His interest shifted to the sciences, and in 1853, following graduate study at Brown University, he returned to Franklin as professor of agricultural chemistry and kindred sciences. Hougham retired in 1863 after serving as acting president of Franklin College but, too young for permanent retirement, accepted an appointment in 1868 as the first professor of sciences and agriculture at Kansas State College. In 1872, at the age of fifty, he answered a call to return to his home state in Purdue's first professorship, ostensibly to guide the building program.

As a scholar of wide interests—the classics and literature as well as the natural sciences—Hougham considered himself at least slightly above the ability and scholarship of his Purdue colleagues, which did not endear him to the faculty. Nor did he have any greater ability than Shortridge in straightening out what Sears and Hepburn called "the kinks of human nature." The responsibilities of being the university's chief executive never appealed to Hougham, and business interests beckoned him back to Manhattan, Kansas, in 1876. He devoted the rest of his life to the manufacture of physical and chemical laboratory apparatus. Hougham died in 1894, an honored citizen of Kansas.

•　　•　　•

As Purdue's second year began in the fall of 1875, sixty-six students appeared: sixteen in regular college-level classes, one special student in drawing, and forty-nine, as in the previous year, in the preparatory classes. Again, most of the students were from Tippecanoe County. The year was Purdue's second, but the first year that it admitted women. Women were admitted with "no distinction in examinations, expense or classes." Whereas the previous year the university denied admission to eight young women, in the fall of 1875 it admitted nine, only one of whom was qualified for collegiate work.

The first two women enrolled on September 17, 1875, were Lora Rosser, of Battleground, Indiana, a sixteen-and-a-half-year-old, and Hattie Taylor, not quite eighteen, the daughter of William Taylor of Chauncey, both as seniors in the preparatory academy.

In addition to admitting women, the university also hired its first woman faculty member in 1875, Mrs. Sarah Allen Oren, widow of a Civil War soldier. The trustees employed her in July 1875, as "female teacher of the university" at $1,000 annually, to begin September 15 of the same year. Before that date, Shortridge found the title awkward and changed it to "assistant professor of mathematics." On August 31, the board decided to appoint her as professor of botany and raised her salary to $1,500. She accepted that offer by letter.

Not much seems to be known about Sarah Oren, but she must be considered, at least in Indiana history, as a woman who was able to make some substantial gains for women in what then was a world nearly, if not totally, dominated by men.

She was educated at Antioch College where she was influenced greatly by the famed American educator Horace Mann, who had been a president of the college. She went to Indianapolis in 1868 as preceptress of the City Academy and a year later joined the faculty at Indianapolis High School—later named for the man who employed her at Purdue. Mrs. Oren taught in Indianapolis until 1873 when the Indiana legislature selected her as the first woman state librarian, where her work in reforming a badly neglected facility was of heroic proportion. She held that position for two years but was not reappointed because of statehouse political changes. In 1875, Shortridge asked her to come to Purdue.

She took her work as professor of botany seriously and less than a month after she came to the campus reported to the trustees with a plan for an orchard for experimental work. The board took her just as seriously, evidently, by approving her plan and designating approximately an acre northeast of the dormitory (Purdue Hall) for the plantings. When it came time to codify rules for student conduct, the faculty as a whole asked her, with Harvey Wiley and John Hougham, to draft them.

In April 1876, Professor Oren was asked to serve as "oversight" (faculty sponsor) for the first women's literary society; the following November, she was given general supervision of young ladies in the boarding house and designated associate principal of the academy.

Mrs. Oren lived with her daughter, Cata, a teenager and Purdue student in the years her mother was a faculty member. They occupied two rooms of the Boarding Hall (Ladies Hall). But in 1878, she resigned her Purdue post to marry Wesley Haines and moved to his farm near Peru in Miami County. When he died a year later, she moved to Sault St. Marie, Michigan, and lived with Cata until her own death in April 1907. She was succeeded at Purdue by Olivia T. Alderman of Eaton, Ohio, paid $1,000 per year.

Not only was Sarah Oren the first woman state librarian and the first woman faculty member at Purdue, she was also the first faculty member, man or woman, to receive a board of trustees citation in appreciation of her work on behalf of the university.

Newly elected President White was not above voicing his biases, one of which was his opposition to women in the college setting. But it was his bias against secret societies—essentially, fraternities—that got him into trouble and eventually brought about his downfall as the university's president.

•　　•　　•

In the years since Purdue opened, White's seven years as president may well have been Purdue's most critical. Not long after he took office in May 1876, White, already a widely known educator from Ohio, came out swinging. His inaugural address on July 16, 1876, epochal in the university's history, laid the philosophic foundations for the academic thrust and direction Purdue still follows as one of the world's most successful engineering-agricultural institutions. He at once attacked the ambivalence of the Morrill Act as being an "educational Babel. No other statute relating to education has disclosed such a diversity, or occasioned such a confusion of ideas. The plans submitted have been sufficiently numerous to bear scattering upon the face of the whole earth!"

White's speech was a lengthy one but it is worthy of reading in its entirety. Only the most significant portions follow verbatim:

> It must suffice to say that the act of Congress, referred to, clearly expresses three things. The first is that the grant was intended to endow a "college for the benefit of agriculture and the

mechanic arts." The second is that "the leading object" of the college, thus endowed, is "to teach such branches of learning as are related to agriculture and the mechanic arts." The third is that this is to be done without excluding other scientific and classical studies, and "in order to promote the liberal and practical education of the industrial classes in the several pursuits and professions of life. . . . "

The one imperative condition is that the teaching of the branches relating to agriculture and the mechanic arts, shall be the *leading* object, and, as a consequence, that the teaching of other branches shall be made a *subordinate* object.

It is unnecessary to make a more exhaustive analysis of the provisions of the act, since it expressly leaves the *manner* in which these two great ends shall be secured, to the several States. Each college is left free to determine for itself how the two classes of studies specified shall be taught, and how the required subordination of one to the other shall be effected. This is the practical question which now confronts us. How shall this University be organized to meet its obligation to the great industrial interests of agriculture and the mechanic arts? What course of study and instruction will secure the two ends proposed and, at the same time, meet the imperative condition prescribed?

It will assist us in answering these questions if we first settle two other inquiries, which are preliminary and fundamental. What "branches of learning" are related to agriculture and the mechanic arts? Can these branches be made the leading element in the required course of liberal education for the industrial classes?

The branches of learning most directly and closely related to agriculture and the mechanic arts, are the natural and physical sciences, and next to these is the science of mathematics. Inasmuch as mathematics underlie all the other sciences, as well as every agricultural and mechanical process, the closer relation may be claimed for this science, but no practical error will be made in assigning the natural and physical sciences, with their many applications, the nearest place.

Can these sciences be made a leading element in the "liberal" education demanded for the industrial classes by the act? This will depend on the sense in which the term "liberal" is used. A liberal education is one that includes a knowledge of literature and the sciences generally, and hence there may be two kinds of liberal education. In the one, literature has the leading place and the sciences are subordinate; in the other, the sciences have the leading place, and literature is subordinate. The former is usually called a classical education and the latter a scientific education, the name being determined by the leading element in the course.

It is true that the word liberal, when applied to education, is often used in the narrow sense of classical, but this is not the necessary meaning of the term in the act. It is there used in a more general sense to designate an education that extends beyond the branches relating to the industrial arts, and includes "other scientific and classical studies." A course of higher instruction including the sciences as a leading element, and the languages, literature, and history as a subordinate element, would certainly afford a liberal education for the industrial classes. . . .

I have led my audience to this conclusion with some care, for just here arises one of the most serious difficulties that beset the land-grant institutions. It is supposed by some that the terms of the grant require these colleges to teach every branch of learning, and, as a consequence, several of them are making a wide and, may I add, very thin spread of their teaching. They are attempting to do the work of the classical colleges, of schools of science, of polytechnic schools, and, at the same time, to beat about over a large experimental farm. The instruction is cut up into an appalling number of parallel courses, general and special, and the few half-paid professors are used over and over, if not used up. It is true that there is nothing in the provisions of the grant to prevent an institution, with a limited endowment, from attempting to play university, but there is also nothing that demands such folly. The common-sense view of the grant is that it requires no college, endowed by it, to attempt to do what it can not do well. If such a college can do anything to meet its obligation to the industrial classes, it can provide facilities for acquiring a thorough scientific education—at once liberal and practical. . . .

It is now conceded that the weak point in the educational system of the West is the absence of schools of Science and Technology. The public schools, academies, and colleges, are supplying facilities for general education, and they are also doing something in the teaching of general science. What is needed, to supplement these, is a few well-endowed and well-equipped institutions, which shall not only teach general science thoroughly, with so much of language and history as may be needed for efficiency and completeness. . . . It is better to teach a few applied sciences well than to teach many in a superficial manner. . . .

A student can not study everything in the brief period of four or six years, and, as a rule, he will receive the greatest benefit by taking a well-arranged course and mastering it. The vital thing is thorough and inspiring instruction in the course pursued, and no aggregation of schools, or courses, or professors, or students can take its place or compensate for its absence. What the interests of higher education most imperatively demand, is not so much a consolidation of our schools and colleges as their proper classification and adjustment—the confining of each to the work which it can do creditably and thoroughly with the resources at its command.

Whatever may be true of other institutions, the policy thus indicated is believed to be the true one for Purdue University. Instead of exhausting its limited resources in doing what is now done by the State University, and the classical colleges, it should make the best possible use of its means in meeting the demand for scientific and technical instruction. It must, of course, meet its obligation to provide a liberal education for the industrial classes, but, as already shown, this imposed obligation does not require it to spread over the entire ground of general education.

White then launched into a lengthy criticism of existing Indiana common (public) schools and preparatory academies as too few and not adequate in preparing pupils for college or university academic rigor.

"The fact has been recognized," he declared, "that while the State of Indiana has an ample number of colleges, it has few preparatory schools where country youth can make [the] necessary preparation for admission to either classical or scientific colleges. Most of the few academies now sustained, either take it for granted that the common schools in the country teach reading and spelling and the other common branches thoroughly, or knowing better, they yield to the foolish desire of pupils and permit them to leave needed elementary training and enter upon higher studies. The result is that after a few months of skimming, they are either satisfied with their attainments, or, having lost all interest in their studies, they abandon [any] effort to obtain a thorough education."

Nor did White think schools in Hoosier cities and towns were much better, and besides, he said, "few farmers will be at the expense or will take the risk of sending their children into cities and large towns to prepare for college or special schools."

Hence, he explained, the "plan of reorganization" he proposed would embrace three departments: the University Academy for preparation for entry into a College of General Science, and the Special Schools of Science and Technology which would include programs of study in agriculture, horticulture, civil engineering, physics and mechanics, chemistry and metallurgy, and natural history. All were, White said, areas in which "the instruction offered can be provided."

In explaining the need for a well-established preparatory academy, White voiced a complaint made by university and college administrators since the beginning of higher education in the tenth and eleventh centuries and into the 1980s. In fact, White's words on the subject seem to be repeated almost verbatim from several contemporary federal reports on the state of education in America: "Whatever may be the explanation, the fact remains that the academies and public schools are sending comparatively few well-prepared students to college. Nearly all of the colleges of the West [western United States] find it necessary to sustain preparatory schools and statistics show that more than half of their students come from the schools thus organized. . . . The only alternative suggested is to let the standard of admission down to the low preparation afforded by the country schools, and to this there are serious objections to which I will not take time to state. . . . "

White spent a good portion of his speech on the details of his reorganization plan but, unlike Owen, stuck to academics. The College of General Science would instruct young men, he said, in the sciences as a preparation for the applied sciences they would get in the special schools of science and technology. Secondarily, he stressed, would be studies in English, Latin or German, and history. The senior year would be largely elective in White's scheme, with the possibility to devote half of senior course work in general scientific courses, half in the specialized courses. This would enable a student, after graduation from the College of General Science, to complete any one of the special applied courses in one year.

White also discussed what he described as special courses in agriculture, an area for which an outline of course work had yet to be completed. But he saw a need "to get beneath pretentious courses and plans and get to the actual work accomplished." He saw a need to teach practical farming methods as well as an approach to experimental agriculture.

"It is not a difficult thing," he said, "to keep up a show of agricultural instruction by means of an experimental farm and paper courses of study, but Purdue University proposes to play no such part. It will aim to meet its obligation to agriculture by practical and effective measures, if such measures can be discovered." There was no question in his mind, he went on, that if students are taught farming by actual practice, "this practice must be on a farm which is managed on business as well as scientific principles."

In his concluding remarks, White made it clear that he did not believe that an education should be narrowed to those specialized courses of study directly relating to some future career, but rather be at once specialized while broadly based also with general studies:

It is sometimes urged that every boy's education should be narrowed to those branches that directly relate to his future pursuit or calling. Such an education defeats itself, and, besides, it is only feasible where the occupations of life are inherited and predetermined. In this country, a child is not necessarily born into the occupation of his father. Here the different pursuits stand with open doors, and, as a rule, neither the child nor his parents know which he will enter nor how long he will remain. How few Americans find themselves at forty in the pursuit which gilded their boyish day-dreams at fifteen!

These facts answer an objection to a prescribed course of study. The majority of students come to the beginning of their college course not only ignorant of their aptitude or power, but by no calculation of chances can they foretell what knowledge they will need in the affairs of life. It is only after a varied trial of their powers in the mastery of representative studies in all the great departments of knowledge, that they find out the studies and pursuits for which they have special taste or fitness. It is one of the purposes of general education to disclose to a student his bent and mission.

Moreover, were it possible to groove the education of every youth to his future calling, such a course would not be desirable. "Man does not live by bread alone." The farmer and the mechanic must also be the guide of the family, a member of society, a citizen of the State, the guardian of liberty, and out of these relations flow duties which are the highest concern of education. In educating an American citizen we are not training an English operative or a Chinese coolie. He may be a hewer of wood, but if his life answers life's great end, he will also be a hewer of error and wrong. Every child born into American citizenship is confronted by the grandest political and social problems of earth's history, demanding a breadth of information, a ripeness of judgment, and a catholicity of spirit.

In all of our schemes of education, let us not forget that *man* is more important than his work. The engineer must be swifter than his engine, the plowman wider and deeper than his furrow, and the merchant longer than his yard-stick.In education, culture must never stand before knowledge, and character before artizanship. The highest result of education is manhood.

When White spoke, people listened. He brought to Purdue solid credentials as an educator, widely known and greatly respected. A native of Mantua, Ohio, born January 10, 1829, the son of a farmer of "moderate circumstance," he had risen to prominence as an educator in Cleveland and Portsmouth schools, had owned two educational journals, and was state superintendent of schools in Ohio. His highest recognition had been his election as president of the National Education Association. White authored two grade-school texts, one in geography in 1854, the other an 1870 arithmetic book. He attended Trowasberg Academy and graduated from Cleveland University in 1851 but, inexplicably, without a degree. Yet at twenty-two, he was temporarily in charge of the department of mathematics at Cleveland University and principal of Cleveland public grammar schools. He was also a high-school principal in both Cleveland and Portsmouth, Ohio.

In Ohio and Indiana he had been a popular, much-in-demand speaker at teacher institutes and meetings and in 1872, while in Lafayette for just such a meeting, had become acquainted with John Purdue. Coincidentally but also conveniently, he was conducting a Tippecanoe County Teacher Institute in Lafayette in December 1875, when Shortridge's administration came to a close. He was asked by Purdue and John Coffroth, trustee board president, whether he was interested in the Purdue presidency—and he obviously was—but for $3,500 annually instead of the $3,000 Shortridge was paid. He was also to be given the same boarding-house privileges as other members of the faculty.

The trustees elected White as Purdue's third president by a four to one vote, then quickly moved to make his election unanimous. The single vote against White had been cast for Daniel Reed, then the president of the University of Missouri, though the record is frustratingly blank as to how individual trustees voted.

White was married July 27, 1853, to Mary Ann Sabin of Huron, Ohio, and they had three sons and a daughter. Edward Sabin White was fifteen when he enrolled in Purdue's preparatory academy in 1876. He attended intermittently thereafter, obtained his bachelor of science degree in 1882, and is believed to have died that same year.

Another son, Albert B. White, did not attend Purdue but after John Purdue's death in 1876 purchased one-third interest in the Lafayette *Journal* from Purdue's estate. The other two-thirds was owned by Purdue's partner in that venture, Septimus Vater, the editor. The paper was sold in 1882, and Albert White went to Parkersburg, West Virginia, for his health. There he entered politics and was later elected governor of West Virginia.

Another son, William E., at age fourteen also entered the preparatory academy in 1877 and graduated from Purdue in 1881 with a bachelor of science degree. The daughter, Mrs. Alice White DeVol, entered as a special student (and thus was not required to register her age), attended sixteen meetings of Professor Harvey Wiley's chemistry class, and scored seventy-six on the final examination.

Although White was aware of the shabby treatment Owen and Shortridge were accorded, he was a fighter; to him Purdue became an overriding challenge, a place where he could test his own ideas about democratic, egalitarian education. He was determined to make Purdue a technical institution. In White's opinion, the impulses set in motion by the Morrill Act were already being dissipated in flim-flam, flummery, and several other varieties of educational nonsense. The ordinary people for whom the land-grant colleges were supposed to have been established were being cheated, he felt, of a right that a great many people had sacrificed to bring about. The White paradox was his dictatorial approach in bringing egalitarian change to traditional higher education.

About eighteen months after he became president, White made clear his views of those who would hinder the educational development of the working classes in an address to the State Agricultural Society of Indiana at Indianapolis. It was entitled "The Education of Labor."

"Aristocracy," he declared in his opening, "has always opposed the education of labor. This opposition may vary in form, but its aim is always the same. Each of the three great aristocracies has its own pet dogma on the subject." He continued:

> The aristocracy of Caste asserts that the great mass of mankind are born to serve, and since the less intelligent the servant the more docile the service, it declares that education unfits the children of toil for their lot in life.
>
> The aristocracy of Capital asserts that intelligence increases the price of labor, and hence it opposes popular education as a tax on capital. The more intelligent a man is, the greater are his wants, and the higher must be his wages, in order to meet his increased necessities. Ignorant labor has few wants to supply, and hence is content with low wages.
>
> The aristocracy of Culture asserts that the great mass of mankind are born dullards, and all attempts to educate them are futile. The few on whom God has bestowed the gift of brains, are commissioned to do the world's thinking, and they thus monopolize the right to education. This is the doctrine of the hero-worshiper, Carlisle, and it is asserted more or less clearly by many devotees of culture, who have lost all sympathy for the people.
>
> These three aristocracies unite in opposing all efforts to uplift the laborer by the power of education. Schooling, they assert, spoils children for labor; it makes them discontented with their lot; fills them with vain ambitions; makes them idle, etc., etc. These assertions are now more frequently aimed at higher education, and especially at the high schools; but they were once urged, with as great earnestness, against the elementary schools of the

The Memorial Gymnasium became not
only the university's sports center, but
also its social facility—evidenced by
the first Junior Prom there in 1909.

The Memorial Gymnasium was
dedicated in 1908 in memory of those
who died in the Indianapolis train
wreck of 1903 that killed football
team members and fans. Now the
Computer Sciences Building, the gymnasium was the first campus building
funded through popular subscription.

Extracurricular activities at Purdue
early in the twentieth century varied.
Two at opposite ends of the spectrum:
(above) the annual May Day festivity
on the Oval (now Memorial Mall) and
(right) the Tank Scrap at the North
Salisbury Street water tank of the West
Lafayette Water Company.

Carolyn Shoemaker: "Be a man, Miss Shoemaker! Be a man."

John H. Skinner: A battleship in Purdue's academic armada.

Two major buildings of the Stone administration were Eliza Fowler Hall (above), built in 1903, and Agricultural Hall (below), built in 1902.

An electrical engineering laboratory,
circa 1923. The "Louisiana" traction
car is in the background.

Michael Golden Laboratories building
was torn down in 1982 to make way
for the new M. G. Knoy Hall of
Technology. The original Golden
building was built as the Practical
Mechanics Building in 1910 and later
was renamed for the revered
instructor.

George Ade, '87, is Purdue's most famous man of letters. The Hoosier humorist, playwright, and author was a member of the board of trustees, but his disagreements with President Stone led him to resign in protest.

The first aeroplane at Purdue University appeared at an "aeroplane demonstration" at 1911 Gala Week on Stuart Field, now the site of the Elliott Hall of Music. The board of trustees prohibited President Stone and George Ade from taking offered rides, labelling such activity as too dangerous.

W. C. Latta and Virginia C. Meredith pose on the State Street lawn of Agricultural Hall in the early 1900s. Latta was an early member of the agricultural faculty in teaching, research, and extension activities. Mrs. Meredith, widow of a Hartford City, Indiana, rancher, became known as "Queen of American Agriculture." She was the first woman member of the board of trustees and was instrumental in founding the Purdue School of Home Economics.

The "Lions" stand in silent solitude. A gift of the Purdue Class of 1909, the "Lions" are a fixture at one of the highest student traffic points on campus—and the subject of considerable blue humor. Stanley Coulter Hall is in the background.

Henry W. Marshall, the publisher of the Lafayette *Journal and Courier* and a member of the board of trustees, was elected acting president of the university following Stone's death, pending the ultimate appointment of Edward C. Elliott as sixth president of the university.

Headlines tell their shocking story of President Stone's death in the Canadian Rockies.

people. Reading and writing have received many a blow as the dreaded enemy of Capital and Caste.

The power and eloquence of White's speeches were impressive; he was considered an authority on education in the United States. But his listeners were equally impressed by his down-to-earth philosophy and his readiness to stand up for his convictions. He was relatively new as the university president, but he had already demonstrated powers of mind and spirit that made him one of the most commanding and inspirational leaders among all of the university's presidents before or since.

White demonstrated for all time that traditional ways of classical education were not what the framers of the land-grant legislation had in mind. On the other hand, he felt compelled to define a kind of university-level education that would be both liberal and practical; he could not believe that the only kind of liberal education was classical. He intended to demonstrate—and did—that it was possible to provide an education based in science that was fully as liberal as one based in literature, history, and language.

If the will of the people—as reflected in the intent of the Morrill Act—was followed, the sciences would have precedence in the land-grant schools, he declared. Further, he believed, since the legislation has stipulated college-level training, Purdue should not attempt to do anything it could not do well. It should stop "playing" at being a university and get down to those areas in which it could offer superior education.

In the first year of White's administration, the college population was sparse: one senior, one junior, six sophomores, eight freshmen (four of them not in all subjects with their class). In the preparatory academy were thirteen seniors, twenty-two juniors, fourteen underclassmen, and one special student.

On the financial side, resources were "modest but secure": an endowment fund of $300,000 with an annual yield of $20,000; lands, buildings, and fixtures accounted for $250,000; two remaining installments from the John Purdue estate brought the total value of the university property to about $600,000. State appropriations were considered generous for the time: $6,500 for general expenses; $2,500 for apparatus and scientific cabinets; another $1,000 for the library of "several hundred carefully selected volumes, including valuable reference books"; $1,500 for campus improvements and experiments in agriculture; and an added $1,500 for the trustees and their secretary.

Student life of the time was considered rather gray—for the college student of the 1980s, no life at all, probably. But fees were quite modest. For a thirty-eight week residence, fees whether for the college or the academy were $169. Entrance and incidental fees were $14; table board (meals) $123.50; room, heat, and light $19; and laundry $12.50.

Yet, for such modest beginnings, Purdue was destined to grow and become, at last, the land-grant college that the Morrill Act intended and as White literally interpreted the legislation. Much of what occurred in White's administration was based on the philosophy underscored in his early presidential speeches, especially his inaugural address. No other president of the university has had any greater influence on the principal thrust, direction, and guiding philosophy of Purdue University than Emerson E. White. He took an institution foundering, drifting toward the rocks of failure, and set it on the course from which it has deviated little in more than a century.

On the other hand, White went too far with his idea of the land-grant university which he envisioned as a sort of industrial-agricultural monastery. It proved to be his downfall. Yet, he built well. In specific accomplishments, he brought from the Massachusetts Institute of Technology the hard-working W. F. M. Goss, who founded the School of Mechanics in 1879; sponsored Professor Langdon S. Thompson's vigorous development of industrial arts; in 1882 established a full curriculum in mechanical engineering with Lieutenant William R. Hamilton as instructor; and brought Charles E. Ingersoll in 1879 as professor of agriculture and horticulture. White thus established the momentum for the university's astounding progress, especially in engineering, that occurred under his successor, James H. Smart.

His unceremonious end grew out of his obsessive effort to build "industrial" courses for students with "industrial" interests, his sometimes stubborn self-righteousness, his pervasive dislike of the classical system in education, and finally his insistence that the university permit no fraternities or other secret societies. The latter eventually got him into trouble and resulted in his resignation.

Purdue, he believed, should stand alone to seek its own destiny within the literal framework of the Morrill Act. He regretted those students who came to Purdue with no interest in technology. Women, he thought, really had no place in this university; the presence of a score of "fashionable young ladies would be sufficient to give the young men in the manual training courses the chills—social, if not malarial." Had they then been students, it is quite likely he would not have welcomed four Purdue students who later ranked among the university's most famous men of letters: George Ade, John T. McCutcheon, Bruce Rogers, and Booth Tarkington.

It is a delicious irony that although White wanted none of the classical subjects taught, he himself carried the faculty title of professor of English literature (though it is not likely he ever taught it at Purdue).

Even after he had set Purdue on a scientific-technical-agricultural direction, White continued to rail against the classical system as late as 1882—the year before his untimely exit from the university. His position was not unlike that of William Hazlitt, the essayist who once concluded that anyone who had been exposed to a classical education and not been made a fool could consider himself lucky.

Technical education, President White declared, had been slow in developing primarily because "its progress had been choked by customs, practices, and other hindrances copied from the classical system, many of these being poor imitations of the stale mummeries of the aristocratic universities of Oxford and Cambridge."

White's true feelings on "industrial education" were nowhere as foursquare as in his final report to the board of trustees after his resignation in 1883 over the fraternity issue. It was a moment when an outgoing president's opinion could be uncolored by the need not to fail. White wrote (in part):

> I have been fully satisfied from the first, not only that the organization of a classical department at Purdue would defeat its industrial departments, but that any organic connection of the institution with the classical colleges of the State would jeopardize, if not subvert, its highest success as an industrial college, and this opinion has been generally shared by my colleagues in the Faculty and the Trustees. Hence the anti-fraternity rule, the severing of all connection with the State Oratorical Association, and the recent dropping of Latin from the course of study. These and other like measures have been adopted to insure the success of industrial education at Purdue—the leading and paramount end and work of the institution. Our entire policy has been based on the firm and clear conviction that the essential condition of success in an industrial college is a central, vigorous, all-controlling industrial life and spirit, and that this depends on freedom from the dominancy of the classical system.

Hence, he built a sort of spiritual wall around the university to prevent its being invaded by the classics which would, in his mind, make it simply another university. He was probably justified in suggesting that the Indiana county appointments of students to university scholarships be either mechanical or agricultural students, but to withdraw the university's membership from the Indiana Oratorical Association was probably questionable. He intimated such activity would have a contaminating classical influence on the university. When the language instructor, Annie E. Peck, resigned in 1883, White saw to it that Latin and German were dropped from the curriculum as having given the university "a classical tinge." More significantly, fatally, White banned student membership in Greek-letter societies; Sigma Chi fraternity immediately declared war on him. For White's presidency, his edict was suicidal.

White did see value in the literary societies as adding a needed dimension to an educational atmosphere mostly technical. The first of these were the Irving and Philalethean societies, the first for men, the second for women. Both had quarters on the third floor of University Hall, and their exercises consisted principally of essays, declamations, debates, and orations. Each society held "annuals," bringing out the best in student deportment, talent, dress, and poise. For example, at one of the later groups, called the Carlyle Society, a student named Ben Taylor declaimed on "Culture in Common Life," wherein he demonstrated that "socialism and a hundred evils can be prevented by liberally educating the working man." The annuals were high points in the university's early social life. The societies began to die out in the immediate post-World War I years, a curio of a much different, bygone age.

•   •   •

Harvey Washington Wiley came to Purdue at the urging of President Shortridge only a few days before the university opened in the fall of 1874. He was a member of the original faculty and still must be ranked as one of the most interesting, if not famous, characters ever to have graced a Purdue faculty chair.

Wiley claimed birth in a log cabin near the small hamlet of Kent, Jefferson County, a few miles east of Madison, Indiana. As a farmboy, he was sixth in line of a family of seven children, four sons and three daughters, of Preston P. Wiley and Lucinda Weir Maxwell Wiley. His father was a $1.50-a-day plasterer and schoolmaster who reared his children in stern Calvinistic discipline but in a household dominated by a love of learning. At the age of three, Wiley was once taken to the schoolhouse where his father taught school. The elder Wiley drew a three-foot square on the floor in chalk, plopped his son in the middle of it, and admonished him not to move out of it. He did not.

By the age of seven, young Wiley was a voracious reader, mostly of history. Thus began a life of the mind that led him through classic studies at nearby Hanover College; a short-term enlistment in the Union Army in the Civil War; a school principalship at Lowell, Indiana; and a medical degree from Indiana Medical College in Indianapolis. He was also an instructor and tutor in Latin and Greek at Northwestern Christian University while studying medicine. Eventually, he went on to the Lawrence Scientific School at Harvard and earned a bachelor of science degree. He returned to Indianapolis and was elected to the chair of chemistry at Northwestern Christian and as a professor of chemistry at the Indiana Medical College. In addition, he assumed teaching duties in physiology at the Indianapolis High School and considered himself on the road to early wealth because he had three teaching salaries totaling $1,400-a-year.

But the strenuous schedule sapped Wiley's strength, and he became critically ill with cerebrospinal meningitis. He was unconscious for three weeks, and his right leg developed erysipelas below the knee, an infection in those days usually corrected by amputation. Wiley talked the surgeon out of that drastic cure, and he eventually recovered, though he was terribly weakened. Wiley spent most of the summer of 1874 invalided at his parents' farm, where he did what chores he was able to perform in his weakened condition. His savings gone because of the expense of his illness, Wiley did not enter private medical practice and prepared to return to teaching in the fall, when in late August 1874, he received a letter from John Stein, then secretary-treasurer of the board of trustees, informing him that he had been elected professor of chemistry at Purdue.

In his autobiography, Wiley said he owed his appointment as professor of chemistry to President Shortridge, who had only recently resigned as superintendent of Indianapolis schools to become the university's second president. "I shall," Wiley wrote in his later years, "always be grateful to him for the chance he gave me to cast my lot with this new university."

The fact that at age thirty Wiley was the youngest member of the new faculty may have had something to do with his popularity among the students. More likely, they respected him because of his innate curiosity about almost everything. His experience in the Civil War led him to become the organizer and first instructor in Purdue's first effort at ROTC; he was also the coach of the first baseball team at Purdue. When differences flared between almost everybody on the campus—trustees, faculty, and students—

and Shortridge, Wiley remained neutral. Yet, from his perspective, he saw much of the source of the trouble as John Purdue himself with Shortridge as a victim without the administrative savvy to properly handle it. While attrition and dissatisfaction took most of the original faculty not long after the first year, Wiley remained nine years.

John B. Harper, Wiley's close friend, was the university's lone senior in 1874 and the only graduate a year later. Although at Purdue only one year, he became the star catcher on Wiley's first Purdue baseball team. Harper left Purdue, immediately became an engineer, and pursued civil rather than chemical engineering. He spent most of his short career in railroad engineering or in land reclamation in the Corps of Engineers and died in government service while still a young man.

Following that commencement at which the trustees, including Indiana Governor Thomas A. Hendricks, were present, Wiley had a private session with the governor, who told him: "The only professor who has given entire satisfaction during the past year is yourself. If you were married and were a little older we would make you president of the school today."

"I thank you for the compliment," Wiley replied. "I have no desire to be president of this school. My desire is to build up a chemical department here that will be efficient and do honor and service to the state. I feel that if I should undertake administrative work [that] would be . . . a field in which I am wholly unskilled and it would probably result in disaster." (Wiley recalled that conversation in his autobiography published in 1930.)

Not long afterward, Shortridge resigned, and White was elected to the Purdue presidency. Under White, Wiley's rising star began to soar. At the time he arrived in 1874, Wiley was already considered a distinguished food chemist. White admired him professionally, and his colleagues believed he was by far the most competent person in the entire faculty. If he was not, then certainly he was the busiest. In addition to teaching chemistry, coaching baseball, and serving as ROTC instructor, he was asked to teach the physics courses. This led to his interest in things electrical, thence to the development of the early courses which ultimately became electrical engineering.

In the summer of 1876, with a thousand dollars of university money in his pocket, Wiley spent six weeks at the Centennial Exposition in Philadelphia, studying its scientific exhibits. He had been instructed to purchase scientific equipment and materials for the university. Wiley spent many hours studying the mineral collections. He taught a course in mineralogy and was interested in obtaining a good collection for the university. At the exposition, he became acquainted with a penniless youth who indicated a willingness to sell Wiley his own collection for $30 merely to obtain survival funds. Wiley looked at it and decided it was certainly worth the price for Purdue's purposes. The young man's name was George F. Kunz. The name meant little to Wiley then, but the youth went on to become the world's most eminent judge of precious stones and a high official of Tiffany and Company.

More significant was Wiley's purchase of the smaller of two Gramme dynamos on exhibit. The larger was purchased by the University of Pennsylvania. The dynamo reached the campus late in November, and Wiley worked night and day harnessing a steam engine to it. He then fashioned a lamp with two sticks of gas carbon, placed it in the tower of the chemical building, and thus produced the first electric light from a dynamo ever seen west of the Allegheny Mountains. With a reflector, the light could be directed to various parts of the city. Moses Fowler often marveled that he could sit on his front porch in Lafayette at night two miles distance from the light and read his newspaper by it.

The project so enthralled Wiley that he began to do research on two principal carbon-arc problems—the too-rapid combustion of the carbons and the brilliancy and steadiness of the light. These he solved by using copper-plated carbons. Though he undoubtedly could have made a fortune from that solution alone, his first love was chemistry, especially the chemistry of foods, the area of research that eventually earned him fame as the "father of the United States Pure Food and Drug Act."

Wiley once observed that any Purdue immortality he might gain would not stem from the fact that he had started and presided over the university's first chemical laboratory but because of what he called the "bicycle incident." Wiley scandalized the faculty as well as the local community when he purchased a nickel-plated Harvard roadster bicycle—the old high-wheeled variety that, as Wiley described it, "made one feel as if he were riding through thin air."

Wiley was so popular with the students there was little they would not do for him; he recruited several to help him learn to ride his new purchase. One group would hold the bike while he mounted it; another group at the end of a sidewalk alongside some bushes helped him stop. That failing, he would plop himself and bicycle into the bushes to avoid injury. Eventually, as in all of his endeavors, Wiley perfected his cycling skills.

"I acquired a bicycle uniform with knee breeches, and I rode daily through the streets of Lafayette, over the bridge across the Wabash, and up to the university, frightening horses, attracting attention and grieving the hearts of the staid president and the professors, as well as the members of the board of trustees," Wiley wrote in his book, *An Autobiography.*

Wiley knew that the bicycle would bring him to grief; it was just a matter of time. At last came a summons by way of a note to appear before the board of trustees. Wiley said he rather looked forward to hearing that his salary had been increased, but when he entered the room, he was amazed by the "density of the silence" (as he put it) and the straight faces of "the mourners."

"I sat in mute expectancy," Wiley remembered. "Finally Mr. Doblebower, a trustee and Lafayette newspaper man, arose to break the silence." John Colcord Doblebower was the Democratic publisher of the Lafayette *Dispatch,* a party newspaper several prominent Lafayette Democrats had urged him to come to Lafayette to found and edit. He had been named to the trustee board by Governor James D. "Blue Jeans" Williams. Doblebower was a tall, intimidating, and solemn-looking gentleman, a native Philadelphian with a well curried beard and a sonorous oratorical voice. His speech to the unrepentant Wiley was about as follows (according to Wiley):

> The disagreeable duty has been assigned to me to tell Professor Wiley the cause of his appearance before us. We have been greatly pleased with the popularity he enjoys among his pupils. We are deeply grieved, however, at his conduct. He has put on a uniform and played baseball with the boys, much to the discredit of the dignity of a professor. But the most grave offense of all has lately come to our attention. Professor Wiley has bought a bicycle. Imagine my feelings and those of other members of the board upon seeing one of our professors dressed up like a monkey and astride a cartwheel riding along our streets. Imagine my feelings when some astonished observer says to me, "Who is that?" and I am compelled to say, "He is a professor in our university!" It is with the greatest pain that I feel it is my duty to make these statements in his presence and before this board.

Wiley had long forgotten about the possibility of a salary increase, and it was all he could do to restrain his laughter.

"Gentlemen," Wiley replied to Doblebower's presentation, "I am extremely sorry that my conduct has met with your disapproval. I desire to relieve you of all embarrassment on these points. If you will give me pen and paper I shall proceed to do so." Wiley then sat down, wrote a brief letter of resignation, handed it to the board secretary, John A. Stein, and quietly left the board room—not only without a salary increase but also without a job. The next day, he received a letter from the secretary of the board— a straightaway, succinct note signed by Stein which read:

> Dear Sir:
> The board of trustees unanimously refuses to accept your resignation.
>
> Respectfully,
John A. Stein,
Secretary

The call of the Washington scene plus the prodigious amount of work that needed to be done to correct mounting food adulteration practices in the nation was too much for the professor in the then struggling young university in Indiana. On June 15, 1883, Wiley was sworn in as chief of the Division of Chemistry of the USDA, and the star that soared over the West Lafayette campus for nine years thus began its ascent over the national capital.

•　　•　　•

Wiley's troubles with the trustees (and some of his more hair-shirted colleagues) in no way compared to those of President White whose antifraternity, anti-Greek-letter-society stance ultimately brought about his resignation.

On the constructive side, White's program, though conservative, brought progress and stability to Purdue. The appointments of Goss in mechanics and that of Ingersoll as professor of agriculture and horticulture marked an important step in the reorganization of the university along the lines that White had repeatedly advocated since his own appointment in 1876. White did not hesitate to state in his 1878 annual report that Purdue had been "notably deficient" in agricultural training and education. And so a beginning had been made— perhaps better than even White could imagine since both Goss and Ingersoll, especially, gavè many years of distinguished service to the university and made a marked difference in the progress and quality of education for which Purdue became noted in future years.

The industrial arts showed great promise, but practical mechanics needed fostering in White's view. In establishing a School of Applied Mechanics, the faculty and administration made it clear that Purdue would adopt what was then called the "Russian System," one that chiefly stressed processes and the use of tools rather than their finished products.

White advocated a practical approach in agriculture also, advocating the employment of "a thoroughly trained man" to direct it. "I repeat the remark I made in my inaugural address, that a superficial empiric in such a position would do more harm than good." White's practical agriculturalist should have at least a 5-to-10 acre plot of ground as an "agricultural laboratory" and in addition 150 acres or so to be operated as a model farm for large-scale experiments in stock feeding, crop rotation, and crop yield research. The farm, he believed, had to be an integral part of the School of Agriculture and not separated from it; the latter would destroy its value as an academic tool.

The program White outlined was carried out essentially as he devised it. The Indiana General Assembly of 1879 provided a two-year appropriation of $9,000, calling for $4,000 for current expenses, $4,000 for machinery and improvements and for the School of Agriculture, and $1,000 for books and periodicals for the library. With the arrivals of Professors Ingersoll and Goss (originally appointed not as a professor but as an instructor) in the summer of 1879, schools of agriculture and mechanics were in operation.

Previously, Professor John Hussey, an original member of the faculty, had lectured on horticulture to a freshman class, and the university had employed George Vestal of Wayne County, a "practical horticulturist," to take charge of the nursery and the grounds.

The first experimental plot in agriculture was laid out previous to Ingersoll's arrival. The site was the present location along the east side of Memorial Mall where Stewart Center and the Undergraduate Library now stand. But it was quickly abandoned in favor of a plot along the west side of what is now Marsteller Street on the site of the present Agricultural Administration Building and annex. Later still, a series of experimental plots were laid out further west where present Smith Hall and the Entomology and Agricultural Research buildings were built.

The president's report of December 1880 expressed optimism about the young university. The auspicious and solid beginnings for agriculture and mechanics, which became the foundation for the later engineering "superstructure," increased enrollment, a seemingly harmonious faculty and their loyalty and enthusiasm all were a part of White's report. "The resources so far at its command have enabled Purdue University to pass in six years from a hopeful possibility to a recognized success," White wrote, but he noted that the university had reached the limit of its existing resources and that further progress would depend upon the Indiana legislature's largess.

"Surely," he said, "Indiana is ready to do as much for her own industrial college as the nation has done for it." In the same report, White praised his faculty—but also made a point about the need for additional financial support from the State of Indiana. "It affords me special pleasure," White wrote, "to bear testimony to the faithful manner in which my colleagues in the faculty are discharging their duties. It is believed that there is not a harder working faculty in the country, and if my information is not at fault, no other land-grant institution in the West pays its professors as low a salary as Purdue."

Although White's steadying hand guided the young university on a progressive and stable course, and while the organization of the academics now held great promise for the future, White and the trustees were heavy-handed. Nearly every facet of student life was under the watchful eye or tight control of the administration. The extreme limit of restriction of student life was an 1877 regulation that "no student is permitted to join or be connected as a member, or otherwise, with any so-called Greek or other college secret society; and, as a condition of admission to the University or promotion therein, each student is required to give a written pledge that he or she will observe this regulation. A violation of this regulation and pledge forfeits the right of any student to class promotion at the end of the year and to an honorable dismissal."

Sears and Hepburn observed that the severity of the rule reflected White's conviction of the principle he espoused—that the Greek-letter societies tended to give the "industrial college" (White's favorite name for the land-grant school) a "classical tinge." To White it was as if the classics were a form of toxic mold, a fungus. The rule's harshness also reflected White's willingness to stand or fall upon it as a symbol of his own educational philosophy.

Too, White's insistence on continued tight admission standards brought on declines in enrollment—a fact which detracted from his popularity. His critics used that as a sign of his waning popularity as the university's president.

A precursor of the 1883 debacle which climaxed in White's resignation could be found in the 1877 legislature which attempted to reduce the annual salaries of the Purdue president and the faculty to $2,500 and $1,500 respectively, which may have been aimed directly at Purdue and White—though the proposed legislation applied to all of the state institutions. The wording of the act was found to be faulty, and Purdue and its sister state-supported institutions thus escaped its penalties. But White, the fighter, voiced his protest at such outrage by resigning, though afterward he was induced to remain.

Financially, the situation began to appear more optimistic; $12,000 in endowment funds, borrowed to repair the boiler and gas house after a fire, were repaid—with interest—from two tardy but welcome final installments on John Purdue's original pledge to the university. An enlightened 1881 General Assembly, which in 1879 had appropriated a minuscule $9,000 for Purdue for two years, increased it to $20,000 for each of the two years and gave carte blanche to the trustees in how it was to be used.

It was a rare time of solid, well-entrenched goodwill for Purdue with the state and the community (White notwithstanding). But it was also brief.

On March 9, 1875, Purdue's first fraternity, Delta Delta chapter of Sigma Chi, was organized secretly. Gradually, the fraternity made itself known and began to pledge several students a year. Under President Shortridge, the fraternity was not appreciated by his administration or the trustees—though it was tolerated because the university was having difficulty attracting students; perhaps the existence of the fraternity, such as those existing at the eastern colleges and Ivy League schools, would help recruit more young students.

When in 1877 the prohibition against the Greek-letter societies was adopted as university policy, Sigma Chi, though firmly implanted as a part of the Purdue culture, went underground because of the new rule and White's widely known vehemence in enforcing it. Yet, the fraternity men felt the rule to be unjust; they began to make plans for a legal fight with the White administration and the trustees.

In the fall of 1881 Thomas P. Hawley applied for admission to begin graduate studies. He had been initiated earlier into Sigma Chi, and when he was asked to sign the antifraternity pledge, literally a denunciation of his own fraternity, he refused. Purdue made the near-fatal mistake of denying Hawley admission. The Sigma Chi lawyers included a young man named John S. McMillin, a Sigma Chi from DePauw University; John Coffroth, a Pennsylvanian, who had come to Lafayette in 1870 to practice law and who had been a Purdue trustee for seven years, the last two, 1875–77, as president of the board; and Thomas B. Ward, a member of Phi Delta Theta fraternity.

So confident of a legal victory was this trio of fraternity lawyers that when Tippecanoe Circuit Judge David P. Vinton ruled in favor of White, they were stunned and immediately filed an appeal to the Indiana Supreme Court. While this legal battle was under way, another battle was being fought on the campus. The administration apparently had surveillance teams at work watching the student body for illegal fraternity activities. At one point five students, all members of Sigma Chi, were expelled, leaving only one active member on the Purdue campus.

Although Purdue had won the first court battle, on June 21, 1882, the Indiana Supreme Court ruled that "there was no impropriety in either becoming a member of, or otherwise being connected with the Sigma Chi fraternity . . . and that the objection seemingly entertained by the faculty against other fraternities of the same class was unfounded."

Had the court opinion gone the other way, it could have stymied the entire Greek-letter movement because any institution then could have made fraternity membership difficult if not impossible.

No one was, of course, more upset by the supreme court decision than President White, who countered by immediately publishing a new set of rules which allowed fraternity membership but which prohibited members from receiving honors and enjoying opportunities made available to other students.

The profraternity people were not yet finished. The Indiana General Assembly in 1883 ruined White's plan by attaching a rider to the appropriations bill which forced faculties of state-supported institutions to repeal any and all antifraternity regulations before funds would be released by the state.

White quickly resigned, realizing that his antifraternity stance was to do serious harm to the university financially. His resignation failed to sway the legislature, and in 1883, no state funds were made available for Purdue University.

It was the university's darkest day, having lost in one disastrous stroke its leadership and its principal financial support. For the next two years, the university stood on the brink of financial starvation, moving forward by and large on the contagious enthusiasm of White's successor, James Henry Smart, the redoubtable New Hampshireman who left high school after one year but later became one of the most extraordinary educators of his time.

White did agree to stay on through the summer of 1883 at the request of the board of trustees and newly elected President Smart to smooth the transfer of presidential authority. Mainly, the two completed work White had begun earlier toward revising the course of study. Prior to 1876, most of the emphasis—nearly a monopoly—was on the fundamental scientific courses. Both Smart and White agreed on the need for a shift in emphasis. Not until then had the special schools played more than a secondary role, their courses having been mainly added here and there to core requirements. Not until the School of Mechanical Engineering was outlined in 1882 had any of them constituted a four-year program.

A four-year course in mechanical engineering consisted of two years in the School of Mechanics, established in 1879, followed by two years of engineering and related sciences under the direction of Lieutenant W. R. Hamilton of the United States Army, who after dividing his time previously between Purdue and Asbury (DePauw) universities joined the Purdue faculty fulltime as an instructor in engineering and military tactics (ROTC). In 1882, Hamilton had fourteen students; the following year he was succeeded by Lieutenant Albert W. Stahl of the United States Navy, who held the rank of professor. Twenty-five students were enrolled. The same year, Goss was given full professorial rank and provided with an assistant, Joseph E. Clapper, in the winter term, and an early alumnus, Elroy A. Dillon, in the spring term.

When White finally quit, he left with his head held high, proud of his Purdue record, unashamed of the defeat which cost him his job. His last report to the trustees contained one poignant personal note in which he wished the university well in its future endeavor:

> In taking leave of Purdue University I sever, probably permanently, my official connection with the American industrial college, and the great educational problem committed to it. To the solution of this problem I have devoted the best thought and effort of my life. The work here accomplished has been done under. . .very great embarrassment and difficulty, and it is gratifying to be permitted to see indications of near success.

White moved to Cincinnati and served briefly as superintendent of public schools. Later he severed most of his connection as an active school administrator and continued his writing and editing for educational journals and the educational press. He often returned to visit the university, a venerated former president, who more often than not was hailed by faculty and students, Greeks and non-Greeks alike. White made his last appearance at Purdue in 1894 when he was invited to deliver the baccalaureate address to graduating seniors. He died October 21, 1902, in Columbus, Ohio.

His greatest problem as president had been that he wanted a university climate of solemnity—more, obviously, than young folk were willing to endure. He was a man of high principles for which he was willing to fight. In retrospect, he picked the wrong battlefield—the fraternities. Too, defending his principle was more important than achieving his goal of a purely scientific-technological university which he believed the land-grant act mandated.

Though he bowed out under a cloud, White's contribution to the university and its ultimate growth is not lessened, and he must be considered one of the most important of the university's nine presidents. He not only laid the groundwork well for the years of his enthusiastic successor, but he also gave Purdue permanent direction without which it might not have survived.

Chapter VI

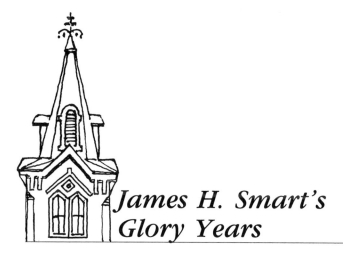

James H. Smart's Glory Years

Whereas White was the determined, cantankerous, often ill-tempered, quarrelsome conservative, James H. Smart was entirely the opposite. High-strung, gregarious, optimistic, fast paced, he was an enthusiastic risk-taker who throve on the challenges tendered by the university's poverty of the 1880s and basked in its relative prosperity and gaiety in the 1890s.

As H. B. Knoll put it in his 1963 volume *The Story of Purdue Engineering*, "Perhaps in no other period in [Purdue] history were the students so happy, rowdy, and creative, and the staff so badly paid, ambitious, and inspired."

If White had the vision, Smart had the inspiration. In his seventeen years as president, before his death in office in 1900, Smart more than any other Purdue president pushed the university onto the educational stage as one of the nation's leading land-grant institutions, especially in engineering. Smart followed the academic blueprint White had drawn, but he paid little if any attention to White's belief in an austere, solemn, and Spartan campus life. Under Smart, the university began to flourish, and the general public began to accept, although slowly, the idea of formal engineering education. The old and pervasive public view had been that engineers ran trains. And what was the point, anyway, of offering formal college training for mechanics?

Smart encouraged a climate of exhilaration—although in his first half-dozen years as president he may have wondered at times where the next payroll was coming from, and the professors may have wondered when. However, the encouragement he gave his faculty in engineering and all that he did to enhance the university's growing reputation as an engineering school assured the success of the new School of Mechanical Engineering and led to the later founding of the schools of Civil Engineering (1887) and Electrical Engineering (1888).

Smart was one of the most unusual educators in American history. He had comparatively little formal schooling and in today's world might even be classed as a high school dropout. He was born June 30, 1841, at Center Harbor, New Hampshire, a small village at the head of Lake Winnepesaukee ("smile of the Great Spirit"), a large body of water in the southern foothills of the rugged White Mountains. When Smart was seven, the family moved to Concord. His father was a high-school teacher who later became a physician. From him, Smart received his early schooling and was a precocious child who entered Concord High School at the age of eleven. But he decided after one year that school was not for him, that his future interests were in business— a belief perhaps engendered by his previous experience as a grocery clerk and delivery boy.

For several years—until he was about seventeen or eighteen— he worked as a clerk, preparing himself for the adventure of Boston. He left New Hampshire with high hopes but returned to Concord in despair; there were no big opportunities for a small-town youngster in the big city.

Eventually, he decided that he should become a school-teacher despite his own meagre schooling. He returned to high school with a zeal of the kind that Purdue University became acquainted with in later years. He seemed to be motivated by the success of some of his former classmates, now schoolteachers. He joined the growing number of young New Englanders who migrated from their Yankee surroundings to the centers of learning elsewhere in an expanding nation.

Smart was an excellent scholar and applied himself rigorously to his studies; he became highly regarded as a student and in the absence of the principal was often placed in charge of the classes in mathematics and English. Later, he taught sixteen boys and girls for nine weeks in a district school near Tilton, New Hampshire, then returned with a small fortune in gold, $36, and spent three more months in the high school. So ended his formal schooling. Smart became self-taught, developing his writing skills and learning to control the subtlety and power of language. He became a writer and speaker of lucid and inspiring eloquence. Eventually, Dartmouth College awarded him an honorary A.M.

degree in 1874 and Indiana University the LL.D. in 1883, the same year he took office as Purdue's president.

After his last three months in high school, Smart moved to Laconia, New Hampshire, and eventually became principal of the grade school and later of the high school at Claremont in the same state. He served a brief interlude as a teacher at Sanbornton, a village near Laconia.

Sixteen-hour workdays of teaching and studying were the rule for Smart, and because of bad lighting, he probably severely damaged his eyesight. At Purdue, those who observed him often said that while reading Smart would hold a book nearly to his nose to read the type.

After Claremont, Smart moved to Toledo, Ohio, for two years of teaching and administration. Eventually, he went to Fort Wayne, Indiana, where at twenty-four he became widely known as superintendent of schools and a member of the State Board of Education. He was instrumental in the reorganization of the Indiana public school system and was elected for three consecutive terms as state superintendent of public instruction as a Democrat. He published two definitive books, *The Indiana Schools and the Men Who Have Worked in Them* in 1876 and *Commentary on the School Law of Indiana* in 1881. He was also author of an earlier, smaller volume, *Gymnastics and Dumb-Bell Exercises* (1863).

Few people had Smart's knowledge and understanding of Indiana's schools and their particular problems, and no one seemed as able as he to do something about them. His temperament and experience in public school education fit him ideally for the Purdue presidency.

Smart was married in 1870 at the age of twenty-nine to Mary H. Swan of Albany, New York. Her father had been a member of the faculty at Grinnell College in Iowa. She served well as a great support in the toughest, lowest-paying job on any college or university campus—the president's wife. They had two children, Richard A., who became a professor of experimental engineering at Purdue, and a daughter, Mary F.

Smart's reputation as an excellent public school executive grew. He represented Indiana at international expositions in Vienna in 1872; Philadelphia in 1876; and Paris in 1878. His eminence among his colleagues probably was the major factor in his election in 1881 as president of the National Education Association, an honor also accorded his predecessor at Purdue.

His appointment as Purdue's president in 1883 was a wise choice by the trustees; he justified their confidence in him by serving with unequalled vigor and brilliance until his death in office in 1900.

Despite his abilities, Smart was plagued with a disorder still common to university and college presidents—lack of money. Yet, he did not panic and with cheerful mien in his first report remarked that "I found the institution in good condition except that there was no money in the treasury." It was Smart's way of saying that a good school was temporarily broke. Most of that problem could be associated with the state legislature's refusal in 1883 to appropriate any money for Purdue because of White's antifraternity stance. But there was also considerable and highly vocal opposition to higher education in the legislature, a situation not at all aided by White's continued tightening of entrance requirements and his apparent indifference to public expressions for higher enrollment. Worse, there was grassroots apathy, a condition totally foreign to Smart and his scheme of things; he set about to change it. He did, but it took the first six years of his administration.

White's departure in 1883 was accompanied by the resignations of several faculty stalwarts. Not the least was H. W. Wiley of the original teaching staff whose new position as chemist for the United States Department of Agriculture eventually led to his national prominence in establishing the original United States Pure Food and Drug Act.

Others also departed, including Professor David G. Herron, who had come in 1875 to teach mathematics, astronomy, and civil engineering (and until Goss arrived, mechanics), and Professor John A. Maxwell, who arrived in 1879 to teach English and mathematics. The year 1883 was also the year of the departure of Annie S. Peck who had come in 1881 to teach Latin. It was a vacancy not filled in line with Purdue's newly defined emphasis and specialization in technology and science. Miss Peck and Wiley were considered by students as two of the university's truly excellent teachers.

Although Smart may have regretted their leaving, he promptly filled the vacancies and opened his administration with a faculty of fifteen (including himself). Robert B. Warder became professor of chemistry (and thus the second state chemist). Edward E. Smith was transferred from the preparatory academy to teach English and history; Oscar J. Craig then directed the preparatory class; Moses C. "Towser" Stevens, who had been librarian and registrar, became professor of mathematics; Richard W. Swan, Smart's father-in-law, assumed duties that included librarian, registrar, and secretary to the president.

Other faculty in Smart's opening years included Professors Langdon Thompson, the industrial arts leader; Charles R. Barnes, lecturer in chemistry and botany; W. F. M. Goss, the engineering founder; William Carroll Latta, in agronomy, who later became a living legend in agricultural extension; Navy Lieutenant Albert W. Stahl, in mechanics; Army Lieutenant Hamilton, the ROTC commandant who was also the first professor of mechanical engineering; John Hussey, in botany (and later geology); Charles Ingersoll, in agriculture and horticulture; and Edna D. Baker, associate instructor in the preparatory academy and assistant principal matron of Ladies Hall.

In contrast to most of the first faculty under Shortridge, the new faculty became imbued with Smart's inspiration, spirit, and enthusiasm and gave the university "its best year" as Joseph E. Ratcliff, president of the board of trustees put it in his report for 1883. A new spirit of harmony prevailed among the faculty; student discipline and behavior were satisfactory; the general tone of the university's scholarship had improved. Even the fraternity trouble seemed to have disappeared. A new conciliatory atmosphere existed between the trustees and faculty on the one hand and fraternity men on the other. But the overriding problem of funding the university on a continuing, regular basis—such as Indiana University and the State Normal School at Terre Haute enjoyed—remained. Purdue stood alone at the mercy of legislative caprice. So critical was financing that the university's obligations began to mount. On October 9, 1883, Smart detailed the Purdue financial situation in a letter to the governor and indicated that he would attempt to keep Purdue's doors open for one year with $17,000—but only with the most stringent economies, concluding his report with a plea to find the wherewithal to save the institution.

Meanwhile, several wealthy Lafayette citizens advanced the university money, and local merchants extended credit. In 1885, Smart asked the legislature to honor the university's obligations; opponents of the university in the legislature asked by what authority the university had incurred such debts. Eventually the General Assembly agreed to appropriate funds to handle them, but not before requiring Smart to submit a detailed report listing the names and addresses of all faculty, employees, students, the cost of boarding them, the amount of money in the university treasury, and many other matters. Smart submitted his report, concluding with this vehement statement: "You ask by what authority debts have been created. I answer: In obedience to public law, plighted faith, sworn duty, and imperious necessity, as herein set forth."

Unthinkable today is the amount of venom spewed out of the university's private college and sectional opponents in the legislature—vociferous rancor from a small number who contended that not half of Indiana's ninety-two counties were represented in the student body, that few sons of farmers attended, that no one had ever known a farmer who benefitted from the university, and that Purdue served Tippecanoe County alone. Therefore the state should not fund it. One member of the state house of representatives said, "I'm not in favor of strangling Purdue, but I want it to take care of itself." Said another, " . . . this is the last year for Purdue. It will die, never to rise again."

In the face of such hatred, it is no wonder that Purdue lost its appropriations not only in 1883 but again in 1887. Smart weathered that drought, too, his optimism still intact. His persistence paid off. After years of Smart's pleading and politicking, continued appropriations for Purdue became assured in 1889—public backing that guaranteed at least the university's continuance if not its prosperity. Federal funding legislation—the passage of the Hatch Act of 1887 and the second Morrill Act of 1890—provided additional financial support. After fire destroyed the new engineering laboratory, Heavilon Hall, in 1894, a generous appropriation from the Indiana General Assembly made rebuilding that magnificient educational structure possible. And in 1895 Indiana tax laws were amended to relate size of appropriations to the wealth of the state.

President Smart was proud that among his many assets was his well-tested ability to work with legislators and to convince them that Purdue deserved their support. Still, even after public financing with continuing appropriations helped stabilize the university's situation after 1889, financial uncertainty was always present. Smart held to his policy of progress and expansion. He added to the organizational structure, fully supported W. F. M. Goss's efforts in the development of engineering laboratories, and repeated his strong belief that Purdue belonged at the top and, therefore, deserved the best that the State of Indiana could provide.

Of Smart, Goss once wrote that even "in the years of financial emergency, Smart was not above using his own personal credit. For example, a large dynamo was delivered to the electrical laboratory; a 300,000-pound testing machine stood on a flatcar, addressed to the applied mechanics laboratory with more [equipment] on the way. Students and faculty, seeing new foundations going in and machines being created, concluded that Purdue University was not dead and that its work was broadened and advanced during what had promised to be a period [of austerity]."

•   •   •

Smart was more than an academic impresario. He was a master at achieving enthusiastic performance from those around him, but he never demanded more of others than he demanded of himself. Important to remember is that, like White, Smart was motivated by a deeply held philosophical commitment to the value of what was then considered a new (and to some, therefore, suspect) academic development—technical education. Also like White, Smart wholly disagreed with those who believed that a scientific-technical education could not, or would not, have room for inculcating in the young high moral precepts and the logic of positive human and cultural values.

On the contrary, Smart believed in a "new education" for a "new time" in history, a belief partially based on his perception of a pervasive and revolutionary change in the way America viewed itself in the postbellum period of the American Civil War. He revealed his beliefs in a banquet speech given January 4, 1896, four years prior to his death, before the Lehigh University Club in Chicago:

> We were provincials before the war. We suddenly discovered ourselves. Columbus discovered only the shore of this continent, but during the war period every man, woman, every child, both north and south, took up the morning newspaper and went out on a voyage of discovery with keener interest than ever Columbus exhibited. The path of the soldier boy was traced from his home along every line of railroad, down every river, across every border, around every inlet and bay, and thus the amplitude of the western empire was revealed to us in a manner that could not have been secured in a hundred years under ordinary conditions. . . .
>
> We then realized that enlargement, which comes with the feeling of ownership, and through this feeling every man became a hundred times bigger than he was before. Thus was born that true national spirit which heralded a revolution in American thought and feeling.
>
> Some other very important things happened during this period. The rapid multiplication of means of communication, not only among ourselves, but among the people of the earth,—the railroad, the submarine cable, the ocean flyer, and that greatest of all engines of modern civilization, the newspaper, has brought distant peoples into touch with us, and consequently has enlarged the American into a universal. By these means the heritage of the

race has become his heritage. All science is his. All art is his. The best thought of the world is his.

In this way the world has become a very much larger world than the one in which you and I were born. It is practically a new world. We not only have a new world, but we have a new boy, and the modern boy is, in his possibilities, a hundred times bigger than the boy of thirty years ago. These things must be taken into account when we try to educate him. The old education will not fit him any more than a suit of clothes made for a pigmy will fit a giant. New conditions require new methods, hence the technical school.

If you ask me what are the characteristics of the new education, I reply that they are the characteristics of the ages in which we live. New problems concerning good citizenship, new theories of economics and sociology, and the new theology, all demand a new education. This age is, in a large sense, an industrial age. So if you will tell me how to make a man most active in employing these for the benefit of his fellows, you will explain the new education.

The thought is this: Man is not to be, but to be able to do. It is not the possession of knowledge, but the right application of knowledge. The man who has money and does not use it, is called a miser. The man who has knowledge and does not use it, is meaner than a miser. Educated selfishness is monstrous. . . .

If you will find me a man who through the application of sanitary science, will add a year to the average of human life, you will find a man who will bless the human race. If you will find me a man who will show us how to prevent insect ravages and fungus diseases in plants, you will find a man who will save six hundred millions of dollars annually for this country alone. If you will find me a man who will show us how to use coal in a locomotive and develop thirty percent of its possible power, instead of five percent, as at present, you will find a man who can build for himself a monument as high as the Eiffel tower, all of gold, and pay for it out of the proceeds of his discovery. . . .

• • •

Despite the hindrances of the financial crises of the 1880s and the university's problems with the Indiana legislature, growth in enrollment as well as programs, attendant resources, and facilities for instruction grew at an astonishing rate; enrollment doubled twice between Smart's first year, 1883, and 1891. As gratifying as such growth was, it placed increasingly burdensome financial problems upon the university. But, by comparison, the problems of growth were much more pleasant to deal with than those of raw survival.

Smart had an expansive mind—the kind of person who, shown an egg, could envision a chicken ranch. His confidence seemed infinite, and he believed in spending what comparatively little money the institution had on big things—such as $4,000 for a Corliss engine—when there were other dire needs. But he looked beyond the matters of the moment and saw in such purchases investments that would, in the long run, pay off in prestige for the university and boost morale among the students and staff. Purdue was going to be a winner, not a loser; few ever worked as hard as Smart to fulfill his predecessor's admonition that Purdue must get down to business in the areas where it could offer superior education.

The School of Mechanical Engineering made early gains under Lieutenant Hamilton, but Hamilton left in 1883 and was succeeded by Lieutenant Stahl. The first graduate in engineering at Purdue was Charles L. Ratcliff of Spiceland, an eastern Indiana hamlet. Ratcliff was awarded the B.M.E. (Bachelor of Mechanical Engineering) degree in 1885. In the following year James F. Bruff, Arthur L. King, Scott Mead, and Joseph Swearingen received the same degree.

The course in mechanical engineering as originally established included some branches of civil engineering. Its details changed from year to year and in the 1885–86 school year included some senior electives—applied chemistry, general literature, and German.

The bulwark of engineering education in its first six years consisted primarily of practical mechanics. Drawing, descriptive geometry, and shop work were the bases for its course work, and the high spirits of Smart, Dean Goss, and Michael Joseph Golden, among others, were its driving force. By the mid-to-late-1880s, the drawing classes and manual training shops were filled throughout the day with engineering students.

William Freeman Myrick Goss came to Purdue in 1879 under White. He was a Massachusetts Yankee from Cape Cod where his father owned and edited a newspaper at Barnstable. Goss had two years of formal schooling in mechanic arts at the Massachusetts Institute of Technology before arriving at Purdue as an instructor at $600 per year—$100 more than the board of trustees thought he ought to be paid. Goss then was not yet twenty-nine years old, but before the turn of the century, backed by Smart, he had done the work that indelibly stamped Purdue as a true pioneer in engineering education west of the Hudson River.

When he arrived, Goss must have been appalled to find that no shop in practical mechanics had been established and that it was to be built in a less than ideal place: the basement of Science Hall, directly beneath Harvey Wiley's chemistry laboratory. Goss set about the work himself, wielding hammer and saw to install a floor and, more importantly, a ceiling to prevent the dust from Wiley's chemistry lab from sifting through the floor on to his five students and into the machinery.

Throughout much of the fall of 1879, Goss worked at carpentry to make some semblance of a laboratory in practical mechanics. Power for his machines was supplied by an underground shaft from the nearby engine and gas house and a large pulley installed just inside the wall of the basement. From this source, a jungle of belting powered Goss's shop tools—thus making possible the first real moves toward what ultimately became one of the world's largest engineering schools.

• • •

An interesting sidelight to Goss's basement shop and laboratory is told in *The Story of Purdue Engineering.* There is some belief, not proven, that Goss had some distinguished carpentry help when he established his first laboratory. George Lyman Kittridge, so the story goes, came west with his close friend, Goss, to help in the carpentry work in the Science Hall basement and worked alongside him to complete the work. Young Kittridge, then only nineteen himself, became one of America's best known Shakespearean scholars and a noted authority on the English language as well as Chaucerian literature. He was a member of the Harvard faculty from 1888 to 1936. Goss, on the other hand, became one of the leading United States authorities on locomotives and railroads. Both men became renowned in their professional fields and were close companions in retirement at Cape Cod.

• • •

Smart became known in Purdue history as "the engineers' president." He tended to bend the university's efforts toward the building and reinforcement of engineering, although not, as some contend, to the exclusion of agriculture. Under Smart, engineering flourished before the turn of the century; agriculture had to wait until 1902 before it had a major building. Smart did not necessarily plan it that way. In fact, he believed he had two main tasks as president—one in agriculture, the other in engineering. Both were unified by the general concept that they were educational mainstreams for the so-called "industrial classes."

As Smart explained toward the end of his career, his efforts in agriculture met with little public response. Purdue would be ready for agriculture, he said, when agriculture was ready for Purdue. The times were such that farmers as a group generally did not believe that any university would be helpful to farming, and many farmers' sons saw no point in going into farming when the prospects seemed so much brighter in engineering. Smart therefore concentrated the university's precious resources where he felt they would do the greatest good for the greatest number. At the peak of the American Industrial Revolution, could there be any doubt?

Work went on in agriculture, but it seemed to be Purdue's poor cousin by comparison. Not until 1902, when Agriculture Hall (now the Entomology Hall) was erected, did Purdue begin to make real headway in agriculture.

If there is a single element in the Purdue heritage that is unique among land-grant institutions, it is very likely Purdue's early stress on the practical mechanics. Subsequently, that emphasis led to the development of engineering at a time when agriculture was dominant at other land-grant institutions.

Where there was a need or demand, however, Smart was responsive. In his first year as president, he unhesitatingly (though informally) endorsed the idea of adding courses in pharmacy to the Purdue curricula. The idea, legend has it, was given to Smart as a chance, albeit appropriate, remark by the owner of a corner drugstore in Indianapolis where Smart and other professional cronies occasionally met for talk and companionship. Smart was chatting with the drugstore's owner, John Newell Hurty, a Philadelphia-trained pharmacist and analytical chemist. Although Purdue was only fourteen years beyond its founding, Hurty asked Smart whether it would not be a good idea for Purdue to add at least some pharmacal courses in keeping with its scientific-technical basis, if not its land-grant philosophy.

Smart pounced on the idea with his usual vigor. "I'm for it good and strong," he is reported to have replied to Hurty, "[I] will present the matter to the next board meeting." But, he added, Hurty would have to agree to serve at least two years as professor of pharmacy. Hurty accepted and is credited with being the founder of Purdue's School of Pharmacy, though not its first dean.

There was no great public outcry for pharmacy training at Purdue. But the state's professional pharmacists saw the need and expressed an active concern for just such a course of study proposed for Purdue. Hurty did help organize a plan of study designed for students wishing to pursue a course in professional pharmacy, but the establishment of the school and its setting was a matter that had to be determined by Smart and the trustees. On December 13, 1883, the board adopted two resolutions, one directing the president to ask Professors R. B. Warder and C. R. Barnes to prepare a plan "for a course of instruction in pharmaceutical chemistry" for the board's consideration; the other resolution requested the president to prepare a circular announcing that "a School of Pharmacy will be opened in Purdue University in the fall of 1884"—provided there were enough qualified applicants to warrant creating a school.

Seven was the magic number; that was the number enrolled that fall, but only for the junior, or first, course. The school's literature for the first year bravely proclaimed that students "would be well prepared and their course of training . . . will compare well with the opportunities offered in other Schools of Pharmacy." Students were selected from among those who had already completed twenty-four months as apprentices in dispensing pharmacies or in a manufacturing pharmaceutical laboratory. The course lasted twenty weeks with classes and laboratory work on a rigorous 8:30 A.M.-5:30 P.M. schedule. Instruction was considered free with only a $28 fee covering materials used in the laboratory, incidentals, and matriculation; $125 was charged for lodging, food, and other costs.

Hurty, Warder, and Barnes, together with an Indianapolis physician, A. W. Brayton, did their work well. Students studied botany, the *Pharmacopoeia,* and how to weigh, measure, and compound prescriptions. A senior course leading to the Graduate in Pharmacy (Ph.G.) completed the program—a degree granted only after rigorous examinations and evidence that the student had worked for forty-two months in a drugstore or for a pharmaceutical manufacturer under a qualified preceptor.

The professional response in Indiana was enthusiastic. The editor of the *Indiana Pharmacist,* Joseph R. Perry, visited the new school, read the questions on the final examination, and talked to Hurty, Brayton, and Warder. Then he wrote grandly, "The facilities for acquiring a thorough pharmaceutical education at Purdue are not excelled by another institution anywhere in the country."

The rapport which developed between the Purdue School of Pharmacy and the profession in Indiana undoubtedly contributed to the swift progress and excellence of the school which today is considered to be among the best in the western world. Although the credit for its development and growth as a quality program belongs to others, Smart must be given full credit for his vision, enthusiasm, and support. Had he not quickly grasped the import of Hurty's concern in an Indianapolis drugstore, the story of pharmacy at Purdue might have been different.

●   ●   ●

Among many of the brilliant moves Goss made, as it turned out, was in bringing to Purdue in 1884 two legendary faculty characters, Michael Joseph Golden and William Payson Turner. Like Goss, they were eastern youngsters who had completed the two-year School of Mechanics at the Massachusetts Institute of Technology. Golden and Turner shared many career parallels, but were exact opposites in temperament. Golden was the flamboyant, athletic, fiery Boston Irishman who managed to strike fear into every freshman mechanics student who ever stepped across his classroom threshold. Turner was quiet, working faithfully in the machine shop and forge, a man whose principal claim to being a faculty celebrity was as the marshal who led the faculty procession on commencement day for so many years.

Golden's immortality was represented by the engineering building which commanded the corner of Northwestern and Grant streets for nearly seventy-two years and bore his name for more than sixty years. The new building was first officially named the Practical Mechanics Building when it was constructed in 1910 in the Stone administration. Engineering alumni venerated Golden in 1920 by seeking a name change to Michael Golden Shops (and later, after 1950, to Michael Golden Laboratories), but engineering students gave it their own name by which it became best known: Mike's Castle. Although the main part of the building was razed in 1982 to make way for a new technology building, Maurice G. Knoy Hall of Technology, the laboratories attached to the original building, modernized and updated, remain.

Golden ranks alongside Harvey Wiley in his energy and enthusiasm as a teacher; though he struck fear into his new students at the outset of each semester, he became a beloved faculty character. The *Purdue Exponent* once said freshmen hated him, sophomores respected him, juniors appreciated him, seniors loved him, and alumni revered him.

A poor Irish lad who had worked as a mill boy in Lawrence, Massachusetts, Golden was determined to get an education. He enrolled with $60 and conditional grades in two subjects. His tuition money came from earnings as a sparring partner in Boston's famed boxing parlors of that era.

Golden had flaming red hair, parted on dead center, and an Irish temper to match its color. Through a thick brogue, he made it painfully and repeatedly clear as to who ran his classroom. To most of the engineering students in his classes, he was hardly beloved. Fear—cold, clammy-handed fear—was how it was described by students later in life. However, almost to a man, they were also willing to concede that though he was unanimously feared, he was probably the best instructor at Purdue. Few completed his course without knowing what practical mechanics was all about.

He could be arbitrary and threatening with such first-day speeches as, "I'll flunk ye if I can, and I can if I want to," or "I'll flunk ye just as soon as I can get me pencil out." Above all, he would tell his new classes that he expected them to be to class on time, to stay "aware," to behave themselves, and not to "monkey."

The 1905 *Debris* wrote of him: "If it suits his fancy to call a geometrical solid as large as a peck measure a point, it is a point, so don't think it is a pussy cat, and if he says that 'dynamite' is toothpaste or a steam engine is a flock of ponies, put it down for it's so and 'ye needn't bother yer head about it because I know and could flunk the bunch of ye by raisin' me little finger. Now that's straight.'"

Golden had a standing offer to put on the gloves with any recalcitrant or argumentative student brave or foolish enough to accept the challenge. One did, but wisely failed to show up. Once on a daily quiz, a student in Golden's class, totally baffled by his assignment, turned in a blank paper with only his name on it. Golden graded it minus ten—for spoiling an otherwise clean sheet of paper.

Yet Golden became warmly woven into the rich tapestry of the Purdue legend—despite such performances as the one in which he, a minority of one of the Purdue Athletic Association, managed to hold up the awarding of varsity letters to the 1910 football team. They had, he said in a speech at an association meeting, lost all but one game; they were lazy, he believed, and did not deserve to wear the gold "P" of a Boilermaker. He was met with boos and hisses, but he clenched his fists, stood his ground, and finally won his point.

That year's team went letterless for nearly a quarter of a century until letters were awarded in 1934 on the grounds that Golden, though convincing, was wrong.

While a faculty member, Golden was also a student and earned two degrees at Purdue, a bachelor of mechanical engineering and the professional M.E. degree. He directed practical mechanics from 1890 to 1916 when he retired, worn out and weary.

Golden was a Renaissance man. A superb athlete, he was exceptionally good as a wrestler and fencer in addition to his boxing prowess. He was also a rabid Purdue sports fan, attending nearly every varsity sporting event. He kept baseball alive at Purdue and even played in the faculty backfield for the annual faculty-seniors football game.

He was also an accomplished musician on the flute, piccolo, and violin. He collected old books and works of art, was a good photographer, and invented many of the machines used by manual training schools of that day.

John L. Sullivan, the colorful heavyweight boxing champion, had known him in Boston. Years later, Sullivan said that he regretted Golden's decision to become a college professor when he could have been a great boxer and "made something of himself."

In later years, Golden's two sisters, Katherine and Helen, followed their brother to West Lafayette and became students and later Purdue instructors in their own right. Both women earned B.S. and M.S. degrees in 1890 and 1892 respectively, and Katherine soon afterward became an instructor in biology. Helen began as an assistant in 1906 in the practical mechanics department headed by her brother and in 1907 became an instructor.

For a time, Katherine lived with her brother in a dwelling at 128 South Grant Street and Helen lived alone at 306 State Street, both addresses near the campus. But Katherine met, fell in love with, and married Arvill Wayne Bitting, a veterinarian who was professor of veterinary science. The couple finally took jobs in the United States Department of Agriculture in Washington. Katherine, under the tutelage of another Purdue "great," Harvey Wiley, the USDA's chief chemist, became a microanalyst in the chemistry division and was honored by her alma mater in 1935 with an honorary doctorate in science.

Turner was obviously more mellow than Golden in his approach to teaching and became known among his students as "Deacon" Turner. He earned a unique place in Purdue faculty history as the commencement marshal, his ruddy-faced, white-haired countenance standing out as he led commencement processions. Though he never obtained a bachelor's degree, President Edward C. Elliott asked that he wear the Purdue gown. Through the long succession of annual commencement processions that Turner marshalled, not one was ever rained out.

Turner always used the language of his native Maine coast and always insisted that his shop be kept "shipshape." He was not as insistent about the time required by students to complete a project as he was about its craftsmanship and quality. His policy was that "we can do no more than work all the time." He was credited with foreseeing the close tolerances which industry would require in its tooling and machinery and with preparing students for engineering problems they would face in future careers.

Turner, as did Golden, made a major contribution to the evolution of practical mechanics into industrial engineering. One of his efforts, the design of a four-horsepower marine engine, gave his students the kind of production problem they would find in industry. The engine was even tested on the Wabash River and worked well. Some consideration was given to its commercial production. But there the matter remained—possibly because production of the engine would have been more commercial than educational.

Turner spent his summers at Isle Au Haut off the coast of Maine and lived next door to his close friend Harlan Stone, the United States Supreme Court chief justice who was the brother of Purdue's fifth president, Winthrop Ellsworth Stone. Turner perforce retired in 1938 at age seventy after fifty-two years of service at Purdue in practical mechanics.

•   •   •

Smart's first major engineering triumph, of which there were many, was the construction of Mechanics Hall, the first new building on the campus following the completion of the original buildings in 1877.

Only two years after the political hostilities of 1883, when the Indiana General Assembly had made no appropriation whatsoever for Purdue, Smart won $12,500 for construction of the building on the site of the present Stanley Coulter Hall. President White had sought $10,000 for the same building in the last days of his administration, but his woes in the fraternity dispute virtually assured that he would not get it or any other sum from the state coffers. Smart, however, had a totally different relationship with the Indiana General Assembly and imperatively demanded the funds—and got them.

At the time it was planned, Mechanics Hall (later called Mechanics Laboratory) seemed adequate, but before construction was completed, it was obvious that it was inadequate. The surge in the numbers of students wanting practical mechanics courses was clear evidence of a pervasive and growing enthusiasm for the kind of industrial education Purdue provided. The engineering programs were developing, and students in these courses were required to take practical mechanics courses—drawing, woodworking, machine shop, forge, and foundry. The new building also included facilities for steam engineering and materials testing.

In his constant search for funds, Smart quickly announced that enrollment was burgeoning—to the extent that one hundred twenty drawing students were trying to use a facility with accommodations for forty.

Although the School of Civil Engineering was established a year before the School of Electrical Engineering, the latter was given its own building first. Smart's influence with legislators widened in the late 1880s because, after the School of Electrical Engineering was established in 1888 under Louis Bell, he got state funds and built a new electrical engineering building a year later. The facility, its high tower a prominence on the campus skyline, stood alone at the head of Memorial Drive on the northeast corner of the Oval (Memorial Mall) on a site now occupied by the west half of the Wetherill Chemistry Laboratories building.

Electrical apparatus for the new building was somehow obtained from a variety of sources, and electrical engineering education in this Indiana academic outpost become a marvel of the time. By contrast, Professor Henry A. Huston several years earlier had had difficulty obtaining a single electric motor for classroom use and finally rented one from a New York company for three dollars a month. The first one on the Purdue campus, the motor was rated at one-eighth horsepower.

•   •   •

Henry Augustus Huston, a redoubtable Maine Yankee, had come west to teach science at Lafayette High School, then a part of the old Ford "graded" school, high atop a bluff at the head of South Street hill. A graduate of Bowdoin College, he was described by H. B. Knoll as a "bundle of barbed wire and good humor."

Had it not been for Harvey Wiley, whom he greatly admired, it is quite likely Huston would never have associated himself with Purdue, mostly because of his intense dislike of White. But eventually, as a stalwart faculty member, he served as a professor in both engineering and agriculture. He became a memorable, if not always lovable, faculty character, not altogether unlike Michael Golden. Huston lived to be ninety-nine and was able to celebrate

E. C. Elliott, president (above left), R. B. Stewart, comptroller (left), and David E. Ross, the Lafayette industrialist-inventor (above), were a threesome who during the 1920s and 1930s pushed Purdue University toward a new greatness with Elliott's political finesse, Stewart's financial genius, and Ross's enthusiastic largess.

Amelia Earhart from 1935 to 1937 was a member of the Purdue staff as a visiting consultant in women's careers. The famed American aviatrix flew the Lockheed Electra (below) on her ill-fated around-the-world flight when she was lost in the South Pacific. The plane was a gift of Purdue Research Foundation and was on display at the Purdue Airport a few weeks before her departure.

Lillian Gilbreth, a famed industrial engineer, was a visiting professor at Purdue for many years, beginning her association with Purdue in 1935.

Harry Reed, dean of agriculture succeeding John Skinner, served on the committee that oversaw university affairs in the absence of President Elliott in the early years of World War II.

A. A. Potter, the dean of engineering at Purdue from 1921 to his retirement in the 1950s, was considered the "dean of deans" of American engineering education. He was acting president from June 1945 to January 1946, between the Elliott and Hovde administrations.

Dorothy Stratton succeeded Carolyn Shoemaker as dean of women in 1933. She became head of the women's auxiliary of the United States Coast Guard (SPARS) in World War II and never returned to the deanship.

Martin Fisher served as the second dean of men, following Stanley Coulter.

Professor R. G. Dukes became Purdue's first dean of the Graduate School when it was founded in 1929.

The Old Oaken Bucket, instituted as the symbol of Purdue-Indiana University football rivalry in 1925, came from an old well on a farm near North Vernon, Indiana. Local legend has it that Morgan's Raiders, a ragtag band of Confederate sympathizers who roamed north of the Ohio River, once used it to get drinking water on a sortie through southern Indiana.

The Old Oaken Bucket was presented to the two schools at halftime ceremonies of the 1925 game at IU Memorial Stadium. George Ade represented Purdue alumni, and Harry Kurrie, president of the Monon Railroad, represented IU alumni. Others are game officials. The Purdue team captain, Harold Harmeson, is second from left. The IU captain is third from right.

The Purdue Memorial Union as
originally built had a look of
dominating and monolithic stability
that represented a new beginning in
Purdue University academic and social
life. Later additions doubled its size.
But even the Union had its hard times,
evidenced by this sign hung over the
State Street sidewalk in front of the
building to attract meal customers.

G. A. Young, head of the School of Mechanical Engineering, was devoted to Purdue and to teaching. He also once directed the Purdue band.

Harry Creighton Peffer was the stormy head of the School of Chemical Engineering, which he founded and nourished into one of the best nationally.

William Kendrick Hatt was the argumentive but brilliant head of the School of Civil Engineering—and fought with nearly everybody else on the faculty

C. Francis Harding was a member of the faculty of the School of Electrical Engineering from 1908, and its head when he died unexpectedly in 1942.

The Edward C. Elliott Hall of Music today (above) and as it appeared while under construction in the late 1930s. The music hall was the high point of the career of President Edward C. Elliott who with R. B. Stewart did the necessary background work enabling Purdue to build it. The board of trustees named it for Elliott in 1958.

the golden anniversary of his Purdue resignation, crediting his longevity to, among other things, daily breakfasts of Danish blue cheese and string beans followed by a glass of sherry.

As a high-school science teacher, Huston arranged his schedule so that his afternoons were free to come across the Wabash to work in Wiley's laboratory. The two became fast friends, and Wiley suggested to Huston that he ought to plan to take a Purdue degree since he was already doing the necessary work. "Who'd want a degree from that dump?" Huston asked when Wiley brought up the matter. Wiley explained that, at the time, President White was critical of him and that if he could direct Huston's studies toward an advanced degree, it might put him back in White's good graces. Huston would do almost anything to help his friend Wiley—or almost anything to spite President White.

Huston received an analytical chemist degree in 1882 and continued to teach at the old Ford school, advancing to the principalship. After White left Purdue in 1884, Huston joined the Purdue faculty. Before he resigned in 1903 to enter the potash industry, he had been professor of physics and electricity, professor of agricultural chemistry, director of the Indiana Weather Service, and director of the Agricultural Experiment Station.

He recalled that he had once had to teach political economy and psychology from two "dismal and antiquated" textbooks chosen by White before he left office and that they had been the cause of the "most distressing events" of what he called "my unimportant teaching career."

One of Huston's principal reasons for disliking White was that he had been a fraternity man while a student at Bowdoin and was diametrically opposite White in the president's intense campaign against secret societies. When Huston climbed the chapel stairs to receive his diploma at commencement, he defiantly wore his old Bowdoin fraternity pin, hoping White would see it.

In his reminiscences written years later, Huston recalled another Purdue "great," Reginald Aubrey Fessenden, the first of the Purdue faculty to have the title of professor of electrical engineering. Huston labeled Fessenden, though with obvious affection, "a typical example of the absent-minded college professor." Whether real or apocryphal, two stories attributed to Huston about Fessenden are worth repeating. One concerned the time that Fessenden, obviously preoccupied, poured his cream into his napkin ring instead of his coffee cup at the Stockton House where many early faculty boarded. Another time, Fessenden came down to breakfast one morning without his necktie. His wife asked him to go back upstairs and put one on. When he did not return, she went up and found that he had undressed and gone back to bed.

For all of that, Fessenden was lured away from Purdue after only one year (1892–93) to Western University (now the University of Pittsburgh) by a higher salary and a $1,000 "bonus" check from George Westinghouse, to be cashed only if he accepted the new offer.

On Cobb Island (in the Potomac River south of Washington, D.C.) in December 1900, Fessenden was the first man in history to broadcast human speech by wireless telephony. The event culminated years of work he first began in a Purdue laboratory. The experiment in broadcasting took place between two fifty-foot masts a mile apart. The transmission was poor in quality but at least intelligible.

Another beloved individual who became one of Purdue's legends was Stanley Coulter, who joined the university in 1887. Coulter, a teacher who had left the profession to become a lawyer in 1880, decided after five years of practice at Logansport that he much preferred education. Coulter, the teacher, had not gone unnoticed by Smart, who had served as state superintendent of public instruction.

The year 1887 had been tough on the Smart administration. The legislature had made no operating appropriation to the university, and many unpaid faculty simply resigned. Smart, in Europe at the time, returned to find his faculty decimated.

Coulter was on vacation at Lake Maxinkuckee that same summer when a youngster rowed out from shore to his fishing scow to deliver a telegram from Smart. It was an offer of a professorship in zoology and assistant principalship of the preparatory academy. Coulter read it, stuck it in his pocket, lit up his pipe, and went on fishing.

Purdue at the time was a new and unorthodox school with no academic standing. It had not yet been received into the fellowship of other established colleges in Indiana. Coulter viewed it as a trade school. But the lure of a professorship in zoology, plus a role in the academic direction of preparatory students, was too much of a challenge, so he accepted. Coulter spent thirty-nine years at Purdue in varied jobs that all had a marked effect on the university's direction.

Nor would a Purdue history be complete without some mention of Benjamin Harrison, the former United States president and grandson of another president, William Henry Harrison, the hero of the Battle of Tippecanoe. Benjamin Harrison served on the board of trustees for six years from 1895 until 1901. An Ohioan, he came to Indianapolis to practice law and served a term as a United states senator from Indiana from 1881 to 1887. Harrison ran as the Republican presidential candidate against Grover Cleveland, won one term, was renominated in 1892, then was defeated by Cleveland.

Harrison is considered by many historians to have been a colorless president, though he had an illustrious Civil War record and was retired as a brigadier general. Following his presidency, he returned to corporate law practice in Indianapolis and was appointed to the Purdue board in 1895. Harrison lent a great deal of expertise on widely differing matters to the board and often lectured to Purdue classes on world affairs and public life in America. When Smart died in 1900, Harrison presided at campus memorial services. He himself died a little more than a year later on March 13, 1901, at Indianapolis, while still a board member.

• • •

Smart, at the suggestion of Lieutenant Albert W. Stahl who directed mechanical engineering, wrote a large number of letters, in longhand, to railroads, quarrymen, industries, and builders, describing the materials testing capabilities at the university.

In subsequent times, Purdue did large amounts of commercial work from outside the university—businesses which sent specimens from various regions of the nation to be tested. That work pioneered an entirely new dimension for the land-grant philosophy.

Goss and Smart were a team. Goss had worked primarily in practical mechanics and by 1890 had achieved enough educationally to satisfy most academicians for a lifetime. In 1890, he began a year of travel and study and returned to Purdue to make new and important contributions to the university in engineering research. He became, as Knoll described him, "the powerhouse of the whole engineering program." But the magic came from Smart; together the two made things happen, the first evidence of which was the purchase of a Corliss steam engine, a marvel of its time and a magnificent laboratory addition for Purdue engineering.

Smart, influenced by Goss, decided to bring a locomotive to the campus as a part of engineering laboratory equipment. The imaginative Smart could have easily decided that he was doing enough to create a technical university without bringing a steam locomotive to the campus. But that was not his way; Smart set seemingly insurmountable goals, then immersed himself in achieving them. He reached for the stars when the university treasury could not afford stepladders. Such were his and Goss's touches of genius in bringing the *Schenectady* to the campus—though pulled by horses, its firebox and boiler stone cold. Once installed as a test locomotive, it became the symbol, the beacon, "the distinguishing mark, the thundering reason (as Knoll wrote) why engineering students were glad to be at Purdue."

Just such decisions marked Smart's administration—the reason why history must show that Smart and White were probably the two most important leaders in the university's more than 119-year existence. For Smart, just over the horizon was the capstone of his career. The construction of Heavilon Hall ultimately symbolized what he meant in his succinct statement to the Indiana General Assembly: "It has been our ambition to make Purdue University one of the most thorough and best equipped technical schools in the country. The State of Indiana can afford nothing less."

•   •   •

Smart did not altogether ignore agriculture, but there is no denying that agriculture did not begin to match engineering's strides until after Winthrop E. Stone became president in 1900. The 150-acre Purdue model farm showed a $759.83 profit in 1874–75—which was the good news. The bad news was that as late as 1879–80, agriculture had only three faculty—one of them being the "university farmer"—and eleven students.

Ten of the 150 acres comprising the model farm were set aside as an "experimental station," and provisions were made for three years of study in crop rotation, farm management, horticulture, stockbreeding, entomology, dairying, and drainage.

In 1880, the profits from the model farm increased to $1,000 per year; two years later, the first graduate in agriculture study, William P. Driscoll, was awarded a diploma. Special diplomas in addition to those in science were also awarded to Henry A. Beck and Elwood Mead. Mead had taken courses in horticulture as well as agriculture and got a B.S. degree with a certificate in agriculture and science. He also took a special course in agriculture mechanics offered by engineering's Goss and, after leaving Purdue, earned a civil engineering degree at Iowa State University. He returned to Purdue and earned a master's degree in civil engineering in 1884. Later he was the first person to receive a Purdue honorary doctorate in engineering (1904).

Mead became one of the nation's best known agricultural engineers and had an outstanding career as commissioner of reclamation in the United States Department of the Interior. Lake Mead, the huge body of water impounded behind Hoover Dam in Nevada and Arizona, was named for this early Purdue alumnus.

John Hussey had been appointed the university's first professor of natural sciences and specifically taught subjects in horticulture and botany. He also lectured on various agriculturally related topics simply because there was no one else qualified to do so.

But White's vision for agriculture and engineering began to take substantive form when he brought Goss from MIT and Charles L. Ingersoll from Michigan State College. Ingersoll began the first experimental test plots the same year he arrived at Purdue, and when in 1882 he was summoned to become president of Colorado Agricultural College, the work was taken over and expanded by one of Purdue's most eminent agriculturists, Professor William Carroll Latta.

Latta served Purdue for more than a half century, from his appointment in 1882 as an instructor and superintendent of the farm in White's administration until his death at age eighty-five in 1935. Like Ingersoll, Latta had been educated at Michigan State College and arrived at Purdue with an M.S. degree. During his career, he served not only as a professor of agriculture but also as director of the experiment station, consulting agriculturalist, and consulting specialist for the farmers' institutes, one of the early agricultural extension activities. In fact, Latta's role in agriculture at Purdue is more nearly tied to his activities in the experiment station and to the general development of cooperative extension than anything else.

Latta moved the experimental plots that Ingersoll had begun on land north of State Street to the so-called "agriculture campus" south of that thoroughfare, then found himself moving them westward in the early 1900s as agriculture underwent accelerated expansion in the Stone administration. Latta continued Ingersoll's experiments with wheat and other grains, using varied types of fertilizers and manures.

In 1882, the first agricultural hall was built, and in 1884, the first agricultural bulletin, "The Hession Fly" by J. M. Webster, was issued. Webster was an agent of the United States Bureau of Entomology who became a fixture in Purdue agricultural research activity in the years after that first bulletin. Through 1887, twelve more bulletins were issued to Indiana farmers by Latta and Webster, James Croop, and others.

Agriculture was greatly enhanced in 1882 not only by Latta's arrival but also by the construction of that first major agriculture building south of State Street—a project requiring the second move of the experimental plots, this time to an area west of the new structure. In 1884, the "experimental farm" and the "university farm" were combined, and a year later Purdue dropped its two-year undergraduate course for a four-year program. In 1887, the federal Hatch Act brought $15,000 each year to Purdue for an Agricultural Experiment Station. The developments the Hatch Act funds permitted, together with the growth in numbers of agricultural bulletins, began to change the strained climate between Purdue agriculture and the Hoosier farming community. Smart organized the station on the foundation of experimental work already under way. J. W. Sanborn was named the first director but resigned before taking up his duties and was succeeded by Horace Stockbridge.

Progress in agriculture was in contrast to the spectacular things occurring in engineering and science north of State Street; progress was made but seemed almost imperceptible.

•   •   •

Although President Smart had appealed to the legislature for a staggering appropriation—$60,000—to build the new engineering laboratory, a less-than-enthused Indiana General Assembly finally allocated a disappointing $12,000. Undaunted, Smart went ahead with the building of the central unit of the future engineering laboratory; the arrival of the glorious dream was postponed until funds could be found.

Meanwhile, the new central unit was built, and the Corliss engine and experimental *Schenectady* were installed. It was formally opened on January 11, 1892, and a day later—to let the public know that Purdue was moving forward—experimental tests were run for railroad officials, master mechanics, and engineers. Smart admitted the building was not very impressive, but instead he emphasized the Corliss engine and the *Schenectady,* which he termed "the largest and most expensive machinery ever put into an engineering laboratory."

In the fall of 1892, a wealthy Frankfort bachelor, Amos Heavilon, was on hand at the campus when President Smart announced that Heavilon had made gifts of $35,000 toward the completion of the Purdue goal of an engineering laboratory second to none anywhere. The occasion was daily chapel, and Heavilon received a standing ovation from the student body for his largess.

The Indiana General Assembly added the kind of support the following year that Smart had always hoped for—a $50,000 appropriation for construction of Smart's engineering dream, and wasting no time, Smart saw to it that construction got under way by March 23. The work moved rapidly, and on January 19, 1894, the mighty engineering laboratory that was given Amos Heavilon's name was dedicated.

The building, its high tower dominating the rather plain campus, symbolized the attainment of what, only a few years earlier, would have been considered the unattainable. Now, the unreachable was reached. It was Purdue's moment of triumph, and Smart saw to it that the university basked in the light at the summit, its students assured that now they had engineering facilities unexcelled anywhere.

Governor Claude Matthews appeared as the dedication speaker, and that evening the new laboratory was the scene of a happy, celebrational ball. Later, when nearly all was lost in the holocaust which consumed the new building, antidance elements in the Lafayette community made it quite clear that the calamity was a result of divine punishment deserved for holding a dance.

Even the university catalogue, by its very nature the dreariest of all publications, gloated:

> The entire structure has floor space of more than an acre, and its extreme limits are 388 feet from east to west and 234 feet from north to south.
>
> A 100-horsepower Harriss-Corliss triple expansion engine has been designed and constructed especially for this laboratory. . . .
>
> The wood-working room has in it fifty benches, furnished with separate tools for 150 students. . . .
>
> The forge room contains thirty forges, equipped with smithing tools and fitted with blast and exhaust pipe systems and fans.

After the joy of the celebration came total gloom. Only four days after the dedication, the triumphant symbol, except for its west wing, lay in bleak, charred ruin following a fearful night of fire and smoke and desperate, vain efforts to extinguish it.

The fire began as a gas explosion in the new laboratory's boiler room. It soon enveloped almost the entire building, including its proud tower. In Lafayette, the entire western sky seemed aglow; men, women, and children rushed to witness the catastrophe, and playgoers in the old downtown Opera House left the theatre in droves to witness a greater drama west of the Wabash River. A horse-drawn fire engine was dispatched from Oakland Hill in Lafayette, but the team could not complete the long run, giving out as they tried to pull the heavy fire apparatus up State Street hill. Finally, a fire hose was brought in but had to be laid all the way to a cistern near Purdue Hall; there was little water pressure.

Smart, of course, was at the scene, tears in his eyes. Later he wrote, "Heavilon Hall had been beautiful four days before: it was infinitely more beautiful now, but the crowds this time were speechless with grief, and in a few hours only a pitiful mass of blackened ruins remained to mark the spot where Purdue's greatest pride once stood."

In the morning, students and staff wept. Fears were expressed for President Smart's health; he had been in preparation for a well-earned rest when the disaster struck. Building Heavilon Hall had become a part of his life. Would Heavilon Hall's disaster also destroy it?

Smart was an extraordinary human being. He had already begun to plan anew before the ruins cooled, and appeared on the rostrum at chapel the day after with the ringing announcement, the echoes of which have resounded across the years to become Purdue's rallying cry, a symbol of its spirit, a reminder of its heritage. "I have shed all my tears for our loss last night," Smart began. "We are looking to the future, not to the past. I am thankful no one was injured." Then, although exhausted from the wearying night's work, he straightened himself to his full height, and his voice took on a new and determined tone: "But I tell you, young men, that tower shall go up one brick higher."

Smart's health had suffered because of overwork. He had planned to take a year's rest. Now he rallied his strength and immediately began planning to rebuild what had become central to the engineering education supremacy that he, with Goss and others, had struggled for so long and so enthusiastically to achieve.

The day after the fire, removal of the debris had begun. Within a week, Smart had mailed an appeal to "friends of the university" telling of the catastrophe and asking for a continuation of the "interest that has heretofore been accorded us." Insurance and the salvage of equipment amounted to about $100,000, leaving a net loss of $75,000. Students and faculty competed with one another to do extra work so that smaller machines could be restored and returned to service. The feeling across the small campus was that while something precious had been lost, cooperation, industry, and school loyalty would somehow bring it back. The common fear that because the new laboratory was demolished students would leave for other schools turned out to be unfounded.

Left unburned in the fire were the foundry and the wood shop. At their entrance, Smart saw to it that a newly acquired 300,000-pound Riehle testing machine was prominently placed. The machine had been exhibited at a world's fair and at the time was considered to be the largest upright machine of its kind in the world, able to accommodate specimens up to ten feet in length, either for compression or tension testing. The machine became a rallying point for reconstruction efforts and symbolized the hope Smart tried to sustain among faculty, staff, alumni, and the community.

Of all the reconstruction tasks, perhaps the most emotionally difficult was the demolition of the blackened, forlorn Heavilon Hall tower. It had been cracked so badly by the heat that it could not be salvaged and had to be razed. But even after a heavy charge of dynamite had been detonated on one side of the tower, it stood fast for another thirty minutes, then slowly toppled in a choke of black dust. In *The Story of Purdue Engineering,* author H. B. Knoll described that moment: "In this bitter fall came to an end the symbol of the first great dream."

•　　•　　•

Reconstruction of Heavilon Hall was swift. Shops and laboratories were rebuilt first. Industries throughout the United States offered help in refurbishing or repairing machinery, or gave free or liberal price discounts on other equipment. The *Schenectady* locomotive, which had been installed in one of the testing laboratories, was so badly damaged after falling from its mounts that it had to be removed to Indianapolis for extensive repairs.

As a part of the "one brick higher" reconstruction, a new building solely for the refurbished *Schenectady* was built just north of the Heavilon laboratories and became the terminus of the now-extinct Purdue Railroad, a spur from the testing plant through the campus and southwest to a connection with the Lake Erie and Western Railroad near the present Purdue University Airport. Instead of being pulled by teams of horses as on its first trip to the campus, a rebuilt *Schenectady* steamed triumphantly to its new home by way of what was once hailed as the world's shortest railroad.

Other new machinery which went into the reconstruction included equipment and experimental engines that even the most prosperous engineering schools envied.

Because of the quick response and cooperation of businesses, the rebuilding of the new engineering laboratory moved rapidly; in 1895, the Indiana legislature appropriated $36,000 to rebuild and $25,000 to replace funds spent from general operating funds. On December 4 of that year, Heavilon Hall was formally opened with its restoration virtually complete.

Smart emphasized the role of industry in the restoration, citing more than fifty companies that made cash donations, rebuilt or replaced damaged machinery free of charge, or gave extraordinary discounts.

The eternal trivia question: was Heavilon Hall actually built "one brick higher"? The best intelligence says it was actually nine bricks higher, but the most visible change in Heavilon Hall was the purchase and installation on April 8, 1896, of the fondly remembered clock and bells in its landmark tower. Funds for the project came from $800 in contributions from the Class of 1895 and Lafayette citizens, $600 from the Ladies' Matinee Musicale of Lafayette, and $10 from the student Mandolin Club.

The restoration of Heavilon Hall was the final large undertaking of the Smart administration. Tired and ill, Smart had functioned under intense and constant pressure since he had assumed the presidency in 1883; his were years, comparatively speaking, of Purdue's greatest growth, albeit an unbalanced growth which made its engineering schools highly ranked nationally.

Smart sacrificed himself in his last year to rebuild Heavilon Hall, the centerpiece of the entire engineering education structure and the symbol of its quality. He spent his final years preparing for the future, and his colleagues—students as well— were saddened by his slowing down and his seeming physical weaknesses.

Smart had, in an earlier period, acted not only in behalf of engineering but also carried on a great number of other detailed duties as president. He was his own director of admissions and insisted on reviewing the applications of prospective students. If they appeared to have academic weaknesses, he would personally write to them advising them on further preparation they needed or remedial courses they should take to assure them of success at Purdue.

Smart also meted out student punishment as his own dean of students. Students caught smoking on "university premises" received his personal, sternly written warning to quit the practice or risk being asked to leave the university. Two major disciplinary "problems" during his administration were George Ade and John T. McCutcheon, famed alumni who went on to achieve immortality in literature and journalism. He reprimanded both for having visited the ladies' literary society without permission and later fired McCutcheon from the staff of the *Purdue,* the student newspaper (forerunner of the *Purdue Exponent*), after an "unauthorized and derisive" issue. McCutcheon tried to return to the staff in the following school year but was told by Smart that his disconnection from the paper was permanent.

Though everything moved fast and furiously in Smart's years, it was also one of enjoyment and youthful exuberance—an atmosphere Smart approved and encouraged despite the need for student discipline. Smart himself became a victim, tradition has it, of that exuberance. A favorite trick of the "dorm devils," a group of pranksters who lived in Purdue Hall, the men's dormitory in those years, was to hide in the bushes and grab some unsuspecting student passerby and douse him under the campus water pump near Ladies Hall. On one occasion, they seized Smart himself and had him under the pump before his own protestations—"I'm President Smart! I'm President Smart!"—told them they had made a grievous error. Smart did not punish anyone for this outrage, but the students involved later said they felt sure that Smart knew who they were by the sound of their voices.

Such was part of a wide variety of student mischief of the day—farm animals left on the roof of the dormitory, roosters in the chapel organ, and the president's chair at chapel enclosed in a square of railroad ties that reached the ceiling. Most of such stunts were good-natured, but George Ade in later years, as a somewhat self-righteous alumni, wrote that it was not much more than plain rowdyism.

Yet, Purdue began to enjoy the developments that make campus life complete. In 1889, the *Debris,* the senior yearbook, first appeared. The same year the *Purdue Exponent* evolved from the *Purdue.* Purdue first fielded a football team in Smart's administration in 1887. Purdue then was only thirteen years old, a "prehistoric era of pompadours, polkas, tight trousers, mandolins, and Sweet Caporal cigarettes," as George Ade described the times. It was also the year Ade graduated, and unable to perform the honest work of the engineer or farmer, he went into writing for a living at $10-per-week but eventually won world recognition as an author and playwright, and local fame as a Purdue benefactor. As Ade put it, after Purdue began football in 1887, he loved the sport so much he "became a sophomore for forty years."

•   •   •

Jacob M. Sholl never received the fame he so richly deserved. He graduated in 1889 with a B.S. degree in mechanical engineering, and that is about all known about him. But he earned his fame in Indianapolis on a Saturday afternoon, October 19, 1887, when he scored the first points ever made for Purdue in its first game of football against Butler University.

Sholl won hero status in a game situation where the tide was against Purdue. In fact, the tide began to rise the moment Purdue showed up. On the other hand, it was perhaps a necessary bloodletting to introduce Purdue to football and vice versa. The lads from West Lafayette were "tall, skinny boys who wore spectacles and had the biceps of a sandhill crane," as Ade described them. Purdue was young; the plaster on the walls of the forlorn collection of plain, red-brick buildings was hardly dry when the call went out for all those willing to sacrifice their bodies to the violence made acceptable by the rules of royal rugby employed for Purdue's first football game. Any youth who wished to play football made the team merely by signing his name to the notice in the dormitory. Some signed for the glory of old Purdue; others did so to get a free train ride to Indianapolis and back.

But what about a coach? Someone remembered there was a deaf-mute in Lafayette who had just returned from an institute for the deaf in the East where the game of football had been at least investigated. So Albert Berg, a smiling young man who could not speak a word or hear what was said to him, came across the Wabash each afternoon "to take charge of the halt, the lame, the blind, and the perniciously anemic," Ade recalled, "to imbue them with stamina, courage, and strategy." His coaching consisted of excited sign language and some rather bizarre sounds from his throat which his players correctly translated as pure profanity. They trained on pie and donuts and never seemed to grasp the importance of keeping one's personal center of gravity as close to the earth as possible to minimize the possibility of injury. The only thing they seemed to do well was clench their fists—not because they were tough, but to keep their fingers from getting stepped on.

Practice went on for an entire week.

When the Purdue boys showed up, Butler was more than ready. A sophisticated young aristocrat named Evans Woolen was Butler's coach. He had taken his B.A. degree at Yale in 1886, was familiar with the tricks of the game, and came home to coach the Butler eleven, which even then was the football power of the midwest region. Woolen went on to become a high-powered banker and even ran for the United States Senate from Indiana at a time when, Ade observed, an Indiana Democrat could not get a break.

Things just did not go right for Purdue, and the Purdues were soundly thrashed, 48–6, at a time when touchdowns were four points, field goals five points, and points-after-touchdowns and safeties two points. Somewhere during the game—described by Ade as a low-comedy reproduction of the Custer massacre at Little Big Horn—Sholl did the unexpected and scored for Purdue. He never played again.

Football returned to Purdue in 1889. Under Coach G. A. Reisner, the team played three games, winning two. In 1890, Purdue won three and lost three, but in 1891, it won all four games, holding all of its opponents—Wabash College, DePauw University, Indiana, and Butler—scoreless while making 192 points. Purdue was a member of a league called the Indiana Intercollegiate Athletic Association in the early years. At Smart's urging, representatives of Purdue, the University of Chicago, University of Illinois, Lake Forest College, Northwestern University, University of Wisconsin, and University of Minnesota met January 11, 1895 to form the Western Conference, now popularly called the Big Ten. Lake Forest and the University of Chicago dropped out, and the University of Michigan, Michigan State University, Ohio State University, University of Iowa, and Indiana University joined later.

''Boilermakers'' was first a derisive term used by Crawfordsville writer Jesse Greene in reporting Purdue's lopsided 18–4 victory over Wabash College in 1889. It may have been a pejoration of the more rough-hewn Purdue players. The name was probably inspired by the play of Robert A. Lackey, a right halfback, a giant of a man with long black hair and flashing eyes who seemed to delight in committing all of the mayhem permitted by the rules of the game. Lackey for years was considered as the greatest Purdue player to ever take the field. On that particular fall day in 1889, Lackey crashed through the classical aristocrats of the Wabash line time and again, suggesting to Greene that he was ''the irresistible leader of the mob in a French revolution.'' Lackey captained the Boilermakers in 1890.

After Lackey's demolition of the Wabash line, Greene called the visiting Purdue team ''Boilermakers'' and gleefully reported that Wabash fans were also calling the toughs from up the Monon line at Lafayette ''pumpkin shuckers,'' ''cornfield sailors,'' ''railsplitters,'' ''farmers,'' and similar plebeian occupations.

But it was "Boilermakers" that caught the players' fancies. It has stuck. One unsubstantiated story has it that Purdue actually enrolled eight large, rough-and-tough Monon Railroad shops employees for a season simply to play football. It was a recruiting violation before there were rules governing such matters. Perhaps the term "Boilermakers" was more accusatory than derisive.

The Purdue colors, old gold and black, were adopted in 1887 minutes before the first Purdue football game with Butler. Until then Purdue had no traditional colors. A team did not, however, enter into an intercollegiate fray of any kind without school colors. A hurried meeting of ten students and faculty was called for the main floor hallway of University Hall just before students left for the game at Butler. They came from the meeting three minutes later, having decided to adopt Princeton University's colors, gold and black, with one variation: "old gold" was substituted for Princeton gold. The old gold and black colors, decided upon in three minutes, have remained firmly a part of Purdue for more than a hundred years.

Smart was enthusiastic about Purdue athletics, football in particular, and cheered wildly in the stands, hugging fellow spectators—typical of a rabid fan—when the team scored or made a good play.

Basketball began late in Smart's administration in 1896–97 when a Purdue team played two games, beating the Lafayette Young Men's Christian Association, 34–19, in a game played in the old gymnasium and military drill hall. The second game, played at Wabash College, was a defeat for Purdue, 23–19. Clarence H. "Big Robbie" Robertson was captain of the team. F. Homer Curtis was the coach.

Purdue played no basketball games in 1897–98 or 1898–99. The game was revived again in 1899–1900 with Alpha Jamison as coach. But the Purdues played only one game—and lost, 16–11, to the Lafayette YMCA.

In the 1900–1901 season, under Jamison, the entire basketball season was a glorious one; the Boilermakers won all twelve games, losing none. Their schedule included three games with Lafayette High School and one with Danville (Indiana) High School, in which Purdue won, 25–4. In one of three lopsided games with the Lafayette High School team, Purdue won 77–9. Against a Logansport team, Purdue won 19–5. They also ran up substantial scores against Wabash, Indiana University, and Butler.

Even in 1901–2, playing with no coach assigned, the Purdue team won ten and lost only two games. But a winning

Purdue basketball tradition was born and maintained through a number of coaches and players. In the 1916–17 season, a young former chemistry instructor, Ward L. "Piggy" Lambert, arrived from Wabash College and carried Purdue to athletic glory, winning more Big Ten championships than any other of the schools. Lambert, a small, wiry man, was considered America's premiere coach, the man who invented the "fast-break" style of play. Lambert coached through the 1944–45 season, then retired to coach freshman basketball for several years.

Lambert was a forthright character who could kid colleagues and players with a solemn, straight face. Once, at a half-time ceremony honoring his many years of successful coaching, Lambert stood as he was presented with an engraved watch fob. The basketball crowd roared when Piggy in jest responded, "This is nice, but where in the hell is the watch?"

•   •   •

In 1894, the old preparatory academy was abandoned because it had been straining the university's resources severely. The university student population had grown substantially, and students were coming to the university much better prepared than in earlier times. In its final year, the academy enrolled only 56 students while the regular university student population had risen by 626.

The academic atmosphere in the 1890s seemed pleasant enough. Faculty-student relationships by and large were close and friendly; most professors knew all of their students by name. The rapport between teachers and students remained high in and out of the classroom. The earliest tennis courts were on the Oval (now Memorial Mall) and became a kind of campus gathering place for both students and faculty and their families.

Raymond C. Ewry, a mechanical engineering student who earned his B.S.M.E. degree in 1897, was usually on hand as either official or participant in the 1890s Purdue field days. Ewry is a nearly forgotten sports hero. As of 1980, he was still listed as the only American to ever win ten individual gold medals in the Olympic track-and-field games of 1900, 1904, 1906, and 1908 in Paris, St. Louis, Athens, and London respectively. More remarkable than Ewry's Olympic records was the fact that as a youngster he was a polio victim and was told by one physician that he would spend the rest of his life in a wheelchair. Another, however, suggested a series of leg exercises which Ewry performed faithfully; he soon found himself not only able to walk but to run. Ewry was a long-legged, six-foot-three inch sophomore when he began his athletic career as a high and long jumper and started to win at track meets throughout the nation. Ewry was also a good student; as a senior he taught engineering drawing.

Field day events included the one-mile run; the baseball throw; batting the baseball; a potato race; hammer throw; running hop, skip, and jump; standing broad jump; running broad jump; Indian wrestle; high kick; 120-yard hurdles; something called catch-as-catch-can wrestle; the 100-yard dash; the 100-yard three-legged race; and the finale, the tug-of-war.

The 1891 field day was held on the gravel drive that encompassed the Oval. The dashes were held on the long north-south drive beginning at State Street and ending at the then Electrical Engineering Building. The meet was a close and friendly association of faculty and students. Meet officials included, beside, Ewry, Goss and Winthrop E. Stone—later the president—among time-keepers and judges. George Ashley, the first graduate in electrical engineering, was chief marshal. Another student, Newton Booth Tarkington, was clerk of the race course. Prizes included a flannel shirt from Vernon's Clothing Store for the winner of the mile run and a dozen glasses of soda water at Haworth's Drug Store for the high-jump winner.

•   •   •

At the time, Tarkington was only another student. He had come to Purdue from Indianapolis ostensibly to study pen-and-ink drawing under Professor Ernest Knaufft; the real reason, however, was a one-sided affair of the heart described by his grand-niece, Susannah Mayberry in her 1983 book, *My Amiable Uncle.* Tarkington was a young man when he went to Lake Maxinkuckee in northern Indiana in the summer of 1890. There he met Geneve Reynolds, a ravishing Lafayette beauty with whom he played tennis, discussed writers (chiefly Robert Browning and George Meredith), and fell hopelessly in love.

Tarkington cajoled his puzzled parents into allowing him to enroll at Purdue that fall instead of at Princeton as the family had planned. At Purdue, he was a B student and wrote for the *Purdue Exponent* and the Lafayette *Sunday Times.* A part of Tarkington's education at Purdue included learning that Miss Reynolds was also pursued by young bachelor professors and instructors, not to mention a former Lafayette mayor, William Vaughn Stuart. Stuart was a prominent local attorney who later served three terms on the Purdue board of trustees and as its president and vice president at various times. He later married her.

The experience made Tarkington despondent, and as he later recalled, "I sometimes devoted myself to the curriculum and even slightly to athletics." At Purdue, Tarkington met Ade and John McCutcheon, who were to become men of letters in their own right, men Tarkington greatly admired.

They, he once said, "were brilliancies out of another world, and long evenings with them were amelioration for what I suffered from professional and other rivals." Tarkington spent only one year at West Lafayette, and after Miss Reynolds became engaged to marry Stuart, he abruptly left Purdue and enrolled at Princeton.

The late Elmer Waters, an 1891 graduate whose reminiscences are the basis for a great many colorful anecdotes about early Purdue, once said that Tarkington was an "expressionless young man" who, in a game of pick-up football did not seem to care whether he lost ten yards or scored a touchdown. In class, Waters recalled, Tarkington "got away with murder," loafing, observing, and commenting—obviously already displaying his gift for stating obvious truths in a wry manner that always seemed to provoke laughter.

In 1940, nearly twenty years after Tarkington had won two Pulitzer Prizes—in 1919 for *The Magnificent Ambersons* and in 1922 for *Alice Adams*—Purdue President Edward C. Elliott and twenty berobed Purdue professors traveled to Tarkington's Indianapolis home to award him an honorary doctor of humane letters degree. In ill health, Tarkington had been unable to travel to West Lafayette for the ceremony, so the ceremony was held on his front porch. Afterward, either deeply moved or chagrined by the affair, Tarkington said quite simply, "Thank you."

• • •

The earliest organized music activity at Purdue goes back nearly to the university's beginnings when a circular was passed among students listing William Mohr as an instructor in piano or organ; he charged $15 for twenty-four lessons, including use of the organ for practice. Mohr also listed instruction for an hour a day at 35 cents per week.

The *Purdue Exponent* of September 27, 1895, announced a new school of music at Purdue—but emphasized that though it was independent of the university, the university endorsed it. The announcement listed Miss Ruth L. Putnam as instructor in piano, harmony, and musical history; Miss Elizabeth M. Millspaugh as instructor in "singing and voice culture"; and Miss Effa V. Louis as instructor in guitar and mandolin.

A month later, a "student brass band" was organized within the military department at Purdue and listed its first players as "Floyd and Lutz, cornets; Hicks, baritone; Remster, alto; and Butterworth, tuba."

Such were the times at Purdue under Smart. He did everything possible to maintain student and staff enthusiasm and to encourage creativity throughout the campus—music and drama and literary societies and student athletics—moving away from the more somber philosophy of his predecessor, Emerson E. White.

•   •   •

After the reconstruction of Heavilon Hall, Smart seemed to grow weaker physically day by day, but his spirit remained vital and his encouragement to the faculty and students to continue their old enthusiasm never wavered. His eloquent appeals for support of all kinds from the university's growing constituency remained strong. Smart was ahead of his time in many respects; and his perspective on higher education was shaped not by questions of its cost but by questions of its *worth* to a kaleidoscopic society that needed it worse than it knew.

Few opportunities passed in which Smart was not able to point out the value of Purdue University in a convincing way. Not as widely known as his deathless "one brick higher" chapel speech the day after the Heavilon Hall catastrophe is an equally significant expression he penned shortly before his death: "If the technical schools will turn out one man who will show us how to use coal in a locomotive and develop ten percent of its possible power instead of five percent, as at present, they will produce a man who will be worth as much to the community as the cost of all the technical schools in the United States for the past twenty-five years."

President Smart died on February 21, 1900. He was only fifty-eight, but his seventeen years as Purdue's president-on-the-run had sapped his strength though not his will. Evidence of Smart's achievements were everywhere. During his last year, Purdue enrollment rose beyond 700 compared to the 100 or so students on the campus the year after he arrived. The faculty had increased from fifteen to more than seventy. The value of buildings and equipment, a mere $322,000 when he arrived, more than doubled to $655,000. Income for the teaching staff increased nearly fourfold from $38,000 in 1884 to $150,000. He had stabilized a critical financial situation. The university was now receiving regular income from four sources: the endowment fund, the

Hatch Act fund, the Second Morrill Act fund, and the educational tax fund of the State of Indiana. Smart also had done a splendid job of convincing the Indiana legislature of the worth of the new school and was able to get occasional appropriations for new buildings.

Far more important, of course, was the growing esteem for Purdue that Smart was able to generate not only among Indiana residents but also throughout the United States and even in foreign lands. That alone assured the university's continued progress; the only question was the rate of speed of whatever advances Purdue would make in the future.

Under Smart, the forces White had worked so arduously to organize became effective, giving the struggling young college, once uncertain of survival, full university status. Smart had devoted his life to giving the infant school the ability to surge forward into a new century with strength, confidence, and no little prestige.

Most importantly, his work widened the gateway of opportunity for hundreds of youths and helped them to become activists in a new and wondrous world of technological advance.

Chapter VII

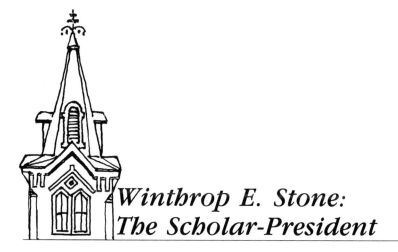

Winthrop E. Stone: The Scholar-President

In his eulogy to Winthrop Ellsworth Stone, Purdue Trustee James W. Noel called him "a piece of New England granite transferred to this [Indiana] soil." And so he was.

Noel's was an appropriate description of Stone who, like Smart, was a native New Hampshireman, the son of farmers who spent their lives tilling New England's thin, rocky soil. He grew up surrounded by that region's craggy ruggedness; early in life he acquired a love of the out-of-doors and a curiosity about the secrets of nature to which he steadfastly held until his tragic death in 1921 in a mountain climbing accident in the Canadian Rockies.

Stone came to Purdue in 1889 as a professor of chemistry, an emerging scientist-scholar with a growing reputation as an organic chemist, especially known among colleagues for his comprehensive research in the chemistry of sugars. Only three years into his Purdue career, Stone became the faculty member Smart relied upon to assume administrative authority in his absence. Goss had held that position but became so engrossed in his engineering experimental work that Stone began to assume an increasing share of the presidential duties. In the last five years of Smart's life Stone took over most of the tedium of administrative detail, leaving Smart time for the determination of major policies.

Ultimately, Smart named Stone as vice president of the university (Purdue's first), and upon Smart's death in 1900, the board of trustees named Stone as Purdue's acting president and shortly thereafter elected him to the university's fifth presidency.

In personality and administrative style, Stone bore little resemblance to his predecessor and mentor Smart, the effusive, impulsive, take-a-chance president who pulled and shoved the small college, kicking and screaming at times, into universityhood. Nor was he at all like Smart's predecessor, Emerson White, the starchy, stubborn, argumentative, and cantankerous educator.

•   •   •

Stone was born June 12, 1862, at Chesterfield, New Hampshire, a hill town in the southwestern corner of the state on Spofford Lake, nestled among the Pisgah mountains. His birth occurred, coincidentally, within the same week that the United States Congress passed the Morrill Act which Lincoln later signed into law on July 2, 1862.

Until he was twenty-four, Stone remained close to the soil on the family's farms, first in New Hampshire, later in Massachusetts. He put in the long hours of work that farm chores required and kept a meticulous vegetable garden for the family. Still, he found time to tramp the rugged wilderness hills near his home, and whether it was the tedium of farm work or the sheer joy of the long walks, he maintained his passionate interest in the dynamics of living things.

When he was twelve, the family moved to a new farm in Mill Valley, within the broader limits of Amherst, Massachusetts. One of the chief reasons for the move was the determination of his father, Frederick, and mother, Ann Sophia Butler Stone, that their two sons, Winthrop and Harlan Fiske (the latter born just before they moved from Chesterfield), would have an education beyond that offered by the district school in New Hampshire. At Amherst were Amherst College and the Massachusetts Agricultural College, which became the land-grant school now known as the University of Massachusetts.

Stone first attended Amherst High School, then enrolled in the agricultural college. He seems to have begun his education rather slowly, but by the time he was an upperclassman, he had won a prestigious academic award—and most of the other scholastic prizes for which he was eligible. In his senior year, he was class president. Stone graduated at the age of twenty with a bachelor of science degree in chemistry and immediately began work as a chemist at a state experimental farm at Mountainville, New York, and later as an assistant chemist at his alma mater in Amherst. (Some accounts indicate that Stone also attended Boston University, possibly at some period during his undergraduate years before he received his B.S. degree.) In 1886, he went to the University of Göttingen, Germany, for graduate study in chemistry. He returned home in 1888 with his doctorate and worked for a year at the State of Tennessee Agricultural Experiment Station.

Stone came to Purdue as a professor of chemistry in 1889, the same year he married Victoria Heitmueller, a woman from Göttingen. Their first son, David Frederick, was born a year later, and their second, Richard Harlan, in 1892. David eventually went on to Harvard, graduated cum laude, and taught German several years before going into the insurance business in New York. Richard followed his father's scientific footsteps, becoming a chemical engineer after receiving his B.S. in chemical engineering at Purdue in 1914.

Stone faced a traumatic personal problem in the first half of his administration when his wife became infatuated with yoga philosophy and left him to return to Europe in 1907 to join a religious cult. Left with two teen-age sons, Stone divorced her in 1911, gaining custody of Richard, at age nineteen still a minor. He married Margaret Winters of West Lafayette in 1912. She was with him in the Canadian Rockies nine years later when he met death in the accident that also nearly took her life.

Stone's brother, Harlan, ten years his junior, went into law, having studied at both Amherst and Yale Law School. He eventually became dean of the Columbia University Law School and served as United States attorney general under Calvin Coolidge, who appointed him to the United States Supreme Court in 1925. Justice Stone was appointed as chief justice of the high court in 1941 by Franklin D. Roosevelt. He died in office in 1946.

President Stone had an even younger brother, Lauson, and a sister, Helen Stone (Mrs. J. D.) Willard, of Amherst. Lauson came to Purdue, served as an undergraduate assistant in his senior year, and graduated in 1905 with a B.S. in mechanical engineering.

•   •   •

In temperament, Stone was considered to be stern, aloof, and reserved; conversely, he sometimes displayed flashes of temper. But as an academic administrator, he had few peers and was highly respected by most of the faculty, although he could be painfully tightfisted while demanding high academic standards and behavior.

Professor G. W. Munro once described Stone ("after long thought") as "a conscientious New Englander who tried, with little success, to adapt himself to a somewhat hilarious world."

In the style of another New Englander, Calvin Coolidge, Stone was erudite though he did not talk much. He seemed unconcerned about personal popularity. Most often visitors to his office talked while he listened, and even when it was appropriate for him to speak, he often remained silent—frequently to their embarrassment. What mattered most to Stone was his and the university's duty to provide first-class education for Purdue's students.

Most of the characterizations of Stone emphasize his direct approach, his slow but ultimately certain decision making, his unshakable insistence on actions based upon principle, and his towering sense of duty. As a scholar, an intellectual, and an administrator, he seemed generally admired throughout the university, despite the fact that he was not always amiable—but of little wonder for one of such intensity, one so burdened with work and so absorbed in it. He had a capacity for righteous indignation, especially when it came to sham. His abhorrence of it could stir him into activity terrible in its directness, and he did not hesitate to reprimand when he believed such duty was required. Yet, he bore few grudges. Although the dignity and reserve in his bearing did not invite familiarity, for those who eventually came to know him well, he had an engaging quality of friendliness and an attractive, quiet personality. Yet, Stone often antagonized where others would have compromised in clear conscience.

Stone assumed the Purdue presidency at the age of thirty-eight. As vice president, he had handled myriad daily details and this routine carried over into his presidency. To say that he was conservative barely describes his managerial style. Little went on at the campus that he was not aware of in seemingly infinite detail. The Department of Modern Languages needed a typewriter. Stone remembered one stored in an obscure closet on the campus south of State Street; it, Stone told the department, "would do." A new grand piano had been obtained for Eliza Fowler Hall. Stone ordered the piano locked and personally kept the key. He exercised control over the university's finances to an astonishing degree and carried a small black book listing the name and salary of every faculty member (about one hundred fifty, not counting support staff).

He once told C. Francis Harding, head of the School of Electrical Engineering, to go ahead and employ a stenographer in June provided he paid her no more than 20 cents per hour and had her wait, if possible, until September for her first pay. Professor Herbert Creek, head of the English department, once asked for screens for his office windows in the basement of Stanley Coulter Hall; clouds of flies were attracted to the malodorous fumes emanating from the biology laboratories in the same building. "There are," Stone casually replied, gesturing with a wave of his hand toward the windows of his Fowler Hall office, "no screens on my windows." In a campus-wide memorandum in 1916, Stone said he saw no reason why towels should be furnished in the restrooms for use of faculty and staff at university expense. He allowed that the university could install paper towel containers— provided that faculty and staff pay for the towels.

Although such episodes did not exactly endear Stone's Yankee thrift to all of the faculty, his overall insistence upon academic quality earned him the respect, grudging at times, of almost everyone, students and faculty alike. Faculty, most of all, liked Stone because he was a scholar—'one of us." Yet, he did have his serious detractors. Among them was a group of alumni of whom the most vociferous was George Ade, the Purdue graduate (1887) who went on to world fame as author and playwright and who eventually became a generous Purdue benefactor with David Ross. Ade served briefly as editor of the *Purdue Alumnus,* the organ of the Purdue Alumni Association, and used it as a platform to air his opinions about the perceived faults of the university under Stone. Most notably, Ade felt Stone had effectively stifled student and faculty spirit and initiative and said so in clear terms. He even staged a one-man campaign among the Indiana political powers and some state legislators to have Stone fired.

Stone, of course, overcame such difficulty by simply ignoring it. He was far too busy attempting to guide the direction of a university which in the first two decades of the new century was challenged as never before in its first twenty-six years. Purdue had made giant strides under Stone's predecessors. Now the university found in Stone a leader who not only could hold these gains but also could guide the inevitably swift growth Purdue would experience in the transitional decades between 1900 and 1920.

Stone's tasks were formidable, yet he managed to complete most of them during his twenty-one years as president. Despite what may have seemed a preoccupation with the smallest details of day-to-day administration, Stone had a broad, well-defined, far-seeing view of Purdue's road ahead. Though he may not have wished for it, he was thrust into the role of builder. At the outset of his administration, he was also determined to do something about the imbalance between agriculture and engineering he had inherited from Smart. And before his death in 1921, he had accomplished an important goal: keeping engineering strong while ensuring the role for agriculture intended by the Morrill Act. Stone's emphasis was to bring Purdue engineering and Purdue agriculture into at least a semblance of equilibrium, although undergraduate enrollments in engineering have always been consistently higher than in agriculture.

He had three unwritten tenets that governed his actions as president: one, that university finances be sound and above any possible reproach; two, that the highest standards of scholarship and behavior be maintained; and three, that intercollegiate athletics—the importance of which among some students and alumni had become overinflated—remain secondary to the main purpose of higher education.

As for more immediate goals, Stone in his first year listed for the General Assembly what he considered the university's most pressing needs: improvement in facilities for the School of Pharmacy and extension of shops and laboratories; increased annual income, preferably by state appropriation; a new agricultural hall and better provisions for agriculture generally; a new assembly hall; a new power and heating plant; and a gymnasium.

Results were achieved first for the pharmacy school when a second-floor addition was constructed for $2,528 on the rear wing of its building (last known as Building No. 2). Pharmacy had been its sole occupant since 1894 when chemistry, physics, mechanics, and civil engineering moved to other facilities. The rear wing had been added in 1889. Pharmacy, which had begun as a worktable with seven students in a corner of the chemistry laboratory, enrolled more than 90 students in 1900–01. There could be no doubt of the need for expansion of the building. Growth and expansion had become a central activity in the Stone administration.

General attitudes were changing rapidly, especially in the public perception of the need for education. The number of high schools was increasing throughout the Midwest—schools that were, in turn, graduating greater numbers of students qualified and prepared for college study. A new time was arriving. The economy was expanding. So was the nation's population and a concurrent demand for higher education, especially at the land-grant institutions.

The pressures on Purdue became external; qualified young people now demanded that higher institutions welcome them. The universities did, but in doing so, they created dilemmas for themselves. As the Purdue reputation grew, for example, it blended with a growing public realization that a college education was a matter of earnest necessity and not merely a pleasant interlude for rich adolescents. This assured a phenomenal expansion in the university's enrollment—beyond 3,000—in Stone's years. In 1900, when Stone began his administration, Purdue enrollment passed the 1,000 mark, contrasted to the 214 students at Purdue when Smart took over in 1883, or the 140 when White became president in 1876.

Fortunately, Stone had fruitful soil with which to work in Indiana. Whereas Smart had worked assiduously to bring about a statewide willingness to maintain Purdue as a high-grade university, Stone now had the willingness plus the wherewithal. The combination accomplished wonders for the university. The population of the state was, for example, 25 percent greater than in 1880; the value of its manufactured products had risen by more than 150 percent; the value of farm property had gone up by 35 percent. Progress seemed continuous and without limit. In Stone's administration, farm values went up by 200 percent and manufactured products by 400 percent. Those figures meant more funds in the tax coffers and therefore an unprecedented generosity on the part of legislators.

Still, there was much to be done. Though Purdue was only twenty-six years of age at the time, many of its laboratories and classrooms were too small, obsolete, or worn out. Besides expansion of Science Hall (then the Pharmacy Building), in 1903 the venerated men's dormitory was converted to classrooms and renamed Purdue Hall. The third floor of Heavilon Hall was altered (for $790) into a room for engineering drawing.

Three years earlier, a legislative committee came to the campus to delve into Stone's "wish list" and almost immediately recommended that funds be appropriated for a new agricultural hall—thereby denying for the moment the other requests. Building needs were met later; operating funds remained a chronic need. (American educator and former president of the University of Chicago, Robert M. Hutchins, believed that the college or university which was not short of money really was not doing anything.)

The need for an assembly hall was filled by the gift of Eliza Fowler, the widow of Moses Fowler, John Purdue's original partner in the late 1830s. On November 27, 1901, in chapel, President Stone held up a check for $60,000 signed by Mrs. Fowler, who later increased the gift to $70,000. Her munificence was the largest single private gift to the university in the thirty-two years since Purdue himself agreed to give $150,000 for its beginning.

University Hall served as Purdue's all-purpose structure; it housed administrative offices, chapel, library, and classrooms. A new building that would seat about 500 and accommodate commencement exercises was urgently needed. From 1895 to 1902, commencement had been held in a large tent pitched on the Oval (now called Memorial Mall). The need for a permanent building became all too apparent in June 1898, when a sudden spring storm blew down the tent during the ceremonies, drenched audience, graduates, and faculty, and caused a postponement, not to mention temporary chaos.

Though Eliza Fowler Hall was not entirely complete, 1903 commencement exercises were held in it. The new hall was a campus showcase. Mrs. Fowler's son, James M. Fowler, installed a pipe organ in the main auditorium. Fowler Hall was more than an assembly building; it also included the president's office and space for board of trustees and faculty meetings, thereby relieving congestion in University Hall.

Increased income came in the form of action by the Indiana legislature in 1903 that doubled the tax rate earmarked for university appropriations from one-twentieth to one-tenth of a mill on the dollar—or from one-half cent to one cent of each one hundred dollars of taxables. Income from that tax increase did not come until a year later—and none too soon since income from state sources had remained unchanged from 1895 while student enrollments ballooned. The fund increase came after Stone warned in a message to the legislature that "we must turn away students unless we have a larger income for the purpose of instruction and maintenance and additional facilities in the way of buildings and equipment."

At the time that the General Assembly increased the tax rate for the university, it also appropriated a specific sum, $75,000, to be made available at once for construction of a new power and heating plant, a legislative response to Stone's forceful plea that the old plant was wasteful and that on extremely cold days classes in some buildings had to be dismissed.

Stone had also campaigned for better recreational facilities for the students. The old gymnasium had by 1900 become a forlorn rattletrap hardly worthy of the name. As early as 1902, he had proposed a student union building—to be built (he hoped) by some generous philanthropist. Instead, Purdue obtained a new gymnasium by way of memorial funds raised by popular subscription to commemorate the seventeen persons killed in the university's most tragic event, a train wreck on the outskirts of Indianapolis on October 31, 1903.

• • •

All things considered, the 1903 Purdue football season was not going too badly. The Boilermakers had lost only to the University of Chicago and the University of Illinois.

Purdue had soundly defeated such grid powers as Englewood High School, 34–0; Wabash College, 18–0; Beloit College, 17–0;

and Oberlin, 18–2. Under a new coach, Oliver F. Cutts, the team was headed for a showdown with Indiana University for the mythical championship of Indiana colleges and universities in a game scheduled for Indianapolis's Washington Park on Saturday afternoon, October 31.

The football rivalry between Purdue and Indiana even in those years was so intense that special trains were chartered for the student body and fans. The day at Lafayette was a festive one as more than nine hundred fifty students, fans, team members, faculty, and townspeople boarded the first of two sections of a special train and at 8:15 A.M. chuffed away from the Big Four station at the foot of First Street. Less than two hours later the happy, festive football outing had turned into a nightmarish scene.

Traveling at about twenty-five miles per hour, the fourteen-car first section rounded a curve four miles northwest of Indianapolis and crashed head on into a "cut" of seven coal cars being switched from a siding. The first car behind the locomotive, containing the team, coaches, and trainer, was instantly demolished. Fifteen students, most of them team members, were killed outright or died soon afterward in local hospitals. The second car, carrying the Purdue band, was overturned and slid partially down an embankment, destroyed; many bandsmen were seriously injured. The third car was also badly damaged, riding up and over the remains of the first two and the coal cars. In all, more than one hundred were severely injured. The final death toll: seventeen.

Like most of the other passengers in the rear cars, President Stone at first seemed barely aware of what had happened. He debarked from his car and worked his way toward the damage scene. There, he blanched at the nightmarish carnage of twisted, piled railroad cars; the strewn body parts lying about the grisly scene; the moans of the injured trapped in the wreckage. The uninjured as well as bystanders and employees of nearby factories worked desperately, wading through the catastrophe in search of survivors—or the dead.

Stone spent most of the next several days in Indianapolis at the scene, at local hospitals, or directing the monumental task of attempting to contact relatives and parents of students. He comforted friends and relatives of those already in the city, though he, too, was emotionally exhausted.

The blame-fixing for the tragedy went on for years afterwards. The conductor and engineer of the Purdue special contended their train orders said nothing about giving right-of-way to any other trains or going onto a siding for car-switching in the Indianapolis railroad yards.

The campus—for that matter the entire Lafayette community—was utterly stunned by the catastrophe. The *Daily Courier* issued three extra editions on October 31, the day of the crash, and the Indianapolis *Sunday Journal* devoted nearly its entire front page and several inside pages to pictures and stories on the wreck.

Coach Cutts, himself injured, was also in shock over the deaths of many player-friends and the team's longtime trainer, Pat McClaire, who died shortly after removal to a city hospital. Cutts, thrown free of the wreckage, awoke from momentary unconsciousness beside the track, his hair and scalp full of bloody cinders. He remained at the scene for nearly a day, unaware until later that he had a serious left leg injury. Team captain I. S. Osborn sustained a broken left leg; many other members of the team—those who were not killed—suffered permanently crippling injuries.

Harry G. Leslie, who had been a star fullback and left end in 1900 and 1901, and captain in 1902, was team manager in 1903. He was removed from the wreckage, believed to be among the dead. Later, as he lay unconscious in a nearby temporary morgue, someone noticed his right arm move slightly. Leslie was taken to a local hospital, gravely injured, but he slowly recovered. Later, he served briefly as alumni secretary and went on to became governor of Indiana, serving from 1929 to 1933. He spent the rest of his life with a decided limp, a lifelong reminder of the Purdue tragedy.

In the aftermath, no one expected Purdue to field a varsity football team for years if ever again. But a year later, the Boilermakers played a twelve-game schedule, winning nine including a 27–0 victory over Indiana University—at Indianapolis—and a 36–0 win over Notre Dame at Purdue's Stuart Field (site of the Elliott Hall of Music).

The Memorial Gymnasium, converted in 1985 to the Computer Sciences Building, was funded by popular subscription and built as a monument to the memory of those killed in the train wreck. Completed in 1909 at a cost of $88,000—a substantial part of which was a gift of the Big Four Railroad—the gymnasium was headquarters for physical education for men and intercollegiate athletics until the completion of Lambert Fieldhouse in the late 1930s.

●　　　●　　　●

The train wreck and its aftermath left an entire academic community in a state of shock—but campus life and classes had to go on. Despite his deep sorrow over the train accident, Stone had a great many problems to deal with that did not allow prolonged mourning.

In 1903, he had announced an all-embracing university policy that included two principal points. The first was to foster closer relations with the commercial world "to the end that our instructors may be in touch with the latest progress in the industries, in order to make the technical instruction of the greatest possible value." The second point dealt directly with the problem of crowded enrollment versus the university's original charge: "To keep the opportunities of the university within reach of the great class of young men and women of limited means to whom such training is of the greatest value."

As Stone reported, the university's facilities, classrooms especially, were "crowded beyond all limits of comfort, sanitary conditions, or effective work. . . . Growth and development for the institution is impossible under these conditions, but not to make growth in a technological institution is as fatal as to eliminate progress from any enterprise." From such a dilemma, he could only conclude that the prospect of excluding a worthy applicant simply because the university did not have the room was not acceptable. Therefore, the Indiana legislature again widened the tax base to find university operating funds and began to appropriate larger sums for the additional buildings the growing university needed if it was to remain a first-class institution.

Because of rising enrollments and newer sophistication in the high-school curricula, plane geometry was added in 1903 as a requirement for admission to Purdue. A year earlier, military training (ROTC) was reinstituted at the university and greeted, apparently, with a great deal of enthusiasm by most students. Compulsory military training, instituted at Purdue in 1891, had been interrupted in 1898 with the outbreak of the Spanish-American War because the United States Department of War had recalled Lieutenant Matt R. Petersen for active duty and sent no replacement.

Under Stone, the university's most pressing needs were steadily met, and by 1910, some semblance of balance between university resources and student population had once again been established. Physics got its first building in 1904 at a cost of $60,000; later it came to be called the Biology Annex, then Stanley Coulter Annex, and finally Peirce Hall. It honored the venerated member and secretary of one of the earliest boards of trustees who had spent much of his own money, time, and perspiration in the university's earliest landscaping. In 1906, civil engineering received a building of its own ($40,000), and electrical engineering, which already had an imposing structure, received a laboratory wing for that building. In 1907, the Chemistry Building was constructed for $60,000 just north of the original Science Hall. It is now the Education Building. New structures were also going up on the south side of State Street on the agricultural campus—that is a story in itself.

Regardless of the new buildings, the situation always seemed desperate. For many years, there was an obvious need for a new library; the first phase was constructed in 1911—a small building but designed for later symmetrical additions. Until then, the library was located in a small, central section of University Hall. How Professor William Hepburn, the university librarian, managed in such cramped quarters when book circulation had increased by 90 percent is one of those mysteries to which he, in his own individual resourcefulness, was privy.

The biological sciences, in those days known simply as biology, also had facilities-lag problems. In 1912, biology was housed in Science Hall, built in 1885 as Mechanics Hall, Purdue's first engineering building. Biology suffered through its deprivations until 1916 when the building was razed to make way for Stanley Coulter Hall.

The needs for such an extensive program were everywhere evident. Both faculty and student body were growing so rapidly as to defy any sort of ordinary and reasonable management. Yet Stone was a calm man and with his New England aplomb met the growth problem while maintaining academic quality. Between 1903 and 1909, the faculty and staff rose from 104 to 147; in the same period the student population rose from 1,440 to 1,940, a growth of 35 percent. Accordingly, the program presented to the Indiana legislature in 1909 was the most ambitious in university history: for the engineering departments, $345,000; for the School of Agriculture, $100,000; and for the Agricultural Experiment Station and extension, $50,000 annually. The 1909 program also asked for capital sums to build the first wing of the Library, an armory for ROTC, and a dairy building. The legislature (as Sears and Hepburn put it) "responded nobly" and therein, at least partially, lies the tremendous expansion of agriculture under Stone that paralleled that of engineering under Smart.

•   •   •

The Purdue School of Medicine was a short-lived educational anomaly of the Stone administration. Purdue had no ambitions in medical education and probably had never considered such a possibility, at least not officially. But in 1905, the Medical College of Indiana at Indianapolis, a private school, made overtures to Purdue, proposing to turn over to Purdue its property and assets in Indianapolis, its goodwill, and the services of its faculty to establish a high-order medical school under Purdue (i.e., state) auspices.

Until 1905, medical education in Indiana was carried on by several private medical schools. The medical community believed that the merger of some of the small private schools with one of the state schools would advance not only the interests of medicine but also public health. Earlier negotiations by the Indianapolis school with Indiana University had failed. Stone, however, made certain that Purdue would not be intruding upon IU's interests, then took the proposal to the board of trustees. In September 1905, board action established the Indiana Medical College, the School of Medicine of Purdue University. The plan was, of course, subject to legislative approval. Simultaneously, two other private medical schools, the Central College of Physicians and Surgeons, also at Indianapolis, and the Fort Wayne College of Medicine, arranged a similar union with Purdue.

In 1906, the Purdue School of Medicine under Dean Henry Jameson, M.D., granted degrees to 122 medical students, (5 of them women) and a year later to 70. However, the legislature was confronted with grave policy questions. Should it favor or disapprove the steps already taken? And to what extent should the state assume direction in medical education? The questions were complicated by Indiana University's attitude. Though it had rejected the private school's original overtures, it did not favor such an expansion by its upstate rival and established a medical school of its own, claiming it had priority in the field of medicine. It attempted to win legislative recognition in the 1907 Indiana General Assembly and at the same time to bring about a disapproval of the existing arrangements for medical education by Purdue.

For a time, feeling ran high, and the legislature was at an impasse. Stone stepped into the confusion, and in 1908, Purdue agreed to withdraw, leaving medicine in the care of Indiana University. In 1909, the Indiana General Assembly mandated that Indiana University assume total responsibility for the public medical school. Stone had followed an original course that at the time seemed a way to improve medical education in Indiana—in the absence of any other proposal. His action no doubt stimulated public medical education, but it has since been a Hoosier truism that "IU does not graduate engineers and Purdue does not graduate medical doctors."

Fortunately, Stone's action probably headed off what might have been years of tenacious academic rivalry instead of the generally cooperative attitude which, with rare exceptions, prevails between the two schools to this day and confines the rivalry to the basketball court and to certain Saturday afternoons in November.

•　　•　　•

Stone is given most of the credit for the swift rise in agriculture in the opening years of the twentieth century, but the fact is that it would have probably risen rapidly anyway. The interest of the Indiana agricultural community in Purdue developed steadily with the advent of farmer's institutes, short courses (from 1888), and extension tied to the agricultural experiment station.

Indiana farmers began to see the advantages of the "new" agriculture that Purdue agricultural teachers and scientists advocated; they wanted it for themselves, and they wanted it for their sons. Hence, the rise in undergraduate enrollment. In 1900, 1901, and 1902, the graduating classes in agriculture numbered 4, 9, and 3 respectively; in 1919, 1920, and 1921, the comparable numbers were 69, 100, and 97.

If, as some charged, Stone's predecessor, Smart, "neglected" agriculture, it was in its facilities. Arthur Goss, who became experiment station director in 1903, remarked years later that when he took over the Agricultural Experiment Station—reflecting the general condition of the School of Agriculture—it "had a small plant of a few, poorly equipped . . . laboratories, located in what was without a doubt the worst building in the United States devoted to [agricultural experiment station] work."

Goss (not to be confused with W. F. M. Goss in engineering) was an early agriculture graduate. One source, in fact, contends he is the first graduate with the bachelor of science degree in agriculture (1888) although two other students earned B.S. degrees and were awarded certificates for special work in agriculture.

Nevertheless, Goss was considered one of Purdue's "brightest students and brightest poker players" and in the Stone administration was another of the president's chief lieutenants in extracting state appropriations for new buildings—especially for the Agricultural Experiment Station—in the halls of the state capitol.

Stone went to work to bring about the necessary balance between engineering and agriculture with nearly the same zeal that Smart had shown in developing the engineering programs. The new Agriculture Hall (now the Entomology Building) did for agriculture what Heavilon Hall had done for engineering. It was a dream of the longtime (1882–1935) Purdue agriculture professor, W. C. Latta, who held every important job in the School of Agriculture over his many years on the Purdue staff save one: dean. Latta and Stone virtually drew Agriculture Hall's plans themselves.

Though their temperaments differed widely, Stone was as aggressive as Smart when it came to Purdue's needs. Stone once said that "the conservative attitude of the farmer toward the various progressive movements relating to that industry, especially technical education, must be overcome." He believed the antidote for such apathy (if not hostility) was to provide such exceptional facilities that Indiana farmers would gain a new pride and confidence in their school. With that as the impetus, together with a slow but steady growth in the acceptance of technical agriculture, the purse strings of the Indiana General Assembly again loosened. The 1901 legislative session responded to Stone with a $60,000 grant, plus $10,000 for each of the two years of the biennium toward equipment, and instruction. The new Agriculture Hall was completed in September 1902. Though it was without a private benefactor such as Amos Heavilon, and apparently was greeted with much less fanfare than the "temple" Smart built for engineering, the building nevertheless added a new dimension to agricultural education at Purdue and symbolized the beginning of a growth that placed it on par with engineering, and in some respects surpassed it.

Purdue's requests to the legislature in 1906 also reflected the emergence of the "university" from the "college" with the continued rise in enrollments and widening of curricula. The university asked not only for funds for a new Agricultural Experiment Station building but also for a separate library building and new laboratories for steam engineering, hydraulics, and materials testing. An appropriation of $100,000 assured completion of the experiment station in 1908; funds for the other needs were to come in 1909, thereby making 1910 the most active construction year since the founding in 1869. The 1909 appropriations were utilized almost immediately. A new farm mechanics building was completed in January of that year, a livestock pavilion in March, and the Practical Mechanics Building, later renamed to honor the venerable Michael Golden, also was completed.

Architecturally, the Golden building, which dominated the intersection of Northwestern Avenue and Grant Street for so many years, was perhaps the least graceful of all of Purdue's buildings. Yet, it was like Heavilon Hall in its importance to the growth of engineering and was also considered an engineering education marvel for its time.

Though strictly utilitarian for the most part—with the possible exception of Eliza Fowler Hall and Memorial Gymnasium—the new structures symbolized not only the growth in physical plant but also the overall growth of the university in enrollment and programs and the impact of Stone's administration on guiding that growth. Of the university's nineteen buildings listed in the 1910 catalog, twelve had been built since 1900.

While Stone paid particular attention to the needs of agriculture, he did not neglect the needs of the rest of the university, evidenced by new facilities in both engineering and science, a new library, and the Memorial Gym. The biggest strides were, nevertheless, in agriculture in Stone's administration. As his predecessor Smart had predicted, Purdue was ready for agriculture when agriculture was ready for Purdue. The state farming industry, began to realize, perhaps too slowly for some, that Purdue could or should play an essential leadership role in the well-being and development of Indiana agriculture. Stone had correctly assessed that development. By 1910, Purdue had reached a condition of equilibrium between its facilities and faculty, and a student population of between 1,800 and 2,000. Ironically, such equilibrium raised a profoundly significant issue: whether to maintain a certain maximum efficiency by restricting enrollment or aspire to continuing expansion consistent with the growth of the constituency (however defined) which it serves and to which it is obligated.

Experience proves that (whether for Purdue or for any other institution) a discrepancy always exists between obligations and resources. The difficulties such a gap produces often bring on unproductive crises of major proportions. Yet, the risks of growth must be taken; the college or university which may choose to maintain a status quo by restricting its growth and its outlook—even in the face of the demands of a growing, complex constituency—wins only brief reprieve from an inevitably bleak outcome. Purdue chose to continue to grow. In less than three years, the so-called equilibrium of 1910 had all but disappeared, and the university was (happily or unhappily, depending upon one's point of view) once again in a state of imbalance between what it needed to do and how much it could do well. In that sense, Purdue never again reached "equilibrium." Nor could it, even if it had wanted to.

The sentiment throughout Indiana, turned 180 degrees since the 1870s, favored offering public higher education to the greatest number without reference to high educational standards or the possibilities inherent in research or graduate study. Such a consensus was, of course, contrary to the academic one that it was possible to simultaneously grow, maintain and improve scholarly standards, and widen the university's educational sphere through research and advanced study.

Few disagreed that an income adequate to meet burgeoning needs of a growing Purdue must continue if the university's reputation was to be maintained. Yet as early as 1910, there was some serious thought that enrollment should be restricted to 2,000 students. A decade later, however, Purdue enrolled 3,000 students with relative ease.

The striking growth of the century's first decade was matched only by that of the second. The beginning of World War I and America's entry in 1917 brought about an entirely new consensus about the value of public higher education, and such a national awakening was shared by Purdue. It brought new pressures for a campus turned into a military training camp. The university's normal progress was speeded; the school operated (as Sears and Hepburn put it) "under forced draught."

Even earlier, the legislature increased Purdue's share of the state educational tax generously making possible funds for operations far beyond even the expectations of the administration. But the gain was considered moderate inasmuch as there were higher service and utility costs for a physical plant that had grown by twelve new major buildings, an enrollment increased by 50 percent, and a faculty expanded by 70 percent. Despite what had to be considered intelligent legislative magnanimity, Stone stepped forward and, in a speech to the Indiana Manufacturers Bureau in 1909, displayed rare Stonian humor, "At Purdue we do not receive much encouragement. People are friendly to the institution; they wish us well; but they want us to make bricks without straw, and gentlemen, that question was settled many hundreds of years ago."

His bricks-without-straw metaphor illustrated Stone's belief that the university needed a stable, permanent income based upon operating costs. Rather than give any appearance that it was succumbing to the whims of college presidents, the General Assembly contended that it was bringing a system to the financing of state educational institutions when it raised a state educational levy to 7 cents on each $100 of taxables. It then assigned Purdue and Indiana universities each 2.8 cents of the levy with the understanding that that would cover all of the two schools' future funding needs for operations.

Though generous, the results were disappointing because both Purdue and Indiana were growing so rapidly as to make the income from that increase inadequate almost from the beginning. That financial shortfall was complicated additionally by a dispute between the Purdue administration and the State Board of Finance over the validity of two statutes, (1900 and 1910), governing the required appropriation of funds restricted for the use of the Agricultural Experiment Station and the extension service. The argument precipitated a legal spat over which fund the specific 1913 appropriations were to be paid from—if they were to be paid at all. An agreement to settle the matter was not reached until 1919 when the Indiana Supreme Court ruled in favor of the university. But accruals over the years of the disagreement by then totaled $726,000, a substantial amount which, had it been paid in lump sum, could have disturbed the state's entire financial condition. Thus, the amount paid in increments of $100,000 over three years was a compromise.

•   •   •

The struggles over financing higher education then seem fundamentally little different today. Although many would argue that society has not truly improved, certainly the world has changed, and the contrast between chauvinist community attitudes of the early years of the twentieth century contrast starkly with those of its latter years. The sharp difference between campus attitudes then and now is vividly shown in a description of Gala Week activities in the 1912 *Debris*, the senior yearbook. The account includes observations of exhibition baseball between Purdue and a touring team from Waseda University, Japan, the previous year: "Our baseball fans were impressed with the ability shown by the little dark-skinned men from across the waters and Japanese field talk furnished no little amusement for the spectators . . . (Purdue won, 5–1)."

The *Debris* described the evening event following the game—readings and birdcalls by Dr. S. H. Clark. The "aeroplane exhibition" of Tuesday also was subject for the *Debris's* quaint prose. That occasion contrasts with today's university which has furnished at least sixteen of its sons to American space flight programs: "The aeroplane exhibition of Tuesday afternoon was a splendid success. Thousands of people saw for the first time machines able to convey man through the air, circling about, and finally coming to earth again."

The next year, 1913, marked the tragic end of one of the most foolish and dangerous Purdue "traditions," the old Tank Scrap which took place between undergraduate men each year at the water reservoir tank of the West Lafayette Water Company at the crest of Salisbury Street hill northeast of the campus. In a former time, the tank was the spot where male students went to "untangle disputes." Later, it became the site of an annual melee between freshmen and sophomores who attempted to paint their class numerals on the tank, then keep the other class from removing them. The idea was that during the brawl, each class tried to take prisoners who were then roped together and marched to the courthouse square in downtown Lafayette to be held up to public ridicule. The rules of mayhem only prohibited using closed fists, clubs, and/or knives.

In the aftermath of the brawl on September 19, 1913, lay the lifeless body of Francis Walter Obenchain, a freshman, who had died of a broken neck. How it occurred remains a mystery. The following day the student body met early in the morning and unanimously voted to "abolish it forever." The custom was never revived. The Tank Scrap had begun twenty years previously and never had the endorsement of the university; the administration simply looked the other way. The death that resulted changed forever the ways that Purdue administrations view the antics and follies of those of the student body afflicted with acute immaturity.

Less violent student activities followed the accident and even the ancient rite of the Mechanics Burnings—when freshmen burned their first-year mechanics textbooks in a Stuart Field ceremony—died out. In their stead came the Purdue Circus and May Day rite when women students danced around a maypole on the Oval (Memorial Mall), reigned over by a May Queen. Both of those activities also went the eventual way of all such "traditions." Mechanics Burning was stopped when its ceremonies began to take on some characteristics of the occult—on a campus that at the time was considered to be Bible-belted.

Another daring student stunt occurred in 1911 when a majority of the student body, at a peak of ebullience, turned out for a nightshirt parade that snaked its way through the campus and the Lafayette community until the wee hours of the morning in celebration of a 12–5 football victory over Indiana University.

•   •   •

The university's building program submitted to the legislature in 1913 had the specific objectives of adding more land for the Agricultural Experiment Station and School of Agriculture, $50,000; five buildings for agriculture, $145,000; and for a new biology building, an armory for ROTC, and a "women's building," $250,000. The legislature found that Purdue had grown so large and complex that it was impossible from a distance to pass upon the merits of specific capital requests but appropriated, in what it considered a "final grant for a specific purpose," $125,000 for lands for the experiment station and agriculture school; $30,000 for new greenhouses; and $28,000 for equipping Smith Hall for the dairy husbandry and dairy manufacture programs.

Smith Hall was built with a bequest from William C. Smith of Williamsport, Indiana, a benefactor who had earlier given the university wilderness land in Minnesota. (Its remoteness ruled out its use by Purdue.) Smith Hall was the third building funded by private munificence of a single individual, not counting, of course, the six original buildings for the most part paid from John Purdue's original gift. The other two were Fowler Hall and Heavilon Hall.

At about the same time, the initial phase of the new University Library was built—the first on the campus to depart from the traditional red brick in favor of a blond brick exterior.

In the decade from 1913, the building program was for its time nearly as spectacular as those of the administrations of Frederick L. Hovde between 1946 and 1971 and his successor, Arthur G. Hansen, between 1971 and 1982. The Stone building program included horticultural greenhouses, 1915; the Veterinary Science Building, 1916; Stanley Coulter Hall, 1917; the Purdue Armory, 1918; and livestock barns, 1919. Plans were underway for the Home Economics Building (Matthews Hall) and the Recitation Building built in 1922 and 1923, respectively, after Stone's death.

Stone's enthusiasm for agriculture was symbolized by his own interest in research, and he undoubtedly had a special interest in the work of the Agricultural Experiment Station because of his own closely allied field, organic chemistry. When Stone became president, the experiment station occupied a building at the southwest corner of State and Marsteller streets. Hurriedly built in 1881, the structure was as poorly planned as it was poorly constructed and almost unusable for the kind of research contemplated by the station staff.

In 1907, the trio of Stone, newly appointed Dean of Agriculture John Harrison Skinner, and Arthur Goss, director of the Agricultural Experiment Station, worked on plans for a new and impressive experiment station. In the halls of the state capitol, they also eagerly sought legislative approval of an appropriation for the building to replace the old structure. Their efforts paid off with a $100,000 appropriation in 1907. The work began immediately, and the new structure was dedicated in January 1909. More impressive than the building has been the work done there in the years since.

A generous legislature had not yet exhausted its largess; because of a new and larger building, the experiment station work also expanded—as did the corresponding financial needs. In that same year, the legislature agreed to raise operating appropriations for the station from $25,000 to $75,000, thereby tripling in a period of five years the scope and equipment of the station and its operations. The payoff to Indiana agriculture has been incalculable; Indiana is one of the few states with no need for a separate state department of agriculture. Instead, the typical functions of such a department are carried on in Purdue's agricultural complex—state inspection and control of fertilizer quality, animal feedstuffs quality control, the state cholera serum laboratory, creamery licensing, seed inspection, and, at one point in history, stallion registration—not to mention the office of the state chemist.

Early farmlands used by the School of Agriculture and the experiment facility were in the campus peripheral area—most of it west of the campus on the south side of what is now Indiana 26 or State Street. Additions had been made from contiguous lands for the most part, but acreage was acquired later in other parts of Tippecanoe County and in nearby counties and eventually across the entire state. For example, Purdue acquired what was called the Moses Fell Annex in Lawrence County, a 678-acre farm given in 1914 by Moses Fell Dunn. Other gifts were the Davis Forestry Farm in Randolph County in 1917 and the Pinney Farm in 1919 in Porter and LaPorte counties near Wanatah. At the end of Stone's administration, Purdue agricultural lands for teaching, research, and service totaled more than 2,000 acres; with the West Lafayette campus included, the university's total acreage amounted to more than 4,300 acres.

Stone's desires for agriculture at Purdue—indeed, Indiana agriculture's desires for agriculture at Purdue—were carried forward under many capable individuals, not the least of whom was the venerable Dean Skinner. Without Skinner, Stone may not have been able to accomplish quality growth in Purdue agriculture. In addition, the Agricultural Experiment Station in Stone's administration had a series of able directors, and to them in no small way must be credited the unusual rapport that the university had with not only the agricultural community in Indiana but the legislature as well—a benefit that accrued to agriculture as well as to the whole university.

Clearly, the instruction of resident students was never the sole concern of agricultural faculty; their common interest included research and dissemination of their findings to the agriculture industry throughout the state. The business of the School of

Agriculture, the Agricultural Experiment Station, and the Cooperative Extension Service, which had their beginnings prior to the twentieth century, was that of agricultural department to the entire state. Purdue agriculture has always seemed to acquire dedicated and able leaders—Latta; Horace Stockbridge; Charles S. Plumb; Arthur Goss; Charles G. Woodbury; George I. Christie, the first director of the then emerging extension department; and, of course, the steadying, stern hand of the indomitable John Skinner. With a basket of Purdue apples, sincere logic, and persistence, he was probably Stone's most effective lobbyist in the capitol.

Among others who gave their best to Indiana agriculture in those formative years under Stone and his predecessor Smart, were James Troop, professor of horticulture and later entomology, and Joseph Charles Arthur, specialist in vegetable physiology and pathology and head of botany from 1887 to 1915. Arthur's worldwide research in wheat rusts led in the 1880s to the establishment at Purdue of the Arthur Herbarium, today the world's largest collection of wheat rusts. It includes more than 90,000 specimens from throughout the world. More importantly, rust research using that resource has saved Indiana and the nation many millions of dollars.

The rapid growth in agriculture and agricultural extension was due not only to the dedication of the staff and faculty but also to a series of statutes and federal laws which provided new and additional sums of money. Most notable was the Smith-Lever Act of 1914 which increased the dollars and expanded the scope of extension at Purdue and at other state universities and land-grant colleges. Between 1905 and 1923, extension at Purdue included the Farmers' Institutes, 4-H (then called Boys' and Girls' Clubs), short courses, exhibits, and the county extension agents. Most spectacular were the educational trains which travelled the rails to bring to the attention of the Indiana public, particularly farmers, the new methods developed by the work of the experiment station.

The Department of Home Economics was the creation of Stone's administration in 1905, an outgrowth undoubtedly of early 1880s lectures by Virginia C. Meredith of Cambridge City, Indiana, on the Farmers' Institute circuit. She was Purdue's first woman member of the board of trustees. The position resulted from an amendment to the law governing appointments to the Purdue board which required at least one woman member. The modification in the law reflected the strong feminist movement of the early years of the century which brought about passage in 1920 of the

Nineteenth Amendment to the United States Constitution (woman suffrage).

Mrs. Meredith, widow of a wealthy Cambridge City stockman, learned well the lessons of public agriculture and became a noted national lecturer. She organized and taught in the School of Home Economics at the University of Minnesota and organized the Indiana Federation of Women's Clubs, as well as the first home economics clubs in Indiana. At Vicksburg, Mississippi, in 1889, she was actually crowned "Queen of American Agriculture." Eventually a resident of West Lafayette, she served on the Purdue board from 1921 to 1936 when she died at the age of eighty-eight.

The first Department of Home Economics (later, the School of Home Economics) was an example of Purdue's tardiness in an area where it could well have been first. The university can only claim that it made up in early developmental fervor what it perhaps lost in having a late start. Stone pushed the department forward but not until a year after his death in 1921 was the new Home Economics Building (Matthews Hall) completed. Still, the home economics curriculum grew rapidly in its early years.

Until home economics, women students for the most part enrolled in general science courses, apparently uninterested in an 1886 attempt to begin a "cooking school" known as the "School of Domestic Economy under Professor Emma P. Ewing." It did not last. The early success of home economics was due in part to Stone's endorsement and backing, although its organization in the beginning was by Ivy Frances Harner, who must get part of the credit. She was followed by Henrietta Calvin in 1908 and in 1912 by Mary L. Matthews, who served under three presidents until her retirement in 1952. The 1922 home economics building, which she had been so instrumental in planning, was named to honor her memory as one of the strong pillars of American home economics education. The Home Economics Administration Building, constructed in the 1950s roughly on the site of the old Boarding (Ladies) Hall, was named for Stone, honoring his role in the school's establishment and early growth.

Another significant development at Purdue during Stone's years was the formation of the Department of Education, albeit a one-man department, in 1908. Stone's administration paralleled the expansion of public secondary education in the United States. Great enthusiasm (at least among the educators of the day) began to develop for educational techniques as distinct from pure scholarship.

The public began to demand professional training for teachers; more and more Purdue graduates were going into public school teaching; the number of new high schools burgeoned. Thus, in 1907, a new state teacher-training law was passed, requiring at least twelve semester hours of professional education for all beginning teachers. One did not have to hold the degree to begin to teach, but to obtain a life, high-school-teaching license required at least a baccalaureate degree. The law also provided opportunity for Indiana's colleges and universities to establish baccalaureate-level courses. The statute thus became the reason for the establishment in 1908 of Purdue's "one-man" Department of Education.

The stroke of the governor's pen also now required all teachers, elementary as well as high school, to be at least high school graduates, and townships without high schools began to establish them.

In Indiana in 1908, nearly 750 high schools were in operation, either commissioned or noncommissioned. Of this number, 507 were township or rural high schools—three-teacher schools for the most part with perhaps a travelling music teacher who made weekly rounds to each. More than half of Indiana's 1,016 townships had no high schools at all, and the trustees of these townships were required by law to transfer their students who were ready for high school to good (presumably meaning nearby) high schools at township expense.

The state superintendent of public instruction reported in 1908 that then existing Hoosier high schools had a total of 2,054 teachers—one in five of whom did not hold a baccalaureate degree. Spearheading public agitation for professional training for all high-school teachers were Indiana colleges and universities which admitted students without examination from the commissioned high schools. The same agitation also specified that teacher training for high school (and elementary school) teachers include practice teaching under expert supervision. Hence, a year after passage of the 1907 law, an education department began at Purdue.

The state's total public involvement in teacher training had been one two-year normal college, Indiana State Normal College, at Terre Haute (now Indiana State University). Dozens of privately owned normal schools existed, but, public or private, the normal schools in Indiana were oriented toward the training of elementary teachers. Thus a controversy arose as to whether the normal schools were even competent to train high school teachers, and the most vociferous opponents believed that high school teacher training should be done only by the universities.

The demand for high school teachers who had baccalaureate degrees was nearly insatiable. In 1900, Indiana had 162 commissioned high schools; by 1908, there were 375 plus 374 of lower or noncommissioned grade. In that eight-year period, the number of Indiana high schools had increased fourfold.

State school officials questioned whether, because of the lack of high schools, adequate provisions for secondary education were being made in Indiana. They were also highly critical of what they termed the "wretched" academic and college-oriented instruction given in many of the smaller high schools. Another problem was retaining Indiana youngsters in high school. A total of 21,168 graduates of the common schools in 1907 were ready for high school, but the number of graduates from commissioned high schools in Indiana that same year was only 4,627; that is, about one in five of those who completed the eighth grade also finished high school.

To head Purdue's education program, Stone appointed George L. Roberts as professor of industrial education, and for six years, Roberts was the Department of Education until 1914 when the Vocational Act of 1913 made it financially feasible to employ additional faculty.

Roberts was forty-seven when he came to Purdue and had had twenty-seven years' experience in education as a teacher, principal, and superintendent in Indiana public schools. A Decatur County farm boy, Roberts began as a teacher in a one-room school near Greensburg before he had graduated from high school. He later qualified for entry into the College of Liberal Arts at Indiana University and got a bachelor of arts degree at the age of twenty-four. He returned to Greensburg, taught in that community's school system, and advanced from teacher to principal to superintendent. From Greensburg, he went to Frankfort as superintendent of schools and later to the same position in the Muncie public schools. During the summer months, Roberts studied educational psychology at both Clark University and Columbia and subsequently earned a master's diploma in education from the Teachers College at Columbia. Two years after joining the Purdue faculty, he received a degree from Purdue.

Stone described him to the board of trustees as a "student of the science of education." Though Roberts did not publish a great number of scholarly papers, he was busy as an administrator and organizer; he taught five classes himself. He was a good selection as first head of the department. Known among students as "Daddy" Roberts, he carried off his academic role with aplomb and confidence. More than six feet tall, he parted his thick, silvery hair in the middle, wore pince-nez glasses, and was always impeccably dressed. But his role as an organizer and his prestige in professional activities beyond the boundaries of the campus helped give Purdue an outstanding reputation in teacher training and educational psychology from the beginning.

•   •   •

In 1907, engineering dean W. F. M. Goss resigned to become engineering dean at the University of Illinois. In his twenty-eight years at Purdue, Goss had shaped Purdue undergraduate engineering from literally nothing in an unimproved basement in old Science Hall into a national educational treasure. In that effort, he always had the full backing and contagious enthusiasm of President Smart, and he may have felt he had much less than that under Stone. At the least, there seems little doubt that Stone did not support engineering in the fashion of Smart. Goss was a popular teacher, but he had no love for its inevitable routine and much preferred to spend his hours in experimentation and research. Despite his own feeling that he perhaps was no longer appreciated, Goss was so highly respected that Stone accepted without question his only recommendation for his successor. He was Charles Henry Benjamin who had been head of mechanical engineering.

Benjamin functioned leisurely and amiably, practiced the art of the possible with great success, and carried on the heritage established by Goss with a sense of humor and humanity. Indeed, he introduced himself as the new dean to an audience of faculty and students with a hilarious talk on what the world would be like were it run by the efficiency experts. Benjamin wrote poetry and mystery fiction and was a water colorist of gallery quality. Many of his works, however, when they did not grace the walls of his West Lafayette friends, wound up in Benjamin's own bonfires.

As the second engineering dean, Benjamin held several other responsible posts on the campus with, as the late Professor R. G. Dukes, head of applied mechanics, put it, "scandalous inefficiency, by the standards of some engineers." Dukes was the scholar who, like Benjamin, had come to Purdue from Case Institute of Technology (now Case Western University). Dukes went on to become the university's first graduate dean and was a good friend of Benjamin.

Despite Benjamin's easy administrative style, engineering flourished just as it had under Goss. In 1911, for example, the School of Chemical Engineering was founded to meet growing needs of a new and thriving United States industry. It had fiery Harry C. Peffer as its first head and seventy-nine students when it opened. In 1917, under Benjamin, the Engineering Experiment Station was founded.

In 1920, when Benjamin resigned, Stone soon found his successor in the remarkable man who served as dean of engineering thirty-three years, turned Purdue into one of America's truly prestigious engineering schools, and had become a national figure in engineering and scientific education. He was Andrey Abraham Potter, the Lithuanian immigrant who played an ocarina, venerated Benjamin Franklin, and firmly believed that being a patriotic, Christian gentleman, which he was, was life's most important success.

Three men became a formidable triumvirate under Stone. They were Potter, even though new to the university; John Skinner, who had become first dean of agriculture; and Stanley Coulter, the Renaissance man who came to Purdue in 1887 as professor of zoology, was founding dean of the School of Science (1907), and the first dean of men in 1919. They were the academic dreadnoughts in the Purdue armada that helped carry Purdue through the perilous waters of the 1920s and 1930s and into the successes of the 1940s under the twenty-three-year "admiralty" of Edward Charles Elliott. They were first, however, men of Stone—farseeing individuals whose integrity made them impervious to the weathering of provincial, vested interest or the caprices of often shortsighted constituencies.

•   •   •

There were also women of Stone at Purdue, one of them Carolyn Ernestine Shoemaker, who served as Purdue's first appointed dean of women from 1913 until her unexpected death of nephritis in 1933.

Miss Shoemaker entered Purdue in 1884 and received a bachelor of science degree in 1888. In 1889, she completed her master's degree. Then 21, she had hoped to embark upon a teaching career, but for the next eleven years, she felt duty-bound to care for her invalid mother. When her mother died in 1900, she joined the faculty as an instructor in English literature and soon became a favorite of all of the students. Stanley Coulter, the dean of men and the dean of the School of Science, recalled that she was in the first class he taught after coming to Purdue and that "she immediately attracted my attention by her magnificent physique, her serious demeanor, and her perfect poise. . . . Ordinarily, she seemed quite composed with something of a philosophic calm in her face and her manner. Calm as she might seem [however], she had a deeply emotional life. . . . her power as a teacher and as a woman lay in the warmth of her feelings."

Dean Shoemaker often credited another Purdue woman as the greatest influence in her adult life. She was Emma Montgomery McRae, known to most of the undergraduate women students as simply "Mother." She was also a professor of English literature and had employed Dean Shoemaker in 1900 as a new instructor. But in the years before that, they had studied and even traveled to Europe together. At Purdue, "Mother" McRae was the dean of women, in fact if not in title.

Mrs. McRae was born in Loveland, Ohio, had done her undergraduate work at Brookville College, taught school at Vevay, Indiana, and later served as a high school principal, first at Muncie, then at Marion, Indiana. She came to Purdue in 1887 under President Smart, taught, and served as an unofficial counselor on every conceivable academic and personal problem of women students. Even with that heavy responsibility, she found time to attend Wooster College, Ohio, to earn a master of arts degree in 1896. She retired from the university in 1912 and was one of the first (if not the first) woman staff member to receive a Carnegie Foundation retirement grant.

One day in 1913, Miss Shoemaker was summoned to President Stone's office where he immediately offered her the position (in addition to teaching) of dean of women. Many universities were appointing deans of women, and as he told her, he guessed Purdue ought to have one, too. She was astonished by the offer and expressed awe at the nature of the task, saying she was not at all sure she could adequately handle such a job. "Be a man, Miss Shoemaker! Be a man!" Stone admonished her. She became a "man" and accepted the university's first women's deanship, serving under Presidents Stone and Elliott.

Dean Shoemaker was more than a faculty member and dean of women. As Coulter once said, "Purdue was not a part of her life. Purdue was her life." Whenever the university called, she was there. She was instrumental in keeping the alumni association active and in getting Purdue clubs organized in the major cities across the nation. She was also a major leader in the organization of the Purdue Union and in the drive which raised funds for the construction of the Memorial Union. Revealed after her death was the fact that she gave $5,000 of her own funds for the drive.

Another early faculty member in the Stone administration was Professor Laura Anne Fry. Though she had none of the conventional college degrees, Professor Fry was an extremely talented New Yorker who had been a pupil of William H. Fry in wood carving, William Chase in painting, Kenyon Cox in drawing, and Lewis T. Rebisso in sculpture. She lived in Ladies Hall, the name given to what had been known originally as the Boarding Hall and what had become essentially the women students' residence on the campus.

•   •   •

The music for Purdue's famed song of loyalty, "Hail Purdue," was written in 1912 by Edward J. Wotawa, then a senior in the School of Science. The words were by James Morrison, then a sophomore in the School of Science, a science graduate of 1915. Written as "The Purdue War Song," Wotawa and Morrison changed the title to "Hail Purdue" when they published it in 1913. Wotawa was student director of the Purdue Glee and Mandolin Club in his junior and senior years and dedicated the song to that group. The original manuscript, penciled on both sides of two sheets of paper, is in possession of the the Purdue Musical Organizations today. Wotawa died in 1963, Morrison in 1929.

•   •   •

Stone guided Purdue through the rear echelon perils of World War I as the university diverted its attention momentarily from its normal peacetime missions to provide support to the United States war effort.

Purdue's first reaction was to offer to the military a full regiment of ROTC-trained field artillery, nearly 1,300 men. The offer was turned down, not unappreciated, by the United States War Department as not being consistent with the federal government's plans for universal military training by conscription.

Yet Purdue's contributions were substantial and included volunteer war work by staff members who served on many wartime bureaus and committees. The main thrust of the Purdue war effort was the Student Army Training Corps (SATC), organized in the summer of 1918 by way of a university contract with the United States War Department. Under it, the university agreed to train, subsist, and house 1,500 men from October 1, 1918, to June 30, 1919, the government pledging a dollar a day per man for housing and subsistence and twelve cents per man for tuition.

The community's ardor for the wartime military grew stronger. Many students joined active military groups, such as the two Purdue ambulance units which served on the French and Italian fronts. Patriotic exercises and military ceremonies were held on the flimsiest of excuses; Purdue was totally pledged to support of the war effort and diverted nearly all of the university's efforts to it. Under contracts with the War Department, Purdue trained several vocational units: 1,634 auto mechanics, 1,278 truck

Steamshovels pour out black smoke as they dig out the tough clay on the Tilt Farm hillside for Ross-Ade Stadium in 1923. An aerial photo by the U.S. Army Air Service in 1924 shows the completed stadium, although the north curve was left incomplete. In near background, neighborhood now known as Hills and Dales was a series of streets in the countryside.

Mary L. Matthews, the first dean of
Home Economics, served under three
Purdue presidents (Smart, Elliott, and
Hovde) before her retirement in 1952.

Duhme Hall, known simply as South
Hall when built in the early 1930s,
represented a growing awareness that
women's role in Purdue University
was integral to its viability.

The new Electrical Engineering
Building was built about 1930 to meet
the demands of the growing
enrollments. Towers were transmitting
antennae for Radio Station WBAA,
Indiana's oldest radio outlet.

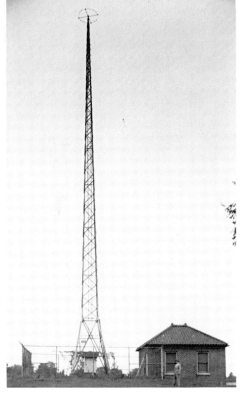

A small television transmitter at the
northeast corner of Ross-Ade Stadium
allowed Professors Roscoe George and
Howard Heim to do pioneering
transmission work that led to the
development of a black-and-white
television tube that up to then had
been cathode green.

In World War II, with President Elliott in Washington as a consultant, the university's affairs were handled by a committee composed of, from left, Executive Dean Frank Hockema, Comptroller R. B. Stewart, Dean of Agriculture Harry Reed, and Dean of Engineering A. A. Potter.

The U.S. Naval Training School was commissioned in June 1942 to train naval electronics mates, the beginning of Purdue's World War II service to various aspects of military training for the armed forces. (Tippecanoe Historical Association Archives)

Cary Hall East was the first unit of the eventual Cary Quadrangle completed about 1939. Cary East represented a new era in student residences. The building was the gift of Mr. and Mrs. Frank C. Cary of Lafayette, honoring the memory of their young son, Franklin Levering Cary. Cary East opened in 1928.

The university celebrated the fiftieth anniversary of the opening of its doors in 1874 with several solemn academic events. The occasion was marked for most, however, by this imposing frame structure over State Street at Marsteller Street.

Student life at Purdue in the 1930s mixed the hectic frustrations of registration in the Purdue Armory at one extreme with pleasant times over soft drinks in a Sweet Shop booth in Purdue Memorial Union at the other.

Hovde Hall, then and now. Then
known as the Executive Building, the
starkness of its white limestone trim
and lack of plantings are in contrast to
today's setting. The hall was renamed
for President Emeritus Frederick L.
Hovde in 1975.

Whether vocal or instrumental, when music at Purdue is mentioned, two prominent names come to mind: Albert P. Stewart (above), founder of Purdue Musical Organizations including the Varsity Men's Glee Club, and Paul Spotts Emrick (left), director of Purdue University Bands from the early 1900s until he retired in the 1950s. Music is important in the life of Purdue University—which has no school of music.

masters, 750 radio operators, and 201 concrete workers who became a special section of the SATC.

The SATC required new, temporary buildings, which were built on what had been known as Stuart Field along the south side of Stadium Avenue They included five military barracks buildings, each housing 250 men, equipment sheds, a 336-foot-long building to house twenty-six army trucks, and a recreation building for the men.

If the complex of military buildings went up rather hurriedly, it also came down shortly thereafter just as hurriedly. What had cost the university nearly $150,000 to build was sold for $9,742.37—to the same contractor, Leslie Colvin, who had put up the buildings in the first place. Their use ceased with the 1918 Armistice. The process was costly for the university, although it did increase enrollment by 1,400. Also in war training at Purdue was a special unit of the United States Naval Reserve; men who had registered for the draft prior to September 12, 1918, and awaited call; and a third group physically disqualified for military service but admitted to the SATC for limited service. A considerable body of male students under eighteen years of age was also enrolled. Proportionately, the War to End All Wars crowded the campus with war activities almost as much as did World War II nearly a quarter of a century later when the military campus scenario was essentially repeated.

World War I took its toll in Purdue lives; sixty-seven died in service, seventeen in action. The Purdue Memorial Union was begun and remains forever as a memorial to those who served and died in that war. Overall, more than 4,000 faculty and students served in the World War I armed forces; 628 of them in overseas posts. Besides those who gave their lives, one student survived a German war prison and twenty-six others were wounded.

Stone paid tribute in a postwar speech to not only those Purdue people who had assisted in the war effort or been in the service but also to the memories of those who died: "Purdue mourns for those as a mother for her sons, comforted by the knowledge that their loss was the price of liberty which will ever be more precious by virtue of its cost."

World War I was also the impetus for construction in 1918 of the Armory along the east edge of University Street, north of Memorial Gymnasium. It replaced a 50- by 100-foot wooden structure built when the university opened its doors in 1874. The old structure had been the social and cultural center of the university as well as the gymnasium and drill hall for ROTC. It gloried as the site of the university's first commencement in 1875 but in its later years had become obsolete for anything but storage of ROTC supplies. Except for chapel exercises, held in University Hall, the old armory was at one time the site of nearly all Purdue indoor public gatherings until Eliza Flower Hall was built in 1902.

The new Armory, just north of the site of its antecedent, became the center for all university ROTC activity which peaked in World War I and thereafter. The structure cost $198,000 to build and still serves not only as the headquarters, classrooms, and drill area for ROTC activities but also for a great number of other activities drawing large crowds. The Armory has possibly the worst acoustics of any building on the West Lafayette campus.

•   •   •

Through Stone's twenty-one years as president, he had his way most of the time. But he had his detractors. Unfortunately, his most formidable antagonist was one of Purdue's most illustrious alumni, George Ade, '87, renowned writer and playwright, who was a member of the board of trustees (1909–16) and dabbled dangerously in behind-the-scenes Republican state politics in which he was nominally influential. He was also one of the university's substantial benefactors in his time, a staunch and loyal member of Sigma Chi fraternity, and to a stable, conservative, and rather monolithic administration, something of a gadfly. From President Stone's standpoint, it did not help matters that Ade was for a period of time editor of the *Purdue Alumnus*. What Ade wrote, people read.

Of his relationship with David Ross, probably the university's most generous benefactor, Ade wrote, "Old maids adopt cats and canaries. Dave Ross and I adopted Purdue." Both were bachelors. Ade had been generous to the university, having contributed the $2,500 needed to complete private subscriptions for the construction of the Memorial Gymnasium in 1908. Ade had also contributed almost the entire $25,000 needed to build a new Sigma Chi fraternity house on Littleton Street, and when the Purdue Harlequin Show needed funds to purchase staging materials, he cheerfully put up $2,000. Later, after he and Ross paid $40,000 for the hillside hollow in a dairy pasture to build Ross-Ade Stadium, Ade teamed with Ross to contribute nearly $70,000 (with much more from friends and alumni) toward its construction.

But Ade did not like Stone, and he did not believe Stone had any inclination to like him. In a letter to former Governor Samuel M. Ralston in 1919, Ade attempted to garner Ralston's political support with other alumni to persuade the trustees not to renew Stone's presidency. Ade's feelings were so bitter that at one point in the letter he wrote, "I am taking an awful chance in writing this letter because I don't know what you think about Doctor Stone of Purdue. What I think about him cannot be set forth in this letter as I do not wish to violate the federal statute against sending profane matter through the mail."

Ostensibly, the difference between Stone and those alumni who stood with Ade was over athletics, then under direction of Hugh Nicol, who had come to Purdue in 1904. Stone was proud of the fact that north of Central Drive the university had an excellent outdoor athletic plant of six baseball diamonds, six football fields, ten tennis courts, a quarter-mile running track, a 220-yard straightaway track, and permanent seats for nearly 3,000 spectators. Stone supported a program of intramural sports fully and spiritedly, believing such activity to be of great benefit and an essential part of the educational maturity of every student. Intercollegiate athletics were something else; unless they were a natural development of the general sports program, they did not receive his full respect or attention.

The issues which divided Stone and the alumni were more deeply fundamental than athletics. Stone, it is true, raised much alumni and student ire when a promising football coach, Andred L. B. Smith, was dismissed after three seasons, 1913, 1914, and 1915, in which his teams won twelve games, lost six, and tied three. To alumni, Stone compounded his sin of firing Smith by hiring Cleo A. O'Donnell of Everett, Massachusetts, who was able to do no better than five wins, eight losses, and one tie in the two seasons he coached at Purdue.

Worse, Stone had also wrested authority for intercollegiate athletics from an autonomous athletic association (which included alumni) and placed it under a newly established Department of Physical Education under the president's office. That action was hardly a popular move, and more resentment developed over matters pertaining to the student union, the band, the *Exponent,* and the *Purdue Alumnus.* The dissidents, of whom Ade was one of the most vociferous, believed they should have a greater voice in the formation of university policy. There was even some irresponsible talk of firing Stone. Ade was all for it.

Although Ade was beloved and highly respected, he may have been a sufferer of an academic syndrome confined to alumni that American educator Robert M. Hutchins was fond of describing: "All alumni are dangerous . . . the more sentimental an alumnus is, the more dangerous he is. . . . He sees a beautiful uniqueness about the period when he was in college. That period has never been equalled before or since, and the sole object of the institution should be to return to those glorious days that produced him."

Stone, being Stone, seemed oblivious to alumni interests and concerns. He was wary of what he felt was too much emphasis on extracurricular activities—"the multiplication and exaggeration," he said, "of every conceivable form of amusement, distraction, and recreation in connection with student life."

Frustrated, Ade resigned from the board of trustees in the first year of his second term and gave his reasons in a frank and open letter. Purdue under Stone, he wrote, was being committed to a course of mediocrity. Further, Ade believed that student resourcefulness and talent were being molded into conformity and graduates from the "repressive program" could not be expected to hold more than routine jobs after graduating. To the liberal, free-spirited author of *Fables in Slang,* the seeming authoritarian Stone administration had become intolerable.

After Ade resigned from the board, his siege continued, and in 1918, as editor of the *Alumnus,* he began to use its pages as his personal soapbox, though his manner was gentlemanly and restrained. He continued his insistence that Purdue should become a livelier, more imaginative school—such as it no doubt had been when he was a student in the administration of Stone's predecessor, the irrepressible Smart.

Ade once wrote that there were two extremes in the polemic which had developed at Purdue, "Those who believe that Purdue is being put into a category with the penitentiaries at Michigan City and the Plainfield Reform School, and the grim disciplinarians who cannot see beyond the campus's iron fence and who say that any who argue against any established policy are misinformed mischief-makers and enemies of the University."

Ade used often-repeated apocrypha about the Purdue professor who was assigned to make up a list of convocation speakers. Three of them suggested by Ade were successful graduates who had become vice presidents, respectively, of a railroad, a steel company, and a multi-million-dollar corporation. The professor was enthused and asked Ade if he believed they would come to the campus as speakers. Only one reason, Ade told the professor, why they might not: all had been kicked out of Purdue at one time or another.

"Life at Purdue," Ade said resignedly in later years of the struggle, "had been just one misunderstanding after another." The alumni had been estranged, student morale had deteriorated—even the faculty had begun to feel the effect, he said, of Stone's heavy-handed authoritarian ways. Stone had, Ade wrote, one solution to every university problem, "Sterner discipline and more hours of work." And, he added, Stone liked only those athletic coaches who "did not cost much money" and could be hired so long as they were "obedient and respectful—regardless of whether they knew anything about coaching." What the alumni wanted, Ade believed, was "every tonic influence which would make Purdue men and women proud of their school . . . a revivified sentiment of loyalty to the school and its associations."

The onslaught of Ade's forces against Stone was terrible to behold. He resisted it with grace until his life ended in a nearly inaccessible reach of the Canadian Rockies.

As with everything else he accomplished in his life, President Stone approached mountain climbing almost as an obsession. It became his mistress away from the demands of his many-faceted role as the president of a burgeoning university. He loved and worshipped the mountains, although his familiarity with the ranges of the western North American continent did not come about until the middle years of his life in 1906.

Stone, the New Hampshireman, was familiar with the gentle, worn-down mountains of the East Coast. He had come to love the out-of-doors and the panorama of living things he found in his youthful wanderings through that region as a New England farm lad. His love of mountain climbing was a refreshing and vivid revival of an earlier memory.

He first became enthralled with the mountains of the West in 1906 on a trip to Glacier, British Columbia, where a Professor Freeborn whetted his interest in mountaineering. Stone later expressed his debt to Freeborn for revealing to him the wonder and mystery of the mountains. Stone once said he could do no better service to mankind than pass along and stimulate interest in the sport of mountain climbing.

In the years after 1906, he became an active member in the Appalachian Mountain Club, the American Alpine Club, the Mazamas of Portland, Oregon, and the Alpine Club of Canada. In 1911, Stone attended the camp of the Alpine Club of Canada and climbed Mt. Daly and several other peaks, though he had fully met the requirements for active membership by having climbed Mt. Baker, Washington, several years earlier.

In 1915 and 1916, accompanied by Mrs. Stone, he spent five summer weeks in exploration with many first ascents of major peaks in the Purcell Range. His notes and photographs on those trips were the basis of two highly regarded articles he wrote for the *A.A.C. Journal.* Stone was considered an ideal mountain climbing companion, and as one fellow climber regarded him, "he was an ideal comrade around the camp fire and no man could have been a more thoughtful and safe climber to be with on a rope." Except for the World War I years of 1917 and 1918 when extra Purdue duties kept him on the campus, the Stones headed for the western Canadian ranges each summer.

On the morning of July 1, 1921, Stone had a routine meeting with the trustees, then began preparations for his summer trip with Mrs. Stone to the Banff region, west of Calgary, Alberta. His last act in West Lafayette had been to pick a basket of roses from the garden he kept at his large white-frame home which faced the campus from the east side of Grant Street. He personally delivered the roses to Blanche Miller at the university library. Miss Miller was the library staff member who was a friend of, and unofficial advisor to, Purdue Presidents Smart, Stone, Elliott, and Hovde. (She held the longest Purdue staff tenure without interruption from the 1890s into the 1950s.) Stone's gift of roses to her was one of the friendly and thoughtful deeds that his colleagues and friends loved to recall about him.

On July 15, the Stones began what became their last try at the heights when they left their base camp at Assiniboine, south of Banff. Their objective was to climb unscaled Mt. Eon, a 10,860-foot peak along the boundary between Alberta and British Columbia and just south of its sister peak, Mt. Assiniboine, which commanded the range at 11,870 feet.

At about 6 P.M., Sunday, July 17, the Stones were within fifty feet of the summit. The president was in the lead, testing the footing, and had called back to warn his wife of the danger from a change in the rock structure which had gone from solid footing to a loose, friable, disintegrating material. She shouted to him to ask whether he was near the top, and he replied, "I see nothing higher."

Without warning, the rock broke away beneath him. He fell almost 1,000 feet to his death.

Dazed and stunned, Mrs. Stone climbed gingerly down the mountain as far as possible and ultimately found a small shelf from which she could neither climb nor descend. There she survived for nearly a week on only a small trickle of water from a crack in the rock wall until she was rescued by a party led by Rudolph Aemmer, a widely known Swiss Alpine guide. She was carried to the base of the mountain for emergency treatment by a doctor-nurse team and removed to a hospital at Banff, forty-five miles to the north, for treatment of superficial injuries and the extended exposure.

Mrs. Stone's first instruction was to have a telegram sent to her late husband's secretary, Helen Hand, informing her official-ly of the president's death. Except for an Associated Press dispatch, the telegram was the first word to reach the campus community about the tragedy.

Meanwhile, Aemmer's rescue party pushed ahead with the search for Stone's body, found on August 5, 1921, jammed be-tween the sides of a seventeen-foot-deep crevice. Before taking the body down the mountain, Aemmer and his crew climbed to Eon's summit and built a rock cairn crowned with Stone's ice axe and containing a small metal box in which they left a paper inscribed:

Friday, August 5, 1921

This monument was built by the undersigned in tribute to their comrade of the mountains, Dr. Winthrop E. Stone, President of Purdue University, Lafayette, Indiana, U.S.A., who on July 16, 1921 [actually, it was July 17] with his wife, virtually completed the first ascent, reaching a point not more than fifty feet from this spot. Dr. Stone's ice axe crowned this monument.

Albert H. MacCarthy, A.C.C.
Lennox H. Lindsay
Edward Feuz
Conrad Cain
Rudolph Aemmer

Mrs. Stone returned to Lafayette where her husband's funeral was held on August 13. He was fifty-nine at his death.

Stone belonged to the nation; he was much admired and respected in the national circles of higher education management and the world of scientists and scholars. Tributes to his memory poured in from all over the country. His tragic death had stunned the community and even his most vociferous detractor, George Ade, wrote, "Like everyone else who knew Dr. Stone intimately, I am much grieved to learn of his death. We all recognize his great devotion to the university and its interests and realize at the same time that the university has suffered a loss which will be hard to repair."

Trustee Noel, in the same eulogy in which he termed Stone a piece of New England granite transplanted to Indiana soil, paid him most fitting tribute, "He wore honor with dignity; he met duty with courage; his life comported with the ideals of his New England ancestors; his heart was both strong and tender; he was sound in his philosophy and adamant against wrong; he was loyal to his country and he feared God. I pray you, what more could one desire in greatness?"

Chapter VIII

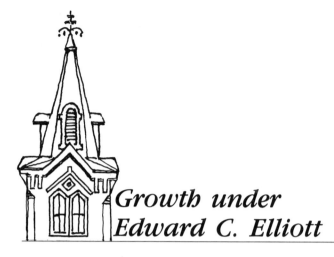

Growth under Edward C. Elliott

Rescuers had yet to reach the broken body of President Stone in the Canadian Rockies wilderness when Joseph D. Oliver, president of the board of trustees, called from his South Bend office to ask Lafayette publisher Henry Wright Marshall to "look after matters at the university until [we can take] other action." At the time, Marshall had been a member of the board only since the previous February but already was chairman of the board's executive committee.

The board met at West Lafayette on August 4, 1921, to appoint Marshall as the vice president of the university and, subsequently, as acting president until Stone's successor was found. Oliver appointed a search committee composed of himself; Marshall; James W. Noel, trustee from Indianapolis; and David E. Ross and Perry Crane of Lafayette and Lebanon respectively, both alumni members of the trustee board.

The following day, August 5, Stone's body was carried down from the mountain.

Marshall, publisher of the Lafayette *Journal and Courier,* was an Ohioan who had had many years' business experience in Lafayette and Evansville. He also had extensive farming interests, owning fifteen farms totaling 4,550 acres, all near Lafayette. Marshall was also a Republican politician, had served six years in the Indiana General Assembly, and as speaker of the assembly's House of Representatives in 1903 and 1905. He had also been a delegate to four national Republican conventions.

Then fifty-six, Marshall had been associated with the university little more than six months when he found himself its acting president. Although he was widely known as a somewhat crusty, opinionated conservative, his business acumen worked well for him and for Purdue. During his year as acting president, Marshall stayed in the background, quietly handling the university's business matters with little wasted motion.

Meanwhile, the respected Stanley Coulter presided as chairman of the faculty. The two worked well together in a spirit of mutual respect; Marshall was astute enough not to attempt to dabble in faculty and academic affairs where he might have appeared to be a midget among some academic giants. Marshall and Coulter ably carried on the administrative leadership of the university and even assisted in the presidential search, Marshall especially, as the trustees traveled throughout the nation to talk to potential candidates.

Eventually the board narrowed its choices to four men, and in April 1922—eight months after the search—the trustees unanimously elected Edward Charles Elliott. The names of the three other candidates were never officially presented nor revealed.

Elliott, then forty-seven, was chancellor of the University of Montana and at midlife embarked on his third career—one that turned out to be a twenty-three-year love affair between Purdue and one of America's educational notables. Whereas Shortridge managed to get the doors of the university open and classes started, whereas White once and for all answered the question of what Purdue was going to be, whereas Smart picked up its tempo and made it into a nationally and even internationally recognized engineering institution before the turn of the century, and whereas Stone brought balance to the academic scale and insisted on scholarly standards of high order, it was Elliott's charisma, savvy, and administrative brilliance that carried Purdue far beyond the wildest imaginings of any of his predecessors.

Elliott was born in Chicago on December 21, 1874, the first son of Frederick and Susan Petts Elliott. His father was a blacksmith who had immigrated to the United States four years previously and had worked at his trade in several eastern and midwestern cities. He returned early in 1874 to his native Ramsgate, England, to marry Susan Petts. They came to Chicago and in 1878 moved to Cedar Rapids, Iowa, where Frederick worked in the shops of the Northwestern Railroad. His son Edward was not quite five years old when he started to school in Cedar Rapids in 1879. Edward's younger brother Frederick, Jr. was five years of age or so when in 1881 the family moved to North Platte, Nebraska. The father became a blacksmith and later foreman in the shops of the Union Pacific Railroad. Two younger children—a daughter, Edith, and a son, Frank—died during the family's first year in North Platte. A much younger brother, Ben, was born in 1889.

The town became the family home for fifty years. In Elliott's youth, North Platte was a frontier town of perhaps 1,500—a place where his family life revolved around organized labor and the local politics of his father and the devout Episcopalianism of his mother. Edward was baptized as an Episcopalian but was never confirmed by membership.

A highlight of Elliott's youth was a family trip when he was twelve to Ramsgate to visit his grandmother. The year was 1887, Queen Victoria's Jubilee. As if an Atlantic voyage were not enough excitement for a landlubbing lad of a dozen years, Edward was thrilled by a trip to London to see former North Platte resident William Frederick "Buffalo Bill" Cody and his Wild West Show. Cody for thirty years had made his home on the outskirts of North Platte not far from one of the two forks, north and south, which converge east of town to form the Platte River. As a youngster, Elliott and his friends played on the river ice. He recalled once falling through into the icy waters and, rescued by his friends, warming himself back to life before a roaring fireplace in the famed buffalo hunter's home. In London, Cody repeated the same kind of courtesy by inviting the Elliotts to dine with him, his daughter Arta, and performers Annie Oakley and Johnny Baker.

Young Edward Elliott graduated in 1890 from North Platte's three-year high school about the time the local school board added a fourth year to qualify its graduates for the University of Nebraska. Elliott went the extra year, graduated again in 1891, and headed that fall for Lincoln and the University of Nebraska. He graduated with a bachelor of science degree in chemistry in 1895. In his undergraduate years, Elliott worked as a ranch hand to earn enough money to stay in school. Though he loved football, he never played in college. Still, throughout his life, Elliott carried the erect, wiry, square-jawed, raw-boned, and clear-eyed image of the outdoorsman and athlete.

Even in those young years, Elliott, who eventually stood as a respected leader of American education in his own right, brushed other greatness. One of the sixty-six members of his college graduating class was Willa Cather of American literary fame. As an ROTC cadet, Elliott had been under the command of then Lieutenant John J. Pershing, with whom he developed a lifelong friendship. "Black Jack" Pershing became the general who led the American Expeditionary Force in Europe in World War I.

Following his undergraduate years at Nebraska, Elliott stayed two more years in a chemistry teaching assistantship and earned his master of arts degree. He had hoped for further study in Germany. Times were hard, however, and he had little choice but to seek a job. He wanted to teach. A high school teaching job in chemistry, physics, and mathematics opened in Omaha, and he jumped at it—only to be beaten out by another man. Later that year, 1897, Elliott got a one-year contract to teach science at Leadville, Colorado, a high-country, silver-mining town that had boomed, busted, and was on the comeback as a more stable community with a renewed interest in its public schools. Yet, it was still a rough, frontier town, and it must have looked depressing to young Elliott when he arrived on August 30, 1897, aboard an open freight car in an unseasonal snowstorm. He had five dollars in his pocket and had been forced to ride on a freight train after a wreck had torn out track a few miles down the mountain. At an elevation of 10,200 feet, Leadville lies astride the spine of the Rocky Mountains through Colorado. Its population varied, depending upon the silver market, but when Elliott arrived, there were about 10,000 citizens.

After finding a single room, he immediately focused his attention on the high-school facilities where he was to teach. He was appalled to find his laboratory equipment consisted solely of a dozen Bunsen burners.

Leadville was pivotal in Elliott's life in at least two respects. There, he met his future wife, Elizabeth Nowland, daughter of school board member and local publisher John Nowland. Elliott was also promoted to superintendent of the Leadville school system, comprised of a three-year high school and five elementary schools. It was a remarkable step up for a young man who at the age of twenty-four was just launching his career. That promotion perhaps more than anything else influenced him to stay in education, rather than pursue a scientific career. Despite rather generous offers for jobs in chemistry elsewhere, the comparatively large sum of $1,500 a year as Leadville school superintendent no doubt influenced him to stay. He spent his summers at his alma mater, the University of Nebraska, taking courses in education and supplemented these with correspondence study in psychology at the University of Colorado.

Elliott's reforms of the Leadville school system were drastic and remarkable for one who had barely completed his first year in teaching. But they were long overdue changes. Before the end of 1899, he had persuaded the school board to institute a four-year high school. By 1900, a new building for it was occupied.

His genius for reorganization and reform in education was already evident in the things he instituted at Leadville.

Elliott had considered the possibilities of further schooling for himself in professional school administration and eventually accepted an offer from Columbia University for a teaching fellowship in educational administration. He spent 1903–4 as an assistant and the following summer went to the University of Jena in Germany, partly to meet graduate language requirements of the Teachers College at Columbia and partly to observe the work of public schools in France, Germany, and Switzerland. He also grew a luxurious beard.

In the second year of his Columbia program, Elliott decided to make educational administration his career. He also befriended Nicholas Murray Butler, the man who recommended him in the spring of 1905 to E. A. Birge, then dean of education at the University of Wisconsin, for the Wisconsin education faculty. He went to Wisconsin that fall as an associate professor. In 1907 Elliott was promoted to full professor—the same year he travelled to Spokane to marry Elizabeth Nowland, the girl he had met and fallen in love with at Leadville many years before and with whom he had since maintained a steady and fervent correspondence. With his new bride, he set up housekeeping at Madison. There, all four of the Elliott children were born—John in 1908, Suzanne in 1910, Marion in 1912, and Edward in 1915.

Elliott spent just a little more than a decade at the University of Wisconsin, turning out prodigious quantities of scholarly work of many varieties— "testimonial," says his biographer, the late Frank K. Burrin (*Edward C. Elliott, Educator*, 1970), "to his apparently boundless energy."

Elliott's reputation as a leader in school administration grew rapidly and widely. When the Wisconsin board of regents in 1908 established a new plan for teacher training, Elliott was named director, a post he held from 1909 to 1916 when he left Wisconsin to become chancellor of the University of Montana system. By that time, Elliott had become one of America's staunchest, most eloquent champions of public school education—from rural schools to the state universities.

The chancellorship at Montana was newly created and at the time unique among United States higher education systems. For Elliott, it was a drastic career change. He had accepted the post with the mixed blessings of friends and colleagues, some urging him to take it, others warning him that it would stretch the Elliott tenacity and pioneering spirit to the breaking point. Going to Montana, he was told, could damage his well-earned reputation and ability to do constructive work because of political feuding, rivalries, and what one of his peers described as "poor organization of the Montana Board of Control."

Despite the administrative caldron Elliott stepped into at Montana, he was always aware of the bleakness of such situations, but as a master of the art of the possible, he was seldom without some kind of solution. Before he agreed to take the Montana position, he specified ten conditions that had to be met. Among them were: his appointment receive unanimous approval of the Montana Board of Education as well as the approval of the presidents of the four Montana institutions; his term be for three years; his salary be $8,000 per year; his term of office begin February 1916; he be provided with adequate office staff, travel expenses, and vacation and permitted to attend appropriate professional association meetings; he be empowered to recommend all nominations for the appointment of new staff members as well as the compensation, promotion, or dismissal of staff members; and he not be expected to make any public addresses for at least six months after beginning his term of office.

The Montana board acceded to these conditions, and they worked well for Elliott—so well that seven years later when he considered the move to Purdue as president, he followed this same pattern by preparing a list of fourteen conditions for the trustees' approval.

Elliott signed his Montana contract in October 1915 and immediately got involved in an imbroglio that had developed over the abrupt firing, apparently without explanation, of three faculty at the State University of Montana at Missoula. The firings had all been at the insistence of one of the members of the board of control. At the time he got into the dispute, Elliott and his family were still in Madison. After his arrival at Helena, Elliott handled the matter with his usual deftness. He then waded into the chaos which permeated the reorganization of the Montana institutions.

Elliott was considered a top-flight educator and administrator; he did not shun controversy. By the end of his six years' effort to provide Montana with a unified and growing system of higher education, though weary and exhausted from the experience, he was ready to embark on a third career, Purdue, where he was to serve nearly a quarter of a century. On May 12, 1922, Elliott sent his letter of resignation as chancellor to the Montana governor. "Now I feel," he concluded his letter, "that I have done my share of the pioneering task and may retire with no sense of remissness."

Four days after he submitted his resignation at Montana, Elliott came to West Lafayette and told the trustees in his unique oratorical style, "Purdue has honored me; I will endeavor to honor Purdue University." Thus began an era of educational leadership at Purdue in which there was never a doubt as to who was doing the leading.

•   •   •

Elliott's appointment climaxed nearly nine months' work by a trustees' search committee. Oliver had been the most active trustee, but Marshall, Noel of Indianapolis, and two alumni members of the board—Ross of Lafayette (who came later to play a major role in the history of Purdue) and Crane of Lebanon, Indiana—were also active. Another trustee, John A. Hillenbrand of Batesville, Indiana, though not a member of the committee, travelled with the committee and assisted in finding the new president.

The search took them to neighboring states and eventually to New York and Washington, D.C., to discuss with other university presidents the possibilities for the Purdue presidency. The candidate list was eventually narrowed to four from among names submitted to the Purdue trustees by the General Education Board.

At a regular meeting of the board of trustees on April 21, 1922, Marshall moved that Oliver, as board president, be authorized to invite Elliott to the Purdue presidency. The vote was unanimous, and there was no discussion of the three other candidates.

Elliott had been encouraged to take the Purdue presidency by several of America's educational pillars—among them Butler of Columbia, Henry S. Pritchett of the Carnegie Foundation for the Advancement of Teaching, and Samuel Capen of the American Council on Education. Capen himself had been suggested for the Purdue presidency but for personal reasons summarily rejected the idea of his own candidacy.

Even more encouraging was Elliott's close friend, Henry Suzzalo, president of the University of Washington, who wrote Elliott that he believed Purdue would suit him better than Montana, both personally and professionally—and his family as well.

At his first meeting with the Purdue trustees in May 1922, Elliott presented a list of conditions under which he would accept the presidency—a list not dissimilar to the one he had presented when he had been invited to the Montana chancellorship six years previously.

His list for Purdue stipulated: his appointment be for an indefinite term; his appointment be approved unanimously, not only by the trustees but also by the officers and staff; his moving expenses between Helena and Lafayette (about $1,800) be paid; his salary be "not less than $12,000" with one month vacation annually; the university provide a residence suitable not only as a home for his large family but also for meeting the social obligations of the presidency; he have an expense account sufficient to cover the cost of "official" entertaining; and all business travel expenses be paid by the university.

Though his stipulations covered the more mundane matters of employment, two other conditions Elliott insisted upon established precedents for his successors at Purdue and have become the basis for the mutual respect and clear understandings Purdue trustees have had with Purdue presidents since. Elliott and the trustees agreed that (1) "the initiative for all nominations for the appointments, and all recommendations for the compensation, promotion, transfer, or dismissal of members of the instructional and scientific staff of the institution, shall rest with the president acting with the advice of the administrative officers immediately concerned," and (2) "the trustees shall have full responsibility for distinctly financial and public policies of the university while the president with the aid of the faculty shall have responsibility for distinctly educational policies, subject to board approval." (The wording of Elliott's presidential acceptance conditions was copied almost exactly in the agreement between Frederick L. Hovde and the board nearly a quarter century later.)

The trustees accepted Elliott's conditions on his first visit to the campus on May 16, except for the $12,000 annual salary; Elliott settled for $10,000, the same as he received at Montana. It was not a terribly important item to Elliott since the trustees had agreed to provide him with a house.

The move to Lafayette from Helena that summer of 1922 was difficult since the university had no house for its president. Mrs. Elliott was concerned about what size it would be; the Elliott family had four children, ranging in age from seven to fourteen, plus Mrs. Elliott's mother, Mrs. Nowland, who lived with the Elliotts after the death of her husband in 1919. Temporary arrangements were finally made for a house at 500 University Street, just north of the Purdue Armory. The dwelling was a turn-of-the-century, gray stucco house (no longer in existence), where the Elliotts lived until August 1, 1923.

The board considered construction of a new presidential manse on the campus. Several locations were considered, and the proposed home became an issue entwined with an overall master development plan for the entire campus. The idea was dropped even though at one point a location on Grant Street between what is now the Purdue Memorial Union and Grissom Hall (then the Civil Engineering Building) was considered. The Elliotts were not particularly enchanted with the thought of living what probably would have been a fishbowl existence had their home been on the campus. That matter was resolved in 1923 when the trustees decided to spend $44,400 for Dr. Guy Levering's home at 515 South Seventh Street, on a high bluff overlooking downtown Lafayette, across the Wabash River as far as the campus. From home to campus was at least two miles and permitted Elliott to indulge himself in his favorite exercise, walking. He made a daily habit of the hike from the Seventh Street residence down the hill, through the Lafayette business district, across the Main Street bridge over the Wabash, and up the State Street incline in West Lafayette to the campus. Occasionally, Elliott also walked home along the same route at the end of the day. Frequently, Elliott turned down offers of rides from motorist friends and acquaintances. He enjoyed the walks because they were a substitute for earlier times with his sons, prowling the Montana mountains on ten- to fifteen-mile weekend hikes.

Another of Elliott's requests to the trustees was that there be no inaugural ceremonies. He apparently believed that money for such a rite should be saved, that he should begin his third career with work, not the trappings of ritual.

Stone's death marked the end of an era in Purdue's existence. The year Elliott came, 1922, was only two years shy of the university's first fifty years. More importantly, the first years of the 1920s marked the beginning of Purdue's modern era. The university had by then emerged from the World War I disturbances and achieved academic equilibrium. In the next twenty-three years under Elliott, Purdue would undergo growth and change unmatched by even the restless, most resourceful years of James Henry Smart's inspirations. Elliott's first decade at Purdue was also one of growing national prosperity. The so-called Roaring Twenties were years of seeming reckless inflation and unbridled frivolity. For Purdue, they were also years when the university walked a fine line between a national prosperity too hastily assimilated and the need to avoid the influences of an overly optimistic period vacant of foresight.

Elliott offered the skilled guidance that steered Purdue on a careful course. The university emerged from its first ten years under Elliott having kept step with the times and showing all evidences of steady growth. He provided the balance and spiritual strength that stood well through the perilous times of the depression years of the 1930s and World War II in the first half of the 1940s.

Yet, in retrospect, one cannot consider the accomplishments of Elliott's presidency without also considering the important contributions of Robert Bruce Stewart, the brilliant college business officer who is credited with developing many standard business and financial practices for the nation's colleges and universities; David E. Ross, a bachelor, the enthusiastic inventor-industrialist-philanthropist who, as an alumnus and member of the board of trustees, made generous contributions to the university over the years totalling more than $2.5 million; Agriculture Dean John Harrison Skinner, the outspoken defender of agriculture at Purdue; and Engineering Dean Andrey A. Potter, the Lithuanian-born MIT graduate who had come to Purdue in 1921 to succeed Charles H. Benjamin and who quickly earned the respect of students, faculty, and nearly everyone he ever met—not only for his sagacity as an engineer, teacher, and administrator, but for his high sense of duty and moral integrity.

This remarkable coterie of five steamed undaunted into the battles against ignorance, Elliott, the flagship, always on the front line. His educational leadership finely honed, Elliott was flanked usually by Ross with his largess and Stewart with his financial genius. The Elliott-Ross-Stewart team was one of the most noteworthy, perhaps phenomenal, combinations of administrators in higher education. Certainly, their impact on the direction Purdue travelled in the 1920s and 1930s is indelible.

●　　●　　●

By its forty-eighth year (that is, since its first classes in 1874) Purdue had, from almost every perspective, burgeoned. Where once it was considered a forlorn little group of homely red-brick buildings on the fringe of the prairie—the personal folly of John Purdue that would last but a few years—the university had in less than fifty years become a major force in American higher education. It was prestigious as an engineering and agricultural school, its enrollment risen from the first 39 enrollees, most of them not really qualified for college-level work, to more than 3,000, and from a faculty of 6 to more than 300.

The Purdue University that Elliott was introduced to in 1922 looked like this:

School of Agriculture—464 undergraduates, 24 graduate students, 55 staff.
Departments of Agricultural Engineering, Agronomy, Animal Husbandry, Dairy Husbandry, Entomology, Farm Management and Rural Economics, Forestry, Horticulture, and Poultry. The dean of the school was also the director of the Agricultural Experiment

Station and the Department of Agricultural Extension. The school offered degrees in agriculture and forestry.

Schools of Engineering

School of Chemical Engineering—183 undergraduates, 1 graduate student, 2 staff.

School of Civil Engineering—417 undergraduates, 10 graduate students, 16 staff.

School of Electrical Engineering—520 undergraduates, 14 graduate students, 17 staff.

School of Mechanical Engineering—603 undergraduates, 16 graduate students, 25 staff.

Department of Applied Mechanics—all engineering undergraduates, 7 staff.

Department of Practical Mechanics—all engineering undergraduates, 29 staff.

School of Home Economics—When Elliott arrived, home economics was a department of the School of Science and was designated a school in 1925–26. Even so, the department had a faculty of eleven with graduate and undergraduate enrollments included as a part of the School of Science. The first bachelor of science in home economics degree was offered in 1927. Still, the school offered options in clothing and textiles, applied design, foods and nutrition, and home administration.

School of Pharmacy—75 two-year undergraduates, 24 four-year undergraduates, 5 staff.

Departments of Materia Medica, Pharmaceutical Chemistry, and Pharmacy.

School of Science—567 undergraduates, 32 graduate students, 137 staff.

Departments of Biology, Chemistry, Education, English, History and Economics, Mathematics, Modern Languages, and Physics.

During Elliott's first decade, departments of Physical Education for Men and Physical Education for Women were established, the former in 1929–30, the latter in 1925–26.

The summer session, a victim of World War I, was revived at Purdue in 1920–21. In the summer of 1920, Purdue enrolled 40 students, but by 1923, that number had increased to 345, a figure more than doubled by 1932 at the end of Elliott's first ten years as president.

The Purdue of Elliott's first year had other "looks." Overall, Purdue had 3,232 students—2,745 men and 487 women—including 76 graduate students. A faculty of 302 taught nearly 600 courses. The main campus was considered to have thirty-one buildings—seventeen of them acquired since 1913 in the Stone administration. Of those seventeen new buildings, thirteen had been acquired for agriculture, either housing for livestock or farm buildings of one kind or another on surrounding university farms.

Only two buildings of the seventeen newest had been built for resident instruction in that 1913–21 period, Stanley Coulter Hall in 1917 and the Armory in 1918. Two other buildings were under construction in 1922 when Elliott arrived: the Home Economics building (now Matthews Hall) and the Recitation Building. In 1923, Elliott's first year, total value of all the buildings, including the two under construction, was $2,407,117.15.

The central campus covered 744 acres, including nearby farms of the School of Agriculture but not including Agricultural Experiment Station lands throughout the county and state, which totalled 2,040 acres on nine experimental farms.

Of the 302 faculty members, 142 held advanced degrees— either Ph.D. or master's degrees in various disciplines. About one-third of the faculty had done their undergraduate work at Purdue.

That was academic Purdue as Elliott found it in 1922. But in a ten-year report he drafted in 1932 for the board of trustees, he described (in part) the physical campus he actually saw when he arrived:

The campus of Purdue University was then as now covered with a great variety of beautiful trees. During these ten years the beauty that nature carefully guided has changed but little; the man-made structures, however, have undergone a veritable metamorphosis. The grounds were crossed in a few places by inadequate concrete walks, the drives were pitted ways of gravel. The course of the supposedly underground steam lines was clearly traced by strips of vivid green in summer and of thawed snow in winter; in some places indeed the joints of the tiles were visible above ground like the vertebrae of some great monster.

Near the southwest corner of the campus stood a quaint dormitory for women built in 1874. Here some few of the nearly four hundred women students slept and ate in draughty and unattractive surroundings. Just west of Ladies Hall, as the dormitory was called, the Home Economics Building was being erected. It was occupied first in the fall of 1923. Until that time all instruction in home economics had been given in Ladies Hall and the Science Annex, a small brick cube directly north of the dormitory. North of the Home Economics Building stood, and still stands, a small brick building also erected in 1874. In that small building all the instruction in pharmacy was given. North of that again were the Chemistry Building, the Memorial Gymnasium, and the Armory, the last of which was the only one rightfully called modern, for the years of building were 1907, 1908, and 1918. Immediately east of the Armory was Stuart Field, on which all athletic contests were held, the spectators, generally what would now be called a mere handful, seated on precarious wooden bleachers. Running before these buildings and curving east in front of the Gymnasium was a service railroad track up which puffed apparently numberless and irresponsible locomotives. The track is still there, but the trains run only in hours when no instruction is being given.

Within the curve of the track stood, and still stands, Purdue Hall, one of the oldest buildings on the campus, built in 1873, the Physics Building, dating from 1904, and Stanley Coulter Hall, the only modern building on the north campus given up to the classroom work of the University. It had been built in 1917. Some way south of Purdue Hall stood University Hall as it stands today.

Before University Hall was the chief beauty and the center of the campus—the great oval around which swept a magnificent cedar hedge, in these latter years becoming a little frayed and withered. On the oval, beside the memorial fountain and the grave of Purdue's generous benefactor, John Purdue, were two stands of pine trees, the removal of which because of disease has impaired the beauty of this part of the campus.

The half of the campus east of the main drive contained all the buildings standing today except the Memorial Union Building in the southeast corner and the new Chemistry Building between Heavilon Hall and what was then called the Electrical Engineering Building. The Civil Engineering Building stood as it now stands save for a wing built in 1927 which furnishes the most beautiful facade on the campus.

To speak of this part as the east half of the campus is justifiable, for in 1922 the northeast quarter of the campus was unworthy to be considered part of it. The main drive ran from the memorial gate given by the class of 1897 to peter out in a jumble of old lumber, bricks, and other debris dumped helter-skelter north of the power plant to form a no-man's land impassable after dark.

Such was the general lay-out of the north campus in 1922. The south campus with the agricultural buildings looked, from State Street, much as it does today, for the buildings since erected on that part of the campus have been placed so far back toward the south as scarcely to show from the street.

What was the condition of these buildings, what facilities and comforts were there for the teachers and the students?

When the decade began, the Departments of Education and of History and Economics were both housed in University Hall. For offices they occupied four cubicles partitioned off at the ends of the main halls. Three of the classrooms in the buildings were great barnlike rooms across the middle of the building. Through these rooms ran a number of steel pillars, originally the supports of the balcony of the first auditorium that in early years occupied a well in the center. These posts were the joy of the students, for behind them they might slumber with little chance of awakening by the instructor. One of these rooms in the basement was floored with creaking and gaping boards, through the holes in which rats would stick inquisitive heads, to flee hurriedly at the thunder of an inspired teacher.

Purdue Hall, a four-story rectangular building, contained the offices of the Departments of Mathematics and of Modern Languages, and, according to the catalog of the year, "other departments." In the basement of Stanley Coulter Hall a classroom had been cleared and partitioned as an office for the Department of English. The classes in English were held in rooms likewise in the basement next to the rooms in which were kept animals for experimental work in biology. And the young instructor was frequently embarrassed by the insinuating laughter of his students when a derisive "baa-a-a" echoed him from an adjoining room.

The only place on the campus where meetings of students could be held was an attic room under the eaves of University Hall. Two steeply spiral stairways led to it, like ladders to a loft.

The engineering departments were more adequately cared for; but the work of the School of Chemical Engineering was scattered among different buildings, and severely handicapped thereby. Each of the other three Schools of Engineering occupied its own building. The School of Electrical Engineering was in the Electrical Engineering Building since turned into the Engineering Administration Building. The School of Mechanical Engineering occupied Heavilon Hall with its imposing tower, and the School of Civil Engineering, its building without the newer wing. Back of Heavilon Hall facing Northwestern Avenue, across the main east and west drive of the campus, were the Michael Golden Shops, just as they are today.

West of the shops and east of the wilderness of debris about the power plant were eight or ten tennis courts where now are the cooling pool and the coal pit. North of the courts was a waste of playing fields with occasional pools in deep hollows after a rain and always soggy in wet weather. A trip across this part of the campus after dark was an adventure to be prepared for with heavy shoes and a flashlight. There was no walk nor gate— entrance to the campus was gained by a scramble over the fence.

Such briefly was the appearance of the campus in the fall of 1922. Changes were to come rapidly, perhaps one of the best of which was the planting of shrubbery at the bases of the buildings that then rose starkly from the ground. The great gap in the southeast corner of the campus was soon to be graced by the Purdue Memorial Union building. The wilderness by the power plant was quickly to be cleaned up and turned into a beautiful mall. The partly exposed steamlines were to be replaced by underground tunnels allowing for more economical operation and furnishing additional walks by their concrete tops. New buildings were to spring up until all departments are housed in offices and classrooms fit for modern instruction.

In those days but an occasional automobile braved the roughness of the campus roads; only a handful of the faculty had cars, and there was no thought even of the problem soon to be created by student automobiles.

The smallness of the numbers of both students and faculty made for a certain informal friendliness impossible for thousands. During commencement week a picnic was held on the oval attended by most of the faculty and visiting alumni. Every year also a faculty picnic was held on the Battlefield of Tippecanoe or at Tecumseh's Trail. Frequently during the year meetings of the University Club were held in Agricultural Hall, Eliza Fowler Hall, or the Armory, at which most of the three hundred or so members of the staff could mingle informally in a way impossible with nearly six hundred.

But to counterbalance an almost sentimental reminiscence one must recall the handicap to a comfortable life for the students. There were no dormitories for men, and every student not a member of a fraternity was forced to find a room in a private home and to eat in one of the two restaurants in "the village." And the housing problem was serious. During the war years, but three buildings had been erected in West Lafayette, and until 1922 there had been little gain. For years after the war a married instructor coming to Purdue had a difficult time finding any place fit for his family to live in. There were no apartments and no houses for rent. Three or four modern rooms in a private home were a luxury.

These physical discomforts, of course, had no bearing on the effectiveness of the university's work save as they caused discontent among the staff and persuaded many to seek positions elsewhere. And the extent to which this operated is shown perhaps by the fact that in 1922 thirteen percent of the staff resigned, whereas in 1931 only nine percent did so.

This then is a sketch of Purdue as it would have appeared in 1922 to a casual visitor who had no way of estimating the spirit and purpose and outlook of the University.

•   •   •

While Elliott limited his public speaking engagements in his first year as Purdue president, he did make a speech to the Purdue Alumni Club of Indianapolis within the week after he officially began his presidency. In it he discussed some of his own philosophy of university administration, pledged to serve the people of Indiana, and disclosed his personal concerns about the physical welfare of students and the athletic program.

He also stole a page from his own inaugural speech at Montana, a theme outlining his presidential responsibilities which he used repeatedly in later speeches before various groups. He came to call this his "personal charter," and later, though he had created it at Montana, he called it his "Purdue Philosophy." It appeared in print many times, though with slight changes:

As president of Purdue I will not consider that I have met my responsibilities until the leadership and the citizenship of the state of Indiana, of whatever class or occupation, continue to recognize that this university is their university; that Purdue University is an integral part of the public school system of the State ever working in its own distinctive and assigned fields; that Purdue is a worthy agency, ever at their disposal for aiding them to meet the needs that determine the happiness, the satisfaction, and the ideals of their lives; until there is firmly established among students and teachers and alumni the enduring principle that the daily work of men makes education possible and pleasurable.

Although he may have wished to spend his first year merely getting acquainted with Purdue, Elliott found himself in an extremely busy period in the university's history. At the same banquet in which he spelled out his "Purdue Philosophy," Trustee Henry Marshall, the man who had served as acting president after Stone's death, announced that David E. Ross, '93, and George Ade, '87—the inventor-industrialist and the playwright-author respectively—had made a gift of sixty-five acres of farmland northwest of the campus for an athletic field and playground for students. The topography, Marshall noted, was ideal for construction of a new stadium with room also for baseball and football fields, tennis courts, and possibly a golf course. Elliott, of course, was delighted.

Elliott, though incredibly busy with the myriad appearances he was expected to make, found time to show up at a pep rally the night before Purdue's football game with James Milliken College on Saturday, October 7. Sleeves rolled up, Elliott talked about the future of Purdue athletics and urged students to get behind the team. "Our future in athletics is tied up in tomorrow's game and we will not be disappointed." The next day, Purdue won, 10 to 0, the team's only victory in a season of seven games.

Less than two years before Elliott arrived, Ross had in mind to buy the old and somewhat neglected Tilt dairy farm, north of the campus, on which to build a new stadium.

One day, Ross showed the site to Walter Scholer, then a young Lafayette architect, a partner in the Lafayette firm of Nicol, Scholer and Hoffman. He asked Scholer to make a sketch showing how the proposed new stadium would look in juxtaposition to the rest of the campus. At the time, the northernmost building was Stanley Coulter Hall; nearly a half mile of cornfields lay between the academic campus and the proposed stadium area.

"I asked Dave what I should show in between the main campus and the stadium and he said, 'Well, just show some buildings. Simple,'" Scholer recalled in interviews before his death in 1972. "It bothered me more than it did him. In about a week I had a little thumbnail sketch of what the buildings might look like as far north as Stadium Avenue [then known as Seventh Street and later as Thornell Avenue]." Ross wanted the sketch to show alumni that Purdue was moving ahead and thinking of the future.

"But in doing it," Scholer said, "I hit on a scheme which Dave got very much interested in and so did I. We worked together that summer and both he and I forgot about the pen-and-ink sketch that he wanted." In March 1922, the trustees authorized its building committee to "submit a comprehensive plan of the grounds, as to driveways, buildings, shrubbery, and pipes" (i.e., underground utility conduits).

The trustees also set in motion other related campus surveys—mostly conducted by faculty committees—as to heating requirements and buildings and grounds. Until the 1920s, even as Purdue neared its fiftieth year, no one had bothered to record on a plat or map the exact positions and dimensions of campus buildings. The entire activity culminated in one of Elliott's earliest official acts as president in October 1922, when he presented the needs for a future development plan for the campus and buildings. The key word was "future"; the other surveys were comprehensive studies of the campus as it existed in 1922.

A month later the board accepted a tentative proposal from Scholer's firm for the master development plan which was to provide details for the future campus—the agricultural complex, the main campus north of State Street, and the proposed Ross-Ade "recreational grounds" which had been announced a month earlier at the same Indianapolis alumni meeting where Elliott made his debut as Purdue president. Ultimately, in April 1924, the trustees approved the Scholer plan, and it was followed in a general way until 1985 when the university adopted a revised master plan.

Elliott's arrival was simultaneous with the arrival of the technical marvel of wireless telephony—radio—and electrical engineering seniors at Purdue were mainly responsible for its enthusiastic pursuit. Purdue had pioneered in the field before the turn of the century in the work of Reginald Aubrey Fessenden, who is believed to have done some of the preliminary research which led to his breakthrough in the year (1892–93) he was on the Purdue faculty.

The first transmitting and receiving radio set at Purdue was built by Professors Raymond V. Schatz and David L. Curtner for the training of soldier operators at Purdue in World War I. Out on Stuart Field, the soldiers went back and forth between the transmitter and receiver to learn that the human voice could be transmitted without the benefit of wires. Curtner, one of Purdue's old reliables, came to Purdue from Gibson County, Indiana, as a freshman in 1907 and retired as a professor of electrical design in 1957. The first day that Schatz and Curtner's home-built radio was in operation, Curtner sang "K-K-K-Katy, Beautiful Katie," a popular World War I song, into the microphone all afternoon— the first radio transmission at the university.

The early work of students with "ham" radios, together with that of Schatz, Curtner, and others, led to the building of Indiana's first radio station, WBAA, licensed April 4, 1922. Its first broadcast was at 9 P.M., April 21 of that year—a program dealing with Arbor Day. The head of electrical engineering, Professor C. Francis Harding, encouraged the development of the station as a technical laboratory; Thomas R. Johnston, the university's public information officer, saw it as a new and wonderful medium for increasing the university's public exposure and providing a useful public relations tool.

The station was first located on the third floor of the old Electrical Engineering Building but was moved to the top floor of the new Electrical Engineering Building in the late 1920s. Its antennae towers atop the building on Northwestern Avenue were familiar landmarks until removed in 1984. They had not been in use since the station was moved in 1940 to new studios in the Hall of Music and a new transmitter was constructed southeast of Lafayette.

Another urgent project for Elliott soon after he arrived was the employment of William T. Middlebrook, a Dartmouth graduate who was with the Chicago industrial engineering firm of Griffenhagen and Associates. Elliott arrived from Montana unaware that his predecessor, Stone, had personally authorized every invoice and every payment from university funds. Middlebrook thus began as the university's controller, an office in which Elliott decided to center all university financial operations except those of the Agricultural Experiment Station and Extension Service. Until Middlebrook arrived, the only business office the university had consisted of a bookkeeper-secretary, Edward Augustus Ellsworth, whose title was bursar.

Once on the scene, Middlebrook learned that the university's funds were in more than 125 separate bank accounts. He immediately established a double-entry bookkeeping system as well as a requisition method that involved his signing every check, but only after it had been checked against his system of approved invoices and requisitions.

Not only had President Stone done much of the bookkeeping and business processing himself, he also carried the keys to every lock on the campus. But Purdue grew, and Elliott had no intention of delving into the day-to-day mundane office details—hence, the need for a university business system under a controller.

Middlebrook resigned after three years and in 1925 accepted the position as the chief financial officer at the University of Minnesota. That set the stage for the entrance onto the Purdue scene of R. B. Stewart, one of Purdue's most influential university administrators and perhaps one of the most important college business personages in America. At the time, young Stewart was business officer at Albion College in Michigan.

Stewart and his wife, Lillian, came to Purdue for an interview at Elliott's invitation. They drove their secondhand Marmon from Albion, hampered along the way by four blown-out tires and a discouraging conversation with a chap in Logansport who did not know where West Lafayette was.

Elliott offered Stewart the job, telling him that he was one of three candidates. "You're the youngest of the three and I can work better with you than if I take those old fellows who will tell me what I should do. I want to make sure that we get things built the way I want them." Stewart agreed, and the trustees on October 14, 1925, confirmed Stewart's appointment as controller effective November 10, at an annual salary of $4,500, about $500 more than he was paid at Albion. Stewart's arrival heralded the beginnings of a solid business organization that included a new system of budgeting, central purchasing, a continuing inventory of university property, and many other fiscal controls to ensure the university's accountability for public funds.

•   •   •

Elliott had been the president only a matter of months when on November 25, 1922, he laid the cornerstone of the new Purdue Memorial Union building during homecoming weekend. The union materialized from a popular subscription campaign among alumni to memorialize Purdue's World War I veterans, especially the sixty-seven Purdue sons who died in the war.

The union began as an undergraduate project of George O. Hays of the class of 1912, who had proposed an assessment of five dollars on each senior henceforth to begin a fund. The project became a campaign following the war for a memorial to Purdue men in the service and in 1920 produced more than $500,000 from alumni and friends. Still, it was not enough to complete construction, and the legal ownership of the facility was transferred to the board of trustees which was enabled, under a new statute, to issue self-liquidating revenue bonds to finance its completion.

In his cornerstone speech, Elliott once again displayed his oratorical flair:

> The Purdue Union embodies more than any other agency, of the present or the future, the inner moving spirit of the University. Here, in this building to be, life will be lived, enriched and humanized by enduring and understanding friendships. This stone, placed in this building today, is at once a symbol of our faith in yesterday, a mark of our might of today, an unfailing sign to the men of tomorrow of duty ever unfulfilled.

• • •

With characteristic Elliott style and energy, the new president quickly involved himself in wide-ranging projects. Two months after the cornerstone laying, Elliott proposed to the trustees that each Purdue staff member be required to submit to the administration a service report form designed to give Elliott and his staff a review of each staff member's performance. He was also busy with travels throughout the Midwest and East to get acquainted with alumni groups and to learn how they felt about the university.

When Elliott arrived, the university was already preparing to celebrate its fiftieth year in 1924—fifty years, that is, since the university doors opened in September 1874. Even before Elliott moved into his Fowler Hall office, a fiftieth anniversary committee of the faculty and trustees had been formed. Elliott quickly involved himself in the planning and was the committee's ex-officio chairman. His influence on the format and general tone of the semicentennial events was obvious: most of the speakers were university or college presidents who were also Elliott's friends and colleagues.

The semicentennial observance was also the occasion of Elliott's most important speech of the year—perhaps in his career—and seemed to take the place of the inaugural address he had eschewed earlier. More importantly, the address reflected Elliott's vision for Purdue. Surely, if 1924 marked a chronological milestone in Purdue history, Elliott's speech on May 3, 1924, must rank as an oratorical one. Delivered from a platform in the Memorial Gymnasium to a crowd mostly of students and faculty, the speech was entitled "Pursuit of Power." The Elliott style was classic. In one passage, he referred to higher education as "the process of the initiation of each generation of youth into the holy order of men."

Yet, Elliott's forecast of the university for 1974 was reminiscent of John Purdue's prediction in the first commencement of 1875 that Purdue would someday become "the most useful high school in Indiana." Said Elliott, "Unless the State of Indiana should repeal its present written and unwritten charters of opportunity for its youth, it is my mature judgment that we must be prepared to care for at least one thousand additional students every five years. This means a slow and gradual increase in the student population. Nevertheless, it means a student body of from twelve to fifteen thousand by 1974."

Elliott could not then, of course, predict the epochal social upheaval of the next five decades which brought about a 1974 enrollment at the West Lafayette campus alone of more than 27,000—though such growth surely would have pleased him.

Elliott began his "Pursuit of Power" address with the oratorical flair that became his trademark over the next twenty-three years as Purdue's president, "Thus we near the end of our triumph for the years that are gone and for the work that has been done. Thus we stand before the tasks of the years to come. The things that are old have been acclaimed. We now consecrate ourselves to the things that will be new." He continued in (part):

> This festival of the years will be merely a vainglorious ceremony unless, with serious resolution, we rededicate Purdue University to the causes of human welfare and progress, unless, with a new hopefulness, we re-enlist ourselves in a crusade for education, ever energized by new wisdom.
>
> The university must always acknowledge its undiminished, nay, its increasing, indebtedness to John Purdue and to his devoted associates during the early struggling years; to that legion of our citizenship who, in private capacity and in public offices, valiantly espoused and defended the University.
>
> This institution owes its life to the belief that labor and learning, intelligence and industry, are inseparable in any form of society where men count themselves free. With the founding of that group of American institutions, of which Purdue University is but a single representative, the potentiality of all education was immeasurably increased for free men and their descendants whose destiny is work.

When forecasting the future, there are certain things that may be taken for granted. The university will continue to grow in numbers and to expand its physical bulk. Unless the State of Indiana should repeal its present written and unwritten charters of opportunity for its youth, it is my mature judgment that we must be prepared for at least one thousand additional students every five years. This means a slow and gradual increase in the student population. Nevertheless, it means a student body of from twelve to fifteen thousand by 1974.

To teach effectively the increasing numbers will mean the doubling, the trebling, and even the quadrupling of the present laboratories, libraries, and shops.

The number of students or the number of buildings, the needed equipment or enlarged funds, are not of essential concern. Of far more consequence is the quality of the performance of the university. On the qualitative and not the quantitative basis must be constructed the formula for the safe guidance through to the future.

The effectiveness with which the foundations are laid in the [high] schools will determine the degree to which Purdue University is able to maintain its present leadership among the higher technical universities of the world.

This is a day of great dreams, but it must also be a day of great deeds. This university was born of the conception that labor was to be made the beneficiary of knowledge. The spirit and the strength which are to be ours and theirs who come to take our places will be dedicated with skill and unstinted devotion to the making of a world that dignifies all of those who work that men may live.

If this institution believes in any one thing above all others, it is in you. We know how much you annoy us at times—sometimes we are weak enough to show how much we are annoyed. Sometimes we scold you, and sometimes we do things even more satisfactory to us than scolding. If you want to do something for me, if you want to do something for the university—and I take it I am speaking to the student body this morning more than to the loyal alumni who have come back, more than to those generous friends who have come from afar to share in our triumph—if you students want to do something, not for me personally but for me representing the institution, will you remember this morning that I give the word of Purdue University for our never-ending faith in the fineness and strength and idealism of you who come every year to renew our strength and enlarge our souls. There is nothing about the university that makes it worthwhile for me and for those whom I represent, for the citizens of the state, to make an effort to provide through this institution great opportunities, unless we have at the same time an abiding faith that the salvation of the world rests upon the new vitality that comes to it every day from this new youth. The university lays the foundation of its future on only one thing, the new youth, and the new truth which is unfolded for us every day.

Elliott's semicentennial address revealed quite clearly that he had examined carefully and critically what he considered Purdue's problems—internal and not external problems, he stressed. Yet, he felt that Purdue had an inescapable obligation to the Indiana public elementary and high schools which produced the students whose preparation therein had profound influence on the academic standards of the university.

Elliott cited ten problems which he felt must be addressed immediately. Certainly, the most important of these, he said, was obtaining the financial support commensurate with the rapidly growing university. And upon the degree of success in solving the financial problems, of course, rested the fate of other problems.

These included adequate living accommodations for the student body. He hoped that the university would be able to provide housing facilities under its own control, and he often noted what he called social and educational "problems" centered in the fraternities. Later, he wrote that he felt the Greek system generally was a "genuine educational asset." The other "problems" involved student social life—to be improved in part, he hoped, by the new Purdue Memorial Union; the need for a more comprehensive physical education program; and the development of ways to provide academically for the individual differences of students.

Elliott also hoped for better coordination of instruction, research, and extension, and a reorganization of the faculty that could bring that about and minimize the administrative chores of professors. He wanted better class scheduling and thus, more efficient use of buildings and facilities, and more systematic supervision of instruction.

Elliott also sought to bring about closer ties with the alumni body of the university to help advance the interests of the university. It was a crucial matter and one of the reasons that he spent what might have seemed an inordinate amount of time travelling throughout the Midwest and East, and eventually the West, to state the Purdue case before alumni groups.

The alumni association was founded in 1912, and G. A. Ross came on the scene as its first full-time executive secretary in 1919. The association itself was only ten years old—and as an active, day-to-day operation under Ross, less than three—when Elliott came to Purdue. His interest in cultivating Purdue alumni in his many trips had a salutary effect on the association which prospered under Elliott more than under any previous president.

Ross left the job in 1924 and was succeeded by Harry G. Leslie, the Purdue football player who was team captain in 1903, the year of the tragic train wreck near Indianapolis which killed seventeen. He himself had been severely injured. Leslie served until 1928 when he ran for governor and was elected. He was succeeded by O. W. Booher who served as association executive director until 1935 when he was replaced by the Ethridge B. Baugh. Baugh served until 1953 when he stepped aside to become the association's director of public relations, and R. J. Rudolph was appointed to the post.

But above all of his other presidential chores, Elliott first pushed to improve academic life for students, based upon his belief in the doctrine of individual differences. The problems of no two students are alike, Elliott stressed. "And that," he wrote in his decennial report in 1932, "is the chief lesson that educational institutions are learning today, a lesson that has vastly increased their difficulties and overthrown their complacency." The university was pledged by the trust imposed in it by the state and its citizens not only to provide students with the competencies of certain chosen professions but also to help fit them to be citizens with sound knowledge, broad culture, good health, and upright character.

Universities had begun to understand the significance of the phrase, "the democratization of education." Thus, they also began to understand the implication of another phrase which was, in a way, a sort of slogan on which Elliott based the changes in the academic profile of Purdue, "the individualization of teaching." To Elliott it meant that every student is entitled to have the educational method matched to his needs "so far as that is possible with thousands streaming through the gate."

The limiting factors to achieving Elliott's ideal were the rapidly increasing numbers of students (every graduate of a commissioned Indiana high school was a potential Purdue student), the limitations on the number of instructors the university could employ plus the limited number of students each instructor could expect to teach at one time, and finally what Elliott described as "the hopelessness, perhaps, of ever fully discovering the individuality of each student."

When Elliott arrived, an antiquated academic rule was still in force: students failing to make a passing grade in twelve hours of classroom work in any one semester were dismissed from the university, unless they failed in only one subject. The rule was inflexible, failing to take into account that many detrimental events that can detract from a student's performance—sickness, financial problems, social worries, and so on. It also failed to take advantage of the benefit to students that might come from warnings. "Being inflexible," Elliott wrote of the old rule, "it considered the students as identical and official mercy was required to offset its inflexibility."

At the beginning of the academic year 1923–24, the university put into effect a new rule designed to cure some of the ills of the old rule: students who did not pass twelve hours of work were warned by being put on probation for the next two semesters for which they were registered—that is, they had to overcome their first failure by passing twelve hours. Failure to pass twelve hours in either of the two semesters meant dismissal from the university.

The plan's detractors believed that the new rule would result in a lowering of academic standards; actually many instructors were hesitant to apply the old rule, because of its inflexibility, and pushed many students over the pass/no-pass line. Under the new system, they were less hesitant to fail students who had been given a second chance, and the academic standards were not only maintained but raised.

The new rule committed the university to a different point of view about students and their learning abilities. The results eventually showed that nearly eighty-five percent of Purdue students who failed were either freshmen or sophomores—a signal to Elliott and his staff that if students survived the first two years, the chances of their success in the junior and senior years, although the subject matter was more difficult, were vastly improved. That meant to Elliott and his staff that something had to be done to help students in the first two years—especially the freshman year.

Their study became the impetus for the establishment of the Purdue orientation program for new students in September 1926, to help freshmen overcome the difficulties inherent in their first year and, for many, their first year away from home. A part of the program was a series of nine placement tests to help the university determine individual proficiency of the new students in mathematics, English, chemistry, and general intelligence. Students were then assigned to courses according to their abilities.

Since the first year, many changes in the program and testing have been made, of course. But the program has continued since and undoubtedly has been of great benefit to the college success of thousands upon thousands of Purdue students. Whatever changes are made, or however it is revised, new student orientation at Purdue will always have the Elliott imprint.

Though the first ten years of his administration brought about rather fundamental academic changes, Elliott believed that Purdue's obligation to students extended to creating an appetite in them for good scholarship.

Sometimes it may have appeared, Elliott once wrote, "that the university considers . . . each student . . . as a Strassburg goose with open bill stretched to receive pellets of learning, that all the university need do is to gauge the diameter of each gullet and the capacity of each crop to guarantee a full store of wisdom." Elliott did several things to promote good scholarship; he even changed the grading system by instituting a new scholarship index system.

Elliott worked courageously to raise scholarship standards and expand course offerings. He also sought to raise the level of instruction and managed to earn the disparagement of some faculty by suggesting in the first six months of his presidency that some departments of the university were overstaffed, that some of the members of the instructional staff had inadequate assignments, and that the overhead costs of some departments were much too high.

He had also said that approvals of promotions in rank and increases in pay would go only to those who had demonstrated a high quality of work. He disturbed some faculty members who had overheard him say that any time a student fails in his work, "we should examine closely to discover whether the institution is not responsible."

Elliott brooked no insubordination nor any nonsense on the part of the faculty, staff, or students. There was little happening within the Purdue campus Elliott was not aware of, and many of the faculty considered him an abrasive taskmaster, dictatorial, if not downright sarcastic at times. He was known to have come perilously close to holding professors up to public ridicule during faculty meetings.

Generally, however, Elliott was liked by the faculty as a whole. Students believed he had their best interests at heart. He came to be dearly beloved by the alumni, in contrast to their feeling toward Stone, and the alumni association in 1929 gave him a new Packard to replace his rather dilapidated 1919 Hudson touring car. The people of Indiana also highly respected Elliott; with the possible exception of James Smart, Elliott had as high a grassroots profile in Indiana as any Purdue president before or since. In 1940, the Indiana Democratic leadership even attempted to persuade Elliott to become the Democratic nominee for governor, a proposal he immediately quashed by announcing he was not and never would be a candidate for any political office, followed by his remark that "I hope there will be no further effort to divert me from the educational things I know how to do, to the political things for which I am not adapted.''

Even after his retirement in 1945, there was another attempt, albeit shortlived, to get Elliott to seek the Democratic nomination for the United States Senate.

•   •   •

Elliott may have been unpopular with some faculty, but the record clearly reveals that Elliott fought battles on their behalf even when they seemed ignorant of any peril.

He recommended and secured approval from the board of trustees for sabbatical leave with pay and significant reduction in fees for dependents of faculty and staff, both achievements in the first year after he arrived. By 1926, he obtained for the faculty a retirement plan tied in with the Carnegie Foundation for the Advancement of Teaching, and in 1929 he instituted a plan for group life insurance to provide sizeable benefits to Purdue staff. Elliott also began the first program to honor faculty who had many years of service.

Elliott obtained most of these benefits from a trustee board with whom he had excellent rapport. The members were highly responsive to his leadership and to the ideas of board president David E. Ross, the alumnus and Lafayette inventor-industrialist.

Financial problems are ubiquitous in the lives of university presidents and universities. They were not different for Purdue, for Elliott, for Elliott's presidential predecessors, nor, for that matter, his successors. In 1921, the Indiana General Assembly had made provisions for a five-mill state tax to support Indiana higher education; Purdue's portion of that levy was two mills per one hundred dollars of taxable property. In 1923, Elliott seemed satisfied that the biennial appropriating body had done as well as it could possibly do for Purdue. The tax was continued through 1924. But the 1925 legislative session took upon itself one of the periodic and seemingly inevitable economic drives characteristic of so many legislative bodies.

In 1923, the legislature had, though revenues had been lower, approved funding for Purdue's new heating and power plant (the present North Power Plant), a necessity before planning other new campus facilities could proceed. Both Purdue and Indiana universities needed expanded campuses and agreed to present budgets to the state based upon a proposed doubling of the tax to ten mills. Even with a reduction in property valuations, the ten-mill tax would not have provided excessive funds to meet the two universities' proposal. Elliott had hoped the increased tax would have provided $2 million annually from that source.

Both universities were appalled when in 1925 the legislature not only turned down the ten-mill tax proposal but repealed the 1921 act which had established the five-mill tax, thus removing the guarantee the universities had enjoyed for four years.

Elliott expressed his disappointment but later concluded—when the legislature appropriated about what the university expected for operating funds and made special funds available for building construction—that the university's constituencies could be optimistic about Purdue's future. Still, Elliott felt a need to take the case for Indiana higher education—Purdue specifically—directly to the people. The case, he felt, was stronger than ever.

One of the profoundest statements Elliott ever made was, "Legislators may come and go, but Purdue is immortal."

Elliott admitted his early encounters with the Indiana General Assembly were a "discouraging experience" but philosophically allowed that "perhaps it's better that the people of Indiana feel that the university is receiving too little rather than too much." As Montana chancellor, Elliott had campaigned for the mill tax as one means of providing financial stability to higher education. He had found that to be the Indiana situation also when he arrived, only to see it abolished three years into his presidency.

By the end of his first decade in 1932, Elliott was able to list the developments he considered the most significant for Purdue. The ten-year report of university activity was published in a hardbound volume, *Purdue University, 1922–1932*, still a valued document from that decade.

Elliott cited as important:

1. The discontinuance of the two- and three-year courses in pharmacy under which students were awarded Graduate in Pharmacy degrees for completion, leaving only the undergraduate B.S. program as well as some graduate study.

2. The establishment of a degree course in physical education.

3. The adoption of a faculty report on the social and moral needs of students.

4. The organization of graduate study in the university into the Graduate School and the appointment of R. G. Dukes as its dean in 1929.

5. The expansion of the Department of Home Economics into the School of Home Economics in 1926 under Dean Mary L. Matthews.

6. The development of a Department of Research Relations with Industry and the establishment of the Purdue Research

Foundation in 1930 by Elliott and the board of trustees. David E. Ross and J. K. Lilly of Indianapolis were the first contributors.

7. The establishment of the Department of Educational Reference under Professor H. H. Remmers, Department of Education, and the establishment in 1925 of the post of university editor. (Professor R. W. Babcock, Department of English, was its first appointee and served until his retirement in 1950 when he was succeeded by William J. Whalen.)

8. The adoption of a long-range campus plan and the inauguration of the physical plant expansion program made possible by a state educational improvement fund established by the 1927 Indiana legislature.

9. The reorganization of administrative control of the Purdue Memorial Union which permitted refinancing and thus continuation of construction, its opening (though not entirely finished) in 1924, and its eventual dedication as a completed building in 1929.

10. A growth in the university library collections from 65,000 to 101,500 volumes, a 56 percent increase, and a growth in circulation from 81,070 to 123,273 annually.

Elliott's popularity continued to grow both inside and outside of the university community. The trustees in 1925 had voted to raise his $10,000 salary to $12,000—a figure Elliott had sought in the negotiations that preceded his appointment in 1922. In 1928, the trustees voted to raise Elliott's salary to $15,000, but he turned it down on the grounds the university's financial condition did not warrant it. A year later, however, the board raised his salary to $15,000 and presented it to him as an accomplished fact.

Elliott presented his first honorary degrees as Purdue president at the 1926 commencement. Three alumni were the recipients— George Ade and John Tinney McCutcheon were given honorary doctor of human letters degrees, and Clarence Hovey ''Big Robbie'' Robertson was awarded an honorary doctor of science degree.

Purdue has granted honorary degrees, although not every year, since 1888 when President Smart presented honorary doctor of science degrees to Alembert Winthrop Brayton and John Newell Hurty. Brayton is probably the only person who has ever been awarded a bachelor of science degree and an honorary doctor of science degree at the same commencement ceremony. Hurty was the Indianapolis druggist Smart brought to Purdue to found the School of Pharmacy.

•   •   •

The idea of affiliate organizations to help Purdue carry out its educational mission originated in the Ross-Ade Foundation, established in 1923 to serve as the receiving entity for the gift from David Ross and George Ade of the Tilt dairy farm, north of the campus and south of Cherry Lane, on which Ross-Ade Stadium and the recreational field were built.

The foundation, incorporated November 26, 1923, was termed by Elliott a "device to do things that Purdue University as a branch of state government could not do." Under the bylaws, Elliott was president of the foundation. Through the years, the "device" has served Purdue well as the receiver of gifts of land and money and as the holder of properties the university might need in later years for educational purposes.

Between its founding and 1932, the Ross-Ade Foundation received more than $109,000 in land gifts from both alumni and friends of the university. Most of the alumni gifts were from Ross himself, including the combined gift of $37,500 that he and George Ade paid for the farm on which Ross-Ade Stadium was built and dedicated in 1924. The gift was a part of an overall $237,500 Purdue alumni and friends contributed for the original 13,500-seat (and standing room for 5,000) athletic facility.

The stadium was perhaps Ross's most spectacular gift to Purdue; it is the one he (and Ade) are best known for. But Ross also gave many other important—and more expensive—gifts, among them, in 1926, the purchase of the land adjacent to his summer home, The Hills, twelve miles southwest of the campus for the Ross Civil Engineering Camp. In 1930, he bought and gave 122 acres of the Neville farm, two miles southwest of the central campus for the Purdue University Airport. The airport was the first anywhere owned by a university and put Purdue far ahead of any other educational institution in providing aeronautical engineering and aviation education. As a result, Purdue is still an aviation leader.

Ross made another major gift to the university in 1928 when he gave the newly founded Purdue Research Foundation 4,420 shares of his own firm, Ross Gear and Tool Company, in Lafayette. The stock was sold for $380,000, and the proceeds were invested in a 4 percent certificate of deposit. To Ross, the reason for the gift was simple: he had discovered that Purdue had no provision to supplement retirement funds for any faculty members. The income from the certificate of deposit was to be used for a retirement fund for certain faculty members—the president, deans of schools, and heads of departments.

Ross also gave his 420-acre Wea farm on South Ninth Street Road, south of Lafayette, to the newly founded Purdue Research

Foundation to make up the difference in value of some corporate stock he had given as his pledge to help start the new agency. Lesser sums he provided included half the price of a lot adjacent to the presidential manse on South Seventh Street and $2,700 to build a swimming pool at the Ross Civil Engineering Camp—a project undertaken by the students themselves.

Ross's involvement in the establishment of the research foundation may be, however, his most significant contribution to the university. Ross had been named to the board of trustees in 1921 and was elected its president in 1927. His interest and contributions to the university and his relationship with Elliott were legendary. After he retired in the mid-1920s as vice president and general manager of Ross Gear and Tool Company, Ross moved his office to a three-story building on Main Street in downtown Lafayette on the north side of the courthouse square. At least one part of his incentive for giving up his industrial life was to devote full time to Purdue University and its needs.

Elliott was known to stop almost every morning at the Ross Building on his daily walk from his Seventh Street home, and Ross often spent evenings with Elliott, trying out new ideas—always involving Purdue—on him.

Ross loved Purdue football, but he refused to find the winning or losing very important. If Purdue lost, he would say, "What of it? They tried hard, didn't they? It doesn't matter if we lose, so long as it wasn't from not trying." Interesting comment from a man who bankrolled the stadium, home ground of the football Boilermakers. At one game he became so absorbed in his own thoughts that he did not know who won. "I was trying," he later explained, "to figure out a better plan for highways to dispose of the automobile traffic quickly when the game is over."

Not many needs, large or small, escaped Ross's attention. Once when he learned of a student who needed surgery but who had no money for it (there was no emergency university fund to meet such needs), Ross immediately gave the university $7,500 in shares of his gear company to establish a special emergency fund "to meet exceptional student needs."

Ade's contributions to Purdue, detailed in the preceding chapter, were not as large as Ross's but were nevertheless as important. In a letter to J. Kirby Risk of Lafayette, Ade admitted he did not keep a very tidy account of his giving to Purdue:

> I have no accurate record of the amount we spent. It is not my desire to blow about the things I have done for Purdue because I derived a real pleasure from getting in on such large and worthy

enterprises. You must remember that Dave Ross and I are old bachelors. Every person who begins to grow old must adopt something. Old maids adopt cats and canaries. Dave Ross and I adopted Purdue. It is only fair to add that Dave has done much more for the university than I have done. The amount of work he has given to the school and the amount of money he has given, without many people knowing about it, entitle him to first place among the alumni and I want it distinctly understood that I am not presuming to put myself in his class as a Purdue benefactor.

The Purdue Research Foundation, with the Ross-Ade Foundation, permitted the university to make strides beyond anything it could expect to do alone.

Elliott became increasingly aware that the rapid growth of the engineering schools brought an increasing number of industrial executives to the campus and that they sought university help in finding answers to some of American industry's most pressing problems. As a consequence the trustees considered the possibility of a new department which would concern itself totally with the development of a continuing relationship between Purdue and industry.

Ross was particularly eager to help develop a plan for industrial research. In April 1926, he and Elliott were instrumental in organizing a national conference of industrial leaders at the West Lafayette campus. Held on June 1 of that year, it attracted industrial representatives from all over the country. They were guests of Ross. Elliott centered the conference discussions on a proposal to establish some sort of advisory body that would link the research laboratories with the problems of industry, most especially Indiana industry.

As a direct result of the conference, Ross, accompanied by Engineering Dean A. A. Potter, visited some of the nation's principal industrial research facilities to find out in what ways Purdue could best serve industries through research. Ross later made an elaborate report to the trustees, advising them that Purdue needed to place greater emphasis on the ways the university could help industries solve problems.

Later in 1927, Elliott presented to the trustees a proposal to create an all-university Department of Research Relations with Industry. The trustees approved Elliott's recommendation in October; Elliott not long afterward appointed G. Stanley Meikle as the first director of research relations. Meikle immediately began an extensive survey of Indiana industries to determine specifically in what ways Purdue could assist. Elliott, Ross, and Meikle eventually concluded that progressive industries were far more interested in the development by the university of creative thinkers capable of solving industrial problems than they were in simply asking the university to solve their problems for them.

The university soon discovered that many aspects of the development of fundamental research activity were beyond its legal pale. The many potential problems all pointed to a need for a separate corporation controlled by the university to prevent adding more financial obligations on the university.

The focal point then became what today is known as the Purdue Research Foundation (PRF), incorporated on December 30, 1930, by the members of the board of trustees and the president. The first two donors were trustees—David Ross and J. K. Lilly of the wealthy pharmaceutical manufacturing family. They each put up $25,000. It was a modest start but one which Ross said was "the best thing that could have happened for Purdue research."

It was also a modest beginning for the foundation which had anticipated prospective generous gifts from other sources. One was a wealthy inventor-industrialist (not Ross) who reportedly agreed to give the new agency an endowment fund between $5 million and $10 million, a small part of his fortune. About the time the gift was forthcoming, the philanthropist was hit by the 1929 financial panic and found himself to be penniless. Another man who had agreed to contribute $25,000 immediately after he returned from Florida never returned; he was taken ill on the way home and died.

Still, Ross was optimistic. "With so much money," he opined, "we'd have been busy planning great laboratories and not given enough thought to picking the right men to do research. Besides, starting in a modest way gives us a better chance for sane, healthy growth."

In 1932, Elliott was able to report that PRF in its first two years had already established more than fifty research projects, involving an equal number of professors and graduate students.

In essence, the new foundation permitted the university to enter into contractual obligations for industrial research—even research of a proprietary nature but which had clear educational objectives as well—with the foundation assuming the legal and financial obligations the university could not take on by reason of restricting statutes.

Ross, Elliott, and Stewart were extremely careful to structure the membership to avoid any possibility that PRF could become a political power base. A major membership category was that of "founder," those who gave $25,000 or more to the foundation.

Other categories included the university board of trustees and the president; ten men selected for their scientific and professional achievement; a fourth group of twenty-five to fifty eminent alumni; and a fifth group of research members, individuals who had made a contribution through some PRF project.

In a publication issued by PRF shortly after its founding, President Elliott in an introductory letter embraced the basic philosophy undergirding the foundation:

> The Purdue Research Foundation is something more than a legal device by which it is possible to undertake activities of fundamental importance, not now clearly within the province of the trustees of the university as defined by federal and state laws. It is something more than a means for focusing the interest of alumni and friends of the university upon a new opportunity for fruitful cooperation, thereby giving new realities to the unselfish strivings of scientific workers.
>
> The Purdue Research Foundation is, above all, concerned to be a creative agency both as to human opportunity and human truth. Within and without the University it should sharpen the senses to the manifold values to be obtained from continued, repeated, and skillful study of the phenomena of nature. By the creation of new knowledge, and the re-creation of old knowledge, the highest purpose of the university will be realized.

PRF more than any other agency has carried the university into the national and international research arenas and has helped Purdue earn its reputation as one of the world's top 100 research institutions.

•   •   •

In his ten-year report, Elliott spotlighted some of the basic changes that contributed to the university's enrollment growth and a general improvement in academics. The report also reflected the physical appearance and growth of the campus. In his first decade, Elliott oversaw the addition of twenty-four buildings, bringing the campus total to fifty-five (buildings, that is, valued at more than $5,000 each). Building projects in that decade also included substantial additions to the mechanical engineering laboratories and the Chemistry Building. The two dozen new facilities compared to seventeen buildings added in the decade prior to Elliott's arrival—thirteen of which were in agriculture.

The net worth of the university (in buildings, grounds, equipment, furniture, and the like) in 1922 was just a little more than $4.7 million; by 1932, that value had increased to more than $10.2 million.

The people Elliott relied on to provide the information for his ten-year report were the same members of the administration in whom he placed the greatest responsibility to carry out his vision for Purdue. In the 1922–32 decade, the major members were Carolyn Shoemaker, the first dean of women; Dean of Agriculture Skinner; Dean of Engineering Potter; and Dean of Men Martin L. Fisher. Fisher, a professor of crop production and farm management, had succeeded the venerable Stanley Coulter when he retired in 1926. Coulter was succeeded in his other job as dean of science by R. B. Moore, who died before the close of the decade. Moore's successor was H. E. Enders, a biologist, named as dean of the School of Science in 1932.

Other stalwarts on the Elliott team in the 1920s were C. B. Jordan, Elliott's appointment as dean of pharmacy in 1924; Mary L. Matthews, who became dean of home economics in 1926; R. G. Dukes, first dean of the newly organized Graduate School in 1929; G. I. Christie, director of the Agricultural Experiment Station; N. A. Kellogg, director of the Department of Athletics; University Librarian W. M. Hepburn; and Professor Robert W. Babcock, the Shakespearean scholar and ex-cowboy, whom Elliott selected as the first university editor.

Two others were making, or were about to make, their indelible marks on the university. The first was Paul Spotts Emrick, who came to Purdue as a freshman from his hometown of Rochester, Indiana, and except for one year after graduation, stayed fifty years to become probably the most innovative college bandsman in history. Emrick graduated in electrical engineering and was a member of the faculty of that school, though most of his attention was devoted to the Purdue University Band. Emrick came from a musical family; his father was an excellent hornplayer and led the Rochester City Band for several years.

At Purdue, Emrick not only developed America's premiere college band; he developed a reputation for toughness sprinkled liberally with some of the saltiest language then heard in West Lafayette. Nor at band practice did Emrick care much who heard him. One bandsman, apparently not playing up to Emrick's standard, took Emrick's blast full on, as Emrick loudly compared the sound the hornsman made with that of a dozen goats flatulating into a downspout.

The second person to make history was a brash young Lafayette voice instructor who in 1930 was asked by Dean of Women Shoemaker to direct the girls' choral group. Albert P. Stewart took on the job, developed the choral group, and eventually got up enough nerve one day to approach Elliott for money to start a university mixed choir. Elliott listened to Stewart's plea from his chair behind the imposing desk in his Fowler Hall office, then as Stewart finished, stood up, slapped the top of the desk with the flat of his hand, and shouted, "Never! Never, as long as I am president will this university ever spend one damn penny on music on this campus, young man! Get that through your head!"

Stewart went on to develop Purdue Musical Organizations, the centerpiece of which was the all-male Varsity Glee Club which brought fame to the university as well as to the music performed by an institution with no music school, and to Stewart himself.

The president who first declared that not "one damn penny" would ever be spent on music came to be, over the years, the No. 1 fan of Stewart's groups, with the ultimate irony that the Hall of Music, built and dedicated in 1940, was eventually named for Elliott.

•   •   •

At the end of his first decade as president, Elliott obviously was in control and enjoyed something few of his predecessors had when they were in office—the nearly unanimous support of all of Purdue's constituencies. Though he was not the unanimous favorite of the faculty, still, he had its respect. And he had excellent support from the student body, alumni, the statehouse politicians with whom he delighted in "mixing it up," and the citizenry in general.

He could relax long enough to watch his children's progress through school and to attend to family matters. His biographer, Frank K. Burrin, in *Edward C. Elliott, Educator,* tells of the Elliott children's delight in the many dinner table exchanges between their parents and their enchantment with their father's penchant for coining new words, as in the phrase he once invented, "her Elliottic mood."

"There's no such word, Ned," Mrs. Elliott would reply, using her nickname for the president. He would counter, "There is now, my dear."

As Elliott's popularity grew, so did his own knowledge of the faculty. He could greet nearly all of them by name, and for many, he had at least some familiarity with their personal backgrounds. In the early years, he made it a point to interview every applicant for a faculty or staff position. Invariably, he had breakfast with them and liked to say—more in jest than anything—that he would not hire anyone who did not eat a hearty breakfast. That particular bit of the Elliott legend was twisted in repeated tellings and eventually resulted in an erroneous story that he refused to hire anyone who ordered prunes for breakfast.

In his first ten years as president, Elliott had pushed the university forward with the same zeal displayed by President Smart and thus had become an irreplaceable part of the Purdue landscape. Elliott's second decade was a more difficult time. The university faced grave problems brought on almost entirely by the Great Depression, and while Elliott never backed away from any university problem, it became evident that he enjoyed the halcyon years of his first decade more than he did the next eight. Despite all the problems—mostly financial—Elliott experienced moments of great brilliance that punctuated the gray years of the depression period prior to 1940.

With rare exception, every problem Elliott faced in the mid-1930s was a financial one; none of them was easily solved. Worse, the bitterness still hung heavily from a 1930 controversy embroiling R. B. Stewart and the Purdue fraternities. Although not as damaging, the fight resembled the one involving President White and the Sigma Chi fraternity in the 1880s, which ultimately led to his resignation.

The Stewart-fraternity fight began in the trustees' concern that the fraternity system at Purdue was overdeveloped and that as new fraternities were built each seemed more luxurious than the last. Investigation of fraternity and sorority building programs and financial plans was carried on by a university committee which included Stewart and Elliott. The committee decided to require all fraternities and sororities to submit building and financial plans to the business office which had the authority to approve only those which were believed to be "sound." The Purdue Greek-letter people were incensed. Since Stewart's office had to enforce the new rule, Greek anger was focused on him. The fraternity-sorority group constituted a powerful bloc; some even felt they were untouchable. The Greeks also directed their anger at Stewart because he was instrumental in the construction of Cary Hall (East) which they felt challenged them in providing student housing.

The apparent mismanagement of intercollegiate athletic funds caused another headache for the Elliott administration in the early 1930s. The department, then headed by N. A. Kellogg, reported a $24,000 deficit at the end of the 1929 football season. Ironically, that season, under Coach James M. Phelan, Purdue fielded one of the best teams in its history and took the undisputed Big Ten championship, winning all eight games, four of them by shutouts. Nevertheless, the trustees ruled that the athletic budget had to be balanced, determined by actual football income. Yet, in the 1930 season, the department showed a $97,000 deficit.

Elliott, Stewart, and Ross became a committee to determine what the problem was and to supervise the department's finances. Stewart and Kellogg were asked to make independent estimates of athletic department expenses. Stewart estimated $19,000 less than Kellogg, and the committee imposed harsh austerity on the athletic program: all minor sports were dropped, Kellogg's proposal to make student ticket purchases compulsory was turned down, and his salary was cut from $5,100 to $3,600 for eleven rather than ten months. The Ross-Ade Foundation advanced the department operating funds and Elliott told Kellogg that if by the end of 1933 athletics was not self-supporting, he faced dismissal. Kellogg had been in bad health and resigned before the deadline. He was succeeded by the legendary head football coach Noble E. Kizer, an assistant to Phelan, who became head coach when Phelan left in 1930 to coach at the University of Washington.

The problems with sports and the fraternities and sororities were miniscule compared to the problems the administration faced because of the depression-caused shortfall in the state funds. The Indiana General Assembly in 1932 was called into special session to deal with money problems. The result was bad so far as Purdue was concerned. The legislature declared a three-year moratorium on the 1929 statute, which had established the special tax for a statewide educational improvement fund. The assembly also approved a 15 percent reduction in state appropriations to the university for operating expenditures and voted to divert interest earned on university funds to a state sinking fund, effectively reducing the number of dollars available to Purdue by 30 percent for 1932–33. That meant across-the-board budget cuts—and certainly no pay increases. On the contrary, Elliott and his staff had the distasteful job of finding ways to cut salaries and wages. Not only were there smaller appropriations, enrollment also began to take a drop—meaning lower income from fees and tuition. The number of students dropped by 600 in the fall of 1931, and the student population decreased by 1,000 students to 3,695 in the fall of 1932.

The year 1932 also was the beginning of a short-lived housing research program that was the promotion of Dave Ross. He bought the Marsteller dairy farm, west of the campus—now the site of Tower Acres and a part of the Purdue south golf course—and gave the land to Purdue. His original plan was to build homes for the faculty with each home's septic system in the front yard so that, Ross speculated, there would never be need to water or fertilize the lawns.

But what occurred was quite different. Ross backed the Purdue Housing Project (underwritten by Purdue Research Foundation) for six homes, all of different construction, each with three bedrooms, each costing $5,000. Ross wanted the houses occupied by members of the university's scientific staff who would continue the research, keep records, and report on all aspects of the buildings and their equipment. The project did not do what Purdue had hoped, and a New York-based corporation, Better Homes in America, moved to the university campus to continue the work. Contributions were slow in coming, and Ross eventually hired a housing researcher and architect, Carl Boester, to take over the project to test his ideas. The program was put on the shelf in 1940 because of the needs of defense research and was never taken down again—although Boester played a heroic role in the chaotic years after World War II in helping Purdue meet a dire housing shortage for faculty and staff.

Despite such diversions, the money problem continued, requiring Stewart to reach deep into his financial bag of tricks to meet at least the university's basic needs. Purdue squeezed a few extra dollars out of various trusts and fixed funds by following Stewart's suggestion to consolidate them for investment purposes and thereby obtain a higher interest rate. But even that was a minor quick-fix.

Though faculty and staff received no pay increases, they still had jobs that paid a steady income—more than great numbers of local people received. Elliott thus proposed a relief fund by which staff members making $350 per month or less would contribute 1 percent and those making more than $350, 2 percent. Collected by Stewart, the funds were then channeled into various Indiana relief agencies. Two checks, $1,000 each, were ultimately sent to Governor Harry G. Leslie for use by the American Red Cross, Salvation Army, and Central State Relief Committee. None of the faculty seemed to object to the gesture, although many were hard pressed to make ends meet themselves and faced the possibility of wage and salary cuts.

In October 1932, the board of trustees finally ordered all Purdue staff and faculty salaries reduced. Elliott was astute. He appointed a faculty committee to come up with proposals on how the salary and wage cuts should be made. The committee argued long and hard, and a young history instructor, Charles B. Murphy, proposed that cuts be from 5 to 35 percent from the low end of the salary range to those with the highest salaries. Immediate outcries arose from committee members on the high salary side.

"But," Murphy argued, "you have some money and those of us in the lower brackets don't have any. I talked to a fellow the other day who said they couldn't cut his salary. He didn't make that much." The upshot was, however, that the committee recommended exactly what Elliott and Stewart hoped it would: a graduated cut in all salaries from 10 to 15 percent, depending upon the amount a staff member received. Elliott himself took a $2,250 pay cut to $12,750 annually.

To cap his woes, Elliott's mother died in August 1932 at North Platte. Elliott later wrote, "Life is just one hard thing after another." It was prophetic. In 1933, the Indiana General Assembly reduced appropriations for Purdue another 6.6 percent, a total reduction from the 1931 appropriations of 21.5 percent because of the 14.9 percent cut by the 1932 special session. Elliott calculated the overall cut was 35.3 percent, including the abolishment of the educational improvement fund.

The sudden death in 1933 of the venerable Carolyn Shoemaker, the first dean of women, shocked the entire university community. Even as her friends and admirers mourned her passing, Elliott looked for her successor. He found her at a San Bernadino, California, high school. Dorothy C. Stratton, a Missourian, educated at Ottawa University, Ottawa, Kansas, was appointed on August 15, 1933. She obtained an M.A. degree at the University of Chicago and her Ph.D. at Columbia. She studied also at the University of Washington, Northwestern University, and the University of California.

Her first task as Purdue dean of women was to move her office from an out-of-the-way, second-floor location into the mainstream of things, something she finally accomplished through a procedure described to her by Elliott himself not long after she arrived: first you ask the president for something, and he says "no." Then you come back again and ask again—and he says "no" again. The third time you come back to ask, you pound on his desk, and he says, "Oh, go ahead and do it!"

Dean Stratton came to Purdue at a critical time, the Depression, and left Purdue on military leave, also at a critical time, World War II. She was named the first director of the women's reserve of the United States Coast Guard, the SPARS, an acronym she coined from the first letters of the Coast Guard motto, "Semper Paratus," plus its translation, "Always Ready." After the war, she was appointed the first director of personnel for the International Monetary Fund and later became national executive director of the Girl Scouts of the United States. She retired in 1960, then for six years she served as representative of the International Federation of University Women at the United Nations.

•　　　•　　　•

On September 12, 1936, a flashfire in the team locker and shower rooms resulted in the death of two star football players and serious burns to four others. The team was in training at Ross Civil Engineering Camp, twelve miles southwest of the campus. It was a normal custom in those years to use gasoline to remove adhesive tape marks from players' bodies after practice. Between fifteen and twenty players were taking showers when the floor drain somehow plugged. Gasoline from the players' bodies formed a thin film over the water which rose dangerously close to a nearby coal-fired hot-water heater. The gasoline film ignited and flashed across the shower-room floor. Some players escaped uninjured. Others were burned mostly about the feet and legs from the flames. But Carl Dahlbeck, a senior guard, Tom McGannon, a sophomore halfback, and Lowell Decker, a junior fullback-halfback, were the most seriously burned. Dahlbeck died the next day of kidney failure; McGannon died the following Thursday of internal bleeding. Decker eventually recovered. Others hospitalized included Paul Malaska, James Maloney, and John Drake, later to become an all-American fullback. The three were hospitalized only briefly with what turned out to be superficial burns.

It would have been easy for the Boilermakers to quit before the 1936 season. They did not. Purdue beat Ohio University, 47–0; took a measure of Wisconsin, 35–14; defeated the University of Chicago, 35–7; lost to Minnesota, 33–0; then went to Carnegie Tech in Pittsburgh and won, 7–6, for the Boilermakers' two-hundredth victory since 1889.

Elliott seemed to overcome the sadness of these tragedies plus his other woes by great determination and hard work. One of his concerns was finding a way to be helpful to unemployed graduates. In 1934, his office initiated a study which sought to obtain information about the occupational status of Purdue graduates of the previous five years. The study was done under Elliott's direction by Frank C. Hockema, a professor of industrial engineering and a part-time Buick salesman, who was Elliott's newly appointed assistant to the president, and Jack E. Walters, personnel director in the Schools of Engineering.

The study showed that of 2,140 Purdue graduates from 1928 and 1934 who were questioned, 90 percent were employed and more than two-thirds were engaged in occupations for which they had studied at Purdue.

Elliott's principal concern was students, and he once said that if ever there were a conflict between faculty and students he would side with the students; hence his concern about such matters as the high dropout rate of freshmen and sophomores in the early 1920s. He firmly believed that if the university adjusted to students and students to the university, there would be fewer student failures. He considered himself as the catalyst in a pressure cooker atmosphere; he was not above arousing the ire of faculty just to keep the pot boiling.

Hockema was easily one of the best known professors at Purdue, and his course in salesmanship for engineers was one of the most popular electives in engineering, attracting standing-room only crowds to an early morning class where he was fond of telling students that "the only difference between a rut and a grave is in the dimensions." A farm lad from nearby West Point, Hockema graduated in engineering in 1918 and became one of the Purdue stalwarts—he was thought of as the most loyal member of the faculty and staff. He was by far the most accessible member of Elliott's administrative team and probably had many opportunities to accept advancement to presidencies at other colleges or universities. But he chose to stay at Purdue.

Hockema also served as secretary of the board of trustees and in 1943 was promoted from assistant to the president to executive dean. At Elliott's "forced" retirement in 1945, Hockema was promoted to vice president and executive dean and Stewart to vice president and controller. The two vice presidential appointments were the first since Stone served in that capacity under President Smart before the turn of the century.

The two appointments, whether inadvertently or on purpose, provided a ready-made staff for President Frederick L. Hovde when he arrived in 1946 to succeed Elliott.

•   •   •

Despite the havoc the depression years played on university finances, Elliott was acutely aware of other fund sources and with Stewart was highly successful in obtaining funds from the federal agencies of the time—the Public Works Administration (PWA), the Works Progress Administration (WPA), and the National Youth Administration (NYA). Between 1933 and 1940, Elliott estimated that federal grants to Purdue totalled approximately $3.75 million.

The same 1932 special session of the legislature that cut Purdue appropriations also aired accusations from an earlier time that Purdue was guilty of much "inbreeding"—employing large numbers of related employees. The public airing of the matter led Purdue to establish an anti-nepotism rule. At the time, it created much consternation, including the dismissal from the faculty of R. B. Stewart's wife, Lillian, who had taught applied design in the School of Home Economics.

The university's austerity brought declining morale among both students and faculty. The board of trustees authorized Elliott to defer student fee payments on an individual basis. Elliott used the authority often but wisely. He also helped foreign students who had not received anticipated funds from their homelands and who were not even able to find jobs because of their alien status.

The federal ruling that all interest garnered by Purdue on federal fund deposits belonged to Washington brought local screams of protest—and an eventual, ill-disguised threat (from Washington) to either pay the interest to the federal government or face the possibility of having all federal funds withheld.

The matter of lost interest on federal funds brought about one of several blunt though polite differences between Stewart and Agriculture Dean Skinner. Skinner told Stewart that if Stewart had let him handle the affair, Purdue might have gotten around the federal demand for the interest funds. "You don't always go to the top dog in the government to get what you want," Skinner chided Stewart. "Sometimes you get a decision you don't want." Skinner was angry, believing that Stewart handled the matter wrongly, thereby costing the Purdue agriculture complex—the school, extension service, and the experiment station—thousands of dollars it had normally counted on.

Another time, when physical plant employees planted ivy so that it would grow on the outside walls of Purdue buildings, Skinner went all the way to the trustee board, protesting that the project was entirely wrong. Reflecting in later years about that and other disagreements with Skinner, Stewart paid him an extraordinary compliment, "You always knew where you stood with Skinner."

A more important difference of opinion developed between the two men when the State Board of Accounts made a survey of Purdue business operations and found much that was unsatisfactory. Among its recommendations the state board suggested that budgetary control of the agriculture accounts be consolidated under Stewart, especially those accounts in the Purdue Creamery, the experiment station, and the extension service. Skinner was livid. He was already under attack from local dairy owners who thought that milk products produced by the creamery should be limited to those the university needed for its own purposes. Too, since the federal funds involved were for direct support of agricultural functions, they should be separate from other accounts, Skinner believed. The State Board of Accounts and Stewart won; the trustees voted to move all agriculture accounts under the university controller despite Skinner's formal protests.

Elliott had a high tolerance threshhold for the spats between his administrators and took in stride Skinner and Stewart's differences; they healed themselves without Elliott's first aid.

Elliott's principal woe, the lack of money to do the things Purdue needed to be doing, was compounded by the tension that often developed between and among department heads over the priorities for dispensing the acutely limited funds to departmental budgets. The four heads of the engineering schools, known as "the Big Four," were not above creating internal strife, especially Harry Creighton Peffer, first head of the School of Chemical Engineering from 1911, and William Kendrick Hatt, appointed head of the School of Civil Engineering in 1906. The other two school heads were Gilbert Amos Young, School of Mechanical Engineering, and Charles Francis Harding, School of Electrical Engineering. Young and Harding handled their problems in a more conservative, more conventional manner, but Peffer and Hatt often fired from the hip—interesting characters among many who from Purdue's beginnings have added savory seasoning to the university's academic heritage.

Young, an 1899 graduate who had also directed the Purdue band, loved to teach, loved the university, and loved to play golf—though he often said he would never pick up a "golf stick" again if it ever interfered with his teaching. He was perhaps overly optimistic at times, once announcing enrollment in mechanical engineering at one thousand when in fact it was just a little more than seven hundred. He was greatly admired by Elliott because he fervently wished and worked to make Purdue engineering the best.

Harding was a much more solemn individual. A tall, lanky man, he was known among students as "Slats." Harding was a kindly, quiet man, though he seemed to glower through his pince nez spectacles. Invariably, in writing his annual report to Elliott, Harding reported in great detail the antics of every "character" on the faculty. In fact, anecdotes of the many strange habits and quirks of personality through Purdue's history could themselves fill a volume.

Peffer and Hatt in many ways symbolize all of the "characters" among us; yet it must also be remembered that they were outstanding and competent men. Each gave more than a measure of service to the Purdue cause.

Hatt was an Easterner who in commencement parades wore the bright red robe of a graduate of New Brunswick University. He was a complex person—"subtle, shrewd, and mischievous," H. B. Knoll described him in *The Story of Purdue Engineering*. He was a man of charm, always impeccably dressed, gracious and even courtly in manner. Yet, as a widower, he was not above the many mundane household chores required to be both father and mother to the four Hatt children.

Hatt was one of Purdue's most formidable figures. As another of Purdue's "battleships," he had the big guns and a great readiness (says Knoll) to fire a broadside. "Hatt was known at Lafayette Stockton House, where many faculty members took their meals, as 'all kinds of Philistine rolled into one,' which meant that he had no intention of ever travelling the rut of conformity."

He was a first-class polemicist who seemed to regard the campus as a battlefield where a war raged between the forces of evil and the forces of good sense which had to be eternally vigilant or face extinction. To defend "good sense," Hatt cheerfully tangled with anyone and would as soon demolish Elliott as he would the lowest ranking member of his staff. At faculty meetings, he nearly always managed to pick a fight with someone and inevitably came out the victor, seemingly impervious to criticism. He could go directly to the core of a problem while his adversaries were left floundering on the periphery. As a consequence, it was inevitable that Hatt came eyeball-to-eyeball with Peffer, who became Hatt's permanent academic adversary. Peffer said the disadvantage in having his office in Heavilon Hall was that it was too far from the Civil Engineering Building for him to spit on Professor Hatt.

Hatt and Peffer both had run-ins with Skinner. Hatt once refused to vote for a Skinner proposal in a faculty meeting. He liked the proposal but refused to vote for it because it was Skinner's.

For all of his boom and blast, Hatt was one of engineering's true contributors. He insisted on high standards for himself and for his faculty and students. Three years after he arrived at Purdue in 1893, he was made chief of civil engineering's testing laboratories. Only an extremely thin book of information on portland cement then existed, and Hatt continued the testing work that contributed significantly to the technical literature on the subject. The thin book turned into several volumes. It contributed to finding many answers about concrete before the consumption of portland cement would be raised from the 8.5 million barrels of 1900 to the 200 million consumed in structural work sixty years later.

Peffer, Hatt's natural enemy, was if anything the more vituperative of the two. He had developed the School of Chemical Engineering and made it without a doubt the toughest, most rigorous
of all the engineering curricula at Purdue. It had Peffer's character.
The development of the school into one of national prominence
was due entirely to his bulldog tenacity and his fiery temperament.
He honed a sharp tongue and his pungent speech bordered on
the scalding. One morning he called his staff to his office and,
obviously upset, pointed out that he had seen one of his best
students holding hands with a girl on the campus and was conducting "his lovings in public when they should be conducted
in private."

At faculty meetings, he was annoyed by garrulous faculty
members who seemed to talk endlessly; "the most unnecessary
noise on the entire campus," he would say. Condemning some
proposal or other at a faculty meeting, Peffer observed that "a
half dozen funerals on this campus would do a hell of a lot more
good."

On another occasion, Peffer conducted a kind of sit-down
strike against a class of seniors who had become rebellious about
one of his course requirements. They were loafing, he said, and
they replied that Peffer wanted them to do too many routine
chores. Peffer stiffened and refused to meet the class, laying the
blame for the impasse on the students. Then Acting President
Marshall became so incensed he demanded Peffer's firing. The
matter was eventually settled, but only after Dean Potter intervened
and put to a severe test his clear thinking, tact, and genuine
affection for human beings.

Knoll tells of another occasion when Peffer ordered a camera
through normal university channels. Purchasing Agent H. C. Mahin
wrote to ask Peffer what he intended to do with it. The implications of Mahin's query so angered Peffer that he fired back one
of the best letters he ever regretted. It was, Peffer wrote to Mahin
in high dudgeon, "none of your goddam business" what he did
with the camera, but since Mahin wanted to know, he intended
to take pictures with it.

Peffer's letter ricocheted, glancing off administrators up the
ladder a rung at a time, until it landed on Elliott's desk. Peffer
was called to the president's office where Elliott told him that
writing such a letter to an administrative officer was the same thing
as writing it to him. Peffer was unimpressed. He pointed out to
Elliott that he too was an administrative officer and that using the
same logic, Elliott could conclude that he had written the letter
to himself.

"Peffer, what am I going to do with you?" the exasperated president asked.

"I haven't the slightest idea," Peffer retorted.

"Get out of here and get back to your office," Elliott said with finality.

Peffer spun and marched out of the office, head held high, a certain satisfied, beatific expression on his face as if he truly belonged to some winged, holy throng. Peffer was easily one of the university's strongest, if not most colorful individuals. He fought tenaciously for his students and for the strengthening of his staff and facilities. The results were clear inasmuch as chemical engineering began confidently and remains one of the best programs of its kind anywhere.

•   •   •

The 1930s were hectic for Purdue. But the general bleakness of the depression era was also punctuated by brilliancies, such as Elliott's and Stewart's fast and furious building program—twelve major buildings between 1929 and 1940 largely financed with federal grants—at a time in history when new construction seemed impossible.

One of Elliott's highest priorities was the development of adequate university-operated student housing. In 1927, the Indiana General Assembly approved legislation permitting state-supported colleges and universities to issue revenue bonds to build and furnish dormitories. At the time, it may have seemed rather an ordinary piece of legislation; actually, it was a landmark statute that made possible many cultural and living improvements most state schools would not have seriously contemplated otherwise.

Within a year, Purdue was attempting to put together the finances for the first new student dormitory to be built since Ladies Hall and Purdue Hall were constructed at the birth of the university between 1869 and 1874. The system Purdue now enjoys began with a proposal by Frank C. Cary, a Lafayette industrialist and entrepreneur, to make a $50,000 gift to the university to honor the memory of his son, Franklin Levering Cary, who died at the age of nineteen in 1912. When Mrs. Cary died in 1927, he pursued the idea of gifts to the university to honor both his wife's and his son's memories. Cary first approached Elliott and Henry Marshall, board of trustees president, about the possibilities and proposed purchase of the southeast corner of Marsteller and State Street for a dormitory for forty men. The trustees earlier had already adopted by resolution a proposal to build a dormitory for between one hundred and one hundred fifty men. Members of the board, Elliott, and other staff members tried to divert Cary's attention to other possible sites without success until Stewart, who knew of Cary's interest in having a dormitory situated where everyone could see it, finally convinced him.

Cary was not impressed with the location between Ross-Ade Stadium and Stadium Avenue, owned by George Spitzer. Stewart remembers that he probably drove Cary by the location "at least one hundred times" in his attempt to convince him that this was where Purdue had planned to build its men's dormitories. The location was even on architect Walter Scholer's 1922 master plan for campus development. "But," Cary protested, "you can't see it. People will drive through the campus and no one will ever see it."

"Give us the $50,000," Stewart replied. "I'll use the university's bonding power and give you a $150,000 building that will be the first thing that anyone going to football games on a Saturday afternoon will see." After Scholer had shown him many sketches and blueprints, Cary became convinced and gave Purdue the $50,000 gift to build Franklin Levering Cary Hall, known also as Cary East. Cary himself became greatly involved in the construction and asked Stewart to name its manager so that he could discuss with him plans for the hall's management. Stewart named Lloyd Vallely to the job. Vallely's imaginative performance at Cary was so impressive that eventually he became director of the Purdue Memorial Union, setting the high standards that have become integral to union operations.

Elliott once summarized federal grants and expenditures made since 1933, part of the national effort to shore up the United States economy. The PWA, for example, had spent $700,000 toward construction of five new buildings—two units of the women's residence halls (Windsor Halls), the Executive Building (Hovde Hall of Administration), a fieldhouse and gymnasium (Lambert Fieldhouse), and an addition to the Purdue Memorial Union. Through the WPA, more than $413,000 had been spent for an airport hangar, an addition to the old Physics Building (Peirce Hall), tennis courts, roadways, sewers, fencing, and sundry other campus improvements. At the same time, the NYA had spent more than $200,000 for needy students for their work at various jobs throughout the university.

In his review in 1939, covering the preceding decade, Elliott pointed to the construction of twelve major buildings and a threefold increase in overall total assets of the university from about $4.5 million in 1929.

But in 1940, Elliott talked of other needs of the university that required, he said, an estimated $10 million to improve and extend the physical plant and to construct and equip buildings. Another $5 million was needed, Elliott contended, for other facilities critical to the university's missions. Late in 1941, Elliott could point to contracts awarded for a final unit of the Electrical Engineering Building, the Duncan High Tension Laboratory, a new Physics Building, and a new transmitter for Radio Station WBAA. Nearly all construction then came to a halt. The winds of war once again stirred the world, and the United States turned its attention to girding for the second War-to-End-All-Wars.

• • •

More than any other, the construction of the Hall of Music now named for him was Elliott's crowning glory, the physical symbol embodying all that he believed Purdue could be. He had talked as early as 1934 about a new auditorium seating 5,000; thus, when federal funds became available, Elliott went after them. One morning in 1938, Elliott told Stewart that the governor had received notice of $75 million in PWA funds for Indiana and that he thought he could get some for the proposed new auditorium. He would supplement that figure by asking for a state appropriation to match a bond issue under the 1927 bond enabling act and make up the rest by increasing student fees.

Again, Elliott was shrewd. He took his plan to Indiana University President Herman B Wells. "I wouldn't think of trying to get something like what we have in mind without giving Indiana University a chance to do the same thing," Elliott told Stewart.

Wells and Elliott together lobbied strongly in Indianapolis. They appeared before a special session of the Indiana legislature in June 1938 and told legislators their plans—a new music hall for Purdue, an auditorium for the IU campus at Bloomington. The special session voted the needed appropriations that day. Elliott also got his PWA grant, and Scholer's crew of forty draftsmen, working in the then unimproved third floor of the Executive Building, began to prepare working drawings. The auditorium steelwork was a textbook in construction engineering for the Purdue community, and local children would gather at a safe distance from the construction site after school just to watch the steel workers throw and catch hot rivets.

The building, the crown jewel of the West Lafayette campus, was dedicated in twin ceremonies May 3 and 4, 1940. Its final cost was $1,205,000. Financing consisted of a $542,000 PWA grant, a $300,000 state appropriation, a $300,000 revenue bond issue, and $62,750 from miscellaneous sources. Elliott did the job right. His consultant on sound, for example, was F. R. Watson of the University of Illinois faculty, an acoustical engineer who had designed the sound system and consulted on acoustics for the Radio City Music Hall in New York.

The actual design included two balconies—cantilevered with no supporting posts. The large balcony beams rested on the rear wall of the auditorium and were hooked to the back wall of the large foyer. At the time, the Hall of Music seated 6,146 (now 6,034 because of minor alterations) and was the largest such hall in the United States—the Radio City Music Hall included. The stage itself was 100 feet wide and 37 feet from the stage to the top of the stage opening.

It was not only Elliott's but the entire community's pride; it is still the principal cultural and entertainment center at Purdue. To construct the same building today would cost more than $18 million. Two years before his death, the trustees suspended the rules governing the naming of university buildings and renamed the Purdue Hall of Music the Edward C. Elliott Hall of Music. From his home, the invalided Elliott expressed his gratitude succinctly, "It is the most exceptional honor to come to me throughout my life."

●   ●   ●

One of Elliott's constant concerns at Purdue was the education of women. At a time when colleges and universities generally did little about it, Elliott was out there on the frontier and made two appointments to the faculty in 1935 that turned out to be educational coups of historic proportions. They were Dr. Lillian M. Gilbreth as professor of industrial engineering and Amelia Earhart, already America's favorite aviatrix, as a consultant on women's careers.

Elliott was extremely sensitive to the needs of women. In the planning of the Executive Building in the early 1930s, Elliott insisted that the architects include a private, back stairway leading to an unobtrusive exit so that young women students, occasionally in tears after a counseling session, could leave the building without having to display their emotions publicly in the main doors. The stairway has since been eliminated through various remodelings.

Elliott explained that the appointments of Earhart and Gilbreth were "made with the intention of introducing new forces for the study of the most important modern unsolved problem of higher education—the effective education of young women."

He had met Miss Earhart at the Fourth Annual Women's Conference on Current Problems sponsored by the New York *Herald-Tribune* where she and Elliott were speakers. She spoke on the future of aviation and the role women were to play in it. Elliott listened with great interest inasmuch as she had just completed her famed flight across the Atlantic. He immediately arranged a luncheon for her and her husband, George Palmer Putnam, to discuss Elliott's idea for some sort of association with Purdue. "I learned," Elliott later revealed, "that her primary interest in life was not in this career of adventure upon which she had embarked, but rather in an effort to find and make some new additions to the eventual solution to the problem of careers for women." That was a philosophy nearly identical to Elliott's, and he immediately asked her to come to the campus and state her philosophy. She was delighted. Within an hour after the luncheon, she had rearranged her busy schedule to make the visit to Purdue. Less than a month passed when she came to the campus to address the faculty and women students on "Opportunities for Women in Aviation."

The visit was her first. She returned in 1935 to discuss with Elliott just what faculty status she was to have. Elliott told her she was to be a "visiting faculty member" with the title of consultant on women's careers and that she was to be paid $2,000 a year.

Her visits were always brief, never more than a few weeks at a time, but they were busy times with a full schedule of conferences with women students and lectures on- and off-campus. While at Purdue, she lived in South Hall (Duhme Hall of the Windsor Halls complex). R. B. Stewart once summed up her job as "motivating the girls to do something more than take home economics courses and work on the (men-women) ratio on the campus."

Her appointment caused only mild dissension on the campus and came, surprisingly, from the most kindly dean of all, A. A. Potter of engineering, who said that he did not think Amelia Earhart was properly educated to be a faculty member at a university. Several faculty wives, local guardians of mores and morals in the conservative 1930s atmosphere of West Lafayette, were mortified by a report that she strolled into the "village" one afternoon in (of all things!) slacks and walked into Bartlett's Drug Store. Unescorted, she mounted a stool at the soda fountain, ordered a soft drink, and lit up a cigarette. Such hussy behavior was barely tolerable in a conservative campus town.

By and large, a majority of the faculty and Purdue community found Miss Earhart charming. A relaxed, tall, willowy woman with pretty features, she had a weathered face from hours out-of-doors in the sun and wind, and short, windblown hair. She got along well with women students and performed at Purdue just as Elliott hoped she would. A woman staff member's reply to Dean Potter's objection to the famed aviatrix was that "the dean is a scholar, and he doesn't understand that you have to motivate kids before you can get them to be scholars."

One evening at a dinner party, she spoke of her dreams of a "flying laboratory" that could help aviation advance. Before the evening was over, she had support for her project from David E. Ross and J. K. Lilly; they offered $50,000 to help make her dream come true. With that beginning, an Amelia Earhart Fund for Aeronautical Research was established within the research foundation and eventually was the repository of funds from Ross, Lilly, and such allied aviation industries as Bendix, Western Electric, Goodrich, and Goodyear. Donations from other friends added cash and equipment of $30,000.

The gifts permitted PRF to purchase and outfit the Lockheed 10 E Electra for her round-the-world flight. Upon her return, she was expected to write a book on her flight and the research activities that were part of it. Her plane was then to become the property of PRF. Income realized from the book and exhibitions of the plane were to be used to advance applied research in aeronautics.

The story of the ill-fated flight, when she and Fred Noonan apparently went down in the Pacific in an attempt to find tiny Howland Island, a refueling stop, is now a part of American history. The theories and stories about her disappearance have kindled a score of books on the subject. In 1939, her husband presented the university with her full-length portrait. It hung in Duhme Hall for many years until it was moved to the foyer of the women's residence hall named for her in 1964.

Not long after Amelia Earhart's appointment, Elliott also announced the faculty appointment of Dr. Lillian M. Gilbreth. She was a famed industrial engineer, author, and widowed mother of twelve children. Her life was the subject of a book, *Cheaper by the Dozen,* as well as a popular movie of the same name produced somewhat later. She was the widow of Frank Gilbreth, an equally famous industrial engineer who pioneered in time-and-motion studies and operational and job efficiency.

Dr. Gilbreth's job at Purdue was similar to Amelia Earhart's. Under her agreement, she was a visiting professor of industrial engineering and spent four or five two-week periods at Purdue to lecture and consult with engineering students. She, too, lived in the women's residences while on campus and later extended her areas of interest to students in home economics and agriculture. In later years, her name now forever linked with Purdue, Dr. Gilbreth gave the university what is known as the Gilbreth Engineering Library. It consists of about 1,500 volumes plus many original research notes related to her husband's time-and-motion studies and his investigations of worker fatigue. Though she retired in 1948 from active association with Purdue, she continued to make visits to the campus through the 1960s.

●   ●   ●

In 1940, at the age of sixty-five, Elliott was still going strong and was able to report that in the past year he had attended and spoken at seventy dinners—fifty of these on the campus and twenty elsewhere in the state and nation.

Thomas R. Johnston, the university publicist whose own colorful career at Purdue began in 1917 under Stone, wrote glowingly of the Elliott achievements: an enrollment that rose from 3,110 in 1922 to 7,121 in 1940; the number coming to the West Lafayette campus for short courses and conferences ballooned from about 4,000 a year to 40,000; expansion of the university's research programs; and a tremendous spurt in building despite the austerity of the times. Johnston came from an Indiana newspaper job as the university's first publicist. A deskman, he had complained to the agricultural extension officials about the poor quality of the material they sent for use on Indiana newspaper farm pages. He was invited to the campus to see whether he could "do better"—and he did for forty-six years. Retiring in 1963, he served the last four years of President Stone's tenure, the entire span of Elliott's administration, and the first seventeen years of Frederick L. Hovde's administration.

For many years, Johnston served as a Purdue lobbyist in the state capitol and became widely known in Indiana political circles. His attempt to seek the Democratic gubernatorial nomination at the state party convention in the late 1950s failed. Johnston probably knew more people in Indiana by their first names than any other person and continued to serve Purdue for thirteen more years until his retirement.

Elliott was an ardent sports fan and in 1940 involved himself deeply in athletic affairs. After the death that year of the beloved Noble E. Kizer, Elliott was forced to assume the duties of the athletic director for several months, naming Allen "Mal" Elward as head football coach and assistant athletic director. Through the experience, Elliott developed a special bond with student athletes and coaches. He was delighted when his youngest son, Edward, played on three championship Purdue basketball teams under Ward "Piggy" Lambert from 1933–34 through 1935–36.

But Elliott was first the educator and second the athletic fan. Questioned by a reporter regarding the news that the University of Chicago had dropped out of the Big Ten conference, Elliott termed the action courageous and told the reporter further that it was "within the range of possibilities that the University of Chicago will demonstrate the possibility of conducting a university without football." He continued, "There have been times that I have wished that we might have colleges and universities without football. This is perhaps a bit too Utopian. Perhaps Chicago will prove that Utopia is possible. But Purdue is not Utopia and intends to continue to play football—and, we hope, good football."

In January 1941, Elliott gave up the acting athletic directorship, naming Elward to the post. The athletic department did what it was in the nature of the the athletic department to do: awarded the president with a "P" sweater and a star (normally given only to the captains of the teams).

•   •   •

Elliott became more and more concerned about Purdue's role in the national defense program in 1941; the university was beginning to be affected since thirty-three staff members had already withdrawn to participate in the program and many leaves of absence were granted to others leaving for military duty. By the end of the following year, Purdue went from a "defense footing" to a "war footing," and the second stage of Elliott's remarkable career as Purdue president ended.

Two weeks after Japan attacked Pearl Harbor on December 7, 1941, Elliott called a special student convocation in the still-new Hall of Music to outline the students' responsibilities as American citizens in a nation at war—'total war," he called it.

"You have a responsibility," he told the students, "for reducing social activities, for rigid economy in your personal affairs, and for maintaining your health and physical fitness." He predicted correctly that the university would make a quick conversion to a wartime footing.

Elliott had cast-iron opinions about military service—ideas that had begun to develop in his own undergraduate years. He supported military training as an essential part of higher education since, he once said, "I served as a more-or-less unwilling member of the cadet battalion at the University of Nebraska."

His real feelings were tested when a Purdue student peace organization requested permission to carry out a nonviolent demonstration against the Selective Service and Training Act of 1940. The group wanted to declare Wednesday, October 16, 1940—the day conscription registration began—as a day of mourning and planned to wear black armbands for the occasion. Elliott quickly and firmly refused the group "the privilege of carrying out this plan." The group tried to schedule a public meeting on the campus for that evening. Elliott also cancelled it. There were no demonstration, no black armbands, and no meeting. And the trustees unanimously backed his decision. The heavy hand of Elliott had fallen.

Within three weeks after Pearl Harbor, the executive committee of the faculty announced the university would operate on an accelerated basis of three sixteen-week semesters per year and eliminate vacations and final examinations. Not long afterward, Elliott was named to serve on a Committee on Wartime Requirements for Specialized Personnel, a subcommittee of the National Resources Planning Board. At still another student convocation in February 1942, Elliott told the students that although they were not in uniform or in a military training camp, they were in a "Purdue training center" where, he admonished, "they should prepare themselves for some meaningful job of war."

Not long afterward, newly appointed War Manpower Commissioner Paul V. McNutt, the former Indiana governor who was Elliott's close friend, invited Elliott to become chief of the Division of Professional and Technical Employment and Training within the War Manpower Commission. Elliott was eager to accept, and the trustees only after considerable discussion reluctantly approved his request for a leave of absence. Elliott left for Washington in June 1942 for his new job; still, he spent much time commuting between Purdue and Washington, even though the university governance—the presidential duties—were turned over to a committee of Hockema, Stewart, Potter, and Agriculture Dean Harry J. Reed, who had succeeded Skinner when he retired in 1939. The group, with Skinner then dean of agriculture, had taken over for Elliott when he was called to the Philippines on a special educational consulting assignment in 1938.

Elliott was not the only senior administrator involved in wartime assignments. The Potter path between Washington and West Lafayette was also well worn. He was in almost constant contact with Washington as chairman of the Advisory Committee on Engineering, Science, and Management Defense Training. Later, he served as executive director of the National Patent Planning

Commission. Stewart also had several government war assignments: special adviser to the director of the Office of Scientific Research and Development, special assistant in the Bureau of Naval Personnel, and specialized training consultant to the United States Army. In 1943, Stewart was named chairman of the Army-Navy Joint Board for Uniform Contracts with College Training Units. His appointment was an outgrowth of Stewart's work with the Navy on a contract for the education and housing of large Navy V12 groups marshalled at Purdue for precommissioning training and technical education. The agreement Stewart authored was so highly regarded by the Navy that it adopted the Stewart format throughout the nation for all of its college and university V12 arrangements.

As the nation mobilized, enrollments at Purdue fluctuated from one academic year to the next. The total number of resident students in 1939–40 was 8,373. In 1940–41, it fell to 8,101 as the Selective Service System began to take its toll among the men students. Enrollment again fell to 7,556 in 1941–42, but rose to 8,161 in the following year as the military programs began to build. It peaked at 9,002 in 1943–44, then took a sharp drop to 6,020 in 1944–45. From fiscal 1942–43 to fiscal 1943–44, the numbers of new undergraduate civilian men declined sharply from 2,700 to 1,236. The metamorphosis from a rather quiet, almost pastoral, campus setting to something akin to a major military training base was well in process.

The university's men's residences in the Cary Quadrangle were taken over by the Navy for its training school for electricians' mates and the Navy College Training Program (V12). The electricians' mates school opened in 1942 and eventually grew to a complement of about 800. More than 6,000 were graduated before the war ended in 1945.

The V12 program was designed to provide a reservoir of trained officers for the rapidly expanding United States fleet. It opened in July 1943, with an enrollment of 1,263, about one-third marines, the rest navy men. In successive semesters, V12 enrollment dropped from 1,251 to 281 before the program was phased out. But it provided education for more than 2,700 navy men and marines. Of that number, about 400 received Purdue bachelor's degrees. The Purdue program was so satisfactory to the Navy that it revised its program following the end of the war and established a Naval Reserve Officers Training Corps at the university.

The United States Army was also prominent on the Purdue scene in World War II. The Army Specialized Training Program (ASTP) began early in 1943 to provide advanced engineering education for about 500. The program later made provision for 125 soldiers in a course in personnel psychology. The trainees were selected from among men already in the Army, and the program eventually grew to a total enrollment of 1,189.

By 1943, the military training facilities at Purdue required housing in the Agricultural Engineering Building as well as the temporary requisition of twenty-one of the community's thirty-five fraternity houses.

Purdue also ran a six-month class for Women's Army Corps officers in personnel administration in 1945. In addition, the Purdue Airport became a center for aviation training—28 pilots for the Army Enlisted Reserve Corps, 534 pilots for the Navy V5 program, and 166 for the War Training Service flight instructors school. The airport also was the site for training 85 pilots from Central and South American countries in airline and fixed-base operations.

Purdue provided training for twenty-five warrant officers for the Navy's diesel engine officer program and offered a three-month course for Army Air Corps squadron engineering officers. Not only the military was involved at Purdue—though it may have appeared to any first-time visitor to the campus to have been quite simply another military installation. Perhaps Purdue's greatest contribution to the World War II effort was the statewide training program in which the university administered training for skilled industrial workers for the war effort.

Readily apparent even before Pearl Harbor was the fact that defense industries would require thousands of skilled workers. Purdue offered three federally financed, college-level training programs, all with different titles but all designed to accomplish the same end. They made Purdue a national leader in training workers for defense industries in World War II. The programs actually began in 1940 and for four-and-a-half years were offered in nearly 100 Indiana cities and towns. As the war progressed, there came numerous requests from industries throughout the state for customized skilled-worker training programs—which led to the development of district offices in Evansville, Fort Wayne, East Chicago, Indianapolis, Lafayette, Muncie, Jeffersonville, Michigan City, Marion, Gary, and Hammond.

The sites at Hammond, Fort Wayne, Indianapolis, and Michigan City developed as bonafide university extension centers after the war, each offering up to two years of most Purdue four-year baccalaureate programs. Ultimately, the center at Hammond became Purdue Calumet campus. The Barker Memorial Center at Michigan City was returned to the Barker estate, and a new site near Westville south of Michigan City became the Purdue North Central campus. At Fort Wayne, the Purdue and Indiana University centers were amalgamated under the direction of the Indiana University-Purdue Foundation at Fort Wayne in a new, joint campus on Fort Wayne's north side. At Indianapolis, Purdue built two buildings on Thirty-eighth Street, moving out of the old Hoosier Athletic Club quarters on Meridian Street, known as the Purdue-Marott Agricultural Center. This regional campus later joined the Indiana University complex at Indianapolis, now known by the ponderous title Indiana University-Purdue University at Indianapolis—abbreviated IUPUI. Each of the regional campuses is now academically independent, and each offers four-year degree-granting programs and some graduate study.

The evolution of the wartime training centers under Purdue management into extensions and eventually into institutions with full academic credentials is one of the most interesting chapters in Purdue history, deserving of its own chronicle, its own volume.

Much of the wartime research and development at Purdue in World War II was secret. Later, it could be revealed that a wide variety of projects and programs, all pertinent to the war effort, were carried on at West Lafayette. A 1945 report revealed that the Purdue Research Foundation and the Department of Research Relations had provided funding of nearly $1.5 million from fifty-one different sources for war research, 60 percent of it in the Department of Chemistry alone. Almost all of the funds were pledges from civilian and military sources in the three years, 1943, 1944, and 1945.

The projects varied all over the campus, however, including housing research carried on in a program begun by Ross in 1932. Chemistry had the largest number of projects, but there was not a school or department at Purdue that did not somehow become involved in some aspect of war training or research.

Which wartime research at Purdue was the most important? Certainly, Purdue's secret work on fluorination and atomic energy was crucial to the war effort. The Purdue Department of Chemistry's experience with fluorine chemistry brought it a contract to investigate the methods for the safe preparation of fluorocarbons, essential in the operation of one of the Oak Ridge, Tennessee, plants where the isotope of uranium 235 was separated from the isotope of uranium 238. Out of this research grew many other investigations involving the study of many useful fluorine-containing compounds.

Purdue in the war years also conducted research contributing to the development of synthetic rubber and its improvement.

Chemists also worked on antimalarial drugs, refrigerants and insecticide carriers, and the extraction of activated carbon from coal.

Undoubtedly, the most dramatic research was that done in the Department of Physics under the direction of Professor Karl Lark-Horowitz on the properties of germanium crystals—fundamental research through which physicists hoped to find better materials for the rectifier crystals in a microwave radar. It resulted in the development of materials which could replace the old silicon crystals. The new material was germanium, a semiconductor. The Purdue research eventually led to the development of the transistor and the establishment of solid-state physics. It is among Purdue's brightest research moments.

More than 450 staff members entered the armed forces. Many of those in the military continued to work at military occupations related to their professional careers at Purdue; still others were involved in civilian war work. At the war's end, the teaching staff was decimated.

More importantly, more than 17,500 alumni, former students who left their studies for the war, and staff members were in the armed forces in World War II. Of these, 500 gave the immeasurable and final contribution.

•   •   •

Though Elliott made regular trips between Washington and Purdue, some faculty, some students, and even some members of the board of trustees felt that Elliott was sorely needed at the campus. In April 1943, he thus resigned his position with the War Manpower Commission and returned to Purdue. He had to make an adjustment to a campus which was somewhat different from the one he had left nearly a year previously. It hardly helped that his close friend and colleague David E. Ross, president of the trustee board since 1927, died of a massive stroke. The team of Elliott and Ross had made things happen at Purdue from the time Elliott arrived in 1922. They were even termed Damon and Pythias by George Ade, and a staff member described Ross as "both an apt student and strong ally" of Elliott. Ross was buried atop a hill overlooking the campus west of what is now the Slayter Center of the Performing Arts, fulfilling a request of many years that his final resting place, like John Purdue's, be on the campus.

Death also came to other Purdue figures in 1943: Dean Emeritus Stanley Coulter, the longtime faculty member and administrator who had come to Purdue, somewhat reluctantly, in Smart's administration in 1887, and Professor G. A. Young, the legendary head of the School of Engineering, a Purdue graduate, and a "holler guy," a Purdue booster who loved his students and teaching as much as he loved the university itself. Not long after these deaths came that of George Ade in May 1944. His death occurred only a month after that of James W. Noel, the trustee who had been elected president of the board immediately following Ross's death.

In the same month that Noel died, the trustees met (April 20, 1944) to inform Elliott that he should plan to terminate his presidency on June 30, 1945, the end of the 1944–45 fiscal year. The reason was that Elliott by then would reach the mandatory retirement age of seventy. Elliott was not really ready to retire; though he had been instrumental in establishing seventy as the retirement age at Purdue, he did not think it applied to him, but resignedly told the board he would be willing to remain until his successor was named. That the decision was final was made clear to him when Trustee John A. Hillenbrand announced at a faculty meeting in December, 1944, that Elliott would retire the following June. The decision was also reinforced by the board's action in appointing two of its members, William A. Hanley of Indianapolis and Allison E. Stuart of Lafayette, to begin the search for Elliott's successor.

In the six months prior to his retirement day, Elliott was honored many times, the climactic event being an assemblage of more than 800 from all over the country to honor him and his family at a farewell banquet in the Purdue Memorial Union ballrooms.

There could be little question that the twenty-three years Elliott served were years of great growth and expansion—whether by Elliott's design is irrelevant. Certainly, he did that which encouraged orderly growth, but it would be a distortion of history to believe that it was solely a result of Elliott. Yet, it is impossible to overlook some of the university's accomplishments under Elliott: a massive building program between 1929 and 1940—from 31 to 59 major buildings—at a time in economic history when the environment was such that capital investment of any kind would have been considered the sheerest folly; an enrollment increase from 3,200 to 8,600 students; the awarding of 20,500-plus undergraduate and more than 2,200 graduate degrees; the establishment of the Graduate School in 1929; an increase in the faculty, administrative, and research staff from 456 in 1922 to 1,217 when he retired; a land acreage increase from 2,784 acres to 6,742 acres—and finally, the most-often used measuring stick, the increase in the value of the physical plant (land, buildings, and equipment) from $3.7 million to $18.7 million.

There were other more subtle, less spectacular changes, among them the employment of the university's first controller; the establishment of a new, more accurate accounting system for university funds; and the beginning of a strict budgeting procedure. More importantly, the Elliott years produced profound changes in admissions and retention policy that had not only a salutary effect on student performance but also on the university's academic standards.

The formation of the allied corporations must be considered, overall, Elliott's single most innovative contribution to higher education. The Ross-Ade Foundation, Purdue Research Foundation, and others became the prototype for nearly fifty others at American universities.

Perhaps the late H. B. Knoll, a faculty member in English who wrote *The Story of Purdue Engineering* in 1963, said it most succinctly, "How anyone could have done more than Elliott did to keep Purdue abreast of times would be difficult to imagine."

At its May 10, 1945, meeting, the board of trustees took unprecedented action by way of three resolutions. The first created the office of President Emeritus of Purdue University and named Elliott to that position. The trustees approved, independent of any other retirement income Elliott may have had, a $7,500 annual pension for Elliott. The second resolution created two new positions of vice president and executive dean, and vice president and controller and named Hockema and Stewart, respectively, to them. The third resolution named Engineering Dean A. A. Potter as acting president until Elliott's successor was named and on the job.

The three actions signalled to Stewart, Hockema, and Potter that they were not being considered as presidential candidates and that the trustees had determined that the new president was going to be someone not previously connected with Purdue. Elliott was not only in complete agreement with the trustees' actions but also assisted, when asked, in finding his successor.

After retirement, Elliott accepted an assignment to direct a national survey of the pharmacy profession, and the Elliotts moved directly from their Seventh Street home to Washington, D.C. Elliott considered retirement "a passport to oblivion" and firmly resisted any sort of inaction; in the next decade he kept busy as a consultant, speaker, and author. In 1948, the Elliotts returned to Lafayette and settled in a comfortable and roomy ground-floor apartment on South Seventh Street in Lafayette, across the street and a few houses south of the presidential home they had occupied for twenty-two years.

Elliott spent about two hours each morning in his Executive Building office in the second-floor presidential office suite and seemed to adapt to a more leisurely pace. Mrs. Elliott died in 1955. In October 1957, Elliott suffered a moderate stroke as he neared his eighty-third birthday, and although he made a partial recovery, he spent the rest of his days partly paralyzed on the right side. Even with that handicap, Elliott managed to get to several Purdue outings and even to football games which he watched either from a wheelchair or through the windshield of his automobile parked above the north end zone. The last game he watched was between Purdue and Nebraska, his alma mater, on September 27, 1958. Purdue won, 28–0.

Elliott's health began to deteriorate more rapidly, and he realized that death could not be far off. On June 16, 1960, at the age of eighty-five, the great, good man died, his fitting and succinct epitaph the words of his successor, Frederick Lawson Hovde: "He made the university live in the hearts and minds of the people of this state."

Chapter IX

Frederick L. Hovde's Environment for Learning

April 25, 1945, was typical for spring in Washington, D.C.— an oppressively warm and muggy day with threatening skies. A handsome, thirty-seven-year-old wartime executive of the National Defense Research Committee (NDRC) walked from his office building on P Street Northwest toward a fateful appointment. The skies suddenly opened and he was caught in an afternoon downpour.

Minutes later he arrived, soaked and steamy, at the office of Kathryn McHale, a Hoosier with a national reputation as a crusader for women's rights. At the time, she was general director of the American Association of University Women and a trustee of Purdue University. (She was a legal resident of Logansport and thus eligible to serve.) She and her visitor exchanged pleasantries; then she came right to the point, seeming to pay little attention to his wet clothing.

"Would you," she began, "be interested in becoming president of Purdue University?"

"Yes, I am very much interested," Frederick Lawson Hovde replied evenly, as his rumpled and sodden suit dripped water into small pools on the floor.

So passed the first moment of Hovde's monumental Purdue career that spanned a quarter century of the university's history.

•　　　•　　　•

246

Hovde made it clear to Kathryn McHale that although he was interested in the Purdue presidency he would not leave the war work to which he had long been committed even before the Japanese attack on Pearl Harbor in 1941. Two days after their meeting, Hovde sent her the usual courtesy note with his resumé and other credentials, thus becoming a candidate for the job President Elliott was about to vacate. It turned out that, actually, he was the only candidate in the collective eyes of the board of trustees.

Hovde was never certain how his name entered the Purdue picture, although he admitted he had an inkling at the time that he had been mentioned in connection with the Purdue presidency. He never really gave it much thought until his rainy-day meeting with Trustee McHale. The evidence suggests that Hovde was first mentioned by his NDRC boss, James B. Conant, the president of Harvard and a leading United States educator. Conant recommended Hovde in response to queries from Elliott, Kathryn McHale, or both. Hovde's name was then, of course, relayed to the trustees who asked her to talk to Hovde.

Meanwhile, the efforts toward a permanent peace began with the groundwork laid at the Dumbarton Oaks Conference that sought the establishment of an international organization generally thought to be needed to keep the peace and bring about a semblance of planetary order. The United Nations Conference on International Organization opened in San Francisco on April 25— the same day Hovde first met Trustee McHale.

The Purdue trustees wasted little time in their presidential search. In the 1940s, faculty-student search committees were unknown. The president was an employee of the board of trustees, and it was, therefore, the trustees' job to hire someone answerable to them.

Hovde was invited to meet with Elliott and Trustees William A. Hanley and Allison Stuart in Indianapolis on May 26. From there, the three made an unpublicized trip to the campus before Hovde returned to Washington and his NDRC duties. The visit was his second; his first was on February 25, 1928, as a member of the University of Minnesota basketball team, playing Purdue in the Memorial Gymnasium. (For the Minnesota Gophers, it was not a memorable trip. Purdue won, 45–27.)

In the ensuing weeks, correspondence flew back and forth between Hanley and Hovde. On July 9, 1945, Hanley called Hovde in Washington to tell him that every trustee had expressed his intention to vote for Hovde when the matter came before the board on July 24. The board on that date, in executive session, selected Frederick L. Hovde as the seventh president of Purdue University.

In a letter to Hanley dated July 28, Hovde accepted the presidency: "To be elected to the presidency of a distinguished university is, indeed, a great honor. Most important to us, however, is the meaning of the act—to have the confidence and esteem of the Trustees of Purdue University. . . . I accept this honor, fully mindful of the duties and obligations involved, with the sincere intention of discharging them to the best of my ability."

Elliott had been intensely involved in Hovde's selection. The board relied heavily on his advice and his deep well of contacts in the world of educators. Elliott had spent a great amount of time in Washington in his own wartime job and inevitably in 1945 was a guest at the Hovdes' home where they discussed the Purdue situation at length. Another Purdue dinner guest at the Hovdes' that summer was R. B. Stewart, also a frequent visitor to wartime Washington.

Elliott also had the chance to discuss Hovde with Alan S. Valentine, the president of the University of Rochester, under whom Hovde served as executive assistant until he joined NDRC's London liaison office in 1940. Elliott was impressed by Hovde; quite likely he enjoyed the heady experience of being instrumental in naming his own successor.

Hovde also wrote to Valentine as soon as he accepted the Purdue presidency:

Dear Alan:

This letter is more than difficult to write for its purpose is to tell you that Priscilla and I shall not return to the university which we loved so much. The reason—a few days ago the Trustees of Purdue University invited me to the presidency of that institution and I have accepted.

You likely know that my negotiations with the Purdue Trustees started shortly after you asked about my interest in Purdue that last time we talked together in Washington. As I said then, I have always been keenly interested in state universities and the problems of public education since my Minnesota days. The opportunity is what I always wanted some day, and the fact that I now have it is due in large measure to you and the advice and training you gave so generously. . . .

Valentine replied (in part):

Of course my reactions to your letter were mixed. I had known of Purdue's interest in you, for President Elliott telephoned me about you, and we had a long conversation a few weeks ago, just before he invited you to Purdue. He told me then that you looked terribly good to him—in fact that you and Priscilla looked so ideal for the

Purdue job that he felt there must be a weakness somewhere, and what was the weakness! I replied that because I very much wanted you back here I almost wished that I could point out some Achilles heel in your armor, but was unable to do so.

•   •   •

Fred Hovde was born February 7, 1908, in Erie, Pennsylvania, the oldest son of Martin Rudolph Hovde and Julia Essidora Larson (later changed to Lawson) Hovde, both of Scandinavian parentage. His paternal grandparents were from Romesdahlen, near Oslo, Norway, and his maternal grandparents immigrated from Vortofta, Sweden.

In Minneapolis, the Lawsons and the Hovdes lived in the same neighborhood. Hovde's mother and father became friends and high school sweethearts. They married when his father was twenty-one and his mother was eighteen. Martin took a job as a $30-a-month office boy and messenger in the United States weather bureau in Minneapolis and eventually, by self-study, passed the civil service examination and became a meteorologist. Soon after, the Hovdes were transferred to Sandusky, Ohio, then to Erie, Pennsylvania. Later, the weather service sent the Hovdes to the bureau at Nashville, Tennessee, and in 1913, when Fred was five years old, to Devils Lake, North Dakota, where Hovde grew up and became a high school scholar and athlete. By then the Hovde family had grown. Fred's brother John was born two years after him; then Elaine, two years younger than John; and Ruth, four years younger than Elaine.

Devils Lake was a city of between 5,000 and 6,000 in Hovde's youth; it is more than 7,000 today, a close-knit community, as self-sufficient as possible, friendly, proud, busy, and progressive, dominating a prosperous, although thinly populated, countryside.

The government-owned dwelling that housed the United States weather station also was the Hovde family home. It had a lawn that covered three-quarters of a city block where Hovde played as a youngster. "I grew up in this house with the huge lawn which became my own football field. The grade school and high school were across the street and the library was just down the street about a block," Hovde recalled. The Hovde lawn became the neighborhood's principal play area. Hovde would say, "Having the lawn as a football field and my own football, I had my own team. I was the captain, coach, and quarterback and I ran the whole show." Hovde was a natural athlete, the ultimate competitor who once said he set twenty-five years as a goal for his Purdue tenure simply because he wanted to break Elliott's record of twenty-three years.

The pay of a United States weatherman was modest to say the least—hardly adequate to save the amount required to provide college educations for four children. But Fred's mother was a shrewd and enterprising person. She saw a need at Devils Lake's Great Northern Hotel, just across the street from the Great Northern Railroad station. The hotel was not only a stopping point for hordes of traveling salesmen, it was a community social center as well. Mrs. Hovde went to the manager of the hotel who agreed to lease lobby space to her. Next, she went to the president of a local bank and without collateral, except a good mind for business and two energetic hands, was able to borrow $600. With it she opened the Lobby Flower Shop, operated it for seven years, and shrewdly sold it just before the crash of 1929. The shop's proceeds were carefully laid aside and used to pay the Hovde children's college expenses.

Fred was a high school football star, but he also excelled in basketball and track. Nonetheless, he was considered a "puny kid," really too small to play. Yet, Hovde went on to lead the Devils Lake High School team to a state football championship.

•   •   •

In September 1925, Hovde entered the University of Minnesota with civil engineering as his first choice. "I also had made up my mind that I would never be able to make the Minnesota football team. I just didn't think I could do it." He arrived at the Minneapolis campus with his boyhood friend Joe O'Brien. To two young lads from a small North Dakota town, the Minnesota campus must have seemed forbidding. In 1925, the University of Minnesota enrolled more than 15,000 students at its Minneapolis and St. Paul campuses. Despite his misgivings, at the end of his first quarter Hovde made a straight-A average, gained new confidence, decided because of his performance in freshman chemistry to take chemical engineering, went out for freshman football, and joined Phi Delta Theta fraternity. Hovde described his undergraduate years at Minnesota merely as "pleasant"—which nowhere even hints at his eventual role as a star football player who won all Big Ten Conference honors in his senior year, was a teammate of the legendary Bronko Nagurski, was elected chairman of the Junior Ball, and won a great number of other academic and athletic honors. He graduated in 1929.

More importantly, as a senior he met Priscilla Boyd on a "blind date," and she eventually became his wife after an on-again, off-again, long-distance romance, complicated while he was at Oxford University as a Rhodes scholar from North Dakota.

Not long after the announcement of Hovde's Rhodes selection, his mother was stopped on a downtown street in Devils Lake by an acquaintance who offered congratulations. But, she added, "I don't see how you can bear to let your son go off to England for two or three years. I just couldn't do that."

"Well," Mrs. Hovde replied, "we just can't stand in the way of our children. We just can't do that, either." And she never did.

When Hovde submitted his application to the North Dakota Rhodes Committee at Grand Forks, he also outlined his proposed plan of study at Oxford University. He wanted to read for the Oxford bachelor of arts in the Final Honors Program in chemistry, taking his final examination at the end of two years, and spend a third year in research for the bachelor of science in physical chemistry. (Advanced degrees at Oxford are the bachelor of science, bachelor of literature, bachelor of civil law, and doctor of philosophy.) He also applied for and received senior standing since much of the work toward the Oxford B.A. degree would be repetitive. Hovde had been admitted to Brasenose College. At Oxford one is not admitted to the university (as is the case in most American universities); one is admitted to one of its many colleges, then is considered to be a student at Oxford University.

Hovde and a fellow Rhodes scholar, Malcolm MacIntyre, a Yale graduate, met on the voyage to England and became lifelong friends. During their Oxford years, they travelled together through Europe during the university's traditionally long vacations. They were especially enchanted by the Tyrolean Alps where they rented quarters to do the prodigious amounts of reading expected of Oxonians on vacation. Hovde also spent the summers of 1930 and 1931 as a tour guide for a European travel agency.

Brasenose College was known among the British as the Oxford college for the "hearties," the English equivalent of the American "jock" or athlete. For Hovde the athlete, it was a happy circumstance. He learned to play the game of English rugby and eventually won the Oxford "blue" for his play in the annual Oxford-Cambridge rugby game in London's Twickenham Stadium. Oxford won, 10–3. Hovde gained whatever immortality one may gain from rugby by scoring the last Oxford "try" (touchdown) for three points. For that game he became only the third American to ever win a "blue" at Oxford. He also won a "half blue" in track, being the only member of the squad fearless enough to compete in the pole vault.

After Hovde completed his B.S. degree in physical chemistry in 1932, he sailed for home and arrived in Minneapolis, where his parents then lived. By mid-September, he had accepted an instructorship in chemical engineering at the University of Minnesota. He anticipated studying the influence of radioactive materials on gaseous reactions with Dr. Samuel C. Lind, a pioneer chemist in radioactive chemistry.

Dr. Malcolm S. MacLean invited Hovde to his campus office one day for a chat that turned into a three-hour debate on the philosophy of education—and another job offer at the university. MacLean had been assigned by then Minnesota President Lotus Delta Coffman to establish a "general college" at Minneapolis. The idea of being on the ground floor of such an adventure with two men whom he so greatly admired appealed to Hovde, and he immediately decided to "throw in" with MacLean and the new General College. The project grew out of Coffman's sensitivity to the need for different approaches to higher education. He recognized new problems and articulated them by noting that "so fragmented have become the fields of knowledge that no student anywhere, anymore, can get a general or liberal education." Coffman thus chose MacLean to see whether such an education could be developed at Minnesota, and MacLean, the effervescent Shakespearean scholar and former cowboy, chose Hovde as his assistant director.

Years later at Purdue, Hovde recalled that he probably learned more about the administration of higher education from Malcolm MacLean than from any other individual. But if he learned about what to do in university administration from MacLean, he learned what not to do from Alan C. Valentine, who at thirty-four years of age became the president of the University of Rochester, New York, late in 1935. Valentine cast about for a presidential assistant who could handle the new Rochester Prize Scholarships. In that search, the first trip he made as president was to visit Fred Hovde at Minneapolis.

Rochester was heavily endowed; it also had Valentine, a young, able, dynamic, imaginative (although steely-cold) administrator. Its faculty included such academic luminaries as physicist Lee DuBridge, geologist Herman Fairchild, and historian Dexter Perkins, all men that Hovde would soon come to know and respect—and they him. Valentine established the Prize Scholarships as a means of attracting students from other than the Rochester metropolitan area; he wanted students from all over the United States, and he needed someone like Hovde to help him achieve that goal. The Hovdes moved to Rochester in 1936.

Hovde was in Chicago in December 1940 to interview prospective scholarship recipients when he received a telephone call from Washington, D.C., asking him of his interest in joining the newly formed National Defense Research Committee (NDRC). The job entailed going to England for a year to expedite the exchange of scientific information between the British and American research establishments. Priscilla was skeptical, but Hovde took the assignment though it meant at least a year's separation from his family. In Washington, he met with Carroll Wilson and his boss, Vannevar Bush, the scientific genius from the Massachusetts Institute of Technology who conceived, created, and ran the United States civilian research effort in World War II. Wilson was Bush's executive assistant. Hovde learned he was to be one of a party of three under Dr. James B. Conant, the Harvard president whom Hovde came to admire so much. The trio was to go to England to establish the liaison office between the two allies.

Hovde took the job—another American deeply involved in World War II nearly a year before the rest of the nation. As a Rhodes scholar, Hovde had developed a deep and abiding respect for the British and a firm belief in British indominability, despite this bleak hour in English history. Beyond that, Hovde saw the war cloud that had darkened the European continent and the British Isles as eventually engulfing America. Hovde could not have picked a worse time to go to England. London lived and died under blitzkrieg conditions with nightly raids by the Nazi bombers. He and Priscilla had married in 1933 and were parents of a young son, Boyd, then six; and Priscilla was pregnant again. Worse, the one-year assignment in London turned into seventeen months.

In the three years after Hovde finally returned to the United States, he served first as executive assistant to Conant, who by then headed NDRC, and later was assigned as chief of NDRC's Division Three, the unit that researched and developed America's early rocket ordnance. He was in that post when the feelers first came his way concerning the Purdue presidency.

•   •   •

Hovde had accepted the Purdue post in the summer of 1945 and was winding down his affairs as chief of rocket ordnance after the Japanese surrender. The Hovdes then lived in Washington and were now the parents of Boyd; Jane, born during his tenure in London; and Linda Ruth, born in Washington about a year before the Hovdes decided to come to Purdue.

Fred and Priscilla made their first appearance in Lafayette as president and wife on October 12, 1945, for homecoming weekend. Purdue put its best foot forward; so did the Hovdes. They sat in the west stands of Ross-Ade Stadium, witnesses to the 40–0 dismantling of the Iowa Hawkeyes. At halftime, the Purdue Military

Marching Band, the nation's first such band to break ranks and form letters, marched proudly up the field in a formation that spelled "Hello Hovde." Hovde was invited down to the field where in a short talk over the public address system he thanked the campus community and the band for their warm welcome, then expressed some of his own philosophy of intercollegiate athletics: "Make no mistake about it—those who participate in intercollegiate athletics learn something from the experience more important than physical skills involved. The American game of football has become a worthwhile part of our university life. Let's keep it that way. I hope the Western Conference will continue to lead the way—stand for the highest standards—in the conduct of amateur intercollegiate sports. May they always do well on the field—and Purdue a little better."

That night Hovde gave a premiere talk at the Founder's Day homecoming banquet in which he asked the alumni to become more active in the affairs of the university:

> In this country we observe "homecoming" in our own unique American way—yet beneath the jollity of the occasion there is something of deeper significance. Every great institution of learning throughout the world, with few exceptions, has a festive time on its calendar when its sons and daughters return to pay homage and respect to alma mater and to renew their youth.
>
> The act of returning somehow enables us to demonstrate to the university and to ourselves, that we appreciate her giving intellectual life to us, that we propose to protect her and aid her against evil days, against all forces restricting her freedom.
>
> The alumni of this institution are loyal and proud to be here, for it is a distinguished institution—made so by the creative labors of many people working as a team. I hope soon to join that team. I expect to be a benchwarmer for some time. I hope that if I work hard, don't flunk my courses, listen to the right coaches, and never miss a practice, I can make the varsity and earn the right to be called a Purdue man. . .

Hovde arrived on the Purdue campus on January 5, 1946, and checked into the Purdue Memorial Union Club. The next morning without ceremony Hovde walked briskly across the campus to the Executive Building—the structure that now bears his name. He entered the second-floor suite of offices at the south end of the building where he was greeted by Edith Blagrave, Elliott's former secretary who would serve in the same capacity for Hovde for the next thirty years.

Then he went to work.

•   •   •

"When I arrived," Hovde said, "it would have been impossible to start any kind of long-range planning. We couldn't buy anything because of the shortages, and we were deluged with the problem of an enrollment about to double and swamped on a day-to-day basis with thousands of minor problems—merely finding, for example, enough beds for everyone."

Purdue was not unlike hundreds of American colleges and universities in the first year following V-J Day, the end of World War II. They had done yeomen's work in training and educating thousands of persons for wartime service, both civilian and military. They had devoted most of their laboratories and other facilities to war-related research. They had, most importantly, "loaned" or otherwise given up most of the nation's best teachers and sharpest minds either to military service or for some duty related to winning the war.

War-weary, with no time to catch an academic breath, the universities turned from the exhausting problems of helping to fight a worldwide conflagration to the equally difficult task of helping a nation to find and embrace world peace. The trouble was that neither people nor facilities were at hand. Instructional facilities and equipment were worn out or obsolete. Nothing had been replaced; repairs and maintenance had been either minimal or in some cases merely patching and repatching. Not helping matters for the universities was that nearly all were about to face the most rapid increase in enrollments in the nation's history, brought about by what came to be popularly known as the GI Bill of Rights. The legislation was by far the most imaginative and wide ranging to affect higher education in the United States since the Morrill Act of 1862.

At Purdue, enrollment suddenly doubled, then nearly tripled, at a time when neither facilities nor faculty was at all prepared for it. The situation was further complicated by having two generations of students on the campus simultaneously—the traditional eighteen-year-olds entering just out of high school and the veterans returning to resume interrupted educations or enroll for the first time.

It was hardly a time for timidity among college administrators, and while lesser managers might have demurred, Hovde relished the challenges. He made his confidence felt throughout the university. He was fortunate in many ways and agreed wholeheartedly with his predecessor, Elliott, who had said in his final speech, "I leave you an excellent university."

Purdue was an excellent university, highly regarded nationally and internationally. Hovde's own assessment of Purdue when he arrived was that it was a well-managed institution. "It had the philanthropy and wise counsel of David Ross; it had pioneered in the development of the Purdue Research Foundation and the Ross-Ade Foundation. It had such marvelous facilities as the Music Hall, a theater which could not possibly be duplicated for even ten times what it cost in 1940."

R. B. Stewart and Frank C. Hockema, appointees originally of Elliott and vice presidents by trustee edict, were already legendary figures when Hovde arrived. Stewart was considered a giant among university business officers in America, a financial genius who virtually wrote the book on financing educational facilities of many kinds with or without the direct use of tax funds. Hockema was the amiable and popular Purdue loyalist.

There was little that Stewart did not know about when it came to the use of academic dollars. The legend of "R. B." in the Purdue community may have grown larger than the man; if so, it did not arise without cause. R. B. Stewart possessed enormous ability and self-confidence that served not only himself but the university as well over his nearly forty years at Purdue. And that does not mention Stewart's considerable philanthropy on behalf of the university.

In his domain, Stewart ruled with an iron fist; he could be domineering and intimidating—not because he tried to be, but just because he seemed so formidable in all that he did. He was a little like General Douglas MacArthur who, it was said, thought he could do everything better than everyone else. The difficulty was that he could.

Hovde, however, took Stewart in stride. "When I first came to Purdue, R. B. wanted to treat me like his little boy," Hovde recalled. "He was by then, of course, a Purdue legend, a man who had learned the ways of two brilliant and strong-minded men—David Ross and President Elliott."

Purdue was fortunate to have Hovde and Stewart for the times. The university would have been hard-pressed to find two men of such tremendous competence who complemented each other so well for the tasks ahead. As closely as the two worked and fought the university's battles, they were never intimate friends, although Stewart was a favorite of the Hovde children and delighted in playing with them on visits to Hovde's home.

Hovde and Stewart were two-thirds of the troika. The other third was Hockema, the foursquare Dutchman who sold Buicks as a sideline and who was a popular professor of industrial engineering. Hovde assessed him as "a good and wonderful man who was well liked, who was a hard worker, loyal to the university—so much so that I believe he would not have left Purdue even if he had been offered a university presidency."

As the senior administrative trio—Hovde liked to call it a team—it led Purdue successfully through one of its most difficult periods and set the stage for the phenomenal growth and greatness that followed.

Three days after he arrived, Hovde outlined his tenets for higher education at an informal convocation in the Hall of Music, then told faculty members what he felt were Purdue's two principal tasks—to educate and to extend human knowledge through research. At Purdue, he said, teaching and research would be equals; in fact, first-class teaching and first-class research were mutually dependent—a statement that absolutely delighted the graduate school staff.

"You cannot have," Hovde said time and again throughout his quarter century at Purdue, "first-class professional schools without research. It's axiomatic. The campus must be, vis-à-vis the student body and faculty, an environment for learning." Such an environment included everything about the university—the classrooms, laboratories, libraries, the residence system, recreational facilities, and cultural and extracurricular activities. Such an environment also included a top-flight faculty and student body. He often said that Purdue must maintain first-class status in all its endeavors, a clear and uncompromising challenge reflecting his own devotion to excellence. For Hovde, anything less than total effort was pointless.

The atmosphere in Hovde's environment for learning had to be such that not only would learning take place, but it would also be stimulated and encouraged. All that the university did eventually had to focus on that single mission: learning—whether learning what is already known or learning what is not known, i.e., research.

Hovde believed learning was an individual matter, a self-energizing process the value of which is directly related to individual motivation. The university cannot force anyone to learn; it can only provide the influences which motivate learning (whether in or out of the classroom).

As a product of a life of competitive athletics, Hovde held the Spartan ethic that valued a strong, healthy body as well as a well-developed mind. He had little tolerance for the "academic snobs who sit on their butts and disparage athletics." (And he had even less patience with snobbery per se. "Snobbery of any kind denies the intellect," he said.) Intercollegiate athletics served as a pivot around which revolved that elusive, nevertheless present, thing called school spirit.

Hovde was pragmatic about intercollegiate athletics. He knew that despite their virtues or vices, they were immensely profitable, permitting the university to channel a large share of those profits into recreational and intramural sports for the benefit of the entire student body. It was a point proven time and again at Purdue where the intramural program was for decades the envy of other comparable universities.

•   •   •

Having set the tone for the long pull ahead, Hovde and his staff turned to Purdue's more immediate postwar problems—a bag of nagging dilemmas that were the outgrowth of the sharpest enrollment increase in the briefest period of time in university history. In 1945–46, Purdue still operated on an accelerated calendar with three terms per year, the first beginning in July, the second in November, the third in March. Resident students in 1945–46 totalled 10,199. In 1946–47, enrollment rose by forty percent to 14,187. But the two-year increase from 1944–45, when enrollment was at or near 6,000, was 130 percent. The enrollment changes during the transitional period from war to peace made orderly planning, as Hovde had said, impossible.

"Obviously," the Purdue annual report for 1946–47 stated, "any institution faced with the problem of such unprecedented growth and yet hampered by the fact that its funds are allocated for a two-year period will find itself in a very difficult position." It was basic understatement.

The veterans flooded in. The admissions office received applications at a peak rate of a hundred a day; during the admissions periods for 1946 summer session and the 1946–47 fall semester, the office handled 20,000 applicants.

A system of preferential admissions was set up to handle the applications. The first preference, to meet its responsibilities under the GI Bill of Rights, was given to veterans; second preference was granted to applicants who ranked in the upper third of their high school graduating classes; all other Indiana applicants were advised to seek admission at one of three extensions the university established out of the wartime training centers at Indianapolis, Hammond, and Fort Wayne. Still, with all of the new restrictions, admissions for the fall of 1946 had to be closed July 1.

Earlier, the board of trustees had given Hovde and Stewart a free hand and what amounted to a blank check to solve the worrisome campus housing shortage. A 1945 federal act, which amended the law establishing the GI Bill of Rights, made federal funds available to universities to defray the cost of moving temporary war housing for veteran students. It was opportune legislation; Purdue had an immediate need for 200 such units for married students and an unspecified number for single students. Without the federal funds, Purdue had nowhere near the wherewithal needed to move the housing units to the campus.

The staff Hovde and Stewart picked to handle the crisis (or crises) was composed of four able and veteran Purdue administrators: R. T. Hamilton, superintendent of the physical plant; Gordon O. Arbuckle, director of men's housing; Inez Canan, women's residences; and Henry B. Abbett, university purchasing agent. The four with Hovde and Stewart took the bold actions required by the enrollment onslaught. From 3,356 students in March 1945, enrollment more than doubled to 7,867 in March 1946.

Cary Quadrangle normally housed 936 students in prewar days, but in 1946, it suddenly bulged with 2,050 male students, a feat made possible by doubling and even tripling some of the single rooms and putting bunk beds in the attics under the sloping roofs of the halls. In the Agricultural Engineering Building on the south campus, 110 bunks were added to the third floor and attic. Space on the second floor of the Purdue Airport Terminal Building was taken over to accommodate 50 students. Across the Wabash River in a northeast neighborhood of Lafayette, Duncan Meter Company had built a small, windowless factory building to fulfill a World War II defense contract for precision instruments. It was unoccupied in 1946, and Purdue took it over to house 300 students in barracks style.

Meanwhile, lockers and double-deck bunks flowed to the campus from Bunker Hill naval installation near Peru, Indiana. These were items all too familiar to an entire generation of veterans. The board of trustees approved contracts for re-erection of other military barracks-type buildings and warehouses. The campus suddenly took on a strange appearance, a conglomeration of red-brick campus and World War II military installation.

Veterans who had vowed they would never again stand in a line suddenly found themselves standing in long registration lines. Their wearing of pieces of their military uniforms—flight and field jackets, P-coats, khaki trousers, olive drab shirts and pants—made the scene complete.

Barracks to house 300 students went up quickly on West Stadium Avenue on what had been known as Russell Field. South of that site on the same field, barracks were erected to accommodate 120 men and women; across from what is now Vawter Hall blossomed buildings for another 300.

On the west edge of what had once been the Purdue poultry farm, barracks went up on what is now the site of Harrison Hall. At the south end of Grant Street, the site of Freehafer Hall, barracks housing 240 men were set up. Each of the various temporary housing units had its own distinctive name—Mohawk for the units on the site of Harrison Hall; Seneca for the units on the site of Tarkington Hall; Bunker Hill, the only non-Indian name, for those across Third Street from Vawter Hall; and Iroquois for those on South Grant Street.

Simultaneously, additional buildings were needed for classrooms and laboratories. To the west side of the University Library was added a gray, warehouse-like building to provide study space. A series of identical warehouse buildings, mostly for use for pharmacy and chemistry laboratories, went up along Stadium Avenue between University Street and Northwestern Avenue. Providing more than 100,000 square feet of floor space, they were "temporary"—but forty-one years later they were still in place, though still considered temporary, as classrooms and offices for the Department of Creative Arts.

One of the young workmen who assisted in erecting the warehouse buildings along Stadium Avenue was a freshly discharged Marine V-12 student, Arthur G. Hansen of Green Bay, Wisconsin, who had earned his B.S. degree in electrical engineering. Hansen bided his time with a summer construction job while waiting to enter graduate school in mathematics in the fall of 1947. Hansen's professional career in higher education culminated in his appointment as president of his alma mater in 1971—the only Purdue alumnus to occupy the president's chair.

A neat row of round-roofed Quonset huts intended as classrooms suddenly appeared north of the Chemical and Metallurgical Engineering Building. A barracks to serve as a student infirmary went up on the street now known as Tower Drive, at the south end of Ross-Ade Stadium.

John C. Smalley, who became vice president for housing and food service, recalled those hectic days as a young member of Arbuckle's staff. Arbuckle was director of men's housing, and Smalley had just returned from European combat service as a field artillery lieutenant colonel. For Smalley, re-entry into civilian life at Purdue was like a new battlefront where he worked from crisis to crisis to help solve the serious and sometimes complex details created by the student housing shortage.

It was a packing-crate existence for nearly everyone, and even Smalley found himself driving to the Duncan building on Elmwood Avenue (then Indiana Avenue) in the wee hours of the morning to help cook breakfast for the 300 housed there. Looking back, Smalley remembered, "There was a lot of grumbling, but no serious protesting. Everyone seemed to get along with the difficulties and took it in the right spirit."

Besides student housing problems, the need for faculty housing added to administrative burdens. West Lafayette was not big enough to accommodate a university that suddenly doubled overnight. New private housing was almost nonexistent; building materials were not available; the nation's conversion from war machine to a peacetime economy moved slowly. Yet, the shortage of faculty housing could tolerate no alibis. Answers were needed and were found.

Hovde and his staff went to Carl F. Boester, a protégé of the late Dave Ross. Boester had come in 1940 at Ross's behest to help him with his pet housing research project, a less-than-successful activity of the Purdue Research Foundation. Could he, the Hovde team asked, build 150 new faculty houses—on a budget of $2,000 per house?

"I had been working on a story-and-a-half house design for postwar use," Boester recalled. "It had two bedrooms and a garage. So I took that plan and stripped it down—removing the garage, of course—and came up with a home costing $2,006." That included the per unit cost of gas mains, water mains, sidewalks, and streets (such as they were). The big problem was getting materials. Building material shortages were a way of life for building contractors; everything from nails to lumber to plumbing supplies, even telephone poles, were on priority allocation. The trustees quickly approved Boester's plans for the homes—affectionately known as the "black-and-whites"—to be constructed along the south side of State Street and west to Airport Road on what was a Purdue cow pasture, a verdant setting of grass dotted with small clumps of trees, once the great pride and joy of Agriculture Dean John Skinner.

Boester called the site "Pasteboard Village," an allusion to the fact that, unable to get either plywood or particle board, Boester had to settle for Upson board, a three-eighths-inch paper product. Unable to get utility poles, electric and telephone lines were strung from house to house through the development.

Boester designed the houses and in addition directed their production and erection on site. The work was under contract to National Homes, a Lafayette-based firm, and the K. H. Kettlehut Company, also of Lafayette. An assembly line was set up in the Purdue Armory where National Homes workmen fabricated the twenty-four components of each dwelling. They were then trucked to the site where Kettlehut's workmen erected them at the rate of four a day. Without footings, the houses rested on concrete blocks. The homes had some interesting and pioneering features, still considered revolutionary in the building trades: two-inch thick walls and two-by-six floor joists on twenty-four-inch centers (the forerunner, one wag quipped, of the trampoline). The buildings were also insulated, two-inches in the walls and four inches in the second-floor ceiling, with fiberglass, a new material invented by a Purdue alumnus, Games Slayter, who later became a university benefactor with his gift of Slayter Center of the Performing Arts.

A good little house, the black-and-white staved off the possibility that West Lafayette and Lafayette together would not be able to house all of the faculty and staff needed for postwar student inundation. The black-and-whites were removed a dozen or so years later in the 1950s to make way for the married student apartment complex. By then, the little house on the Purdue prairie had become popular, mostly because it offered extremely low rent; there was even some mild protest when the last occupants learned they would be forced to move.

The black-and-whites were only a part of the housing solution; in what is now an intramural field along the west edge of Airport Road, sewage and water lines went in to supply another community of wartime barracks turned into apartments for nearly 600 married students and housing for 270 single students. The board of trustees approved a plan for a trailer camp northwest of the campus on Cherry Lane adjacent to a part of what was then known as the Miller farm. The camp was about half filled in 1946 and by the fall of 1947 was operating at its full capacity of 106 trailers. It had a bathhouse and washroom in a day when most house trailers did not have bathrooms.

The stopgap measures Hovde and his staff had to take to solve a desperate problem overlapped the efforts to plan for more permanent quarters. For example, the university badly needed the apartments going up west of Ross-Ade Stadium for a rapidly expanding body of graduate students, from 292 in 1940–41 to a postwar figure of 1,073 for the fall and spring semesters of 1946–47.

Innumerable frustrating problems confronted the new president. He had barely learned where his office was when postwar problems hit him and his staff head-on. Some of the problems the university could control; some the university could not control, such as trade union strikes which delayed completion of several projects. In one case, several large semitrailer loads of badly needed building components from Kingsbury Ordnance Plant in LaPorte

County sat for days on a side street in Knox, Indiana, awaiting settlement of a strike.

But finding the housing needed for the mushrooming enrollment and the corresponding numbers of new faculty and staff was only one of Hovde's problems. Finding enough faculty to teach was also critical. World War II had impaired an excellent faculty, taking some members into the military and others into corporate research. Many never returned to the university, and replacements had to be found.

"We enlisted almost anyone with any teaching experience," Hovde recalled. Retired faculty still living in the area were recalled; faculty wives with any kind of academic credentials were practically drafted for the classroom, as were nonfaculty members who were asked to wear two hats just to help meet the heaviest teaching load in history. C. S. Doan, Purdue athletic ticket manager for many years—a man who took unmerciful verbal beatings about his handling of football and basketball game seating—returned to teach mathematics and became one of the most popular trigonometry teachers in his department. A local coal dealer, J. P. Wayne, former West Lafayette High School principal and teacher, was brought in to teach freshman college algebra. Somehow the classrooms were all supplied with teachers, and it was a marvelously adventurous time in the history of learning at Purdue University.

The housing, classroom, and faculty shortages met, problems of the lack of laboratory equipment remained to be solved; and numerous heroes, through one method or another, got what Purdue needed to carry on its primary missions. One such hero was Professor O. D. Lascoe, who was hired soon after he graduated from Western Kentucky State Teachers College. Dean Potter assigned Lascoe to survey and acquire war-surplus goods that could be used in engineering. Lascoe single-handedly acquired capital equipment ranging from Quonset huts to office furniture to enough canvas to cover a football field. But his major coup was in rounding up a king's ransom in machine tools to set up the central machine shop. Ultimately, his manufacturing engineering laboratory in the southwest bay of Michael Golden Laboratories (once simply called Shops) contained nearly half a million dollars worth of up-to-date machine tools to which industrial and mechanical engineering students were introduced.

Another problem, beyond the housekeeping details and logistics inherent in the influx of veterans, was handling the myriad differences in their academic qualifications, abilities, and needs. Out of the recognition that students, especially the veterans, came from a wide spectrum of backgrounds and experiences grew a special educational program individualized to fit the needs of students who might not otherwise be qualified for traditional college-level work. The program was reminiscent of the one Hovde worked on as assistant to Malcolm MacLean, Hovde's mentor in the University of Minnesota's General College. Nor was it different from many of the practices and procedures postulated by Hovde's predecessor, Elliott. The Purdue program gave students an opportunity to "gain their academic feet" before tackling college-level studies, admitting those for whom it was educationally sound to provide special attention.

Another problem that arose as more veterans enrolled was the slew of students whose difficulties were traced to reading deficiencies. Hovde saw to it that a reading clinic was established to help students overcome such problems.

•   •   •

Three months after he arrived, Hovde's own housing problem was solved with the completion of the redecorating and refurbishing of the president's home at 515 South Seventh Street. The time came to close his Washington residence and move the family belongings to Lafayette. Priscilla, Jane, and Linda came by air to Indianapolis; Fred drove the family car from Washington, accompanied by Boyd, then eleven.

R. B. Stewart offered to meet Priscilla and the children at the Indianapolis Airport and drive them and their luggage to Lafayette. Jane was then four, and Linda a toddler of twenty months. In those years, R. B. was a man on a dead run most of his waking hours. As they left the airport, R. B. told Priscilla he needed to stop at the Eli Lilly Company "for a few minutes" to discuss a university business matter with William A. Hanley, the Purdue trustee. For a harried and preoccupied Stewart, "a few minutes" turned into more than an hour, not the most pleasant introduction to life as a Purdue president's wife for a mother struggling with two restless youngsters in a parked automobile.

Not long after the Hovdes were settled in their new home, the family pet, Dusty, a chow-spitz, arrived by crate and was reunited with the children. In his great joy and frenzied exploration of his new home, Dusty forgot his indoor manners and disgraced himself on the newly decorated walls and new furniture. President and Mrs. Hovde were away from home for the evening, and Mrs. Hovde's mother, Mrs. Boyd, and Fred's sister, Elaine, were visitors. If Dusty's behavior was not trouble enough, someone spilled a bottle of ink on the new carpet and splattered it on a wall. Mrs. Boyd and Elaine rushed to a nearby drugstore and tried to repair the damage before the Hovdes returned. "They were not sure that night," Elaine recalled, "about the blessings of being the new tenants of the university's property."

If all was not going smoothly to put Purdue on a postwar track, neither was all going smoothly for the Hovdes as they tried to make their new house a home.

• • •

With all of the temporary housing in place at West Lafayette, there was still not enough housing or classroom and laboratory facilities to accommodate all of the students who sought admission. Hovde proposed that some students take their freshman year at seven off-campus centers to alleviate crowding at West Lafayette and still meet Purdue's educational obligations.

Earlier, Hovde had met with the presidents of other Indiana state institutions—Herman B Wells of Indiana University, Ralph N. Tirey of Indiana State Teachers, and John R. Emens of Ball State Teachers College. The four agreed that a great number of GI Bill students who sought entry to Indiana public institutions of higher education could be admitted without creating a so-called "GI School."

Hovde obtained authority from the board of trustees to provide the freshman year for up to 1,000 Purdue students at Hammond, Michigan City, LaPorte, East Chicago, Fort Wayne, Indianapolis, and Muncie. He even investigated the possibility of the university operating a center for freshmen at the Bunker Hill Naval Air Station, south of Peru, Indiana. (The proposal was never actively pursued, and the base became an Air Force Strategic Air Command facility.)

Hovde delayed an announcement of his proposal to offer the freshman year at other Indiana sites. At the first meeting of the state presidents, the proposal brought a quick reaction from Wells, who expressed fear that such action by Purdue would bring on "a mushrooming growth of local junior colleges all desiring state financing."

The four presidents met again on May 9, 1946, at Indianapolis to continue their discussions of mutual problems created by the GI enrollment bulge in every school in the state. Hovde reiterated Purdue's critical need to provide an off-campus freshman year for as many as 1,000 students. Wells again expressed his disagreement with the plan, touching off an exchange of correspondence which may have been a crucial point in the future development of working relationships between the two presidents and their schools.

Wells, a native Hoosier of Jamestown (Boone County) and an Indiana University alumnus, had gone far relatively quickly, from assistant cashier of a country bank at Lebanon, Indiana, to the deanship of the IU School of Business Administration, then into the university presidency, all within a little more than a dozen years. Wells was erudite, perceptive, and personable, a portly bachelor who endeared himself to his IU constituencies and soon traveled among the leaders of American higher education.

Wells had worked well with Elliott in the late 1930s. They had, for example, agreed "to walk up and down aisles of the Indiana General Assembly together to get our two auditoriums in the special session of 1938." He referred to the Indiana University Auditorium and Purdue Hall of Music. In Indianapolis, they had worked well together to get the state funds needed to match federal works projects funds granted to both schools.

Elliott and Wells worked on other mutual activities—such as a Joint Committee on Overlapped Curriculum. For all of that, Wells believed that Purdue's schools of engineering and agriculture "would not play ball with us." He resisted repeated attempts to begin an engineering school at Indiana University but wistfully noted that of the twenty states that have separate land-grant universities Indiana alone did not duplicate engineering schools.

The administrations of both IU and Purdue were well aware that despite the vast philosophical differences between the two schools, the best interests of both were more nearly served by policies that encouraged cooperation at every level. The happy result has been a tradition of cooperation between the two, which is a rare situation in higher education today. It has saved the citizens of Indiana untold amounts of money.

In 1946, Hovde tussled with a pressing over-enrollment problem with only one substantive solution at hand: off-campus classes in seven different locations for 1,000 students. He made it clear at the May meeting of the state school presidents that he intended to go ahead with his plan in the absence of anything better.

Wells quickly realized that Hovde was not bluffing and, indeed, had the support of his board of trustees. Wells then wrote to Hovde on May 27, 1946:

> When we discussed the matter, we excluded from our conversations by agreement any discussion of the problems of existing duplication. You volunteered the feeling that Purdue should not as a permanent policy carry on any extensive program in the general urban extension field. I appreciate very much your feeling in that regard, and I assure you of our similar thought with regard to the rights of Purdue in rural extension education.
>
> However, if you develop staffs to teach the usual arts and sciences courses in your extension centers in order to alleviate a

temporary situation it is reasonable to believe that there will be a strong demand from within your institution to continue such offerings after the existing short-lived critical conditions have passed. I need not tell you, for you know as well as I, that university bureaucracies are not different from the governmental bureaucracies and they surrender any areas of activity with the greatest reluctance. . . .

If Wells feared curricular duplication, his greater fear may have been that Purdue would get into the general extension business. Indiana University had carved out its own academic niche in urban areas of the state and believed to some degree that it thus deserved a monopoly. Yet, Purdue had been in agricultural extension almost since its beginnings and had one of the most highly regarded programs of that kind in the nation. IU was not at all enthusiastic at the prospect of Purdue expanding into the same business. But it seemed inevitable: Purdue had established World War II technical training centers and continued these as technical extension centers after the war; local community consensus demanded they remain. Wells's worst fear was about to be realized.

To head off Purdue's entry into urban extension, Wells proposed in the same May 27 letter that IU would be willing to take up to 1,000 first-year students at its centers at East Chicago, South Bend, Fort Wayne, Kokomo, and Indianapolis. Wells said that IU would take on the extra students while explaining to Hovde that it would mean curtailment of some of its own programs. It was a sacrifice, he went on, that IU would make "because we feel so strongly on the question of avoiding duplication and its consequences."

Hovde replied to Wells more than two weeks later on June 15:

> Ever since our Indianapolis discussion on May 9 concerning Purdue's emergency off-campus freshman program in its Technical Extension Centers, I have given much thought to your position that such a program was unwise from the standpoint of public, legislative, and educational policy. Your points were pertinent and well taken. Nevertheless, I have finally come to the definite conclusion that a do-nothing policy is far more dangerous from the same standpoint than going ahead with a definite program of freshman work in our extension centers to take care of the emergency load of veterans who want to start their scientific training but cannot come to the Lafayette campus. Illinois has activated a similar but more extensive plan in fifteen cities to meet its problems.
>
> Actually, I think you really agree with me on this matter, for your splendid and generous offer to train Purdue applicants in

the Indiana Extension Centers—which does what you intimate Purdue should not do—is evidence of our agreement.

The issue of "duplication" in the work of our extension centers does not give me undue worry as long as the educational needs of the state are not being met. Furthermore, our extension programs are largely self-supporting and are not a drain on state funds. It also can be argued that duplication in some instances is both worthwhile and necessary. For instance, certain fundamental studies, such as English, mathematics, and chemistry, are basic to almost all advanced professional courses. Duplication is, of course, wasteful and unwise when our facilities and personnel are not fully used. This is certainly not the case now and is not likely to be true in the future if we plan our program wisely after the emergency is over.

With respect to Purdue University's future extension programs and policy, I am quite clear that our freshman off-campus program is temporary in nature. We know we cannot train engineers, scientists, pharmacists, and agriculturalists in our extension centers. We think we can train them better in the Purdue campus and train enough of them to meet the needs of the state in normal times. Our urban extension programs in the future will be directed primarily at meeting the adult educational needs in engineering, science, pharmacy, and home economics. I look upon the university's future program in adult education, both on the campus here and in our off-campus centers, as one of the most important and far-reaching services this institution can provide in this state. In addition, I see no conflict with Indiana's urban extension programs since our spheres of educational activity are quite distinct . . . .

With respect to the basic issue of responsibility in the Indiana extension field, I cannot accept your position that Indiana University has the sole responsibility for both the arts and science courses. Purdue University is charged with the educational responsibility for engineering, agriculture, pharmacy, and home economics. These pursuits are essentially applied sciences; the basic sciences are fundamental in any course of training for these professions. At any rate we intend to build our adult educational program in the Purdue centers as slowly, carefully, and well as we know how. In this building process we stand ready at all times to collaborate to our mutual advantage with our friends and co-workers of Indiana University. . . .

It was an effective letter. In it, Hovde expressed his gratitude to Wells for his offer to "take" Purdue's freshmen at Indiana Universities centers. The real significance of the exchange, however, went far beyond the matter of the moment. It set the tone for future cooperative effort between Purdue and Indiana University and also put Hovde on record that Purdue would in no way play country cousin to any other institution. Purdue would move forward within the bounds of its traditional mission as Indiana's land-grant institution and would play a leading role in cooperative efforts to develop the best possible public higher educational opportunities throughout the state. Moveover, the Wells and Hovde letters clearly established Hovde as a "no-nonsense" president.

Hovde never felt any competitive power play from Wells and intended that neither should engage in such unproductive activity. "I simply hoped to project an image that was scientific, unpolitical, and of good management," Hovde said. Actually, Wells and Hovde differed only on how the higher educational opportunities would be made available—but never on who would offer them. They were in accord that Purdue and Indiana must walk hand in hand.

Hovde and Wells's spirit of cooperation was a big boost for the newly founded (in 1944) Indiana Conference on Higher Education, an organization of all of the presidents of public and private colleges and universities in Indiana. Hovde became active in it immediately upon assuming the Purdue presidency and served as its president in 1948–49. It was a rare and refreshing organization because it attempted to provide a cooperative spirit among both the public and private institutions of higher education. It worked—in contrast to most other states where the public and private higher educational interests expend much energy groping for one another's throats.

Such a cooperative venture paid big dividends when the Federal Higher Education Facilities Act, signed in 1963, made substantial funds available to both private and public institutions. Rather than squabble over the $5.9 million allocated for institutions in Indiana, the Indiana Conference of Higher Education presented a plan whereby the funds were to be equally distributed on a formula basis.

That and other cooperative ventures were seen as unique in higher education and stem from the rational and gentlemenly way Hovde and Wells treated each other. The development of the regional campus system of both Indiana and Purdue resulted from policies of cooperation that Wells and Hovde adhered to in the post-World War II years.

Wells agreed with Hovde that the rivalry between the two schools was what Wells described as "crazy alumni competition." "The alumni," Wells would say, "look at the appropriations of both schools, and if the total for Indiana is a dollar more than Purdue got, they scream to high heaven. . . ." Hovde and Wells could commiserate—and perhaps did—over the pressures brought to their jobs by well-meaning but misguided alumni. Hovde was philosophical about it, once telling Wells, "Well, Herman, that's just one of the problems we have to live with."

•   •   •

Hovde never fancied himself an orator, at least not in the Elliott oratorical style. Hovde's speeches were usually marked by quiet simplicity, exquisite logic, and clear meaning. He possessed the vocabulary of the learned, and like the learned, he used it masterfully and wisely, never flaunting it. He was never compelled to histrionics, but rather sought emphasis with the correct choice of words or through the sparse beauty of phrasing. A Hovde speech nearly always did what he wanted it to do: say exactly what he meant, devoid of theatrics, leaving no doubt about where he stood.

"I did not put on a show for anyone," Hovde once reflected in retirement. "If you know me, you know I was deadly serious about the business of higher education." In contrast to Elliott, who seemed to relish public appearances and speech-making, at which he was a master, Hovde looked upon speech-making simply as a necessary part of being the president of a large university. "I did not seek it out," Hovde said. "On the other hand, I was certainly aware that a university president is fair game for speech-making."

Hovde's critics believed that he was aloof from both faculty and students, a totally mistaken impression possibly gained from his speaking style. He was believed by some to be a cool, stoic Norseman, difficult to get to know. Hovde was in reality the opposite; if he appeared otherwise, it was because he wasted neither words nor time and had an extremely low tolerance for banality. He may have appeared to be the world's most imperturbable man; he was nonetheless a most sensitive one.

Hovde viewed Purdue students as mature adults and paid them the high compliment of assuming that as rational men and women they should live by rules simply for the protection of the commonweal. Yet he fully understood youthful exuberance and impatience and the consequences thereof. It is a lonely and thankless job to be in a position of one who not only makes the rules but sees that they are enforced. That, too, Hovde accepted philosophically.

Although Hovde did not seek to entertain his audiences, it was not because he had no sense of humor. On the contrary, it is not possible that he or anyone else could have survived twenty-five years in the Purdue presidency without one. But to Hovde, the athlete, the team concept was the important thing. He had no particular desire to develop a charisma, to become the personification of Purdue—a "Mr. Purdue," so to speak. Hovde tried throughout his Purdue years to get across the essential point that while he may have been captain of the team—perhaps its best-known member—he was not the team. The university, he believed, would not be successful except as it sought its goals through well-managed teamwork.

As a speaker, therefore, it was important to Hovde that the focal point for his audiences be Purdue and not Hovde. He knew that his job was, in simplest terms, to interpret and defend the academic life to those who understood it less well.

Even in the early days of his administration, hectic as they were, Hovde managed to find time to think seriously about the future—that someday, after the GI bulge years, the university had to live a much less desperate, hand-to-mouth existence, that it had to do more than merely find enough places for everyone to sleep. Hovde talked of a $15 million building program, $7.5 million for new living quarters for students alone. He talked also of increased graduate study, an attendant increase in research programs, and the need to make Purdue "a more important and efficient center for continuing study."

In his first speech after he was named president in 1945, Hovde had told an alumni audience at a homecoming banquet that he envisioned a new center where Purdue graduates could return for updating of their skills. He talked of the development of continuing education, for Hovde believed above all else that education at every level was a self-energized, lifelong process, not something at which eighteen-year-olds occupied themselves for a specified period at the end of which they received a diploma.

Most importantly, as Hovde reiterated in countless speeches, in whatever effort Purdue engaged it must be the best. Anything less was hardly worthwhile, if not an injustice to the entire constituency which supported it. This became the hallmark by which Hovde guided the affairs of the university for a quarter century.

•　　•　　•

In June 1946, Hovde's sixth month on the job, he addressed his first commencement audience at Purdue. One of the traditions of Purdue commencements is that the president delivers "the charge" to the new graduates. Rarely has Purdue deviated from that pattern, and when it has, the speaker has usually been a close affiliate—a widely known or popular faculty member about to retire, for example.

As commencement speeches go, Hovde's first at Purdue was a good one; it clearly stated his own basic and guiding philosophy of learning and education. He thus began a twenty-five-year series of brief, to-the-point commencement talks heard by thousands of Purdue graduates and best remembered for Hovde's uncanny way of understating his points as a means of emphasizing them:

> In accordance with university custom, it is now both my privilege and duty to close this, your final meeting together as classmates, with friendly words of congratulation and advice befitting the occasion and indicative of the esteem you have earned in the minds and hearts of your faculty. Your teachers honor you today, not only in formal ceremony, splendid with the color of academic finery, but also because they are proud of their handiwork.
>
> The work you have done at this university is but a passing phase in your own personal education, that process of mind-training which results from study and exploration of the fascinating world of ideas. Your teachers have been your partners in the university phase of your education. They have played a necessary and important role, but the vital role has been yours. Your faculty partners in the learning process have set tasks and goals for your minds to prepare you for the more difficult tasks ahead; they have provided some of the stimulus that has catalyzed your own intellectual growth; they have assisted you to learn and, in doing so, have themselves learned how to do their jobs better for those who are to follow you. Throughout all history, educators or teachers have been engaged in what is perhaps the most important of all professions, yet their work has never been satisfactory. To my knowledge, there has never been a civilized society which thought its education was good enough. As a matter of fact, life itself is never good enough and the job of education, which is to make it better, probably cannot be done. To admit the job cannot be done is to admit defeat. Regardless of the difficulties, real or imaginary, the work of education must continue; we must strive with ever-increasing efforts to reach the ultimate goals of real education, for it is in this striving that we grow, even though we never reach perfection.
>
> Our educational problems were just as alive and kicking twenty-four centuries ago as they are today:
>
> Over three hundred years before Christ, Aristotle wrote about education in these words: "There are doubts concerning the business of education, since all people do not agree in those things they would have a child taught, both with respect to improvement in virtue and a happy life; nor is it clear whether the object of it should be to improve the reason or rectify the morals. From the present mode of education we cannot determine with certainty to which men incline, whether to instruct the child in what will be useful to him in life, or what tends to virtue, or what is excellent, for all these things have their separate defenders."

Frederick L. Hovde served as president twenty-five years, the longest of any of Purdue's presidents. He guided the university through its period of greatest growth and change.

Maurice G. Knoy, local industrialist and active alumnus, was president of the board of trustees in the last years of Hovde's administration—and Hovde's most powerful backer.

E. C. Young, who became vice president of research and dean of the Graduate School, was Hovde's confidant and his chief adviser in Hovde's early years as president.

John W. Hicks served as Hovde's executive assistant and the university's lobbyist in the Indiana General Assembly after 1955. A professor of agricultural economics, Hicks served also as executive assistant to Presidents Hansen and Beering and retired in 1987 as senior vice president. He was acting president in 1982–83.

This is the Purdue University campus in May 1947 as the university worked feverishly to catch up with an overnight influx of GI Bill students, veterans of World War II.

Prof. Eric Clitheroe was the university's first philosophy faculty, brought to Purdue in 1951 by Hovde to enhance the humanities offerings. Clitheroe admired Hovde because "he looked like a university president and acted like one."

Prof. Karl Lark-Horovitz headed the Department of Physics and the wartime team at Purdue that did fundamental research on germanium leading to the development of solid-state physics. Lark-Horovitz pitied Hovde for his "boring job."

Paul F. Chenea was considered one of Hovde's most important team members. He was the first vice president for academic affairs but perhaps is best known for his stuffed-shirt-deflating wit.

George A. Hawkins, succeeded A. A. Potter as dean of engineering and later was vice president for academic affairs. Hawkins was instrumental in the curricular changes of the 1950s and 1960s that gave engineering education its scientific emphasis.

Much was going on at Purdue in the 1960s, including this gaping hole in the Purdue Mall at Northwestern Avenue. It was part of a project to install a linear particle accelerator for the Department of Physics in 1968. A year later, Neil A. Armstrong, AE '55, stepped onto the surface of the Moon and into immortality as the first man in history to do so.

President Hovde, right, chats with Indiana University President Herman B Wells at a Purdue-IU football game in the 1950s. Hovde was Purdue's No. 1 football fan. He was an all-conference quarterback at the University of Minnesota in 1928.

Three men Hovde relied on for honesty in all aspects of intercollegiate sports were Guy J. Mackey, director of inter-collegiate athletics and Hovde's frequent golf partner; K. W. "Jack" Mollenkopf who gave Purdue its best football in history plus a Rose Bowl victory; and Stu Holcomb, brought to Purdue in 1947 by Hovde to try to change Boilermaker football fortunes. His most famous win: a 28-14 score over Notre Dame in a striking 1950 upset.

Two scientific stars at Purdue in the Hovde administrations—and later—were Seymour Benzer (right), Stuart Professor of Biophysics, a pioneer in the relatively new discipline, and Herbert C. Brown (above), R. B. Wetherill Research Professor Emeritus. Brown's research in hydroboration brought him a Nobel award in chemistry in 1979.

Student spirit, Hovde always felt, was essential to the proper learning environment. He encouraged such booster groups as the Reamer Club, keeper of the Purdue Special mascot locomotive (above). The paper-strewn aftermath at Ross-Ade Stadium clearly reflects such spirit after the 1966 Boilermakers beat IU in football, 51-19, to retain the Old Oaken Bucket, win Purdue's first trip to the Rose Bowl in Pasadena, and score the highest number of points ever made in Ross-Ade Stadium. At the Rose Bowl, Purdue defeated Southern California, 14-13.

Symbols of two of Hovde's dreams for Purdue are Stewart Center (above) and Lilly Hall of Life Sciences. Hovde wanted Stewart Center as a continuing education center—a place where "education can continue for life." The Lilly Hall epitomized Hovde's idea for a "community of scholars"—men and women who would work together in the last half of the twentieth century, which Hovde believed "belonged to the life scientists."

Today the same old questions plague the educational philosophers, both amateur and professional; only today we use slightly different words and say moral versus intellectual education, or liberal versus technical training. Education has never been right, has never been adequate, has never been complete, despite the fact that to it has been devoted more thought and effort than almost any other profession, save perhaps those of warfare and politics.

This nation of ours has more schools and colleges and universities than the rest of the world combined; yet nobody thinks he is educated. As Mark Van Doren says in his recent excellent book on liberal education: "It is impossible to discover a man who believes the right things were done to his mind. He was forced to learn too many things, or too few. The present was ignored, or the past. Something was left out entirely, or at best skimmed over, mathematics, poetry, the method of science, the secret of religion, the history of this or that. The result is, he will say, that he does not feel at home in the realms of nature and intellect, he is not securely centered between thoughts and things; he is not a philosopher. And whereas once he did not care (during his university career), now—if he is middle-aged—he does. He knows he has missed something, and suspects that all the king's horses and all the king's men could not find it for him again."

These words which Mr. Van Doren puts in the mouth of what we may call our middle-aged university alumnus, may be, and indeed are, an indictment of our schools, but they are also an indictment of our mythical alumnus who has failed to do for himself what he thinks someone else should have done for him thirty years before.

Perhaps it is a good thing that no one thinks he is educated, for, if it is a desirable state and, judging from the amount of concern and criticism about it, it must be, then perhaps some of those who think they are uneducated will seek and strive to obtain what they want under their own power.

I hopefully suspect that some of you are already in the category of our mythical, middle-aged alumnus. If you don't think you are educated, there is some hope and chance that you will now attempt to do for yourself what the university has failed to do. Here is a goal, a personal, individual task for each of you to tackle—the attainment of which will bring more happiness and wisdom than any other pursuit in which you may interest yourself.

Education itself is not wholly to blame for its faults, which admittedly are many. The nature of the learning process involves the learner far more than the teacher. This is the hopeful and saving fact. Even though this university did not "give" you what you think you need or should have in the line of education, you are now sufficiently trained to study and learn, on your own initiative, anything you think you have missed or you may need in the future. If not, then this institution has failed in its primary objective.

Despite its imperfections and failures, education is constantly being asked to save the world—to heal its multiple sicknesses of fear, of organic institutional and political disorders, of spiritual degeneration. What a task to place on education! While education may carry part of this burden, in the last analysis the task is yours. The healing of society's ills depends on the development and mobilization and use of all the knowledge, wisdom, and spiritual power you can develop and command. This is your greatest individual task and duty—university men, of all people, must improve the society which provided the university opportunity for your education.

You have two other tasks ahead which are important—namely, the development of your professional competence for a career of service in the world of work and the development of your social competence as a parent and a member of your future community. There is nothing this world needs or values so much as real competence, no matter what the job may be. You will find no more satisfying experience in life than performing your tasks competently.

And now, in conclusion, one final thought—there is a tendency abroad in the land for people to think our nation owes them a living just because they happened to be born. We live in the finest land, under the finest form of government yet devised by men; what we have is the product of the work and intelligence of all those who have preceded us. To keep our nation healthy, to make it even better requires competent, educated citizens who realize the simple elementary fact that unless somebody works, no one can have all the things that make for the true and good life. Neither this society nor any other owes anything to you or to me that we do not earn. If anything, it owes only the opportunity to do useful, competent work. No one can deny this opportunity is everywhere today when so much needs to be done.

Your faculty believes you will discharge your future tasks and duties with much credit to both Purdue and yourselves. We hope that your university training will make your future careers so fruitful with service and personal happiness that you will always support and help your Purdue continue to do its job.

Goodbye and good luck!

Hovde's first six months as president were probably the most crucial in his quarter century at Purdue's helm. First impressions die hard, and in that tough period of upheaval in 1946, Hovde quickly earned his reputation as a highly respected, quiet, perceptive, and personable educator. His competence and sense of purpose had been amply demonstrated, and into his hands, Purdue was now willing to place its destiny.

Hovde had already dedicated his waking hours to the university, yet, he found time to return to Washington to be recognized for his service in World War II—awards which included the King's Medal in the Cause of Freedom by Great Britain for his work in the year before the United States entered the war and the President's Medal for Merit for his work as a scientist-administrator in American rocket research.

In the fall of 1946, although the activity seemed at a chaotic pitch, the campus began to achieve a curious kind of abnormal normality. Purdue had never experienced such crowding; classrooms were used to capacity from 7 A.M. to 5:30 P.M. and sometimes later; new faculty members were hard to find; scheduling was a virtual nightmare; housing with rare exception was of the packing crate variety; red tape seemed to tangle more readily. While major problems were solved, others had a frustrating way of cropping up almost daily. Abnormality became a background noise; listen to it long enough and you will not hear it. Students then, as now, griped and protested, but not so intensely. For war veteran students—men and women who griped their way through an entire world war mostly because they had to be in it—serious complaining had no real basis. Veterans were at Purdue because they wanted to be. Wanting something badly enough, the human organism is marvelously able to adjust the "barely tolerable" to "minor inconvenience.

But there was the haircut strike when local barbers raised their prices from fifty cents to one dollar. For veterans who were used to the thirty-five-cent shearings of the post exchange or the free haircut from the barrack amateur, the doubling in price was an outrage and resulted in a semi-organized movement and some picketing of local barber shops. A boycott of barbers was attempted. The crew cut was the man's hairstyle of the time, and some Purdue males were notorious for letting their hair grow as long as a freakish two inches in some cases. The strike, like many student protests, eventually settled down to sullen acceptance of the economic fact of higher-priced haircuts.

●　　●　　●

Hovde was, in the parlance of organizational psychology, a high-trust, high-delegatory executive who believed that it was his job to find the best people he could to do the tasks that needed to be done, then stay out of their way and let them perform. In that sense, he was also nondirective. His concept of the team approach required that not only must the men and women he chose be competent in their specialties but also complement others on the team and act in concert with them.

That approach freed him from an excess of administrative details best left to others and gave him opportunity for the more important work of exerting intellectual leadership. The man he most often sought for advice was Ernest C. Young, the hard-working agricultural economist who became Purdue's second dean of the Graduate School, succeeding R. G. Dukes when he retired in 1942.

Young was the founder-developer of the Indiana Farm Management Program, a pioneering Purdue project to help Indiana farmers learn how to keep precise records of their farming operations. Young had previously made major contributions to the Department of Agricultural Economics, which became through his efforts as teacher and researcher probably the best such department anywhere.

Because of Hovde's great admiration for Young, the two spent many after-hours sessions, usually in Young's office, talking about all aspects of the university—its people, organizations, attitudes, and procedures. He came to rely on Young's opinions more than those of others on his staff. "He was," Hovde once said of Young, "one of the truly wise men of Purdue University."

Under Young's influence, Hovde believed that the key to excellence at Purdue was research. He encouraged those with the necessary qualifications and background to continue their studies in graduate school because he wanted Purdue to place more emphasis on scholarly investigation. This, he felt, was essential if the university were to take its rightful place among the world's best scientific and research institutions. He knew that high quality in undergraduate programs would occur if Purdue were willing to take the risk inherent in a strong research effort through the Graduate School. To Hovde, research and undergraduate instruction were not at odds, although widespread and misguided criticism tried to make them seem that way.

For a quarter century, Hovde advocated the university as an agent of change—the very nature of higher education. While he was president of Princeton, Woodrow Wilson was fond of saying that "the object of a university is to make young gentlemen as unlike their fathers as possible."

Philosophically, Hovde agreed with Harold W. Stoke, the ex-university president who wrote *The American College President* in 1959 and who suggested that colleges and universities do not exist merely to serve students but to wage war on ignorance. And (asks Stoke) what army was ever organized merely to serve its recruits? Hovde believed, extending Stoke's metaphor, the recruits were an essential part of the war; they were best prepared to fight it if they not only were taught traditional knowledge but also were put on the front lines of battle—to do research. That was the kind of atmosphere Hovde hoped to bring to Purdue.

He wanted a university in motion. The paradox is that while everything and everyone at a university are in a constant mode of change, nothing really appears to change and Old Siwash always seems to be Old Siwash—mostly to the satisfaction of small groups of alumni. But the motion of all of the elements of a university, the ebb and flow, is a complex system of not easily understood abstract dynamics clearly perceived by only a handful of people. One of them was Hovde. His style and strength as an administrator developed out of his ability to "read" the rhythms of university dynamics and act in concert with them.

Paul F. Chenea, who served as Hovde's vice president for academic affairs from 1961 to 1967, was another of Purdue's wise men, evidenced in a statement he once made apropos direction and motion within the university, "Many times the best speed at which to proceed is the one in which there appears to be no motion at all to the greatest number of people."

Hovde's ability to understand the subtle distinctions among change, progress, and stability gave him a clear vision of the university's purposes and goals. He also displayed seemingly infinite patience in their pursuit. He was realistic and pragmatic; he knew that magic wands exist only in fairy stories. As early as 1947, when he discussed with the trustees the concept and need for a new graduate-faculty-alumni center, he was not thinking one, two, three, or even five years ahead, but far, far beyond. In fact, the facility he had in mind in 1947 did not come into existence until more than a decade later in 1958—the Purdue Memorial Center later renamed to honor Lillian V. O. and R. B. Stewart for their inestimable contributions to the university.

If it was to be worthy of Purdue University, Hovde believed, it was worth whatever the time and effort and patience required to do it right.

•　　•　　•

Monday night, February 24, 1947: the weather in West Lafayette was typical for northwestern Indiana at that time of year—cold, an overcast sky, a remnant of crusty snow underfoot. Thousands of Purdue students ate evening meals hurriedly and trudged eagerly from nearly every direction through the early evening darkness to converge on the Purdue Fieldhouse. Basketball fans anticipated another exciting game in a long, blistering rivalry. The University of Wisconsin Badgers laid a possible conference championship on the line against the Boilermakers, underdogs that season but known to be suddenly explosive, especially against teams with title hopes. Up to that Monday night, Purdue had nine wins and eight losses. It was not the best of the many excellent Purdue teams in the history of Purdue basketball, but Purdue basketball fans are forever fans.

In the last half of the 1940s, a full fieldhouse for a Purdue basketball game was taken for granted. With an enrollment near 14,000, space was at a premium everywhere, whether in dormitory, classroom, laboratory—or the fieldhouse.

That night the crowd hurried faster than usual; the atmosphere was keener, noisier as the 9,000 bleacher seats, as well as the permanent seats on the west, north, and south sides of the fieldhouse, quickly filled. Through the crowd noise and curious smells—a blend of stale popcorn, liniment, and moist sawdust—the eager fans concentrated their attention on the opening tipoff. An exciting first half featured good play and bad, crowd cheers and boos, most of the latter aimed squarely at the hapless men in the striped shirts who get paid to run the game.

The piercing squawk of the official buzzer ended the half, and both teams headed for the locker rooms. A mighty crowd of Purdue partisans rose almost as one in a standing ovation for the Boilermakers who led Wisconsin, 34–33.

Somewhere in the wooden structure of the east bleachers which held nearly 4,000 spectators, a wooden support cracked, unheard in the all-engulfing crowd's roar.

In the west stands, moments earlier, the Hovdes watched their twelve-year-old, Boyd, scramble down from his perch next to them and with some other youngsters of his age head for the east stands. It was a favorite halftime sport for youngsters to retrieve items dropped by spectators. Sometimes they would find small change, or sometimes a generous student would tip them a nickel or a dime for handing up dropped coats, hats, gloves, and the like.

Then it happened: the south central portion of the east stands sank sickeningly, as though some of giant, invisible fist were pressed into a huge pillow. The entire stand with its load of thousands of basketball fans teetered forward and plunged downward and outward toward the basketball floor. The sight was more vivid than the sound. There was a sudden low groan, a sort of eerie, unison sigh, from the crowd, then cracking and rattling of bleacher boards. It was as though 9,000 persons were suddenly stunned into silence. In the confused moments following, hundreds of victims, those least injured or not injured at all, stumbled out on to the basketball court. Others, dazed, wandered aimlessly about. Still others, stunned and confused, seemed to be looking for personal articles.

Ushers and university officials waded into the mess of broken and splintered planks and beams to free the trapped injured. Police Lieutenant Joseph Clark described the scene: "When the east stands collapsed, it was just as if somebody had thrown out a giant box full of matches on the floor."

Still in the west stands, the Hovdes watched in horror, panic tightening their throats; instinctively they thought the unthinkable—Boyd trapped beneath the collapsed bleachers. After a brief, frantic search, the Hovdes found him near the southwest corner of the basketball floor. His parents felt the limp relief that only parents experience in such situations. Happily, Boyd had been unable to get through the milling halftime crowd and missed being involved in the crash by only seconds. Hovde then was able to turn his full attention to the catastrophe which surrounded him.

Doctors and nurses in the stands came down to the floor to aid the injured. Students fashioned makeshift stretchers from bleacher planks. Others offered their winter toggery to cover those in shock. The panic which could have resulted in additional injuries was fortunately absent.

The community responded quickly as appeals for help went out over Radio Station WBAA from sportscaster John R. DeCamp. Ambulances, delivery trucks, school buses—even a hearse or two from local funeral homes—arrived unsolicited to help get the injured to local hospitals and the campus infirmary. Those at the game not injured or not involved in dispensing first aid were asked to leave. They did so quickly, orderly, and quietly.

Fatally injured in the tragedy were Roger Gelhausen, a freshman in physical education from Garrett and a Navy veteran; William J. Feldman of East Chicago, a sophomore aeronautical engineering student; and Ted Norquist, married, a veteran of sixty air missions in Europe, and a senior in mechanical engineering from Gary.

Even in the first confused minutes, Hovde somehow made contact with his key staff members and, before the dawn of the next day, had in his entourage Vice Presidents Hockema and Stewart; George E. Davis, director of the Office of Student Affairs, and members of his staff; and Guy J. "Red" Mackey, director of athletics. The community looked to Fred Hovde for leadership in the terrible situation—and he gave it. "But," he said later, "I found that every action I prescribed and every order that I gave that night had been carried out before I gave it."

Hovde and his staff spent the remainder of the night visiting the injured in the local hospitals and notifying their families of the extent of injuries as that information could be confirmed. The city's and the university's switchboards quickly jammed as the news of the bleacher crash spread across the nation and distraught parents began to respond. A standard telegram was set up for the uninjured. It simply read "Uninjured in bleacher accident" and was designed to ease the telephone congestion.

The fieldhouse was locked, sealed, and placed under guard. That official inquiry would be made into the cause of the accident was a foregone conclusion.

Throughout the night, Hovde spent many hours on the telephone, relaying the facts as he then had them to members of the trustee board. He also briefed Governor Ralph F. Gates; together they began to lay the groundwork for an immediate investigation by a joint committee of state and university officials. They worked swiftly. The committee held its first meeting the afternoon following the accident.

Gates selected Bert J. Westover, director of the State Administrative Building Council; Paul W. Kerr of Elkhart, member of the Indiana Senate; Henry A. Kreft of LaPorte, member of the Indiana House of Representatives; State Fire Marshal Carter Bowser; and G. W. Hadley, assistant attorney general.

The trustees quickly approved Hovde's suggestions for the investigating committee: Professor John L. Bray, head of the School of Chemical and Metallurgical Engineering; R. T. Hamilton, superintendent of the physical plant; R. E. Mills, professor of civil engineering; Professor E. R. Martell, head of the Department of Forestry; Brenton A. Devol, university legal counsel; and Trustee William A. Hanley. The two observers from among student leadership Hovde appointed were Edwin L. Karpick, editor of the *Purdue Exponent,* and Wallace L. Cook, president of the student senate.

The following day, February 25, the campus appeared to be one giant place of hurt. Students went to classes on crutches, huge casts swinging like giant, white pendulums. Bandages and slings of all kinds and sizes dotted the between-classes scene. Bruises, black eyes, welts, and contusions were all postcrash badges, stark reminders that "I was in it." More than 250 spectators, a vast majority of them students, were injured in the crash. Of that number, 110 were hospitalized. The estimates do not, however, take into account the many students who never sought medical help; some did not realize they had a bruise, a wrenched knee, or other painful joint until later.

The investigating committee hurried to the fieldhouse the next afternoon to begin the inquiry, which it did not complete until March 27, 1947. Hovde then personally delivered the two-volume report and its conclusions to Governor Gates. The conclusions were drawn from examinations of virtually every board in the forty-two tiers of bleachers. More than fifty photographs were taken and the committee interviewed more than 200 witnesses.

The basic conclusion was that even though the structure was far from overloaded, a metallic failure in a hook-and-stirrup "sleeper" connection near the south end of the stands was the principal culprit that began the series of events that caused the bleacher collapse. "Sleepers" were the horizontal, longitudinal members designed to prevent upright members from front-to-back movement. When the hook-and-stirrup connectors broke, others failed successively, permitting the structure to be thrust forward and downward by its load.

Ultimately, the trustees ordered payment of all medical expenses of the injured, losses and damage to personal effects, and the funeral costs of the three men who died in the crash.

Later, the university got its bill for the investigation— $24,576.00, or $1,642.00 more than the $22,934.50 the university had paid for the bleachers originally. The original amount was, however, credited when Purdue purchased new steel-supported bleachers. Hovde always considered the monetary amount involved inconsequential compared to the three deaths and injury suffered by nearly 300 students in the accident.

At a Lions Club-sponsored annual basketball banquet honoring the team, Hovde arose to speak and hid his sorrow over the accident with the greatest difficulty. He used the occasion to urge the university community to dedicate itself "to building a stronger and finer university and make up our loss by increased service to all students coming to us in the future. This is in the tradition of 'building one brick higher' after tragedy strikes."

Hovde then turned his attention to those who had provided aid and helped in many other ways in the aftermath, "It was a truly magnificent performance, and I am so proud of the Purdue student body for the way in which it conducted itself and rose to that occasion that I could burst with pride." Hovde's lifelong love for "his" Purdue began to assert itself publicly.

The second half of the interrupted Purdue-Wisconsin game was played three weeks later at Evanston (Illinois) Township High School gymnasium, the outcome almost a certainty before the second-half tipoff. Purdue lost by twelve points, 72–60. In that time, in that place, in that unique situation, Purdue's loss was understandable; no Purdue player really had his heart in it.

•   •   •

Considering the strains under which most of them conducted the business of higher education, America's colleges and universities did a spectacular job in the first half dozen years after World War II. They were overloaded, underfunded, and virtually without the means to catch up, not only with the knowledge explosion that was a byproduct of the war but also with the physical expansion that the huge enrollments demanded. Yet, they made the educational provisions of the GI Bill of Rights work as well as any federal legislation ever has.

The times portended unprecedented social and technical change. The mood reflected on the Purdue campus in the purposeful way most students approached study. Purdue students in the first years following World War II were generally categorized as serious and mature (and thus presumably more studious), but the youthful writers of the 1947 *Debris* did detect some deviation from what seemed to many a sobersided atmosphere:

> For those of us enrolled during the war years, campus life certainly has changed. To the joy of the girls and the dismay of the fellows, the ratio [of boys to girls] has zoomed from an all-time low of 1.25 to 1 to a hearty 4.6 to 1. Everyone has a car, or so it seems, when one is trying to park close to campus. Pep rallies are peppier, and fraternities and sororities are again trying to outdo one another in making victory signs and house decorations. There are more picnics, more parties, and more dances. The tempo of college life is growing faster by the month.

Still, the overriding goal of a majority of Purdue students was to educate themselves in preparation for lives altered by the war. There was no great outcry, no great organized campus movement to solve the world's ills—or even to tell the administration how the university ought to be run. The universal tendency seemed to be that students solved their own problems, ran their own lives, and aimed toward something better than the disorder many knew from their war experiences or from the debilitations of the Great Depression. Higher education was the way up, the way out—the ticket.

Hovde warned 1,085 graduating seniors in the midyear commencement on February 5, 1950, of the danger of placing "order" above freedom and urged them as educated men and women to "minimize regulation by laws and maximize regulation by self-control based on clear understandings of the values of freedom and the rights of others."

In the Hall of Music on that cloudy, gusty February afternoon, Hovde said to the first graduates of the first four-year class in his administration:

> It seems to me that the finest kind of regulation is that which seeks always to encourage and aid the functioning of private enterprise to maximum production for the welfare of society.
>
> Private enterprise is really economic freedom. As students, you have been engaged in the very private enterprise of educating yourselves. While we talk about mass education in a democracy, we mean mass opportunity to have an education. . . . The process itself is individualistic—a person's education cannot be anything but his or her private enterprise.
>
> . . . The Supreme Creator has hidden the truth about nature, man, and his societies so well, and we still know so little, that I for one am not yet ready to accept any other man's word for it. Answers will only be found if we as people are wise enough to give the human mind the complete freedom to seek the truth with every means at our command.

Hovde's words were straight from his own personal philosophy that while order is necessary to preserve freedom, order is not an end to be pursued and achieved at the expense of freedom. They came at a time in history when the ideal of order was worshipped. On a planet in such disarray as in the late 1940s and early 1950s, Hovde's words were particularly apropos when it seemed tempting to many to turn their backs on the world's miasma and to pursue individual destinies—an impossible fantasy if not an utter contradiction.

They were the years of the "Communist threat," beclouded by the McCarthy era, named for Wisconsin's Senator Joseph P. McCarthy. His political life drew sustenance chiefly from the irrational fear of great numbers of Americans that the Russian threat was from within and not from without. It was a time not of reason and rationality but a time of witch-hunting, of accusation and counter-accusation, a time of spiritual and emotional destruction for innocent and guilty alike. It was not a proud time for America. Truth and the First Amendment were severely abused.

The nation's campuses came in for their share of broom flights into political witchery. Hovde publicly decried the internal dangers posed by Communists and communism, but he was equally as vocal about the dangers to individual freedoms from the extreme right and the superpatriots.

In the mid-1950s, Hovde carried on a behind-the-scenes confrontation with the American Legion. The organization had strongly objected to the appearance of Dr. Linus Pauling on the campus as principal speaker for the dedication of the Wetherill Laboratory of Chemistry. Pauling was a distinguished American chemist, a friend and colleague of Hovde's during the war. He was the 1954 Nobel laureate in chemistry, head of the chemistry department at California Institute of Technology, and one of several scientific luminaries who were to attend. The occasion was a scientific highlight for Purdue.

Pauling was among the nation's most famous scientists, but he was also an extremely controversial and outspoken figure whom the American Legion decided it did not officially like. Hovde made several unobtrusive trips to the legion's national headquarters in Indianapolis to meet with the legion's officers. In the deft manner that marked many of his other successes, Hovde won.

"There are undoubtedly lots of people that you don't want allowed to speak on university campuses," Hovde told them. "Give me a list of the names of people you prescribe, and I will then be in a position to do something about seeing to it who is and who is not invited to speak on the campus. And if you will give me such a list, I'll make it public. Everyone should know who it is the American Legion does not want allowed to speak anywhere."

Of course the legion refused to consider Hovde's proposal and quietly dropped their objections to Pauling's visit to Purdue. "I even invited them to come to West Lafayette to hear Pauling's speech," Hovde said. No one knows whether they did.

In a Minneapolis luncheon club speech, Hovde decried "the loose talk about colleges and universities being breeding grounds of the Communists and the Reds. On the contrary," he told his audience, "our universities are the bulwark of defense of the democratic system." However, though he defended the universities, he also condemned the excesses of the few and supported the firing of Communist party members from university faculties on the ground that "no man can subscribe to Communist party ideals and retain his intellectual freedom. If a professor has lost his intellectual freedom, he has no place in this university's [Purdue's] life. It is a sad truth that in order to save your freedom you might have to lose it."

By and large, Purdue escaped the "loose talk" about Communists on the campus. Hovde told the board of trustees late in 1947 that reports of two staff members having "strong leanings toward communism" had reached him. He did not repeat their names publicly, and the trustees conducted their own discreet and confidential investigation under the aegis of a three-member subcommittee. The entire matter died aborning for no record of its outcome is known to exist. The assumption is, therefore, that the committee found no evidence of blatant communism at Purdue—at least none that appeared to be diabolically threatening to the university or to the nation.

•　　•　　•

Hovde also did not mind letting the world know where he stood on intercollegiate athletics, which have the potential for more mischief in higher education than occasional campus witch-hunts or student occupations of the president's office. Because he had been a superb college athlete himself, Hovde was often asked for his views, and he willingly gave them, leaving no doubt that he was the staunchest supporter of intercollegiate athletics and the most articulate critic of their abuse.

He believed it was possible to retain amateurism in collegiate sports provided the rules were properly enforced, and he made it clear on many occasions that he personally would see to it that they were. To Hovde, the idea that a college athlete is entitled to the opportunity to work to help pay his college expenses was acceptable, but he was emphatic in saying that no fakery could be involved, such as in the case of the star lineman at a southern university who was paid rather handsomely to "wind" the campus's electric clocks every day.

"If you pay a student for inferior work, you have done him a disservice. You have taught him dishonesty," Hovde once told an interviewer.

He also believed that coaches should be treated as equals with others of the teaching profession: "The coach must be rated only on his knowledge of his profession and his success in handling young men. He must be given the same security that his professional colleagues enjoy. I played on a basketball team [Minnesota] which won only one conference game in a season. But we were successful in that we learned all that we could absorb from a man who knew as much [about] basketball as any other coach in the profession."

Not often did Hovde display his temper—but he could. Most often he saved his scorn for the Sunday morning quarterbacks and other second-guessing critics afflicted with fire-the-coach syndrome. John W. Hicks, who served the last sixteen years of Hovde's presidency as his executive assistant, can recall one incident when Hovde patiently listened to an alumnus unmercifully berate the

Purdue football team, the coach, his staff, and any other local conditions which, to him, only added to the failure of the Boilermakers to win. Hovde finally interrupted the critic.

"Where," he asked, "did you play your college football?"

"Well," the alum admitted weakly, "I didn't play college football . . ."

"Then," Hovde replied quietly, obviously hot under the collar, "you don't know a goddamn thing about it!" and turned and walked away.

He strove to practice his own belief about coaches and coaching and in 1951 gave Head Football Coach Stuart Holcomb a ten-year-contract. Holcomb, a protégé of West Point's famed Coach Earl Blaik, came to Purdue in 1947 to succeed former Purdue All-American Cecil Isbell.

Holcomb had a so-so record in his nine years at Purdue. His popularity by and large rested on the fact that in 1950 the Boilermakers beat the University of Notre Dame at South Bend, 28–14, to win fleeting national fame for ending Notre Dame's thirty-nine-game winning streak. *Time* magazine quoted the loser, not the winner. "All the world is watching us," Coach Frank Leahy was quoted as saying. Though the Boilermakers were ecstatic and the West Lafayette campus went wild for two days, Coach Holcomb was quoted by *Time* as predicting "We'll probably lose the rest of our games." It was, unfortunately, a nearly perfect prediction. After Notre Dame, Purdue lost five games in a row but did win the Old Oaken Bucket battle with Indiana University in the last game of the season, 13–0.

Hovde's decision to give Holcomb a ten-year-contract following the 1950 season brought the critics out of the woodwork and created as much consternation in big-time college football as did the Boilermakers defeat of Notre Dame the previous season. But it was consistent with his theory about college coaching at the large schools—namely, take the constant win-or-get-fired pressure off the coaches and thereby eliminate some, possibly all, of the unethical practices coaches and schools have been known to employ.

Holcomb left Purdue in 1956 and was succeeded by one of his assistants, a bespectacled, congenial but tough-minded line coach, K. W. "Jack" Mollenkopf who over a span of fourteen years gave Purdue players and fans the best football the university ever experienced—plus the bonus of a Rose Bowl victory over the University of Southern California, 13–12, in 1967.

•   •   •

About a month after Hovde arrived, Nelson M. Parkhurst, a young Purdue alumnus who had taught vocational agriculture and coached high school basketball, sat in the office of Clarence Dammon, then director of admissions. Parkhurst had the distinction of being Hovde's first hire, having approved the appointment as assistant to the director of admissions on his first day in the presidency. With him was another fairly new Purdue staffer, Harland W. White, also assistant director of admissions. Parkhurst, Dammon, and White were contemplating the handling of more than 10,000 applications for new admissions, re-entry, or transfer from other universities and colleges. Vice President Hockema suddenly appeared in the doorway and announced, "You fellows are going to have to give us an estimate of the number of students we're going to have next fall." Dammon gave the assignment to Parkhurst who gathered all the data available and several weeks later came in with his fall enrollment estimate. Dammon looked at it, then instructed Parkhurst, "You'd better show this to Hockema right away." Parkhurst's projection was nearly 11,500 students.

Hockema looked at Parkhurst's report incredulously. "My goodness!" he exclaimed, "we can't possibly have that many students!" He then called in Professor George Sherman from engineering. Sherman was chairman of the university committee on scheduling and prided himself on estimating the upcoming semester's student population. Sherman was an inveterate pipe smoker and, as he looked at Parkhurst's estimate, said through teeth clenched tightly around a pipe stem, "Well, we might have 9,000, but not 12,000."

"I'd say we could have as many as 10,000," Hockema joined in expansively. "But 12,000? Never." Hockema's and Sherman's consternation was understandable; the comparable enrollment in the fall of 1945 had been about 5,803.

"Gentlemen, I've used everything at my command to make these estimates, and if I were to start over, I'd still come out with about this same figure," Parkhurst replied in his own defense. When October 1, 1946, arrived so had 11,472 Purdue students—just a trifle shy of his prediction. Several days later Hockema stuck his head in Parkhurst's office and in mock solemnity pronounced, "Young man, I just want to tell you that the life of a prophet is short."

Parkhurst earned the highest respect at Purdue for his statistical analysis as a means of accurately forecasting enrollment trends; he eventually became university registrar. Contrary to Hockema's jest about the life expectancy of prophets, Parkhurst served more than thirty-five years and, until his retirement, was considered "dean" among American college and university registrars. Later, as the "GI Bulge" enrollment began to drop, finally falling to 9,200 in 1952, Parkhurst predicted that it would rise steadily again for at least two decades and beyond, and his earlier forecasts for enrollment increases through the 1960s were the accurate basis for mapping Purdue's first ten-year building program.

Another element Hovde saw as necessary to meet the certainty of future enrollment growth was wise management of the university's space—the efficient and timely use of classroom, laboratory, and office. Up to 1950, each of the academic schools managed—in effect "owned" its own space. The schools "traded" space as needed, and no classes were without four walls, floor, ceiling, heat, or light. But no one was certain how much space was available or how well it was being used. In 1949, an inventory of campus space was made in a study done by Frank Hart of the University of California, and the *Hart Report* became the basis for designing the specifications needed to mesh the requirements of scheduling with the requirements for space.

To do the job, Hovde picked a new Purdue graduate in mechanical engineering, James F. Blakesley, a twenty-six-year-old Californian who had been a theater manager before the war and a B-24 pilot and squadron commander in World War II. When he joined the university staff in 1950 as executive secretary of the university scheduling committee, Hovde told him that "within ten years or so you'll probably be the nation's expert on university space management." Eventually Blakesley and his staff built a sophisticated system that, as he called it, "built some measuring sticks" to show how the university was using its available space for instructional and research purposes and later for administrative space usage. As the computer began to gain widespread usage, Blakesley quickly incorporated it into his system and began using it for scheduling. As a result of his work, Purdue became in 1957 the nation's first university to use computer-based scheduling of classes.

"It was an invigorating environment," Blakesley says of those early years. "We were out there doing things no one else had done before. It was one of the rare moments in higher education management, and it was Hovde who had given us the opportunity."

Blakesley's unit, now called the Office of Space Management and Academic Scheduling, gave the university the capability to best schedule students to their choice of courses and to get optimal uses of available space and allied resources.

Accurate forecasts of future enrollments, wise and accurate management of space, and a prudent but vigorous legislative program that monitored Purdue's interests in the Indiana General Assembly, all became the basic tools of the Hovde administration. He employed them almost constantly to pursue his goals for Purdue and to meet the logistical problems which arose as the university underwent phenomenal growth in the decades after 1950. Hovde early and repeatedly warned his counterparts in other Indiana private and public colleges and universities that ultimately they would have to reckon with such growth.

Hovde's goals for Purdue were, however, independent of growth and size; these were factors controlled almost solely by demographics and birth rates—the inexorable statistics with which educational institutions must learn to live. Hovde's primary concern, like Elliott's, was that as students arrived they be qualified for the rigors of Purdue curricula and that the university in turn be prepared to offer the best possible environment for learning within whatever means were available. The central problem was organizing and managing all of the elements required not only to meet the quantitative problems of the increasing enrollment but also to provide the best faculty available and the best conditions possible for "quality" education (whatever may be the implications of "quality").

●   ●   ●

The bricks-and-mortar metamorphosis of the West Lafayette campus was symptomatic of inevitable changes in the university academically. The underlying questions dealt with how the university was to prepare the means to provide education for increasing numbers of people in the years ahead. And what would be the nature of that education.

World War II had been the catalyst for tremendous growth and stimulation of science—probably the most significant in the history of civilization. The war was, Hovde would say, "the scientists' war" because of the vast and concerted scientific programs, both applied and fundamental, generated by both sides in the development of war's instrumentalities. Profound changes were thus wrought in the world's scientific perspective and the way nearly everything was viewed. Hovde often pondered the significance of the idea that of all the scientists in recorded history, nearly 95 percent of them were alive in the 1950s. For example, there were a large number of relatively new and unexplored disciplines, among them atomic physics, electronics, computer sciences, genetics, biophysics, and molecular biology. Hovde knew that education to be at all useful had to be geared toward preparation of men and women for a future technologic and scientific world which would never remain static.

You could not, Hovde believed, continue to prepare engineers to do the things they did a decade ago; you had to prepare them to be competent years beyond. The same was true, he often said, of all other professional development. That meant that the traditional educational approach had to change, to be more than merely vocational—that is, to teach what is already known. Rather, education had to emphasize the scientific approach, to discover what is unknown, and, further, to devise ways to make such basic knowledge useful. For Hovde, that was why an extensive research program was necessary. He saw no dichotomy between research and teaching. Indeed, the rapid progress of knowledge demanded educational settings where research and teaching were inextricably linked. Anything less, he often proclaimed, was unworthy of the citizens of Indiana who supported the institution through the appropriations of their tax dollars.

Hovde thus centered his twenty-five-year career at Purdue around what Purdue should be. And that, in his view, was a cohesive collection of strong, science-based professional schools undergirded by the best general education programs that could be developed. To achieve that ambitious goal, Hovde was fortunate to have the full support and enthusiasm of the board of trustees who had the decision-making authority.

With rare exception, Hovde had the backing of all of the trustees throughout his career. He won such support by gaining their full trust. He was meticulously conscientious in insisting that they be kept informed of what was happening within all of the areas of the university. He quickly developed rapport with each new board member by being straightforward in his dealings with him or her, corporately and individually.

He could tell a full board meeting that, "I have told Dean So-and-So that I expect such-and-such results—and I expect this board to back me up." Invariably, it did.

Hovde's working relationship with the trustees came down to the fact that the powers of appointment, the powers of budgeting, and the powers of promotion were essentially delegated to him. With these, he knew he could control the destiny of the university. He insisted that the delegation by the board of its authorities always be clearly spelled out, and he considered that this was the key to his effectiveness as president. Without such clear-cut authority, he knew that he (or any other college or university president for that matter) would have been in for a rough time of it and probably would have been unsuccessful in reaching his goals, regardless of their worth.

The Hovde years were blessed by trustees who, with negligible exception, were vitally interested in the welfare of the university and seriously dedicated to its advancement; many became important benefactors of the university in the spirit of David Ross, probably the most important benefactor in Purdue history in terms of his largess. Rare was the trustee who had an ax to grind or who had ulterior motives beyond the welfare of the university. In his quarter century at Purdue, thirty-nine men and women were at one time or another members of the board of trustees he served. Of that number, only two, while loyal, did not in his view possess the qualities or experience that a Purdue trusteeship demanded. As a matter of personal integrity, Hovde would never reveal their names, although those most intimately associated with him quite easily guessed.

The political climate for higher education in Indiana also was generally favorable. Despite the tightfisted manner in which legislators often seemed to dispense funds for higher education, the truth is that neither the governor nor the legislature interfered in the internal affairs of the university administration. In that milieu, Hovde proceeded to move forward—in the words that often became closely associated with him—"in the pursuit of excellence."

• • •

One of the characteristics that sets Purdue apart from other land-grant institutions is its early stress on engineering. When other land-grant universities stressed agriculture, Purdue under the personal enthusiasm and drive of President Smart was doing great and spectacular things in engineering before 1900. That emphasis continued under Presidents Stone and Elliott and the guiding influence of Dean Potter. Purdue, of course, had an excellent School of Agriculture, developed by some able agriculturists led by John Skinner under President Stone. But the precedents created by the engineering emphasis were impossible to ignore. As early as 1925, Purdue had the largest undergraduate engineering enrollment in the nation, a rank it held well into the 1970s. But that early emphasis did create problems. Eventually, a "barrier," represented by State Street (the main east-west thoroughfare), seemed to divide agriculture from the rest of the campus in ways other than physically.

When he arrived in 1946, Hovde quickly recognized that the life sciences as represented by several scattered departments in the School of Agriculture and the School of Science had for too long been neglected. Some believed that Hovde was "in an angry mood" over the traditional barriers that often exist between academic departments and schools, especially the one represented by State Street. Though he was determined to do something about the problem of the life sciences, he was not in an "angry mood" at all. Hovde was, above all else, cool and approached most problems in that frame of mind. He seldom if ever dealt with any problem with the absolutism often engendered by anger.

Nevertheless, Hovde decided it was time for an amalgamation of smaller departments and course offerings (biology, botany and plant pathology, bacteriology, zoology), a reorganization the board of trustees approved in November 1948, by changing the name of the Department of Biology to Department of Biological Sciences. To pull the scattered departments together into a cohesive unit, Hovde brought to Purdue a gentle Texan, John Karling, a gifted Columbia University research botanist. Karling was intrigued by Hovde's oft-repeated notion that "if the first half of the twentieth century belonged to the physicists, chemists, and engineers, the second half will belong to the biological scientists." It was a notion that, in a real sense, came to pass.

Karling worked arduously toward the development of the biological sciences at Purdue, and from that small number of scattered departments, he built one of the best such departments in America. Much later in his Purdue career, he gave up the departmental headship to return to his research on fungi as Wright Professor of Biology.

Karling's successor was another outstanding biological scientist, Henry E. Koffler, a Viennese who received his undergraduate education at the University of Arizona and his advanced degrees in microbiology and biochemistry at the University of Wisconsin. He came to Purdue in 1947 as an assistant professor and was the key figure in the beginning studies in molecular biology, then a pioneering field. He quickly became the rising star in his discipline and soon caught Hovde's eye. He had been on the campus a dozen years when Karling stepped down, and Koffler's appointment as his successor was inevitable. He astutely guided the department's expansive growth which kept it abreast of almost revolutionary changes in the life sciences and maintained its reputation for excellence. Koffler resigned in 1975 and went on to become the vice president for academic affairs at the University of Minnesota, still later president of the University of Massachusetts, and eventually president of the University of Arizona.

The amalgamation of the biological sciences was the key to Hovde's goal of achieving a superior level of scholarship and top-flight graduate programs that cut across the entire spectrum of those disciplines. But an important element in achieving his goal was the construction of a life sciences building (which became the Lilly Hall of Life Sciences). It was also the keystone in the first ten-year building program he launched at mid-century. Ultimately, the life sciences building complex, built in at least four phases, housed thirteen acres of floor space by the time it was completed in 1959. At the time, it was believed to be the largest building in the Western world devoted to instruction and research in the life sciences.

The bringing together under one huge roof all of the university's life scientists—a community of scholars involved in basic and applied sciences—made the greatest kind of sense to Hovde and contributed much toward destroying the so-called barrier symbolized, for some, by State Street.

In Hovde's years, the Purdue campus was never static. Construction of some variety was always going on somewhere, whether it was a new academic building, a new residence unit, utilities, major landscaping, or a new athletic facility, or remodeling, or expansion.

A major university that is doing its job properly can never have a campus on which somewhere in some way some physical change is not being made. And so the old sod of Purdue—once the hunting ground of the Kickapoo braves, once the farmland of pioneers—has had little rest in more than a century. In 1948, the trustees approved Hovde's building program and asked the Indiana General Assembly for up to $14 million to pay for new capital construction: the first phase of the ten-year program that included the new life sciences facilities, completion of the existing chemistry building which became the Wetherill Chemistry Laboratories, a new building for a proposed School of Veterinary Medicine, and an addition to the Mechanical Engineering Building.

Paradoxically during Hovde's tenure, with the exception of the first unit of the new Civil Engineering Building, a small one-story office building for the School of Aeronautics, Astronautics, and Engineering Sciences, and a collection of modest buildings which comprise the jet laboratories at the west side of the Purdue Airport, no new engineering buildings were constructed at the West Lafayette campus. Instead, the emphasis was on science facilities: Lilly Hall of Life Sciences, the Mathematical Sciences Building, the Wetherill Chemistry Laboratories, and a second new chemistry building named in 1987 for Nobel Laureate Herbert C. Brown. There were also major additions to the Physics Building and its contiguous laboratories, a new Pharmacy Building, a new Home Economics Building (Stone Hall), an expansion of the Biochemistry Building, the School of Veterinary Medicine complex, the Krannert Building for the School of Management—as well as Purdue Memorial Union guestroom additions, the graduate houses, a ninety-bed Purdue University Student Hospital, nearly a quadrupling of the permanent residences for both single and married students, a multiple-phase program for construction of new heating and power plant facilities, and countless new agricultural and farm additions.

The principal reason only a few new engineering facilities were added was because Purdue's were adequate for the time. That does not mean they were neglected, however; major updating, remodeling, and refurbishing cost millions of dollars through the years. It seems to be in the nature of engineering education that its laboratories and other facilities are undergoing constant revision.

The emphasis on new science facilities symbolized Hovde's dream of moving Purdue ahead as a first-class research institution, one that stayed on the cutting edge of new knowledge. He would have never permitted Purdue to dawdle along as merely another good agricultural and mechanical arts college. The new buildings themselves were important only insofar as they symbolized a change in emphasis—science and research—to enhance Purdue's traditional engineering and agricultural missions.

•   •   •

A second part of the Hovde "dream" goes back to the fall of 1945 when, as president-elect, he addressed the homecoming banquet in the Purdue Memorial Union. It was his introduction to the university; he was not to take office for another three months.

"I foresee a great building here," he told his alumni audience. "A busy intellectual center for graduate students, faculty, and you—devoted to serving the people, industry, the agriculture of this state and nation by means of lectures, forums, courses, demonstrations, cooperative projects, symposia, and so on. This is only a dream, but if it is worthwhile I am sure ways can be found to have it."

Hovde held onto his dream for thirteen years, and ways were found to have it, thanks to the financial genius of R. B. Stewart who devised a then unique open-end bond plan that permitted the university to sell self-liquidating bonds to be retired from a portion of student fees and charges in the building.

On May 9, 1958, the center was dedicated. It included the 1,200-seat Loeb Playhouse, the dazzling gift from Bert and June Loeb, Lafayette merchants and philanthropists.

Memorial Center went beyond even Hovde's 1945 dream; it encompassed the theater (which included theatrical shops, rehearsal rooms, and an experimental theater beneath it), as well as the University Library building which was expanded and improved. It also included a new Eliza Fowler Hall, a 400-seat auditorium which replaced the original Fowler Hall, razed to make room for the new center. The huge new building also included facilities for conferences, adult education activities of all kinds, student activity offices, a ballroom, and quarters in the lower levels for audio-visual and educational media production. It is still Purdue's largest academic building with nearly a half million square feet of usable floor space.

Hovde was extremely proud of the center but perhaps prouder still of the fact that it was built without infusion of state tax funds. In addition to gift funds, the university borrowed the balance of the money and repaid it through revenues and user fees. "Therefore," Hovde explained in his dedicatory talk, "all those students and citizens who use this building will pay for it—it now belongs to the taxpayers who didn't have to pay a cent for it. I hope I shall never have to hear again any uninformed citizens say the university spends too much money for buildings."

Before the project was completed, the center had three names, and before it was fifteen years old, it was given its fourth and permanent name, Stewart Center. In the planning, it was called an adult education-student building; then, in a bow to the legalities involved in the financing, the Union-Hall of Music Annex; and when completed, the Memorial Center, a tribute to the university's dead of World War II, as the Memorial Union had been a tribute to Purdue sons and daughters who died in World War I. Fittingly, it was renamed Stewart Center on March 1, 1972, honoring R. B. and Lillian V. O. Stewart for their beneficence to Purdue and the Lafayette community. The act also had special meaning since it was R. B., the university's chief financial officer, who had performed the intricate financial handiwork that made the building possible.

Stewart Center and the Lilly Hall of Life Sciences, the second largest building at the West Lafayette campus with 391,622 square feet of floor area, were the capstones in the intense and feverish building activity that marked Hovde's twenty-five years at Purdue.

Stewart Center has other significance from the standpoint of Hovde's years. It represented his firm and lifelong belief that education was more than a traditional four years in campus classrooms. Education, he said, is for life. The progression of human events and technological change require educated men and women to return to the campus to keep current in their career fields as well as to re-expand horizons narrowed by the intellectual calcification that victimizes almost everyone to varying degrees at some time or other.

Hovde alluded to all of this in his first speech at Purdue in 1945, even before he assumed the office: "In an age of science, the man of science can no longer think only of what he creates. There is evidence from all sides that the scientist is beginning to think more than ever about the effect of his technology on society. He is beginning to worry about and discuss the significance of what he has wrought. . . . Men of science at last are becoming seriously interested in the role they should play in our government, in international relations, in the problems before the psychologist and the sociologist, in the problems of political science."

The university was, Hovde believed, the proper place for the professional to come to discuss and contemplate all of these things and to search for some of the answers. Science and technology were in a headlong rush, and new knowledge was being generated far faster than it could be properly absorbed. The engineer, the scientist, the agriculturalist, the manager—the professional in all fields, including teaching—could not begin to keep up and needed ways to avoid obsolescence. As a result, Purdue's continuing education activities grew phenomenally. By 1987, educational conferences, seminars, short courses, and similar activities attracted on the order of 100,000 annually to the West Lafayette campus; like functions brought large numbers to other campuses in the system.

• • •

Hovde was able to report in 1954, as construction began on Stewart Center, that thirteen major construction and renovation projects had been completed since 1950. The dirt flew everywhere. Hovde's thirteen projects were merely a start. Work was begun on the second unit of the life sciences complex. The Wetherill Chemistry Building, actually the west end of an existing chemistry building, also was under way. An addition of fourteen guest rooms on the north end of the Purdue Memorial Union was in progress, and an 800-student State Street Courts residence system was being built.

Hovde also promised a start on the new intramural and recreational gymnasium, at the time a unique facility which became known among students as the Co-Rec and was financed entirely by the student users from fees and other income.

On July 1, 1956, Hovde reported to the board of trustees that $48 million in new construction was in progress at the West Lafayette campus. Looking ahead, Hovde told the trustees that he hoped the near future would include the completion of the life sciences complex, expanded power and heating plant capacity, the addition of another science classroom and laboratory building, additional residence halls (for at least an expected 2,000 male students), a new pharmacy building, a student hospital to replace a World War II barracks used as a student infirmary, and the facilities for an anticipated new School of Veterinary Science and Medicine (now the School of Veterinary Medicine).

The remaining elements of the first ten-year building program included the new civil engineering building, a forestry building and laboratory, a nuclear engineering building, a laboratory for industrial psychology, an applied art and design building, a new agricultural administration and classroom building, facilities for Purdue's three-service ROTC program, and an addition to the Physics Building.

It was an interesting "shopping list," and the university did not achieve all that it sought. Still, as Hovde was quick to say, "A record? It was damn near a miracle!" that a ten-year building program such as Purdue's in the 1950s was completed within twelve years.

Of course, Hovde knew that such a massive building program would have some trade-offs, some negatives so far as alumni attitudes were concerned. He took the heat from various alumni for the inevitable razing of some campus structures either no longer structurally sound or obsolete for a variety of reasons. Practicality and the cold, hard economic facts of university life had to take precedence over sentimentality. Hovde managed with grace to overcome that rather peculiar phenomenon wherein some alumni become loyally and affectionately attached to certain arrangements of brick and mortar—the buildings that symbolize for them their own years as students. When such buildings are razed, there is an angry reaction, a certain outraged consternation that, somehow, a part of the glorious past (i.e., when they were students) is now doomed to oblivion, beclouded by a choke of demolition dust. So there were scattered outcries when Hovde decided that old Heavilon Hall, that epitome of Purdue's past, had to go to make room for a new building, also to be named Heavilon Hall but without the familiar landmark of the clock-and-bell tower. Heavilon Hall had been less a building than a tradition shaped in brick, mortar, and limestone. For thousands—alumni, students, and the public at large—Heavilon Hall was Purdue. The words of President Smart in 1894 ("But I tell you, young men, that tower shall go up one brick higher!") the morning after fire destroyed the first building became the symbol of Purdue determination and a rallying cry for future generations of Purdue loyals, bringing a tingle to the spine, a lump to the throat, a tear to the eye.

•   •   •

Hovde used to say that he was less interested in what the buildings looked like than what was going on inside them. That was his way of saying that he believed Purdue's predominantly red-brick architecture was just right and that those who argued about it argued in vain since they would have to take their complaints to the university's founders.

Hovde's years as president may always be best known for the remarkable expansion and change in the university's physical plant—a view that misses the mark by a wide margin. The real mark of the Hovde administration was in scholarship—the research and scientific orientation the university acquired under his leadership, a move away from the traditional vocational engineering and technology previously taught. The growth in the physical plant and all of the new buildings was simply a manifestation of that fact. Yet the building program was itself a remarkable achievement. The physical plant grew from a value of $19.5 million when he arrived in 1946 to nearly $300 million when he retired in 1971.

Capacity of university-owned housing increased fourfold from 3,700 to nearly 13,000—an accomplishment Hovde always contended was simply necessary to meet the rising enrollments, independent of anything he or anyone else might have done. The graduate houses, however, were based on Hovde's idea of providing a community for graduate students, who were, in his view, the backbone of the university's research activity. The concept was so successful that a second Graduate House was built and became the third largest building on the West Lafayette campus after the Stewart Center and the Lilly Hall of Life Sciences. Eventually, the two graduate houses were named to honor the memories of two of Hovde's closest aides and friends, Ernest C. Young, the second Graduate School dean, and George A. Hawkins, who served as dean of engineering and eventually as vice president for academic affairs.

•   •   •

Early in his presidency, Hovde displayed a great interest in the galaxy of scientific and educational stars at Purdue. Two of the brightest were Karl Lark-Horovitz, the head of the Department of Physics, and his protégé, Seymour Benzer. Lark-Horovitz had directed the fundamental research at Purdue in World War II on the electrical behavior of germanium and silicon—work without which development of the transistor and the phenomenal growth of the electronics field would not have taken place. Lark-Horovitz and his team quite literally were the frontier of solid-state physics years before it became a "discipline." Benzer, a New Yorker, came to Purdue in 1942 as a graduate student under Lark-Horovitz, participated in the germanium research, and later worked under him as a faculty member.

Lark-Horovitz took an immediate liking to Hovde, and the two developed a deep, mutual admiration. Lark-Horovitz and Benzer both had a built-in disdain for paper shuffling and figured that Hovde must have spent dull day after dull day in that kind of activity when he probably would have much preferred to be out on the campus, poking through someone's laboratory.

"Why don't you go visit President Hovde and tell him about science and research and the research you are doing," Lark-Horovitz suggested to Benzer one day. "The poor guy has such a boring job!"

Benzer did visit Hovde on several occasions, and Hovde said he was always fascinated by Benzer's descriptions of his work. On the other hand, Benzer was impressed by Hovde. "I was always impressed by the piles of papers on his desk and I remember sympathizing with his predicament."

About a year after Benzer received his Ph.D. and an appointment to the physics faculty as an assistant professor, he became interested in another new field, biophysics, and requested a one-year leave of absence. Lark-Horovitz was dismayed. The Purdue physics group was in the vanguard of solid-state physics, and he felt that Benzer had a great future in it simply by "riding the tide." But he eventually acquiesced, and Benzer was granted the one-year leave at Oak Ridge National Laboratory near Knoxville, Tennessee, "to get the feeling" (in Benzer's words) of biophysics.

Benzer was always surprised when requests for extension to stay at Oak Ridge—which he felt certain would be denied—were granted. Benzer spent two additional years at the California Institute of Technology and one at the Pasteur Institute. Then, having stretched a one-year leave into four years, Benzer asked for two additional weeks to attend a conference of biophysicists in Paris.

Lark-Horovitz sighed but took the request to Science Dean William L. Ayres, who shouted, "Fire him!" Nevertheless, Lark-Horovitz got the two-week extension.

When Benzer finally returned to Purdue, he found that Lark-Horovitz had developed a small biophysics section under Lorin Mullins, who had come to the university to do research in membrane physics, a subject of interest to Lark-Horovitz since his early years in Vienna. Benzer's scientific career was the more remarkable because his interest in biophysics (where he studied genetic structures) turned to investigation of neurological phenomena. He was elevated to Stuart Professor of Biophysics in 1961, among the first to hold a distinguished professorship in a program Hovde established in 1959. Until then, Purdue's only named professorship was that held by George A. Hawkins who was Westinghouse Professor of Heat Transfer.

Benzer resisted tempting offers to lure him away from Purdue until 1965, when he took leave to study at Cal Tech. Then, after fifteen years of contributions which led to the development of molecular biology at Purdue, he accepted an appointment as the James G. Boswell Professor of Neuroscience at the California institution. Privately, Hovde hated to see Benzer leave. "But I never begged a man to stay," Hovde explained. "He had to make his decision on his own. But that doesn't mean there weren't some great losses." One of them was Benzer.

At least four major program thrusts received Hovde's primary support: introducing computers and computer sciences; updating the engineering curriculum so that it would be taught as a science rather than an art (i.e., engineering practiced traditionally); founding four new schools (veterinary medicine, management, technology, and humanities); and establishing distinguished professorships.

As early as 1952, Hovde gave eager support to a small group of professors and graduate students who worked with early calculators and computers and in the mid-1950s went as far out on an administrative limb as possible to approve expenditure of $125,000 for the purchase of a Datatron 204—in those days a state-of-the-art machine that was critical to Purdue's pioneering work in the computer sciences. Some of the early names in computers were Carl Kossack, Alan Perlis, Duane Pyle, Paul Brock, Richard Kenyon, George Morgan, Al Lewis, Betty Suddarth (who became a Purdue registrar), Thomas Jones, Sylvia Orgel, Virgil Anderson, James H. Stapleton, Gordon Sherman, John Clark and Robert Burnett (both electrical engineering professors), and Tom Cheatham and L. E. "Gene" Grosh (both graduate students).

The real leaders in the development of computer usage and the beginning of the nation's first undergraduate computer sciences department (although Stanford also makes the claim) were Felix Haas and Samuel Conte. Haas, a mathematics professor, went on to become dean of the School of Science and later, under President Arthur G. Hansen, executive vice president and provost. Coming to Purdue from industry, Conte was founder and head of the computer sciences department.

As the state-of-the-art hardware, not to mention software, in computer development advanced, so did Purdue's emphasis on curricula and facilities. Following the Datatron 204, Purdue installed a Univac Solid-State 80 (a less than successful machine), the IBM 7090, the IBM 7094, the IBM 360/40, and eventually two CDC 6500s and a CDC 660. In the spring of 1983, the long-awaited Cyber 205—known in the industry as a supercomputer—was installed at the Purdue University Computing Center. Purdue became one of the first two universities in the United States to have supercomputers.

Hovde was one of a handful of American leaders who early saw the significance and impact of the computer on civilization. In 1962, at the dedication of the IBM 7090 in the Engineering Administration Building, Hovde said that "the electronic computer may well be the single most important development of the twentieth century in terms of its overall impact on the management of the operating elements of our complex and gigantic society." Several years later in another speech, he reiterated his unshakable belief, declaring that "tomorrow's engineering work will use in a bewildering variety of ways the most important machine of our time—the computer." They were not empty words; in a real sense, Hovde was exactly right. The computer revolution moved quickly. Hovde was always intrigued by the idea that if the eighty-year history of aviation had moved at the same pace as the computer revolution we would have been on the moon in the 1930s. His challenge was to try to keep Purdue ahead of the headlong rush.

Seldom did Hovde speak so confidently or in such absolute terms as he did when he talked about computers. He was so convinced of the computer's vast potential, especially as a tool in research and education, that he enthusiastically fostered not only computer education at several levels at Purdue, but he also encouraged its use in the university's administrative milieu, when elsewhere the computer was viewed somewhat tentatively or timidly. As a result, few universities offer computer education at as many different levels as does Purdue.

•   •   •

Dean Potter's long and illustrious leadership in engineering at Purdue came to a close in 1953 with his retirement. But it only signaled the dean's beginning in a second career in bituminous coal research, in which he became nearly as busy as he had been in his thirty-three years as Purdue's engineering dean. He maintained his interest in the university, and even at the age of ninety-four, the dean emeritus usually walked from his Russell Street home to his office in the Engineering Administration Building.

The appointment of Professor George A. Hawkins to succeed Potter came as no great surprise. Hawkins, a quiet man from Colorado who had transferred to Purdue from the Colorado School of Mines, was Potter's student. He earned all three of his degrees at Purdue in mechanical engineering, receiving his doctorate in 1935—the third individual to be awarded an engineering Ph.D. at Purdue. Hawkins rose swiftly through the faculty chairs after he joined the engineering faculty. In 1938 and 1939, he spent a year in postdoctoral research under Max Jakob at Armour (now Illinois) Institute of Technology. He eventually became widely known as an investigator in heat transfer and thermodynamics, authoring or coauthoring nine textbooks during his career.

In World War II, he directed significant work on the heat transfer problems involved in cooling the barrels of .50-caliber machine guns. This work was done in concrete bunkers built in a swale northeast of Ross-Ade Stadium along the west side of Northwestern Avenue.

Hawkins was director of the Engineering Experiment Station when Hovde tapped him to succeed Potter. It was an unstable time in engineering education; Hawkin's appointment had the effect of propelling him into the maelstrom whirling about the profession. There was a growing ferment nationally for a shift away from the traditional "art" or "practice" of engineering and toward "engineering education in the fundamental principles."

As early as 1929 the controversial and monumental *Wickenden Report* of the American Society of Engineering Education (ASEE) decried the custom of stopping engineering education at graduation and the failure to distinguish between mere preparation for the workaday world and preparation for intellectual leadership. Hawkins himself was on the cutting edge of the trend toward substantive curricular changes in engineering, the need for which clearly emerged from World War II's dominant scientific impetus. The war had quickly produced a tremendous expansion of scientific knowledge the professional engineer would need.

When Hawkins was named engineering dean, "the curricular kettle at Purdue had been boiling and bubbling for five years" (as

H. B. Knoll put it in *The Story of Purdue Engineering*). Hawkins had served on the ASEE's special committee on curricular changes which recommended in 1955: "It is the responsibility of the engineer to recognize those new developments in science and technology that have significant potentialities in engineering. . . . Moreover, the rate at which scientific knowledge will be translated into engineering practice depends, in large measure, upon the engineer's capacity to understand the new science as it develops." Thus, the report concluded, there must be a shift from "teaching . . . engineering methodology."

As Potter retired, so did several other school heads within engineering, and younger scholars helped bring about the transition of the teaching of engineering as "science" instead of "art."

Although the time seemed opportune at Purdue and the arguments overwhelming, the revolution in engineering curricula at Purdue caused tremendous turmoil within the schools and the development of schisms between "older" and "newer" faculty.

Of course, Hovde pushed for curricular change merely by administrative style and demeanor and set the tone for the change. However, he did not dabble in the intricacies of the changes themselves nor in the inevitable dichotomies that resulted where there were sharp differences of opinion and philosophy. Besides, it was an academic area zealously guarded by the faculty bodies. But it was an exhaustive and exhausting test for Hawkins who, as the new dean, guided and directed the engineering education changes that were essential to Purdue's development in the 1950s and 1960s as a major international scientific university.

Though Hawkins had a splendid background for the deanship in engineering, he was enigmatic. He was a brilliant reseacher, an excellent teacher, and had made his mark as an administrator in the curricular changes. In the 1960s, Hawkins was charged with responsibility for the undergraduate portion of another monumental national study of engineering education by the ASEE. Known as the *Goals in Engineering Study*, the report took five years to assemble and write. It called for major revisions in the way engineering was taught, similar to curricular changes that had been made in engineering at Purdue in the 1950s. The report called for an eventual general curricula requiring five years rather than the traditional four years and made the master's the first academic degree for engineering students.

The report created great waves of consternation within the profession and, unfortunately, lost Hawkins many friends. Interviewed just prior to his unexpected death in April 1978, Hawkins admitted that "we took an awful beating on it (the report). Many of my former colleagues and close friends still do not speak to me."

Hawkins had expressed confidence that someday five-year engineering curricula would be the rule in most United States universities. Hovde himself opposed the five-year program in pharmacy (which is now the fact at Purdue and at most pharmacy schools). And he felt that the fifth year in engineering should be a graduate year, that it was possible to maintain a viable, up-to-date four-year program. He also believed that adding a fifth year to engineering, or any other curriculum, only made already costly higher education more so.

Hovde recognized Hawkins as one of the university's most capable staff members. In 1967 when Paul F. Chenea resigned to take a vice presidency in research at General Motors Corporation, Hovde without hesitancy asked Hawkins to succeed Chenea as vice president for academic affairs. Hawkins resigned in 1971 but remained on the campus to assist President Arthur G. Hansen in a variety of administrative posts until 1973.

•   •   •

Hovde was always quick to credit "his" successes to the members of "his" team. The ultimate athlete, he was a competitive figure (in the sense that he always strove for excellence) who as an administrator talked more about his "team" than his "staff." After his biography was published in 1980, he confided to the author that he liked the chapter that described the people around him far more than the chapters about himself. He had brought some unusual and extremely capable people to Purdue. At times, he stood in awe of their competencies and imaginations, and though he may have argued with them on occasion, he never employed anyone, then tried to tell that person how to do his or her job. He let his staff know exactly what results he wanted, then got out of the way to let them do it. One of the rare qualities that permitted Hovde to accomplish so much in his twenty-five years was his ability to delegate responsibility without giving up his authority. As a result, he never lost the loyalty or confidence of any of his senior staff. If Hovde had a weakness, it was his own blind loyalty to those who were a part of his team. It was a very laudable trait, albeit one that did not always do him the greatest justice.

Hovde was zealous in his defense of academic freedom. In the years immediately following World War II, the McCarthy era, queries were often filed with the board of trustees criticizing the selection and use of specific textbooks in certain classes—especially reading lists in English literature. Hovde reacted immediately with certainty, stressing to the board the "importance of intellectual freedom within the university [and] the importance of studying the ideas both true and false—primarily to combat the false—because that is the way of intelligence."

"I have a strong belief in the intellectual maturity of the student body and the fundamental integrity of the faculty, and I consider this matter of vital importance to the welfare of the university," Hovde told the trustees. "I urge you to investigate carefully and give this issue all of the experience and wisdom at your command."

At the same meeting, Hovde proposed and won approval for creation of an additional reserve fund to provide University Research Fellowships ranging from $100 to $1,000 to encourage young staff members to pursue their doctorates.

Hovde also fought for, and obtained, a gamut of faculty and staff benefits over the years. These included increased university contributions to pension funds, a five-day work week, liberalization of sick leave and vacations for clerical and service personnel, and an order (dated September 1, 1948) forbidding racial discrimination of any kind in the Purdue Memorial Union barber shop.

His critics who believed that he was not close to the faculty simply reflected some misunderstanding of what being a college president, at least in the Hovde style, requires. Despite criticism that he was cold and aloof (criticism which never bothered him), Hovde was the kind of compassionate person who in the company of then Vice President and Executive Dean Donald R. Mallett made it a point to spend many Christmas Eves delivering poinsettias to hospitalized or shut-in staff members and students.

In September 1949, Hovde appointed Robert Johns as his first administrative assistant to help remove some of the routine burden and problems of the presidential office. Johns also held a one-fifth time appointment as an assistant professor of education. He had been on the job about two weeks when he came to Hovde's office one day and solemnly announced, "You ought to fire at least half the faculty." The idea seemed to Hovde patently absurd because of his great respect for the faculty. He was momentarily stunned. Then he could only stifle a desire to laugh out loud for fear of embarrassing his brash, young assistant who demonstrated such blunt naivete in such matters.

Johns was described as having most of the attributes of an excellent administrator, if at times he seemed somewhat heavy-handed in his dealings in academic affairs. He left in 1954 to become head of the United States Armed Forces Institute at the University of Wisconsin, thereby setting the stage for the membership on the Hovde administrative team of a young agricultural economics teacher named John William Hicks III.

Over the next thirty-two years, Hicks served not only as adviser, confidant, and good right arm to three Purdue presidents but also as the university's legislative liaison in the state capitol— the lobbyist legislators sought out more than any other for answers to tough educational problems. In good times and bad, it often seemed as if the university would not or could not operate without him.

Hicks was born in Sydney, Australia, the son of an American film distributor. But he grew up in New Rochelle, New York, and studied at Massachusetts State College (the University of Massachusetts). Hick's education was interrupted by a three-year World War II stint as an Army Air Corps aircraft armorer, but he earned his bachelor's degree in 1946, meeting one course requirement at nearby Vassar College. At the behest of Earl L. Butz, Hicks came to Purdue in 1947 as a doctoral student in agricultural economics and was awarded his degree in 1950. He joined the faculty in the Department of Agricultural Economics and quickly won a reputation among students as one of the best teachers in the program.

He was handpicked by Stewart and Young in 1953 for a gubernatorial appointment as executive director of the ad hoc Indiana Commission on State Tax and Financing Policy. His final report for the commission was so impressive that Hovde knew immediately that Hicks was the person he was looking for. Hovde told Hicks that there was no job description for the executive assistant which, recalls Hicks, "was all right with me." That meant that Hicks had a wide latitude in assisting Hovde, who came to trust him implicitly. Through the next seventeen years with Hovde, and fifteen with Hovde's successors, whatever task he was given, glorious or ignominious, Hicks performed with a relaxed, easy grace; he was easily one of the most popular individuals on the West Lafayette campus. He made hundreds of friends, most of them charmed by his warmth, wit, and erudition, and his passion for baseball, epitomized by the San Francisco Giants even though he never forgave that team for leaving New York. The fact that Hicks arrived from Massachusetts somehow outfitted with a superlative Hoosier twang also enhanced his popularity among the native sons and daughters.

As Hovde often said, he "inherited" his senior staff when he arrived in 1946; Stewart and Hockema were both appointees of his predecessor, Elliott. They had been virtually "welded" into their jobs by trustee fiat months before the Hovde name was even mentioned as a possible candidate for the presidency. Hovde had no complaints, however; both were men Hovde might well have chosen himself. Hockema died in 1956 and Stewart announced his resignation in 1961, giving Hovde his first opportunity as president to organize his staff in his own way. The team Hovde put together was, with some exceptions, the same ten years later when he retired—a group of people who, when the going was so grim and hectic in the late 1960s, stood resolutely and without reservation shoulder-to-shoulder with "prexy." Hovde had an uncanny way of selecting the right people for the jobs that needed doing. He was always proud of the fact that issues that came up in staff meetings invariably were thrashed out, often to the point of exhaustion, but still thrashed out to everyone's satisfaction. Hovde often suspected that unanimous agreement over staff matters was often more a case of staff members wanting to keep peace in the family out of loyalty to him, so that he would not have to choose between them on any issue.

In reorganizing his staff in 1961, Hovde chose carefully; he knew that the future of the university for at least a decade would be determined by how well his staff performed individually and corporately. They were Lytle J. Freehafer, who became vice president and treasurer, perhaps the strongest member of the Hovde senior staff; Donald R. Mallett, vice president and executive dean, the former dean of men who had been named executive dean after Hockema's death; Paul F. Chenea, whom Hovde elevated to vice president for academic affairs; and E. C. Young, already dean of the Graduate School, who was given the additional post of vice president for research. When Young retired in 1963, Hovde beckoned Frederick N. Andrews, then head of the Department of Animal Sciences, to the Executive Building to succeed Young, and a year later gave him the additional titles of vice president and general manager of the Purdue Research Foundation.

Because of the growth of Purdue's extension centers at Hammond, Indianapolis, Fort Wayne, and Michigan City into regional campuses, Hovde recognized their essential importance to Purdue by appointing Charles H. Lawshe in 1966 as vice president for regional campus administration. Hovde had picked Lawshe in 1958 to combine the Division of Technical Extension and the Division of Adult Education to put a stop to the jurisdictional disputes the two divisions often engaged in. Until Lawshe combined the two, the atmosphere at Purdue fairly crackled with misguided proprietorship.

Freehafer came to Purdue in 1953 from the state capitol where he was state budget director, a post to which he had been appointed by Governor Henry F. Schricker four years earlier. Born in Oklahoma, he spent his boyhood in Huntington, Indiana, and put himself through DePauw University partly with a scholarship and partly with a job as a brick mason. He graduated cum laude in 1931 with a degree in economics. He worked at several jobs, including brick masonry and bookkeeping for a construction company. After the 1932 Democratic victory in Washington and Indianapolis, Freehafer got a job as supervisor of audits in the state auditor's office. He became deputy state auditor in 1940, and when the United States entered World War II in 1941, he was called to active duty as a reserve officer and served in the Indiana headquarters of the Selective Service System. By the war's end, he had been promoted to colonel in the Army finance department. Freehafer returned to state government as an auditor in the State Board of Accounts and was elevated eventually to the state budget post. At a party following a Purdue-Indiana Old Oaken Bucket game in 1952, Stewart and Raymond W. Kettler, university comptroller, talked Freehafer into joining the Purdue staff. He began work at Purdue the following February as assistant comptroller.

Freehafer moved through the business office chairs rather rapidly and learned his lessons well from Stewart; when R. B. retired in 1961, Freehafer's appointment as his successor was not surprising. Hovde would have had to search long and hard for anyone better suited by either experience or temperament than Freehafer. A tall, imposing man with enormous ability and integrity, he was a zealous guardian of the university's resources and a brilliant innovator. Freehafer continued as vice president and treasurer under Hovde's successor, Arthur G. Hansen, for two years, then at sixty-three decided to retire.

Mallett was thirty-five when he joined the Purdue staff as assistant to George E. Davis, then director of the Office of Student Affairs. An Iowan, Mallett came from a town called Guthrie Center but was reared and schooled in Des Moines. Educated at Drake University, he taught high school physics, freshman mathematics and even coached football, basketball, and wrestling, though he admitted that he was never much of an athlete himself. He went to Iowa City to pursue his master's degree in psychology and education, received his Ph.D. in 1936, and joined the University of Iowa staff as assistant dean of men. Mallett came to Purdue in 1945, and in 1952 when Davis became director of adult education, he was appointed dean of men in a reorganization of that office. Four years later he was elevated to the executive deanship by Hovde.

In Hovde's 1961 reorganization, he added vice president to Mallett's title. Mallett came to Purdue at an opportune time, only months before Hovde's arrival, and was in the first echelon of administrators who were called on to meet the nearly overwhelming challenges and problems during the GI Bill of Rights student years.

Mallett was imaginative and personable, a dynamic administrator sensitive not only to student needs but also to student foibles. He had an uncanny perspective on their problems and a deep and sympathetic understanding of the things that often trouble young people. He met such problems usually with an enormous sense of humor, without which no administrator of student affairs long survives. Shortly after he arrived, Davis asked Mallett to structure the first program of student orientation, a process which up to that time usually consisted of someone asking a group of new students, "Any questions?" He was also involved in the housing shortages of 1945 and 1946 and travelled from door-to-door in West Lafayette asking residents for spare rooms to rent to students.

Mallett was one of the most efficient and effective members of Hovde's staff, though health problems hindered him before he died in 1971. O. D. Roberts, who had been elevated to dean of men when Mallett became executive dean, served a major role with Mallett in the late 1960s in handling a host of problems connected with the years of student unrest.

Another important member of the Hovde team was Helen B. Schleman, who succeeded Dean of Women Dorothy Stratton in 1947. Dean Schleman was a longtime member of the Purdue staff who had come to Purdue at the behest of Miss Stratton in the early 1930s as director of the first women's residence hall built since Ladies Hall had been razed in 1928. Dean Schleman was innovative and hardworking, another link in a heritage of strength and warmth that began with Carolyn Shoemaker.

When she came to Purdue in 1934, Helen Schleman reported to two people, Dean Stratton and then-Controller R. B. Stewart. She still shrugs philosophically and observes that when you report to two bosses "you learn twice as much."

She earned a bachelor of arts degree from Northwestern University and master's degrees from Wellesley College and Purdue. She retired in 1968 and was succeeded by M. Beverley Stone, an associate dean of women who had come to Purdue in 1956 and was the obvious choice for the position.

Chenea was from Oregon and educated at the University of California at Berkeley, where he received his degree in civil engineering in 1940. He worked first as an engineer for a construction firm building Pacific naval bases. He then entered the Army ordnance corps as a second lieutenant and left at the end of the war as a lieutenant colonel. Chenea was an associate professor of engineering mechanics at the University of Michigan, where he had also earned his master's and Ph.D. degrees, before he arrived at Purdue in 1952 as head of the Department of Engineering Mechanics. He came at the urging of the new dean of engineering, George Hawkins. Within two years, Chenea became associate dean of engineering under Hawkins and was the man Hawkins and/or Hovde most often picked to serve as "acting" head of departments to temporarily fill vacancies.

Chenea also served two years as head of the School of Mechanical Engineering and for a part of that period also headed the Department of Mathematics. There seemed to be no academic administrative position Chenea could not fill well, and Hovde had spotted him early as the kind of person who would be an asset in the senior staff. Hence, there was little question about whom Hovde would select in 1961 as the university's first vice president for academic affairs. Chenea, like Hovde, was deadly serious about the business of higher education and the scholarly life. Although normally soft-spoken, he had a razor-sharp but gentle wit that he would use to deflate an overinflated ego or to unstuff a stuffed shirt. Chenea theorized that one of the reasons Hovde assigned him as chairman pro tempore of the university senate, the faculty governing body, instead of serving as chairman himself, was because Hovde, like all athletes, did not like to lose—in this case the possibility of losing arguments in faculty-of-the-whole sessions. The temptation, Chenea would say, to try to win arguments was too great.

Hovde felt that the presence of the presidency often tends to keep faculty from making suggestions or offering views that ought to be made. Yet, the president had to be represented. "Faculties," Hovde would say, "often adopt policies for the administration to enforce which are not enforceable." Hovde occasionally visited senate meetings but never as chairman after he established the academic affairs vice presidency.

When Young decided to retire in 1963, the question was a natural one: whom would Hovde find to replace a man who had become almost irreplaceable? The answer came swiftly— Frederick N. Andrews, the forty-nine-year-old head of the Department of Animal Sciences, a scholar and scientist who had made several far-reaching contributions to the knowledge of animal physiology. Hovde correctly assessed Andrews as an excellent administrator, as well as an outstanding scientist who was also energetic. He called himself a Bostonian, although he spent most of his childhood years at Weymouth, a town about twenty miles south of Boston, down toward Cape Cod. Andrews entered Massachusetts State College in the fall of 1931. He was already interested in animal reproduction, and by the time he was a junior, he knew he wanted to make university teaching and research his lifework.

In the summer of 1936, Andrews entered the University of Missouri to begin his doctoral work; in the mid-1930s, the University of Missouri had one of the nation's best agricultural experiment stations. There and in the Missouri School of Medicine, Andrews did most of his graduate work in physiology, nutrition, and biochemistry. Andrews was asked twice to come to Purdue before he accepted. The second offer was from W. V. Lambert, who came to Purdue as associate director of the Agricultural Experiment Station. He knew Andrews professionally and in 1940 asked him to take on a new teaching position in the physiology of reproduction in domestic animals. Later, Andrews with William E. Fontaine, an ebullient and popular professor of mechanical engineering, teamed up in a new area which quickly won Hovde's support—artificial climate control for farm animals. The work was one of many important research projects in the Herrick Laboratories, named for Ray W. Herrick, founder and chairman of the board of Tecumseh Products Company. Herrick gave $300,000 for the beginning of the laboratories, which were installed in the university's converted horse barns on west State Street.

Andrews involved himself in a wide-ranging number of projects at Purdue and coauthored four textbooks in animal science plus one hundred fifty scientific papers. The enrollment in the Graduate School under Andrews grew phenomenally in the 1960s and 1970s. Andrews, however, was always quick to emphasize not so much the numbers enrolled but the number of degrees actually awarded and the performance of the graduates after they left Purdue. In Andrews's tenure, Purdue was usually ranked thirteenth nationally in the number of Ph.D.s awarded in all academic fields His selection by Hovde in large measure contributed to research and teaching excellence at Purdue and symbolized what Hovde wanted most: good basic research programs—but also strong programs of research which applied basic research to the needs of humanity.

Adult education and the need to extend the university far beyond its walls was far too important to Hovde to permit the internecine warfare he saw begin to develop between the two divisions which ran adult education and technical extension. To correct the situation, he reached into the faculty to find the man who could do it, an organizational genius who became one of the most intriguing administrators in higher education—Lawshe, a professor of industrial psychology when Purdue was considered the mecca of industrial psychologists. Lawshe was one of an elite trio led by F. B. Knight and which included Joseph Tiffin. Later the trio became a quintet with the addition of Ernest J. McCormick and Newell C. Kephart.

Lawshe was a Purdue graduate, a native of Swayzee, Indiana, where his father was the town druggist. His father, too, was a Purdue graduate, having graduated in 1904 when pharmacy was a two-year curriculum. Lawshe had varied employment after he graduated in 1929. It included managing a theater in Logansport and working for his father in the family drugstore in the Depression; teaching in country schools in east central Indiana; obtaining a master's degree in educational administration at the University of Michigan; teaching high school journalism and American literature at Evansville, Indiana; coauthoring a high school journalism text with an uncle; returning to Purdue for his doctorate in psychology; working once again in Evansville where he was a high school principal; and finally returning to Purdue as a staff member. He first served as "guest" professor, a rather precarious position, in the newly created Division of Education and Applied Psychology until a fulltime professorial appointment emerged.

When Lawshe took on an administrative post, he knew his days as a teacher and researcher in industrial psychology were over. Hovde suggested that even though he was going to administer the affairs of adult education and technical extension he could keep one foot in industrial psychology—perhaps teach a graduate seminar. Lawshe made a conscious decision that if he were going to be a Purdue administrator he had to cut all ties with psychology— in effect, end one career and start another at the age of fifty. Beyond the charge to combine the two divisions, Hovde gave Lawshe no particular instructions, only his admonition that whatever he did must be good. While it was Hovde whose vision correctly calculated that the extension centers at Hammond, Fort Wayne, Michigan City, and Indianapolis would someday mature into full-fledged campuses in their own right, perhaps even independent state colleges, it was Lawshe who played the leading role in their guidance to full institutional status. It was an epochal period for Purdue, and Hovde gave Lawshe his total encouragement, support, and trust. Lawshe simultaneously pulled together Purdue's associate degree programs (then administered by the Division of Conferences and Continuation Services, the unit that resulted from the merger of adult education and technical extension), added a new department of nursing, and established what became in 1964 the School of Technology. Lawshe was its first dean, but that was his means of preparing George W. McNelly, his associate dean, for the deanship. When Lawshe became vice president for regional administration in 1966, and thus a member of Hovde's senior staff, McNelly, a talented, mild-mannered Iowan who had his undergraduate degree in chemistry and his doctorate from Purdue in psychology, served the school well. When he stepped down from the deanship in 1987 to return to teaching, the Purdue School of Technology represented one of the nation's outstanding such programs. The school had ventured into a new statewide technology program aimed at helping enhance Indiana's economic competitiveness and prompted President Ronald Reagan's three-hour visit to campus on April 9, 1987, to pay political tribute to the project. It was the first visit to Purdue University by an incumbent American president.

• • •

Hicks, Young, Freehafer, Andrews, Chenea, Mallett, Lawshe, and later Hawkins, were the senior staff Hovde handpicked and upon whom he relied before making any major decision. Toward the end of his presidency, Hovde said that as he thought back upon all of the decisions he made "I cannot think of one that I made solely by myself. I often made the final decision on any given question, but the the process of making that decision always involved many other members of the university."

In the Hovde years, besides the senior staff, some of the "many other members of the university" who played vital roles in Purdue's successes included Dean Potter in engineering and Dean Harry J. Reed in agriculture. Reed was among the deans that Hovde admired most. In 1957 when Reed announced his decision to retire, Hovde chose as his successor Earl L. Butz, the former head of the Department of Agricultural Economics, who was on leave at the time to serve as an assistant secretary of agriculture in the Eisenhower administration.

Butz, a northern Indiana country boy from Noble County, came to Purdue for his education in agricultural economics and remained to become the dean of agriculture, later dean of continuing education, and still later secretary of agriculture under

United States presidents Nixon and Ford. An unfortunate remark he made during the 1976 presidential campaign was his political undoing, and he was forced to resign.

Butz liked Hovde because he was, as Butz said, "easy to work with. He was a tremendous help to me both as a department head and as a dean. He was supportive. He appointed you to a job and let you alone to do it—but he expected results." Agriculture at Purdue was, Butz explained, "an aggregation of practices which were taught—largely vocationally, the application of accepted and traditional methodologies. Hovde insisted that agricultural education become a matter of the application of the basic sciences— that as a professional school, agriculture become an applied school undergirded by the basic sciences."

Hovde had few critics in his years at Purdue, but they did exist, and surprisingly one of them was Dean Potter, who deeply respected Hovde for his abilities and his compassion. In his later years, Potter assessed Hovde as "by far the most civilized man I've ever met." Yet he was critical, especially of his relationship with the faculty. Potter did not believe Hovde paid faculty members the attention they deserved. "He seemed too wrapped up in games and athletics [in which Potter had little or no interest], and the faculty was critical of him for not paying them enough attention." Potter believed that was a factor which may have hampered Hovde's effectiveness as president. But Potter could also be ambivalent on Hovde and took nothing away from his presidency, giving him full credit for Purdue's rapidly growing national and international reputation.

●   ●   ●

Besides the strengthening of the Graduate School, four new schools were added to the university during Hovde's administration—the aforementioned School of Technology in 1964, the School of Veterinary Science and Medicine in 1957, the School of Management in 1958, and the School of Humanities, Social Science, and Education in 1963.

When a report from Hovde indicated mounting pressure for a veterinary school in Indiana, the trustees asked for more information. A later staff report said quite simply that if Purdue developed a school of veterinary medicine, accreditation by the American Veterinary Medical Association (AVMA) would be an absolute requirement. And to gain AVMA accreditation would mean immediate expenditure of $2 million to build new clinical facilities and an animal hospital, and to remodel the veterinary science building on the south edge of the campus.

The report called for state appropriations for the first year of $400,000 in emergency funds to provide facilities for an entering class in 1949, plus operating appropriations that would begin at $72,000 per year and increase to $200,000 per year in 1952. Purdue hoped to have an eventual student body in veterinary medicine of 260, enabling the university to graduate 400 veterinarians in the first decade after the school began to operate and as many as 600 each decade thereafter to fill a desperate shortage of veterinary practitioners in Indiana. In 1948, licensed veterinarians practicing in Indiana numbered 526. Their average age was fifty. Most of them were graduates of the early proprietary, nonpublic schools that eventually all closed, leaving a state with $600 million in annual receipts from animal products without a veterinary medical school.

Another of the men Hovde admired in the university was Leslie M. "Pat" Hutchings, the head of the Department of Veterinary Science, who stood shoulder-to-shoulder with Hovde and stubbornly insisted that no veterinary medical school should be established at Purdue that was not fully funded from the beginning. Theirs was a particularly perilous trail through the political-legislative jungle educators must often travel on their periodic funding safaris; Hovde and Hutching, however, stood firm for more than six years and three sessions of the Indiana General Assembly until they made their point and won the legislature to their view.

Hovde's adamance that Purdue was not interested in trying to start a veterinary school with less-than-adequate funding was another example of his infinite patience. The first sessions of the Indiana legislature considered the veterinary school proposal but flatly refused to do anything at all; the legislators expressed some interest in later sessions, though not enough to provide successful support. In the 1957 session, the legislature bent to the leadership of Governor Harold W. Handley and provided the $2 million needed for buildings and facilities to get the school opened in 1958. Handley was sympathetic to the Purdue point of view; he had served in the legislature many years himself before being elected lieutenant governor in the administration of George Craig. As such, he was also commissioner of agriculture and never missed an opportunity to visit Purdue. Later, Hovde paid Handley the supreme compliment of saying that without Handley's political leadership "we would never have been able to establish this school."

The final triumph for Hovde was the AVMA's accreditation of the school even before the graduation of the first class in

1962—an unprecedented action in academia and a historical "first" among the nation's veterinary schools. It reinforced his belief that holding out for the best pays off. He often cited the case of the University of Minnesota where the state legislature funded about half of the buildings needed for a new veterinary school and ten years later the school still did not have the other half. "It started on a shoestring and remained on a shoestring," Hovde used to say.

Hovde called Hutchings a "first-class teacher, first-class researcher, first-class administrator, first-class politician, first-class human being." Hutchings died prematurely in 1959 of lymphatic cancer before he could enjoy the results of his hard work and the many battles he and Hovde fought and won on behalf of the new veterinary school. At his funeral, the usually stoic Hovde wept openly.

•   •   •

The formation and development of the School of Management and the Krannert Graduate School of Management (originally called Industrial Management and Krannert Graduate School of Industrial Administration, respectively) had some parallels with the establishment of veterinary medicine at Purdue. Again, it was based on Hovde's premise that it was pointless to embark on new academic voyages with second-rate paddles, that settling for less than the best at the outset nearly always guaranteed mediocrity.

Hovde found the "right" man to do the job in a handsome, erudite, and enthusiastic economist, Emmanuel T. Weiler, who came to Purdue in 1953 from the University of Illinois at the behest of William L. Ayres, dean of the School of Science, Education, and Humanities. At the time, economics was a part of the Department of History, Economics, and Philosophy. Ayres convinced Hovde of the need to create a separate department of economics. Weiler was to head it; for Purdue, he was a fortunate choice.

At the time Weiler organized it, the Department of Economics at Purdue was small with about eight faculty members. At roughly the same time, the university organized another new academic department, the Department of Industrial Management and Transportation in the Schools of Engineering; Weiler was asked to head it as well as economics. But the situation was administratively awkward, and Weiler considered himself in an unmanageable situation in which he reported to the dean of science as well as the dean of engineering. An offer to become the dean of the Wharton School of Business at the University of Pennsylvania was almost

more than Weiler could resist But he did. The temptation to bypass
Deans Hawkins and Ayres and go directly to Hovde, normally unthinkable if not downright suicidal in most university pecking
orders, was irresistible. "What I really want," Weiler told Hovde
after he informed him of the Wharton offer, "is to be dean of a
School of Industrial Management at Purdue University."

As he explained later, "I thought it would be more fun to build
something than to take over something already well-established.
Too, I had enormous confidence in Fred Hovde and his willingness
to back me in this new venture. So I stayed. Hovde was the kind
of man who bet on people, and if he had confidence in a person,
he'd back him all the way."

The School of Management was created to offer the B.S. degree in industrial management, a development that caused no little
consternation on the campus at Bloomington, especially in the
IU School of Business Administration. Purdue's interest in a
business school had a totally different justification in Hovde's view.
Purdue's was a school oriented primarily toward the development
of people (i.e., Purdue engineers) as managers of the production
side of the economy, as against the typical business school curricula related to the "service" aspects of the economy. The new
school also had another unique aspect: fostering applications of
the computer to industrial management decision-making and quantitative economics. The requisites for the B.S. in industrial management were also unique; its students were required to have two
majors: one of thirty credit hours in business- and management-
related courses and another of thirty credit hours in a technical
major such as engineering, computer science, physics, or chemistry. "One foot in business, one foot in technology" was how
Weiler put it. Eventually the management school developed a
master's program known as the Master of Science in Industrial
Administration, or M.S.I.A., program. It was popularly known as
the "finishing school" for engineers and, indeed, was limited to
engineering graduates in its early years.

The founding of the Krannert School was, as Weiler assessed
it, "a creation of raw courage." Hovde wangled an introduction
for Weiler to Herman C. Krannert, the Indianapolis industrialist-
philanthropist who made his fortune in founding, developing, and
operating Inland Container Corporation. Krannert admired Weiler
and invited him to join the board of directors of his company.
Eventually Weiler asked Krannert for the money to establish the
Krannert Graduate School of Industrial Administration at Purdue.

"First," Krannert replied, "show me a catalog of what the
school will be." Weiler did, including proposed school policies

and individual course descriptions. Krannert was impressed and agreed to bankroll the new graduate management school venture, providing $2 million as a part of the cost of the building on the southwest corner of State and Grant streets which bears his name. He also put up $300,000 a year for research, continuing education for industrial managers and executives, and supplements to faculty salaries for those already in the top ten percent. "Krannert," Weiler observed candidly, "liked to attach strings." But the Krannert gifts enabled Weiler and Hovde to lure top faculty from such business schools as Harvard, Stanford, and Carnegie-Mellon.

By 1969, Weiler was, as he put it, "tired of being a dean and dealing constantly with faculty. I wanted to return to teaching myself." He told Hovde he wanted to to become a professor again. Hovde made him Krannert Distinguished Professor of Economics and Management, and Weiler returned to teaching freshman economics. His associate dean, John S. Day, was named to succeed him. Day was a good choice; he was qualified to serve as dean of any of the best business schools in the United States.

Weiler was a gadfly academician who once proposed that faculty members be given every second year off to use their expertise to help solve some of society's grave problems. He also stunned an alumni gathering by suggesting that college degrees be somehow revoked after five years unless renewed by further formalized schooling. "An education," he told them, "is a little like a dead mackerel. It must be used and replaced or it begins to smell."

Weiler died on July 1, 1979, after a long bout with cancer and was one of those Hovde paid tribute to when he spoke at his final faculty convocation on May 11, 1971, "my great people of whom I am very proud."

Hovde was always aware of the need to (as he put it) "educate the whole man." To him that meant exactly what it said: Purdue would achieve greatness only when its topflight scientific, engineering, and agricultural programs were accompanied by first-class undergraduate programs in the humanities and social sciences. He stressed undergraduate study, not graduate study, for he saw no purpose in becoming deeply engaged in doctoral programs in the humanities and social sciences. He believed it was impossible in practice to build the library collections required for good graduate research in those areas. He knew that Purdue could never become another Columbia, Yale, or University of Chicago even if it wanted to. And he repeatedly made clear that Purdue did not want to.

Yet Hovde's critics contended in retrospect (that point at which it is safest to be a critic) that without graduate programs in the humanities, a good undergraduate program was not likely to be developed. Indeed, the argument went, how do you propose to provide the "service" courses to meet the English and other nontechnical course requirements for the science, agriculture, and engineering majors unless you have graduate assistants to teach them? And to have graduate assistants, you must have, of course, graduate study.

To Hovde, Purdue's educational mission was clear-cut; it had been spelled out in no uncertain terms ninety years earlier by one of his predecessors, Emerson E. White, and the precedents that made Purdue an outstanding scientific institution were set by White's successor, James H. Smart. History and tradition were on Hovde's side.

He believed earnestly that the humanities were essential to Purdue if it were to maintain its goal of providing students a "total learning environment." As he said in his 1966 commencement address, "Science itself and the pursuit of science have no quarrel with the humanities and the arts, and vice versa—indeed, these three aspects of life flourish best when they flourish together."

Society exists in (for want of a better term) the High Tech Age; Hovde knew, however, that human beings are not technical but social creatures—that most of the decisions people make throughout their lives are political or social. Even when they make technical decisions, in one way or another these impinge upon that which is socio-political and involve human integrity. Hovde was fond of paraphrasing Robert M. Hutchins's cogent observation that "in free systems in which men compete according to the rules, the strain is always on the character, rarely on the intelligence.

One of the requirements for Hovde's "educated man" was that he at least try to understand or recognize the philosophical, cultural, political, emotional, spiritual, and traditional factors involved in the complex processes that underlie the society in which he would be expected to participate. Such understanding by scientists and engineers in an era dominated by accelerating technology was essential.

Chenea, Hovde's perceptive academic vice president, observed that Hovde's most significant contribution to Purdue in his quarter-century presidency was in bringing the humanities to a level of excellence. Yet, whether Hovde's own philosophy, desires, and efforts were clearly or generally understood—especially by the humanist faculty who stood to benefit the most—seems questionable. Of all of his efforts on behalf of Purdue over twenty-five years, those in behalf of the humanities were for him probably the most perplexing. The formation of the School of Humanities, Social Science, and Education in 1963 was not an administrative afterthought, but an inextricable part of the greatness Hovde envisioned for Purdue from the beginning.

In 1946, Hovde's first year, the liberal arts areas were administered through the School of Science. Basically, these areas included English, speech, psychology, education, sociology, history, government, economics, modern languages—and little else. Courses in art and design and in child development were included in the School of Home Economics. No philosophy courses were offered except those noncredit offerings in religious philosophies taught by some of the clergymen from peripheral campus ministries. But it was in this very specific subject area that Hovde chose to make his case for the humanities, and in so doing, personally selected as the first philosopher on the university faculty Eric L. Clitheroe, a loquacious, Presbyterian minister who, when he was offered a position in 1950, was head of the Division of Philosophy, Religion, and Psychology at Coe College, Cedar Rapids, Iowa.

For several years under Dean W. L. Ayres of the School of Science, Clitheroe *was* the philosophy department, although he was listed in the faculty roster in the Department of Sociology. Clitheroe, the philosopher, and Ayres, the mathematician, were never intimates; though they often sharply disagreed, it always stopped short of out-and-out antagonism. But later, Clitheroe recalled, "When Ayres found out I could teach, we became very close friends." As a result, philosophy grew from several courses into a program and finally became a department. Much had changed from Clitheroe's appointment in 1950 until his retirement in 1972.

Early in his presidency, Hovde had approved an experimental plan for exceptional women students in which the liberal arts were emphasized. It began in 1948 and was phased out in 1952 when there was a new, across-the-board emphasis on the humanities. But the liberal sciences (as Purdue called the program) had been successful and proved there was room for a viable and significant humanities offering at Purdue.

In 1953, the name of the School of Science was changed to the School of Science, Education, and the Humanities. Up to that time, the School of Science, by its name, implied exactly that—chemistry, mathematics, biology, and physics. The new name denoted a greater emphasis on the humanities and education. Simultaneously, under the reorganized school, were formed two separate departments of psychology and sociology and the Division of Intercollegiate and Intramural Athletics.

The school's next milestone was the approval by the trustees in 1959 of the bachelor of arts degree—a recognition that the humanities and liberal arts at Purdue had come of age. The B.A. degrees were awarded in June 1960, and a year later, Hovde agreed, though with no great enthusiasm, to seek from the trustees "in principle" approval of a master of arts degree. Purdue purists felt Pandora's box had been opened to graduate study in the humanities, never to close again.

Even with that kind of evidence and encouragement, Ayres was apparently not convinced that he and Hovde had the same goals in mind, though Hovde gave Ayres full support to the end of his (Ayres's) Purdue career. When he left in 1962 to become vice president and provost of Southern Methodist University, Ayres repaid Hovde for his trust by giving a copy of his letter of resignation to the *Purdue Exponent* before Hovde read it.

In it, Ayres revealed a wide variance in his and Hovde's beliefs about the proper role of Purdue in the future. Ayres did not believe that humanities should merely serve a support role to the university's scientific areas but that the humanities and the social sciences themselves represented a broader academic base from which Purdue would achieve greatness. Ayres's abrupt departure presaged some profound administrative changes designed to strengthen not only the humanities and social sciences but the "hard" sciences as well, changes less than a year in the offing and changes Ayres himself likely would have welcomed and applauded.

Hovde immediately appointed Chenea as acting dean of the school and asked him to spend at least eighty percent of his time in it. The School of Science, Education, and the Humanities was so heterogeneous in scholarly interests as to be nearly unmanageable; the school included chemistry, the biological sciences, mathematics (which had briefly been assigned to the Schools of Engineering because of faculty antagonisms with Ayres who at one time had headed the department), and the humanistic and social sciences offerings. Open warfare among these elements seemed imminent, and their separation made sense. Less than a year after Ayres resigned, on November 22, 1962, the trustees approved the major reorganization that established a School of Science and a School of Humanities, Social Science, and Education from the old School of Science, Education, and the Humanities.

The selection of people to administer the new schools far transcended the placement of lines and boxes on an organizational chart. Again, Hovde's long experience at finding the right people provided fortunate choices. To serve as dean of the School of Science, he picked Felix Haas, a strong-minded, MIT-educated mathematician whose first love was teaching, an Austrian who fled his homeland and Hitler at seventeen to work in a New Jersey steel mill. Haas came to Purdue from Wayne State University in 1961 to head the mathematical sciences division.

Hovde selected Marbury B. Ogle as dean of the School of Humanities, Social Science, and Education. Ogle, a perceptive and articulate political scientist and Vermont native, joined the Purdue faculty in 1945 after wartime service in the Office of Strategic Services. He quickly became one of Purdue's most popular and effective teachers.

Both Ogle and Haas were capable deans, and their adroit management of their schools in the early years provided a solid foundation for their successors. Haas moved into the university's second job as executive vice president and provost in the Hansen administration, and Ogle managed the affairs of the humanities school for a decade before retiring.

•   •   •

The 1960s were restless years the world over as we all lived in the shadow of the twin imposters—triumph and tragedy. It was a Dickensian time stamped with our best and our worst. It began in exultation and a piquant anticipation perhaps never equalled in human experience, but it ended as a divisive and mortal pang, a missive of history contained in a bloodied envelope addressed to us all.

To paraphrase H. L. Mencken, the republic trotted before the weary eyes of the world every raucous and bizarre carnival act in its repertoire. Yet, the 1960s were years of great and crowning technological achievement, though they came with no guarantees. A South African surgeon performed the first successful transplantation of a human heart, and other similar surgical feats followed. We had learned to transplant the human heart, but not how to transform it. We sent men to the moon and returned them safely to earth. One of them, Neil A. Armstrong, a 1955 Purdue aeronautical engineering graduate from an Ohio town called Wapakoneta, was immortalized by being the first human being to stamp his footprint on the dusty lunar surface. Another Purdue graduate, Eugene A. Cernan, EE '56, in the following decade commanded the last crew to leave the moon in America's Apollo space program.

There were assassinations and the United States involvement in Vietnam that, as it turned out so tragically, no one wanted. And the young rebelled, especially on the campuses. They marched against their parents; against the established authority of church, school, employer; and against the very government they would one day inherit. The rebellion fed upon itself and eventually, in one way or other and in varying degrees, affected nearly every campus in the land.

Who still wonders why the young rebelled? Who wonders why the young always rebel? But this was a new phenomena. The world watched as we tried to consume our children before they consumed themselves. Seeking happiness, we seemed more willing instead to fulfill our propensity for misery. In whatever state we may have found ourselves in the 1960s, none of us was ever again to be an innocent.

At the end of the decade we could look back upon it as the Great Digression, knowing that despite the bewildering interruptions, the society had done much and gained much. The words Winston Churchill spoke nearly thirty years earlier by short-wave radio from London to a commencement at the University of Rochester, seem apropos of the 1960s. (The words were spoken from a side room of Number 10 Downing Street on June 16, 1941, and young Fred Hovde, then liaison secretary between British and American scientists, was present and had helped make the arrangements): "The destiny of mankind is not decided by material computation. When great causes are on the move in the world . . .we learn that we are spirits, not animals, and that something is going on in space and time, and beyond space and time, which, whether we like it or not, spells duty."

• • •

The early years of the 1960s were happy times at Purdue. Nothing indicated the grimness that lay ahead in eight to ten years. Fall enrollment in 1960 stood at 19,000, and all indications were that it would continue upward for more than twenty years. All planning focussed on that fact. Admissions requirements were tightened, and everything at Purdue was moving or changing. When it was not, Hovde wanted to know why.

Innovation was integral in Hovde's professional philosophy. He liked educational technology that was forward-looking and held promise of advancing the learning environment. He became an early and enthusiastic supporter of what eventually became known as the Midwest Program for Airborne Television (MPATI). The project had great impact on the future of televised instruction generally and proved the effectiveness of using prerecorded, uniformly high quality classroom materials and instructional episodes. These were videotaped for transmission to member public schools over a five-state area from DC-6 transport aircraft flying at an altitude of 23,000 feet over Montpelier, Indiana, broadcasting to the schools on a regular basis. The planes were based at the Purdue University Airport, and MPATI maintained its headquarters in the basement rooms of Stewart Center. MPATI prospered several years before newer video technology and such sophisticated machinery as satellite linkage made the operations obsolete and economically unsuitable. Yet, the program had interesting implications for raising the general quality of education, especially in those areas of the world where economic considerations often make good instruction otherwise impossible.

Hovde liked to indulge occasionally in the delights of Purdue's successes. He was as proud of Purdue's four-time winning team in the GE College Bowl on national television as he was of the 1966 Boilermaker football team which defeated the University of Southern California, 13–12, in the January 1, 1967, Rose Bowl.

He was as pleased as the students were when the Buick Motor and Fisher Body divisions of General Motors Corporation got together to build and present to the student body a new Boilermaker Special motorized "locomotive" which became the rallying point for Purdue spirit.

Such pleasant interludes could not long divert his attention from the serious problems of expansion and progress. The new complex of buildings Hovde and Pat Hutchings had insisted upon for the new School of Veterinary Science and Medicine was dedicated. Merit increases in salaries and wages that amounted to 10 percent for university employees were granted. Benefits of other kinds for university employees at every level continued to be revised and improved.

The university's phenomenal growth in the 1960s followed a trend in higher education nationally and was independent of anything any single person may have done. As John Hicks often said, "Purdue would have had as many students, as many programs, as many buildings, as large a budget with any of a thousand other men in the presidency. What made Fred Hovde so special was his wise and excellent management of this growth— his insistence on staying on a course that lead Purdue to become excellent in all of its endeavors." Size and excellence were two entirely different things and in Hovde's thinking were never to be confused.

As the demands on higher education increased, acquisition of dollars from the state to meet those demands got correspondingly tougher. Criticisms of the way dollars were spent by the colleges and universities were more grist for political mills than substantive reasons. But such charges always made the job of communicating the needs to the state lawmakers difficult, and it is a fact of public educational life that a gap will always exist between the institution's needs and the public's clear understanding of those needs.

In 1957 the Soviet satellite Sputnik reminded Americans once again how important education for competency is to the national well-being and how perilous it is to consider education an expense to be kept as low as possible rather than an investment yielding compound interest. Hovde delivered that message for twenty-five years to anyone who would listen. It certainly reflected a philosophy that his successors repeated and that his successors' successors are forever obligated to continue. In its suspicion of academe's occasional Pecksniffian entrepreneur and/or the retrograde antics of some students, the world overlooks the essentiality of higher education. Hence, the message must go on.

Hicks often explained the financing of higher education as straightforwardly as possible: "It is not the university's function to make money or save money; it is the university's job to spend money. Now you may question how wisely it has been spent, but first-class university education costs a lot of money; a 'cheap' education is no education at all. When higher education is viewed from the perspective of value received and not merely as a cost to be tolerated, it becomes one of society's best uses of its resources."

•   •   •

Other changes occurred in the 1960s that were, at least at the time, controversial. The agitation to abolish the Reserve Officers Training Corps from the nation's campuses gained impetus, and in 1965, new federal legislation changed the law, making ROTC training at American institutions completely voluntary. Purdue traditionally required all underclassmen to take ROTC training, even though the 1862 Morrill Act establishing land-grant colleges and universities required only that the schools offer such programs. At Purdue, ROTC is offered by all three major branches of the American military—the Air Force, Army, and Navy, one of the few American universities still doing so.

Other "liberalization" at Purdue included dropping a 1934 regulation requiring all freshman women, except residents of West Lafayette and Lafayette proper, to live in the women's residence halls. One reason for lifting the rule was to prevent overcrowding in the women's halls brought on by the enrollment increases.

Hovde's support of the humanities brought about rapid growth in the School of Humanities, Social Science, and Education. Even so, there was much grumbling about his refusal to "properly" fund the libraries the school believed it ought to have. Hovde's response was that he built more library space in his years at Purdue than any of his predecessors, although most of it was space for the various school libraries as new buildings were added.

One area of the university where Hovde admitted he failed to achieve significant change was in the School of Home Economics. "It was," he said, "the one academic area at Purdue that stumped me."

In 1952, at the retirement of the revered Dean Matthews, Hovde toyed with the idea of appointing a man to the post, an area normally dominated by women. Instead, however, he appointed Beulah H. Gillaspie, who had headed home economics at the University of Arkansas and had been a vice president of the American Home Economics Association. Dean Gillaspie provided excellent leadership, upgrading the school's program over her decade as dean. As her retirement approached in 1962, Hovde contemplated the appointment of William E. Martin to head home economics. Martin was head of the Department of Child Development and Family Life (now called Child Development and Family Studies) and had a national reputation in his field. He would, Hovde believed, bring Hovde's brand of excellence to the school.

Hovde quickly learned, when the word got around, that the home economics faculty, then almost all women, would probably not give Martin their full support or cooperation. Hovde, like any good general, knew when to retreat. He eventually appointed Professor Gladys Vail, then head of the Department of Foods and Nutrition and acting dean after Dean Gillaspie's retirement. Vail was widely known as a researcher. She was soft-spoken but effective. Her influence had a salutary effect on the school's research program, though her tenure as dean was brief. At her retirement in 1967, she was succeeded by Eva L. Goble who retired in 1973.

Pharmacy was a different matter. When Hovde arrived in 1946, the dean of pharmacy was Glenn L. Jenkins, an appointee of Elliott. He provided excellent leadership, and the school prospered. When Varro E. Tyler arrived in 1966 from the University of Washington, he proved he was an excellent appointment because the school's leadership continued at a high level; he carried on the Jenkins legacy—a reputation as one of the best undergraduate programs in pharmacy and without doubt a top graduate research program in pharmaceutical science. Hovde gave full support to Tyler and stayed out of the way.

Other things were happening: the creation of the Department of Geosciences; the establishment in 1960 of the book-publishing arm of the university, now known as Purdue University Press; the amalgamation of the University Theatre and the Department of Art and Design; and the organization of the Division of Sponsored Programs to administer the university's widening research programs. Purdue was also involved in international programs, especially in Taiwan, Brazil, India, and Afghanistan. In addition, Hovde was proud of the Junior Year Abroad program under which qualified juniors could spend a year at a university in Germany, France, or Spain.

Purdue acquired federal funds to install a new twenty million electron-volt linear accelerator. It went into a special structure under Purdue Mall (at Northwestern Avenue) which created perhaps the most spectacular man-made hole-in-the-ground in Indiana.

The university made moves in environmental engineering, social welfare, and closed-circuit television broadcasting to meet burgeoning needs at the growing system of regional campuses.

No other years in the university's first one hundred were as prosperous or as promising. Yet, the university began to experience the undercurrents of dissatisfaction and foreboding that seemed to be building in the nation as a whole and that reached its frightening crescendo at the close of the decade and into the first year of the next.

Purdue's rapid growth in the 1960s was a identical to what happened all over the United States. The colleges and universities enjoyed great attention and success, partly a result of Sputnik, but mostly because of the coming of age of the first wave of World War II "baby boomers." The prosperity of higher education ultimately made it a victim of its own success. Universities have always played a unique and esteemed role in American life, albeit for the most part their contributions have either been misunderstood or taken for granted.

As the nation began to undergo rather drastic cultural change in the 1960s, academe attempted to respond to newer and expanding national priorities. The lines defining the traditional purposes of higher education became less resolute; the college degree became, for many, a status symbol and economic ticket, not merely the symbol of a prescribed level of scholarly attainment. The universities now began to be oversold as the answer to almost everything that bedeviled society and came to be viewed, quite mistakenly and tragically, as all things to all people. It was a perception as dangerous as it was naive and, alas, one that the colleges and universities, in their scramble for certain kinds of financial goodies from whatever the source, were tempted not to deny.

At that stage, the colleges and universities, Purdue included, became ripe for the one thing that they can least tolerate—politicization. Hovde firmly believed that a university can be many things to many people (though not all things to all people), and he defended the humanist viewpoint of education for education's sake equally with that of the utilitarian idea of education for occupational competency.

Of all places in the world, Hovde believed, the university campus must continue to be the common ground where all philosophies, however repugnant, may be examined and debated rationally without being promulgated. He could become supremely peeved at proposals of all sorts that "Purdue could be somebody's policeman." He viewed the university as a place for discussion of political views, though it was not to be a vehicle, in the official sense, for direct political action. Those who fail to recognize the difference cannot be expected to understand the reason for a university in a free society.

The problems of student unrest and confrontation that occurred throughout the county had their roots, of course, in a nation frustrated, saddened, sickened, and dissatisfied by the war in Vietnam. The campuses, including Purdue, became the arenas of protest, although in retrospect the problems Purdue encountered were not as serious as elsewhere—though serious enough.

The protest problems began as early as 1964 when a small group of students and staff began a campus organization called the Peace Union, the first aim of which was to campaign to abolish compulsory ROTC training for underclassmen at Purdue. The university took no action until the federal act was changed a year later—the administration making the point that it abolished compulsory ROTC because of the federal act and not because of the campaign of the Peace Union. In the following years, the Peace Union leadership organized rallies on the Memorial Mall, a step away from the founder's grave, to protest everything from the Vietnam Way to the presence of Dow Chemical Company and Central Intelligence Agency recruiters in the University Placement Service, the offices of which the group briefly occupied. It also protested racial injustice and a 1969 student fee increase.

Another campus group called the Friends of SNCC (Student Nonviolent Coordinating Committee) petitioned the trustees to take a policy stance against local landlords who practiced discrimination in choosing tenants, to establish an aggressive recruiting effort for black students, and to require integration of all extracurricular activities as well as fraternities and sororities "in practice as well as in policy."

The evening of March 16, 1966, the student chapter of the national Students for a Democratic Society (SDS) met in Memorial Center. The group's visiting speaker was an admitted anarchist-pacifist named Joffre Stewart, popular on the college nihilist speaking circuit. As a part of his harangue, he made his anti-American feelings known by tearing, spitting upon, and stomping a United States flag. Even the members present were stunned by the act which not only violated federal and state laws but also was repugnant to a majority of citizens, including SDS members, and had nothing at all to do with rational, good-faith discourses on the issues of the time.

The reaction was immediate, although the administration seemed to move slowly; never in the history of the university had an administration ever dealt with a problem of this kind. The American Legion with whom Hovde had dealt on Linus Pauling's appearance in the late 1940s, protested the flag desecration and demanded the ouster of a part-time graduate student in sociology, Martin Barroll, the SDS chapter president. Also decrying the act was Indiana Congressman Richard Roudebush, a former national Veterans of Foreign Wars commander, who told Hovde he should ban all "leftist, radical organizations from the Purdue campus."

The flag desecration incident alone was nightmare enough at a university whose principal reputation was as a conservative school. But the real nightmare was for members of the Student Affairs Committee of the Faculty Senate that had been assigned to investigate the incident. Many were personally intimidated. Threats against some members' homes were thinly veiled; another member was nearly run off the road on his way home from a late-night campus meeting. A dean's home was splattered by shotgun pellets. The tension, the unrest, and the divisiveness grew.

Such problems were enough for any administration to grapple with. In addition, at Purdue the American Federation of State, County, and Municipal Employees Union (AFSCME) demanded official recognition. In 1967, the union local, with fewer than 300 of the university's 1,800 clerical and service workers, sought exclusive collective bargaining rights. The board of trustees rejected the request and pointed out that as an agent of the state it had no legal authority to enter into any exclusive bargaining agreement with anyone. The board reaffirmed that stand on February 29, 1968. In the early morning of March 7, the university found itself struck by about 180 workers. Though most employees reported for work, other union members honored the picket lines, and deliveries to the university were almost halted.

University legal counsel George Schilling obtained a temporary restraining order from circuit court by noon, and the picket lines dissolved. Later, a National Labor Relations Board election was called. The clerical and service workers who would have been represented by the AFSCME turned out nearly 90 percent strong and soundly rejected the union.

On May 15, 1968, a group of about one hundred Purdue black students held a quiet but ominous demonstration on the steps of the Executive Building. Each placed a brick on the front steps and left as their leader presented President Hovde with a list of demands aimed at improving the black student's lot at Purdue: a more aggressive recruitment of black faculty; integration of Purdue's "segregated, bigoted, and insulting" United States history courses; integration of all student activities; addition of courses dealing with black culture and arts; a compilation of a list of discriminatory off-campus housing; "more than token" integration of the administration; and addition of a course dealing with distortion (presumably in history and current events) to the core curriculum for all students or, the list of demands concluded, "the fire next time," a phrase from black author James Baldwin. Hovde responded positively to the student demands, not because of implied threats but because they addressed some valid points and listed some areas which, as Hovde admitted, the university had neglected.

The *Purdue Exponent,* long a traditional victim of official neglect, fell into the hands of a few dissidents and tried over about three years to make life tough if not embarrassing for Hovde. One particularly vicious column written by a California couple in graduate school, defiled Hovde in four-letter scatology so offensive that Hovde's senior staff, outraged, met him at his plane as he returned from a business trip. They demanded the firing of the editor, William Smoot, a bright, outspoken young philosophy student from Mayfield, Kentucky. Hovde at first resisted but eventually fired him, an action that eventually led to a legal question of who actually owned the *Exponent*. Several legal opinions later, it was determined that, indeed, the *Exponent* was owned by the university. Meanwhile, Smoot's staff met with Hovde and wore him down. He finally allowed the young man to return to the editorship until a faculty-staff-student committee decided just what the status of the paper was to be. The committee, chaired by Professor John Osmun, head of the Department of Entomology, determined that, indeed, the *Exponent* was owned by the university but that Editor Smoot had been fired "without due process."

Later, the *Exponent* was established under a publishing foundation which became owner and publisher.

The turmoil of the 1960s was punctuated by five separate but not unrelated incidents involving two student takeovers of the Executive Building; a "live-in" in the southwest lounge of the Purdue Memorial Union, which resulted in the on-the-spot arrest of 229 students; a brief takeover of the University Placement Service offices in Stewart Center; and an attempted disruption of the President's Review of ROTC units on May 1, 1970.

The takeover of the placement offices on October 15, 1968, was the first such disruption. The Peace Union protest against job recruiters from Dow Chemical and the CIA ended almost as soon as it began. Vice President Mallett made the strategic mistake of showing up to promise the protesters that no recruiting by either Dow or the CIA would be permitted until after the trustees had a chance to discuss it in the next month. Hovde, to uphold previously stated policies, was forced to countermand Mallett's promise. By then the protesters had left.

Late in April 1969, the student fee increase protesters were at it again and took over corridors of the Executive Building (being careful to stay out of the offices). When they refused to leave, Hicks had to give the order to begin making arrests. It was the most distasteful chore he had to perform in his nearly forty years at Purdue. Seeing that the university would not be intimidated, the protesters left the building—and even left a crew behind to help janitors sweep and clean the hallways.

The third "invasion" followed the Executive Building debacle. Several hundred students decided to "live" in the southwest lounge of the Purdue Memorial Union as a means of protesting whatever there was to protest, since the issues that brought the loudest anguish from students seemed to change daily. The student protesters in the Union were too much for many alumni who had returned for Gala Week activities. Some left in tears. Others were outraged. Still others who had generously provided for alma mater in their wills, changed them. The time was not propitious for Purdue to lose friends; the university's Centennial Fund Drive to raise $25 million for new science and engineering facilities was under way. Though the fund-raisers and Purdue officials eventually termed the drive a success, privately they estimated the student unrest and the turmoil thus created probably cost the drive several millions. In a way, it was a shame. The Centennial Fund Drive was the first general fund campaign of its kind in the university's history. Other previous drives had been held to support a single purpose, such as the funding of the Memorial Union in the post-World War I years and the solicitation following the 1903 train wreck at Indianapolis to build the Memorial Gymnasium.

Hovde privately hated such campaigns and had to be persuaded to approve the centennial campaign by several senior staff members. The Hovde paradox was that he was a good fund-raiser himself and over his twenty-five-year tenure quietly raised millions for the university. He simply did not like the noisy hoopla and arm-twisting involved in some public fund campaigns.

The university made no effort to remove the protesters who had gone a long way toward "trashing" the Union's main floor. When it became apparent that the patience of a majority of students was wearing thin over the Union live-in and that they might take matters into their own hands, Hovde decided on May 5, 1969, to order the Union vacated and locked against the possibility of a bloody riot among the students. Two hundred twenty-nine students refused to leave and were held in the Union ballrooms until booked on trespassing charges and released without bond. (The cases never came to trial.)

The following day, May 6, 1969, the centennial anniversary of the university's founding, the campus swarmed with state and local police. Troopers were on guard against disruption of the official ceremonies in the Elliott Hall of Music. A few minutes after 1 P.M., the protesters marched from their daily rally on the mall to the Executive Building, ostensibly protesting the arrest in the early morning hours of the students who refused to leave the Union. At Hovde's request, Governor Edgar D. Whitcomb ordered in a phalanx of state troopers, unarmed except for cannisters of mace, a substance not unlike tear gas. All staff members were ordered from the building; the troopers entered the building, and the student protesters departed. Several staff automobiles were pushed in front of doors in an attempt to block entrance by police. Tires were slashed, and the crowd seemed in an angry mood. "It was," as one staff member said later, "the only time in the two years of protest that we feared for our personal safety."

On May 1, 1970, another rally took place on the mall, a protest over the United States invasion of Cambodia. Meanwhile, in the Armory, the annual and traditional President's Review of ROTC units was under way. The protesters headed for the Armory to try to break up the review, marching across the campus, arms linked, shouting over and over an obscene antiwar cheer. In the Armory, they sat down throughout the various troop formations. But Purdue University police were on duty and on Hicks's order patiently and slowly herded the mob through a large vehicle door at the north end of the Armory. Although some of the protesters feigned hurts and several heads were in collision with Purdue riot sticks, the few injuries were superficial. More than forty students were arrested; ultimately thirty-five who appealed disciplinary actions were heard by an appeals board and were either expelled or suspended.

Despite the tumult, the daily life of the campus went on unimpeded. Classes met; professors taught; bells rang on time; students scurried across the busy campus, many either unaware of, or ignoring, the dissenting cacophony all around them. Work in the laboratories continued apace; meals in the dormitories were served on time; tests and examinations were scheduled and studied for. All of the daily activities that make a large and diverse university function seemed undisturbed, despite the occasional hoarse and desperate rhetoric emanating from surplus military bullhorns.

The years of protest and revolt against any and all authority were perplexing ones for Hovde. Staff members stood by as he groped for answers to the crises that seemed to emanate from every crack in the woodwork, painfully aware of their own inadequacy in helping him to find meaningful answers.

•   •   •

On December 19, 1969, Hovde appeared routinely at the required first-semester president's convocation, this one billed as the centennial faculty convocation, and stepped to the rostrum as he had done many times before at faculty convocations to report on the state of affairs within the university.

He made an unroutine announcement: he would retire from the university on June 30, 1971, thus completing a personal goal he had long held, to serve in the Purdue presidency twenty-five years, thus topping Elliott's twenty-three years.

In announcing his decision to step down, Hovde made it clear that though he was leaving before the mandatory retirement age of sixty-five, it had nothing to do with student unrest or other issues in the university. To those close to him, however, he seemed weary. He had suffered some respiratory problems, mostly caused by chain-smoking.

His announcement was neither dramatic nor emotional. He simply thanked the faculty for their support and chatted about "the deep personal satisfactions" a quarter century, almost a quarter of the life of the university, had given him:

> All these years I have been privileged to have a part in the preparations of thousands of talented young men and women who have been educated at Purdue and have taken their places in our

society with distinction to themselves and to the university they attended.

In turning over my duties and responsibilities to your next president, my deepest personal satisfaction will come not only from the knowledge that the past is but the prologue to the future and that this institution will unquestioningly continue to grow in excellence, but also from the wonderful people of this university who have been my valued and much admired colleagues and friends through the years of our association in the work of this university.

For the trustees, Maurice J. Knoy, the veteran president of the board of trustees, made an appropriate reply of appreciation for Hovde's years at Purdue, then announced that the search for Hovde's successor would involve not only faculty and trustees but also students and alumni. The task took more than a year and resulted in the appointment in the spring of 1971 of Arthur G. Hansen, then president of the Georgia Institute of Technology.

Hovde made his last appearance at the state capitol on February 10, 1971, at a joint session of the Senate Finance and the House Ways and Means committees and, as he had done at thirteen other legislative sessions over his twenty-six years, appealed to legislators to maintain the quality of Indiana's state-assisted universities. He said (in part):

> My experience has been that, over the years, the Indiana legislature has acted in a most enlightened way with respect to our state system of higher education. You have given us freedom to do the best job we can with the resources you have provided; and over the years you have provided reasonable financial support. As a result the young men and women of our state have been given the opportunity for first-quality higher education. And that, of course, is what it is really all about. All of us want our children and our children's children to be able to compete with the very best in the nation and the world. We certainly do not want them to look back on their education and say, "I was cheated."
>
> We who have the responsibility of managing our state universities have responded to the challenge and have managed our institutions well and efficiently. As a result, while Indiana today stands only 30th among the 50 states in per capita tax appropriations for higher education, we are among the dozen most favored states in the overall quality of opportunity for higher education which we offer our young men and women.   .   .   .
>
> I am, however, deeply concerned about these [proposed] appropriations [for fiscal 1971–72] because I have given my best to the university's development over the past 25 years. And one very great truth about universities is that while it takes many years to develop a first-class institution, that same quality can be lost very quickly.

I know the many demands on the limited resources you have. And I appreciate the concerns of the taxpayers, for I am one myself, just as all of you are. But I would ask that despite these very great problems, you not undo the work that you and your predecessors have done in the past of helping to provide first-quality universities for young Hoosiers. To allow our universities to deteriorate would be tragic for our young people, and, in the long run, for all of our people.

The honors and accolades for Hovde were many. He was feted at several dinners, including a faculty-staff dinner in the ballrooms of the Purdue Memorial Union, where he had made his first public appearance at Purdue at a 1945 homecoming banquet.

Perhaps the most elaborate affair was a state dinner in the Indianapolis Hilton Hotel where Hoosier and national VIPs attended—including President Richard Nixon, who heaped high praise on Hovde as a friend and great American educator. Appropriately, he presented Hovde with a presidential golfball.

Following his retirement, Fred and Priscilla relaxed in a new home in a northeast Lafayette neighborhood near their daughters. They golfed, travelled, and enjoyed their grandchildren. Hovde spent several hours a day in his office, answering his mail and handling the affairs that revolved around his membership on several corporate boards of directors, including General Electric Company, and spent hours with the author of his biography.

Priscilla died in 1980 of complications which arose from hip replacement surgery. Her death left a deep void in his life, but he continued to try to enjoy life until his own respiratory problems put him in the hospital. He died at 10 A.M., March 1, 1983, in Lafayette's Home Hospital, a victim of emphysema.

In its eulogy, *Perspective,* an official university publication circulated to about 250,000 alumni, parents, friends and employees of the university, said of him:

> Suffice it to say, it mattered not at all to him whether we were students or staff members, deans or department heads, or even United States presidents or drivers of campus mail trucks, Fred Hovde's generorsity of spirit brought out the best in each of us.
> And what else could we ask of any man?

Chapter X

The 1970s under Arthur G. Hansen

On June 7, 1970, Arthur Gene Hansen, the newly inaugurated president of the Georgia Institute of Technology, stepped forward on the stage of the Elliott Hall of Music to accept an honorary doctorate in engineering from his alma mater. Hansen had come to Purdue in 1943 as a V12 student in the United States Marines. He received his bachelor's degree in electrical engineering in 1946 and his master's degree in mathematics in 1948. As a graduate student, he had taught freshman mathematics.

During his brief visit to Purdue, Hansen chatted with several members of the board of trustees, notably Maurice G. Knoy, then its president. The university's search for a new president to succeed Frederick L. Hovde had been under way almost from the moment in December 1969 when Hovde announced his intention to retire on June 30, 1971. Was Hansen a candidate? The trustees hoped he was. On the other hand, they knew he had been president of Georgia Tech less than a year and probably would not be interested in leaving there for the Purdue post.

Meanwhile, a trustee-appointed committee of faculty, administrators, alumni, and students continued its work under the chairmanship of Professor Robert W. Johnson of the School of Management. In the aftermath of the problems nearly every campus in the land suffered in the last half of the 1960s, the search for highly qualified candidates for the Purdue presidency was not at all easy. Many who might have aspired to a university presidency before those hectic days reassessed their ambitions. Eventually, however, the committee considered 250 names.

The search continued through 1970 and into 1971. On a night early in 1971, Hansen's telephone rang in Atlanta. It was Knoy. "Are you interested," Knoy asked, "in the Purdue presidency?" The two chatted amiably, but Knoy quickly became aware that Hansen felt he could not leave the Georgia Tech presidency. Hansen declined.

But Knoy's telephone call made Hansen think: Purdue was his alma mater and a much larger school than Georgia Tech, which had about 9,500 students compared to Purdue's four-campus enrollment of 35,000 plus. In Hansen's view, the Purdue position was a big step from the presidency of Georgia Tech, even though it was a prestigious and famous engineering school. Hansen saw Purdue as a comprehensive university, one hundred years old with new and growing dimensions and almost unlimited potential. He decided to take the big step.

Several weeks after he had talked with Hansen, Knoy got a late-night telephone call from Atlanta. "Is the Purdue presidency still open?" Hansen asked. It was, Knoy replied and indicated the trustee board's interest in discussing it further. Later, Hansen met with the full board at the Columbia Club in Indianapolis. From that point, his appointment as the university's eighth president was assured.

Ultimately Hansen became the choice of not only the board of trustees but of the select committee as well. The trustees elected him officially at their meeting June 12, 1971, and approved his five-year contract, beginning with a $45,000 first-year salary. Previously, on April 27, the trustees made a public announcement of Hansen's appointment, and Hansen simultaneously announced his resignation as Georgia Tech president in Atlanta. He arrived in West Lafayette several days later for a brief news conference at the Memorial Union and took time to meet with student and faculty leaders. The Purdue community was impressed by his scholarly but warm and friendly demeanor, a characteristic that served him well in his eleven years as president.

On July 1, 1971, Hansen—as two of his predecessors, Elliott and Hovde, had done in 1922 and 1946 respectively—came to his second-floor office in the Executive Building and went to work, thereby preserving a Purdue custom of not holding formal inaugural ceremonies for its presidents.

•   •   •

Hansen was born February 28, 1925, at Sturgeon Bay, Wisconsin, a Door County town forty miles north of Green Bay. His father and mother were Henry and Ruth Andersen Hansen, both of Scandinavian descent. His mother was the twelfth child of the Gilbert Andersens who had immigrated from Norway. Economically, Hansen always considered he was from a "lower middle-class" home.

Henry Hansen was a hardware store clerk in Sturgeon Bay (and Arthur a fourth-grader) when the family moved in the early 1930s to Green Bay where he bought and operated a small neighborhood grocery. Arthur was thirteen when his mother died. He and his younger brother Henry both helped out in the store as youngsters and on Saturdays used a cherished bicycle to make grocery deliveries. The vehicle was not acquired until Arthur was fourteen, and as he remembers, it cost the princely sum of $13.

He describes his youth as "happy and pleasant," though he has vivid memories of working in the small store when many customers were forced to ask for credit to buy groceries and from whom his father often could not collect.

Hansen recalls being at home one evening when his father phoned and asked him to come to the store immediately—merely to help load the car of a customer who had bought seven dollars worth of groceries. Those were the days when a loaf of bread sold for thirteen cents and cigarettes were two packs for a quarter.

Outside of the family grocery, Hansen earned his first dollar picking fruit in the orchards in the countryside surrounding Green Bay. He also developed an extensive newspaper route. But most of his free time was spent clerking in his father's store. Yet, he found hours for fishing, hunting, and hiking—recreations that he still likes.

More importantly, however, were Hansen's high school days when he was an excellent student, especially in mathematics. His teachers encouraged him to continue his education. Green Bay is, of course, the home of the National Football League's legendary Packers. The entire community of 42,000 was sports-minded, more accurately football-minded, and Arthur remembers the thrill of meeting the train, usually on Sunday nights, which carried the Packers home from an out-of-town game. Yet, he did not play football and chose instead track, in which he lettered in his junior and senior years in the quarter-mile and low hurdles.

Hansen also participated in high school dramatics and forensics, edited the school newspaper, and was class president. He graduated from West Green Bay High School in 1943 as class valedictorian. He probably would have attended the University of Wisconsin at Madison on a scholarship if World War II had not changed his plans.

Though his teachers encouraged him to go on to college, Hansen's father thought differently. "He wanted me to stay in the store and someday take it over," Hansen recalls. "He really didn't think college was worth it."

Not long after his graduation, Hansen joined the Marine Corps Reserve and soon received orders to report to Purdue University at West Lafayette, Indiana, as a V12 student. "The only school I knew anything about was the University of Wisconsin," Hansen says. "I didn't really know anything about Purdue. It was the first time I had been away from home. The farthest I had ever been from Green Bay was Milwaukee. I remember arriving in Lafayette at the New York Central depot and being taken to the Cary Halls where I was to be housed." Later, he was transferred to the Alpha Tau Omega fraternity house on Russell Street, then eventually went back to Cary Hall Southeast. The ATO house, like many others, had been leased by the military for the duration.

Hansen had a choice of engineering study—civil, mechanical, or electrical. He picked electrical engineering, and in the accelerated academic program of the war years at Purdue, he earned his B.S.E.E. degree in two years and nine months and was commissioned a second lieutenant in the United States Marine Corps Reserve. Hansen's was a remarkably rapid undergraduate experience. Even so, he found time to join Phi Gamma Delta social fraternity. (Did the Marines permit its personnel to join fraternities? "I didn't ask," Hansen smiles.) He was a member of the Purdue track squad for two years but, noting the competition, decided he belonged in intramural sports. Because he was a top student, he won membership in Eta Kappa Nu, the electrical engineering honorary, and Tau Beta Pi, the all-engineering honorary. He was active also in the student chapter of the American Institute of Electrical Engineers.

The war ended in the fall of 1945, about nine months before Hansen was to graduate. His memories of those days in the V12 program include the Christmas of 1945 at Cary Hall when the military students were quarantined because of a poliomyelitis scare—not an epidemic, but enough cases in the area to require the quarantine. Hansen recalls that there was a majority of long faces among the V12 contingent confined to Cary Hall that Christmas season. Another Marine V12 student, Bruce "Mickey" McGuire, an enthusiastic Varsity Glee Club member who went on to become assistant to Albert P. Stewart in Purdue Musical Organizations, saved Christmas that year by staging an impromptu Christmas show for his fellow V12 "inmates."

After graduation and commissioning in June 1946, Hansen was sent to Great Lakes Naval Training Station, was placed on inactive status, and returned to civilian life. (Several years later, he was about to be called to active duty in the Korean War, but his work as a research engineer for the federal space agency took priority and his name was removed from the Marine Corps roster.)

Hansen returned to Purdue the fall after graduation to enter graduate school as a master's degree candidate in mathematics with minors in sociology and physics. He was also a teaching assistant in freshman mathematics, and one of his students was a pretty Indianapolis freshman named Nancy Tucker. The two had dated before classes began in the fall of 1946, but no one was more surprised than she when at the first meeting of her algebra class she learned Hansen was her instructor. She recalls that after the class commenced, "He whispered to me gently the suggestion that I ought to drop algebra because I wasn't getting it down too well." Hansen would not let a personal relationship interfere with his integrity; even though she studied harder, she ended up with a "C."

Later, in 1948, Nancy prepared to leave Purdue to continue her studies at Butler University. She and Hansen exchanged farewell gifts—hers Gibran's *The Prophet*, his the sequel, *In the Garden of the Prophet*. She still believes the exchange was prophetic.

She completed her work for the B.S. at Butler, obtained her M.A. degree at Indiana University, then taught chemistry, biology, earth science, creative writing, and advanced composition. Eventually, she taught the physical sciences in the Department of Defense program for the education of United States military personnel in Iceland and the Philippines.

Meanwhile, Hansen met and married Margaret Kuehl of North Platte, Nebraska, a dietitian in the Women's Residence Halls who earned her dietetics degree at the University of Nebraska. The Hansens eventually had two daughters and three sons— Ruth Suzanne, Christine Louise, Geoffrey Allan, James Arthur, and Paul Edward.

After earning a master's degree in mathematics in 1948, Hansen went to work in Cleveland as an aeronautical research scientist at the Lewis Flight Propulsion Laboratory of the National Aeronautics and Space Administration. He suddenly found himself working on compressor and turbine blade design, though he never had taken a single course in fluid mechanics. "It is an understatement to say that I was handicapped," he remarks. In 1949–50, Hansen took a year away from his Lewis Laboratory duties to pursue doctoral studies and to teach mathematics at the University of Maryland. Then returning to Cleveland, he continued to work for the Lewis Laboratory but also taught graduate mathematics at John Carroll University in Cleveland and Baldwin-Wallace College at nearby Berea, Ohio. He continued work on his Ph.D. at Case Institute of Technology (now Case-Western Reserve University).

In 1958, Hansen took a position as head of the newly formed nucleonics department of Cornell Aeronautical Laboratory at Buffalo, New York, but continued his work toward his doctorate, awarded by Case Western in 1959. The same year he accepted an associate professorship in mechanical engineering at the University of Michigan. Curiously, he was employed to teach fluid mechanics and to set up a fluid mechanics laboratory. That meant he conducted a strict, self-imposed self-education while he taught a fundamental fluid mechanics course for undergraduates and developed a graduate course in compressible flow theory—a situation he still calls "a nightmare." Eventually, however, Hansen wrote two books, one an undergraduate text in fluid mechanics, the other a monograph on analytical solutions to fluid mechanics problems. "I just wasn't satisfied with the texts that were available and so I decided to write my own," Hansen explains.

In 1963, Hansen was elevated to a full professorship in mechanical engineering and chairman of graduate studies in mechanical engineering. He also consulted for a variety of firms and served as a special lecturer to staff engineers at Ford Motor Company. He spent the summer of 1964 as a senior research engineer at Douglas Aircraft Corporation in Long Beach, California. In his last year at the University of Michigan (1965–66), he was elevated to chairman of the Department of Mechanical Engineering.

•   •   •

In 1966, Hansen went to the Georgia Institute of Technology as dean of the college of engineering at the behest of E. A. Trabant, vice president of academic affairs. Trabant had served as the second head of Purdue's new School of Engineering Sciences in the 1950s. He left Purdue to become dean of engineering at the State University of New York at Buffalo. In 1966, Trabant became vice president for academic affairs at Georgia Tech. His first act was to hire Hansen as dean of engineering.

Hansen filled a position that previously had been the center of controversy among the engineering faculty. But not long after he appeared on the campus, he overcame that drawback and became one of the most popular administrators at the Atlanta institution. As Robert B. Wallace, Jr., wrote in *Dress Her in White and Gold*, a "biography" of Georgia Tech (1969 by the Georgia Tech

Foundation, Inc.), "few men have achieved such high popularity as did Dean Hansen under the toughest kind of circumstances."

In 1968, then Georgia Tech President Edwin D. Harrison, who had received his Ph.D. degree in engineering from Purdue in 1952, resigned to become an executive vice president of J. P. Stevens and Company. Trabant announced only a short time before that he was leaving Georgia Tech to become president of the University of Delaware.

On May 28, 1969, exactly 328 days after Harrison stepped down at Georgia Tech, George L. Simpson, chancellor of the Georgia University System, announced the appointment of Hansen as Georgia Tech's seventh president.

Dr. Vernon Crawford, the acting president, said of Hansen, "Because of his stature in educational circles, because of his knowledge of the problems and great potentialities of Georgia Tech, and because of the deep respect and warm affection in which he is held by the entire Tech community, he is the ideal choice."

It was also a happy one. Hansen was extremely popular among faculty and staff but especially among students. Indeed, his major strength as he prepared to take office was found among the students. "He is and has been the best man on this campus from my point of view since the day he stepped into the dean's job," one student leader at Tech said. A radical student said, "He doesn't kowtow to students, but he is honest with them and will debate the issues at any time."

Hansen's approach to the Tech presidency was based on his own philosophy made clear in an article in a campus publication less than a month before he was named:

> [The College of Engineering] should encourage the faculty to experiment, innovate, and develop new patterns of education. [It] should be willing and able to list new concepts in interdisciplinary studies, new programs of need satisfaction, and new methods of education.
>
> If we are faulted for any reason it would be that we have not responded to new challenges, clung to the patterns of the past, and failed to justify our educational position as it relates to our unique role in the University System and the unparalleled opportunity that we have to set a pace and lead in engineering education.

Hansen performed well at Georgia Tech; it is quite likely that had the possibility of the Purdue presidency not come up, he would have had a long and fruitful tenure at Georgia Tech. At about that time, Hansen and his wife, Margaret, separated and divorced. He came to the Purdue presidency as a single man. His ex-wife, a professor of foods and nutrition at Spelman College of Atlanta University, died of cancer several years after Hansen returned to his alma mater.

One evening not long after he became Purdue president, Hansen was writing replies to the many congratulatory notes he received. One of them was from Mrs. Carolyn Burres in California, Nancy Tucker's sister. To his reply, Hansen added a postscript: "How is Nancy? Tell her I have by no means forgotten her. She still has a soft spot in my heart." That PS led to the resumption of their college romance.

Miss Tucker returned to Indianapolis from the Philippines in June, and they were married by the Rev. Douglas Dickey, a campus minister. The date was July 26, 1972, the beginning, in a sense, of the first "team presidency" in university history, since of all previous Purdue presidents' wives, she was the most active on the campus and extremely popular with students.

•   •   •

Before they elected him to Purdue's eighth presidency, the trustees made clear to Hansen two areas in which they expected to see his concentration: the restoration of student confidence in the university administration and the institution of a continuing, high-profile program in raising private funds for the university with a strong organization to support it. Hansen did both.

His first public speech as Purdue's president was at a special welcoming convocation sponsored by the student body and open to the general public in Elliott Hall of Music. In his talk, Hansen made clear what his administrative style would be and minced no words in calling for a new assessment of the university's purposes and what Purdue should be doing. He raised tough questions about the future and told students, faculty, staff, and townspeople that Purdue must concern itself with the manner in which it responds to the needs of the world around it:

> The immediate future of society is clouded: If ever society was in need of the special expertise and the special critical and analytical functions that have been characteristic of the university, it is now. On far too may campuses issues that are of genuine concern have been treated in a manner that can only be termed at best, immature or insincere. I want to see an end to game-playing with such issues. I want to see an end to emotionalism that replaces thoughtful, scholarly critiques with collections of cliches and diatribes randomly interspersed with four-letter words.
>
> If a university cannot rise above this, if its members have no greater pride in their ability to reason and to defend a position

with logic and clarity, then the processes of education have been to little avail.

Whatever we may decide a university to be—this one in particular—I would propose that there is one thing it must be: a place where reason prevails, where scholarship is honored in whatever sense that term applies, and a place where all who employ reason and respect scholarship have the opportunity to express themselves freely. Whether this ideal is reached lies squarely in your hands. It is your responsibility to make it what it might best become.

Hansen inherited a tremendous amount of forward momentum from the Hovde years—as well as the remnants of the student unrest period that punctuated the last years of the 1960s. The onset of the new decade was a confusing time. There seemed to be little direction and much tension and disillusionment everywhere. At Purdue, Hansen set out immediately to create a more relaxed, open atmosphere throughout the campus community, beginning with the large and well-appointed office he occupied in the presidential office suite at the south end of the Executive Building's second floor.

On strolls across the campus, Hansen often stopped students to chat, beginning with "Hi. I'm Art Hansen." He was not afraid to ask pointed questions of students. He was deadly serious about learning what was bothering them, what their gripes were, and how they viewed the university's problems. He was open, warm, and sincere, but more importantly he knew how to listen. He knew that Purdue University was a great institution with infinite potential. It required only a few weeks to discern the truth of Fred Hovde's statement when he arrived, "I leave you a fine university"—words that Edward C. Elliott had said to Hovde twenty-five years earlier.

Hansen believed, however, that while Purdue was a "fine university," the university needed to know why. He wanted Purdue once again to define its mission in terms of the times it found itself in, to know insofar as is possible where it was going and whether what it was doing was relevant in a kaleidoscopic society which needed its universities more than ever. With a West Lafayette campus of 26,000 students when he arrived, Hansen was now ready to put his own stamp on the university.

Wisely, he held onto as many members of the old Hovde team as possible. He paid John W. Hicks tribute by continuing him as executive assistant; to Hansen, having Hicks at his side was a foregone conclusion, for he knew that no one knew Purdue and its people better than Hicks, nor was there anyone who knew the Indiana legislature as well as he. He retained Lytle Freehafer, the vice president and treasurer who was considered by many to be the best university financial officer in the nation. Fred Andrews remained at his post as vice president and general manager of the research foundation. George A. Hawkins, the venerated dean of engineering whom Hovde had elevated to vice president for academic affairs in 1967, stepped down. But Hansen asked him to stay on as acting dean of engineering to fill the vacancy created when Richard Grosh left Purdue to become president of Rensselaer Polytechnic (Troy, New York). Donald R. Mallett, under Hovde the vice president and executive dean, was retitled vice president for student services, but illness and subsequent surgery required that former Dean of Men O. D. Roberts fill in for him as acting vice president. Also remaining was another of the best university administrators of the time, Charles H. Lawshe, vice president for regional campus administration.

He had been on the job for two weeks when on July 14 Hansen announced his reorganization of the senior staff. He brought in Harold F. "Cotton" Robinson to fill a new post Hansen created—provost, the chief academic officer of the university, reporting directly to Hansen. Robinson had been a vice-chancellor of the University System of Georgia for more than three years when Hansen picked him. A veteran university administrator, Robinson was a widely known plant geneticist and statistician. He came from a hamlet named Bandana in the western North Carolina Blue Ridge country and won high honors as a student and later as a professor at North Carolina State University where he became administrative dean for research before going to Georgia. The provost position and duties had been those of the vice president for academic affairs.

Under Hansen's plan, he would have only two senior officers reporting to him, the provost and the vice president and treasurer. Three other vice presidents—Mallett in student services, Lawshe in regional campuses, and Andrews in research and dean of the Graduate School—were to report to the provost as were the dean of men, dean of women, and all of the academic deans.

A month after announcing Robinson's appointment, Hansen reached into the faculty to find William J. Fischang, professor of entomology, to be interim vice president for student services, and Donald R. Brown, professor of psychology, to be assistant provost under Robinson.

Simultaneously, Hansen appointed Lindley H. Wagner, M.D., of Lafayette as director of medical education, a new program wherein first-year Indiana University medical students took their course work at Purdue. Wagner had been director of medical education at Lafayette's Saint Elizabeth and Home hospitals. The new program to provide medical education away from the IU School of Medicine was Indiana's alternative to founding a second state-supported medical school.

Fischang was appointed as interim vice president to act for Mallett who was in Houston, Texas, for surgery. Mallett never was able to return to his job. After his death, Fischang was given the job in his own right. He was chosen because of his widely known personal concern for students and teaching. Fischang was recognized as the entomology department's outstanding teacher five years in a row and was also selected as a Danforth Associate in a national teaching and scholarship program.

Brown's selection was based on his experience as an academic administrator, a man who not only was a teacher and researcher but who also had served as associate head of the Department of Psychological Sciences and as an assistant graduate school dean. He was a member of the university senate as well as the faculty governing body of the School of Humanities, Social Science, and Education.

●　　　●　　　●

As a bachelor, Hansen first lived in temporary quarters. R. B. and Lillian V. O. Stewart had conveniently presented the university with their home, Westwood, on the west edge of the campus, on June 12, 1971, and Hansen moved into it in September. Later, when an extensive remodeling and enlargement project was begun, Hansen lived elsewhere but finally ended up in the South Seventh Street home owned by the university and occupied by both the Elliotts and Hovdes for a total of nearly fifty years. After they were married in 1972, the Hansens continued to occupy the Seventh Street home until the work at Westwood was completed.

Over the next ten years, Westwood was not only the presidential manse but also a sort of second Union building; the Hansens virtually opened it to students. The recreation room became a meeting place for several groups such as Iron Key. On other occasions, as many as a hundred students gathered for weiner roasts and similar functions. One year, when Purdue was involved in the NCAA basketball tournament, the Hansens were unable to attend. The Delta Gamma sorority showed up en masse and made an all-day party out of it, making popcorn and other refreshments, as the Hansens and the sorority members watched Purdue play on national television.

The Hansens knew the mood of the students in the early 1970s. In the aftermath of the Vietnam protests of the late 1960s, Hansen felt the distrust and coldness of many students. They were sullen and uncommunicative. Somehow, he believed, that had to be turned around if Purdue was to continue to be an effective university. Moving from the house high atop Lafayette's Seventh Street hill to "back home on the campus" (Hansen's words) was critical to a revival of honest communication between the administration and the student body. Westwood thus became the symbol of a presidency that sought not merely reconciliation but a new enthusiasm and anticipation of what the Purdue community could be.

Hansen had successfully performed that turnaround at Georgia Tech and once received a bronzed freshman beanie honoring him for his interest in students and student participation in the work of Tech.

Another tangible symbol of the general concern about student participation in the governance of the university was passage by the Indiana General Assembly in 1975 of an amendment to the statute governing the university's board of trustees. Under it, the trustee board was to consist of ten members, one of whom had to be a student in good standing. The student trustee term was two years. Governor Otis R. Bowen appointed Larry Greishaber, a graduate student in pharmacy from Hobart, as the university's first student trustee on January 1, 1976.

The Hansens worked assiduously in student activities. In the rest of the university, Hansen attempted, with varying degrees of success, to bring an end to an evident morale problem among clerical and service workers, faculty, and the professional and administrative staff, all of whom work day to day to keep the university running smoothly. Westwood became the scene of many kinds of social activities that at one time or other involved the physical plant workers, or the top 500 students academically, or the new faculty welcoming reception, or a President's Council party, or even an occasional wedding. The Lafayette Symphony Orchestra played on the Westwood lawns, one of the subtle ways by which the Hansens hoped to improve town-and-gown relationships. Indeed, they took on the monumental task of transforming the university's tense atmosphere (a residue of the sixties) into one of optimism and goodwill.

The "new" Westwood became the site also of home tours. The Hansens did not seem to mind, since they recognized that Westwood belonged to the public, that they occupied it only by the grace of the university and the people of Indiana, and that in any case their occupancy was transient. Nancy's enormous sense of humor surfaced often, and a favorite story is told about the visit of an Indianapolis *Star* reporter who was touring the new home. She asked Nancy who owned the furniture. "Anything you can sit on or eat from," Nancy replied, "belongs to the university. Anything pretty, weird, or movable belongs to us." Things that belonged to them included a large collection of chess sets, Nancy's collection of sea shells she had made in her world travels, and a mesmerizing, colorful collection of salt-water tropical fish.

The Hansens were once vaguely criticized for trying to turn Purdue University into the "University of Camelot (where King Arthur held court)." It was an cheap shot—but one the Hansens could laugh about. The president even played the role of King Arthur, and Nancy his Guinevere, in an Agricultural Alumni Association annual fish fry skit. The innate ability to laugh at themselves and their own human foibles endeared them to everyone who took the time and made the effort to get to know them.

Harold W. Stoke, in his 1959 book, *The American College President,* observed that "most college presidents do not really enjoy their glass houses. They are reminded too often that their bounty is not their own." The Hansens seemed to be an exception; they thoroughly enjoyed living in the "glass house" at Westwood.

Although in temperament and style Hansen and his predecessor Hovde were not at all alike, they shared one common and critical belief: above all else a university president does, he must never waver in his task of maintaining the university's commitment to truth. That was a part of the philosophy of every president in Purdue's history. But the uncertainties of the early 1970s required Hansen to reassure a university community, still mindful of the nonsense committed on beleaguered campuses everywhere, that Purdue had not wavered in its commitment. He also found it necessary to persuade the university to regain its confidence, to re-examine its goals and its mission—essentially, to take a hard look at its reason for being. That seemed to be a simple question on the surface, but frustratingly complex when examined closely. Hansen asked students, the faculty, the staff, the townspeople, the alumni—virtually every constituency of the university—to help him. Whether any useful answers ever result from such an exercise, it has the salutary effect of ventilating individual perspectives about what the university is and can be. It is an exercise, however, in which all honest answers are essentially correct.

If the collective perspective of the university was askew, Hansen wanted to right it. In the metaphor of the late Lotus D.

Coffman, a Hoosier who became the esteemed president of the University of Minnesota, a college president is like a hunter in the woods who may spend 95 percent of his time swatting mosquitoes while trying to keep in mind that he is there to get a shot at a moose. Purdue had spent disproportionate time and effort swatting mosquitoes in the late 1960s; Hansen believed it was now time to take aim at a moose.

• • •

"We need," Hansen told an audience at an alumni conference luncheon of the Krannert Graduate School of Industrial Administration, "the help of faculty, students, and alumni to look at our program missions, the level of program emphasis, the appropriate mix of nonvocational aspects, and how total resources can be used more effectively. The goals of a university are not very well defined. You say it should meet society's needs; I'll buy that. But what needs?"

Hansen knew that the trend was toward some kind of universal higher education, some kind of college for everyone. And he raised the question of managing such an enterprise when at the moment the universities and colleges were in a management crisis; the doubling of enrollments and simultaneous rising costs had created educational dilemmas of a major proportion.

"The time has come," he declared, "when the way to meet rising costs has become unclear. There seems to be no way to meet them other than the outstretched hand. We've reached the point where tuition increases cannot continue."

Simultaneously, Hansen continued, the crisis was complicated by demands for new educational programs, noting as examples the regression in the aerospace industry and the simultaneous growth in molecular biology, and no feasible way to shift personnel or equipment, one to the other. But, he concluded proudly, "Purdue is a magnificent university, and if any university can make it, Purdue can. And if we solve the problems here, we'll do much to solve them for higher education in general."

The Krannert speech was typical of those Hansen made in his early years at Purdue and was a portent of the optimism he hoped would spread not only throughout the university community but the state and nation as well.

As he told the board of directors of the Purdue Alumni Association at Gala Week on May 5, 1972, "I must repeat what I have told other groups in and out of the university in the months since I have had an opportunity to inspect the machinery of this university and talk to the many dedicated faculty and staff which really make it go. And that is this: Purdue is truly a fine university. That is not idle flattery; that is what I consider an accurate assessment of the situation. This is not to say we do not have problems. One of the factors which make Purdue a fine university is the willingness of its people to recognize and define its problems and seek solutions for them."

Optimistic or not, Hansen was well aware of the university's problems, and the one that obsessed him was the austerity of the budgets in the years immediately following his arrival. One of the most austere Purdue operating budgets in twenty years was adopted for 1972–73—$77.7 million for the West Lafayette campus and $13.5 million for the regional campuses at Westville, Hammond, and Fort Wayne. On June 30, 1971, Indiana University assumed financial management of Indiana University-Purdue University at Indianapolis under an agreement made earlier between the two schools. It became effective just one day before Hansen took office.

Financially, the 1970s were frustrating years for Purdue and the other state universities. The Middle East oil crisis—created when the world's principal oil-producing nations set new and much higher prices per barrel for crude—brought about rampant worldwide, double-digit inflation. In truth, that created problems within the financial structures of those public universities that depended almost entirely on public funding for their operations—and Purdue was one of them. There was simply no way the public tax base could keep up with the economic spiral. As a result, as early as 1972 the available funds were only about 4.5 percent higher than the previous year. Overall, that meant the university had less than $2.1 million in "new" money, since unavoidable cost increases, employer social security payments, utilities, mandatory supplies, and so on would amount to $1.7 million.

Hansen told the university staff that modest salary and wage increases would be possible, that utility and maintenance support for new buildings at regional campuses would be available, and that some general but modest progress in existing programs could be made, but only by withdrawing funds from other programs. Hansen was deeply concerned that there existed the real possibility of a dent in the armor of Purdue's carefully guarded educational quality—that it was a "standstill" budget that did not permit Purdue to go forward in areas that he saw as critical. These included programs for educationally disadvantaged students, renovation of older buildings, replacement of the many part-time faculty members at regional campuses with full-time faculty, and most importantly, replacement of scientific and technical equipment either worn out or obsolete. Hansen viewed his first

Purdue budget gravely since it would be a portent of a future when inflation would continue to erode the university's purchasing power.

The outlook was bleak despite the fact that $7.5 million in new construction was underway, most of it for the regional campuses and Purdue Airport runway lengthening and widening.

Hansen therefore wasted no time in establishing a new administrative arm to bring about full-time, concerted fund-raising in the private sector. He was convinced beyond any doubt that Purdue could not remain one of the world's great scientific and engineering institutions by relying solely on state appropriations affected by the political vagaries of state legislatures. Purdue would always be a good university, Hansen believed, but it could not achieve the kinds of "cutting edge" programs he envisioned without substantial and continuing infusions of private money. He had only to look back to the end of the university's second decade for a classic lesson of what private finding means. It was a time when President Smart had no luck in persuading the legislature to appropriate funds for a new engineering laboratory. But he triumphed when Amos Heavilon gave $35,000 for the construction of Heavilon Hall and its adjunct laboratories. The state then followed with substantial appropriations; other gifts from industries and individuals provided what was then the best engineering education center west of the Alleghenies. It was a "cutting edge" facility that put Purdue far out in front of any other engineering institution save the Massachusetts Institute of Technology, and even its people looked at Heavilon Hall with considerable envy.

Hansen's mission was one the trustees had outlined to him at the outset. In 1972, he began building a fund-raising organization. To direct it, Hansen selected Stanley E. Hall, a New Yorker and a Purdue alumnus who obtained his electrical engineering degree in 1959. Hall wound up in management and college development (euphemism for fund-raising) and was a vice president at Hiram College, a small eastern Ohio school, when Hansen beckoned him to Purdue. Besides fund-raising, Hall was given the responsibility for the university's public relations, which at the time were carried on primarily by the University News Service and the Office of the University Editor (now the Office of Publications).

Hansen already had a formidable agenda for Hall when he arrived and immediately asked him to set it in motion. The long-range goal was to "awaken a sleeping giant," the metaphor one fund-raising consultant used to describe the alumni body and other constituencies whom Purdue rarely, if ever, asked for private contributions. Except for the money sought through John Purdue Club members for support of intercollegiate athletics and the scholarship foundation, fund-raising among private sources was not a concerted Purdue emphasis. Hansen intended to elevate the fund-raising profile to a level heretofore unknown at Purdue.

Purdue's greatest strides, including its founding, have generally been made possible by the private sector. Heavilon Hall, the Memorial Gymnasium, the Purdue Memorial Union, the first Cary Hall, the first Windsor Hall, Eliza Fowler Hall, Smith Hall, Ross-Ade Stadium, the Wetherill Laboratory of Chemistry, Loeb Playhouse, Slayter Center of the Performing Arts, Lynn Hall of Veterinary Medicine, the Krannert Building, and Lilly Hall of Life Sciences are all examples of Purdue facilities provided either entirely or partially by private gifts. The heritage and the spirit of an alumni body of more than 150,000 was there. The awakening, as gently as possible Hansen hoped, was about to take place.

Hansen approved several suggestions from staff members. A high priority was a periodical designed to reach all alumni, parents of undergraduates, employees, and friends of the university. It began as the joint project of the University News Service and the Office of Publications, a newsprint tabloid-size publication Hansen named *Perspective*. The paper was published six times a year at the outset with interpretive articles and news about the people, projects, and activities of the university. Its philosophy continues to be that well-informed alumni are interested and receptive alumni. *Perspective* was first published in September 1973 and continues quarterly with a circulation on the order of 250,000 per issue under the aegis of the Office of Publications.

Another early program put into place was the Focus on Purdue program which brought as guests to the campus selected alumni and potentially influential citizens from all parts of the state and nation for a weekend of intense but interesting briefings on every aspect of the university. The idea behind it was to develop a well-informed coterie of Purdue boosters who knew Purdue inside out. Other programs brought state legislators to the campus or worked to develop improved internal relations among staff and faculty. Development of an annual giving program began.

Other fund-raising activities that evolved from the Hansen program were an annual student-run Phonathon; the Purdue Annual Fund; a Parents Association; and Purdue Retirees, an organization formed to utilize the talents, loyalty, and energies of many retired faculty and staff otherwise lost through retirement.

But central to the entire Hansen plan was the development of a permanent organization called the President's Council, a group of friends and alumni of the university who not only supported the university monetarily (minimum dues: a $1,000 per year gift to the university) but also lent their support in other ways, such as giving advice the president often sought on wide-ranging matters affecting university policy. It was also a social organization to foster an esprit de corps among those who love the university.

Hansen seemed proudest of the Council for Special Events, a student organization that involved the students in an intense way with not merely fund-raising but in the general boosterism of the university in a constructive way. The group planned and virtually ran the student Phonathon and went about the state giving talks in behalf of the university. Enthusiastic students, Hansen often said, were the best representatives Purdue could possibly have.

•　　•　　•

When Hansen gazed out of the windows of his comfortably appointed second-floor office in Hovde Hall, he could almost feel the strength and stability exuded by the massive, red-brick geometry of Purdue's simple architecture. The broad expanses of campus lawn, well-groomed and manicured, and the shrubs and young trees proffered an aura of warmth and security. The students themselves, each different in countless ways but all with an educationally common goal, to Hansen represented Purdue's innate sense of anticipation and vitality and vision—all fuels that propelled this place from an Indian hunting ground to one of humankind's noblest experiments in civilizing.

Hansen pondered the idea that regardless of the number or profundity of its accomplishments, Purdue should always remain aware of its enormous possibilities. It would never run out of problems to solve or jobs that needed to be done. A favorite Hansen theme was that if universities such as Purdue did not exist, they would have to be created to unlock an infinite number of humankind's seemingly unsolvable puzzles. To Hansen, Purdue had to remain an effective bastion in the never-ending War on Ignorance, a costly and eternal conflict in which the chief weapon is, unlike other wars, human intelligence.

Of Hansen's seven predecessors, none seemed as obsessed about the future of civilization and the university's critical role in it as he—at least not publicly. In his speeches, Hansen often quoted Alvin Toffler, author of *Future Shock,* and would disturb his audience, sometimes to the point of being depressing, by thinking the unthinkable. He would say, for example, that he believed that science and technology would find answers to most of the problems of humanity, while admitting that science and technology, and the results thereof, always raised their own critical problems. But confronting such issues was simply a part of his job, Hansen believed, and he worked almost desperately at times to get others in the university—faculty, staff, students, alumni— to think seriously with him. He may have sometimes viewed the future as bleak, yet he could simultaneously express optimism about it. He must have been frustrated by those who ignored or failed to understand what he was trying to say.

That may explain in part why he worked so diligently with his development staff to insure that the President's Council, the flagship of the university's private funding effort, would not become simply a rich man's college dollar club but rather a forum where all kinds of ideas and problems relevant to the university could be explored. It was to be a place, he hoped, where he could give and receive guidance.

In a simpler time, college faculty and administrators were inclined to hold the alumni at arm's length, content to let them flail away with criticism of—or worse, advice for—the football coach. The point Hansen tried to make throughout his eleven years as Purdue president was that the times were no longer simple. He sought a new kind of enthusiasm, a maturation of the expressions of support that went far beyond simplistic answers and Saturday afternoon cheers. Anything less, Hansen believed, would doom the President's Council to failure. He gambled on the long run and made the President's Council work. It still does.

Although at times Hansen's administrative style may have been criticized, the intellectual leadership he brought to Purdue was crucially important in a decade in which the social pendulum seemed to swing from issues and communal causes of the 1960s to one in which individual interests and achievements prevailed—a time inaccurately labelled the "me generation."

Everywhere Hansen went, he took his Purdue message with him and repeated his belief that higher education itself, with the world in general, was undergoing change "so profound that many may never fully understand what has happened." To an audience of midwestern pharmacists at a Purdue conference, he rejected out-of-hand the then common notion that American colleges and universities were mortally ill and overcome by troubles of their own making.

"I do not for a single moment buy that," Hansen declared. "I do not even entertain the question seriously." He then reiterated his belief that, on the contrary, universities and colleges stood nearly alone as bastions of knowledge and, as they always have, agents of change.

One of the most visible changes in the universities was just such a nontraditional activity as the pharmacists' conference at which he spoke—a place, he said, where professionals could come to keep up with the progress in their own fields. The enormous output of new information and the speed with which it is available required the university to remain relevant and flexible. And Hansen thought that was all to the good.

"Continuing education must be directed clearly toward not only the acquisition of new knowledge and techniques, but their optimal use by the professional to improve his competence in gaining the results he seeks," Hansen said. The words echoed those of his predecessor, Hovde.

• • •

Having waxed eloquently on the purposes and future of Purdue, Hansen was forced by the conditions to deal with what he described as "cultural tensions" developing on the West Lafayette campus as the numbers of blacks and other minorities attending the university began to increase. In 1972, about 700 blacks were enrolled, and they were not satisfied with the conditions they found, mostly because Purdue had traditionally had few black students and was inexperienced in doing the things necessary to meet their needs and bring them into the mainstream of the Purdue community. And, of course, there was just plain, age-old prejudice.In the Elliott era, a young black engineering student once got an audience with then President Elliott to complain about the rather crude and unsatisfactory housing Purdue's few blacks had to endure. Black students at that time were not even permitted to occupy university-owned housing. Elliott's reply to the young student was, in effect, that if he did not find Purdue to his liking (whatever the conditions may have been), then he should leave. The young man did exactly that—and went on to become a federal judge in Philadelphia. He is A. Leon Higgenbotham, who in 1979 returned to the campus to receive an honorary doctor of laws degree.

In Hovde's first year as president in 1946, he was forced to deal with what was called "Jim Crow mentality." The consternation created when a black student applied for admission to Cary Hall rumbled all the way to the board of trustees where, under Hovde's influence, the restriction was lifted for all time. After complaints, Hovde also decreed that blacks were not to be discriminated against in the Purdue Memorial Union barber shop (which closed in the long-hair years of the 1960s).

But it was 1972, and Hansen believed, as did Hovde, that racial discrimination was an irrationality that had no place on a university campus. On the night of February 17, Hansen met with a group of black students in the living room of the Black Cultural Center (BCC) on University Street, a center begun under the aegis of Hovde as one means of alleviating the neglect Purdue blacks had undergone for so long. Hansen received a polite but cool reception, and there was an undercurrent of subdued hostility at the meeting.

He was the first speaker in a series the BCC had planned between black students and university administrators. At the time, the campus racial situation was described by the Lafayette *Journal and Courier* as "not good, but it's not bad, either"—a bit of journalistic ambivalence that reflected the rampant confusion extant throughout much of the community.

One student at the Hansen meeting asked, "You have been here six and one-half months, and you have been trying to define the missions of the university. But it looks to me like blacks have been pushed into the backseat again. Does the university have a definite commitment to black students?"

"Let me say this," Hansen replied. "There has been a commitment [by this administration]. That [includes] the $400,000 for black student programs, and it's rising. There is at least that. That is the only money, to my knowledge, put aside for any special student group. No other single area outside of the budget has occupied my time more than this one."

That was true, though the black students did not believe it. There was, one student at the meeting argued, a lot of talk about commitments, but nothing about a "sense of urgency."

"I sense you don't have that sense of urgency," the student challenged Hansen.

"You are wrong. Wrong. Wrong. Wrong. You are totally wrong," Hansen fired back.

By August of 1972, Hansen was able to announce a program aimed at improving the situation for blacks on the campus. Singer A. Buchanan, a professor of drama who also was coordinator of black student programs, had left to take an academic position at Bowling Green University and the management of the Black Cultural Center was placed under the Purdue Memorial Union. In addition, several new black professors had been employed, and the search for blacks for the central administration continued. Hansen's dilemma was always that the demand for black professors in Purdue's specific academic areas far exceeded the supply. Meanwhile, the search continued for a manager of the Black Cultural Center, a post filled by a quiet but effective spokesman for Purdue black students, Antonio Zamora. Hansen also increased funds to enlarge the staff of the student-services area.

Earlier, Hansen had issued a public plea to students, faculty, staff, and the entire Greater Lafayette community to "face the issues squarely to bring about a reduction in cultural and racial misunderstandings," which he felt were increasing:

> To the degree that a student or any other member of this community feels alienated or frustrated in the pursuit of his or her daily tasks or is unhappy in his or her daily personal relations to the people who surround him or her, the environment for learning has been diminished. It is not enough to say that alienation, frustration, and faulty personal relationships exist in any human community. Rather, it is our obligation and responsibility to effect changes to correct these deficiencies. Within a university . . . it is essential that the social environment be as favorable as possible. It might also be pointed out that the university has far greater intellectual resources to meet this requirement than most social institutions.
>
> In recent years, both the tremendous growth of most universities and the rapidity of social change have made the creation of a stable and satisfactory educational environment a most demanding task. At Purdue, for example, there has been a continuing problem that has centered recently on relations among and between the various people on the campus and students having cultural backgrounds different from the majority of persons comprising the university community.
>
> Tensions have grown and misunderstandings have increased. The time has come for all of us to redouble our efforts to improve the environment for all. To this end I am calling upon members of the university administration, the staff, the faculty, and the student body to consider and respond . . . to proposals to improve the general educational and academic environment.

Hansen then listed a six-point program which included development of "learning seminars [to create understanding] of the university community as a pluralistic society." He also ordered a review of all university rules and regulations "with the intent of repealing or revising those which detract from the creation and maintenance of the desired learning environment." Department heads and administrators involved in student life were asked to analyze and report to him strengths and weaknesses "as these may relate to a sound educational environment." He wanted Provost Robinson to consider how best to insure accountability of all faculty members with teaching responsibilities. He sought ways to provide the resources for meeting the problem of academic deficiencies of minority students and told administrators he expected them to aggressively pursue fairness for "minorities and women when their qualifications are otherwise comparable to other job candidates."

Hansen did not confine his activity in behalf of educational opportunities for minorities to the Purdue campus. He was founder of the National Action Committee for Minorities in Engineering and spearheaded the formation of the Society of Black Engineers at Purdue, a society which soon founded chapters on other engineering campuses throughout the United States.

•　　•　　•

Hansen felt so strongly about the need to re-establish trust among the various elements of the campus community that he decided to return to the classroom to teach one section of a freshman class. On August 28, 1972, he met the first class of the course called "Perspectives on Contemporary Issues," an elective for students in the School of Humanities, Social Science, and Education. The engineer-president of a school, traditionally an engineering school, a man who could have taught most of the mathematics courses and any number of engineering classes, chose instead a humanities course. Hansen, the engineer by profession, the humanist by preference, knew that the School of Humanities, Social Science, and Education had become Purdue's largest school; enrollments in agriculture and engineering had dipped, albeit temporarily, to a worrisome level while humanities grew. But Hansen was willing to face the fact that Purdue had to live with, and act upon, that particular phenomenon.

Mrs. Hansen joined her husband in teaching the class as an unpaid volunteer instructor, and in the event that a demanding schedule kept either or both President and Mrs. Hansen from being present, John Hicks substituted as instructor.

The course strained Hansen's already demanding schedule, but he managed to meet a majority of the classes for the fall semester of 1972. As his work increased and required more of his time, he did not attempt to teach the course again.

What did occupy his rare periods of free time was learning to fly under the tutelage of the Department of Aviation Technology. He was a quick study at the controls of the department's Piper Cherokee 140s, and on February 15, 1972, a chilly and blustery day, Hansen took off from the Purdue Airport's east-west runway and soloed. On July 3, 1973, he passed the required examinations and won his private pilot license—Purdue's first flying president.

Hansen's pilot license added, symbolically at least, to the Purdue heritage in aviation going back to 1911 when two barnstorming planes landed on Stuart Field (now occupied by Elliott Hall of Music and several other buildings) for an aeronautics demonstration. President Stone wanted rather badly to take a ride and was set to do so when some members of the board of trustees prohibited the flight as being too dangerous. The heritage continued under President Elliott who, with the financial help of benefactor David E. Ross, was responsible for the construction of the Purdue Airport, at the time the only university-owned airport in the United States. Elliott fostered aviation and aeronautical engineering, and the nation's first civilian pilot program began in the pre-World War II days of the late 1930s under the direction of Grove Webster.

Aviation continued its growth under Hovde. The Purdue Aeronautics Corporation and the shortlived Purdue Airlines actually provided "live" laboratories for professional pilot students. Aeronautical engineering became a separate school, and from it the first man on the moon, Neil A. Armstrong, graduated in 1955. The Department of Aviation Technology came into existence and later established the nation's first bachelor of science degree in aviation technology under the direction of James R. Maris in the Hovde administration. And though the presidents since Stone fostered Purdue's leadership in aeronautics and aviation, none participated as personally as did Hansen.

But if the atmosphere established by the Hansen administration seemed warm and sunny, there were housekeeping problems that surfaced when Vice President and Treasurer Lytle J. Freehafer notified Hansen in the fall of 1973 that he intended to take early retirement at the end of December. Freehafer, the senior mainstay of the Hovde administration when the campus boiled over in 1969, was as popular as any man can be who also holds the university's purse strings. Freehafer had been state budget director when he came to Purdue under R. B. Stewart and was, in a sense, a Stewart protégé. He learned much about what to do from Stewart and, conversely, what not to do. Freehafer was once described by Hovde as "one of two men whom I have ever known who had absolute total integrity."

In his retirement note to Hansen, Freehafer said that "many of the things that Mrs. Freehafer and I would like to do have not been possible because of my duties [at the university]." Hansen heaped much praise on Freehafer, calling him "one of the truly outstanding business officers in the entire country," which was true.

Freehafer's note and Hansen's tribute, however, failed to cover a schism that had developed between Hansen's two senior officers, Freehafer and Provost Robinson. A personality conflict may have caused the rift between the two. Freehafer was a strong, dominant financial leader. Robinson was a strong, able academic leader with what Hansen described as "unerring instincts for excellence." Their inability to resolve their differences led to Freehafer's early retirement at the end of 1973 and ultimately to Robinson's resignation to become chancellor of Western Carolina University at Cullowhee, North Carolina, only a few miles from his hometown. Their leaving was a blow to Hansen and a loss to the university, since both men were extremely capable.

Freehafer had polished a well-run business and financial machine which had served the university with great efficiency. Robinson, the workaholic, demanded as much of himself as others and perhaps felt the business-academic scale was not in balance. He wanted to be in a position, as the university's chief academic officer, to make some financial decisions traditionally in the purview of the chief financial officer.

"It was one of the most unfortunate episodes while I was the president," Hansen says of the matter. "I tried very hard to bring these two very strong and very talented people together. But I could not. The whole thing was really a lack of communication. Cotton [Robinson] didn't see that the business side was really trying to help him."

Fortunately, Hansen did not have to look outside of the university family for either Freehafer's or Robinson's successors. One was Frederick R. Ford, a Benton County native, who came to Purdue as a freshman in engineering and, quite simply, never left. Ford eventually earned his Ph.D. in management and joined the business office staff. A series of promotions resulted in his appointment as university business manager and assistant treasurer under Freehafer. He, like Freehafer, had studied well, and his experience and ability meant that his appointment as Freehafer's successor was a general expectation.

The other was Felix Haas, the MIT-educated mathematician who had been appointed as dean of the School of Science by President Hovde. His appointment as provost was a logical and wise one and received the nearly unanimous approval of the university community. Haas served throughout Hansen's tenure and into the first years of the administration of Hansen's successor, Steven C. Beering, before retiring to teach mathematics, his first love. Eventually Hansen changed Ford's and Haas's titles to executive vice president and treasurer and executive vice president and provost, respectively. That move permitted a spate of vice presidential appointments under each of the two senior officers—and the

Arthur G. Hansen was the first president who was also an alumnus. He served eleven years before becoming chancellor of the Texas A & M System.

Harold F. "Cotton" Robinson was the first provost in university history. He came in 1971 not long after Hansen assumed the presidency.

Lytle F. Freehafer, retained as vice president and treasurer under Hansen, got his start at Purdue under Hovde. He retired in 1973 after twenty-one years in which he rose rapidly from assistant comptroller.

Steven C. Beering, former dean of the Indiana University Medical School and director of the IU Medical Center at Indianapolis, became the ninth president of Purdue in 1983, succeeding Hansen.

The Executive Building constructed in 1935 was renamed the Frederick L. Hovde Hall of Administration in 1975 to honor the president emeritus. At the same time, Hovde also received an honorary doctorate. He retired in 1971.

Although it was funded from receipts of the 1969 Centennial Fund Drive, the A. A. Potter Engineering Research Center was constructed and occupied in the Hansen administration and was one of its outstanding building achievements.

The men at Hansen's side after Freehafer's retirement and Robinson's resignation were two "inside" appointees as executive vice presidents—Felix Haas (left), the dean of science and brilliant mathematics professor who became executive vice president and provost, and Frederick R. Ford (right), the business manager and assistant treasurer who was groomed by Freehafer for a top university job. Hansen appointed him executive vice president and treasurer.

Capstone of the Hansen administration's extensive construction program was the Life Sciences Research Building, financed entirely with part of the $44 million-plus contributed during Hansen's first fund campaign, the Plan for the Eighties.

Two highlights of Arthur G. Hansen's tenure as Purdue president: crowning in 1978 the first black homecoming queen in university history, Kassandra Agee (above), and the encouragement of the Black Cultural Center on University Street. The BCC was founded in the Hovde administration and received Hansen's full support and personal attention.

The advent of Title IX federal regulations opened the door to women's intercollegiate athletics in the 1970s on about the same basis as men's. The result at Purdue was the fashioning of one of the nation's best collegiate women's volleyball teams. The lower view is of the $9.3 million Undergraduate Library opened in April 1982. Funds for the new facility were partly a result of student lobbying for library appropriations in the Indiana General Assembly.

Hanley Professor of Biological Sciences Michael Rossman (with a colleague) represents a new breed of Purdue scientists on the cutting edge of new knowledge. Rossman used more than 25 percent of Purdue Computing Center power in his graphics mapping of millions of atoms to find fundamental knowledge of the virus. His breakthrough on the common-cold virus brought the university national attention.

Steven C. Beering and his wife, Jane, were greeted at a student reception in the Purdue Memorial Union minutes after the announcement of his election by the board of trustees as ninth president of Purdue University on February 4, 1983.

From six plain buildings on an
originally treeless campus in 1874 to
the sprawling campus of today, Purdue
University at West Lafayette stands as
the achievement of men and women
unafraid to dream.

oddity of an organization sprinkled with as many vice presidents as academic deans.

Besides Robinson and Freehafer, others moved on during the Hansen years. Hall, the director of development, had done a superb job of laying a solid base for the development operations that Hansen envisioned, despite his inability to achieve all he had hoped. He could not bring the alumni association—an old, well-established monolith not administratively tied to the university—within the sphere of influence of his organization, a fact which caused him to seek employment elsewhere.

His successor was Leonard W. Bucklin, a down-easter educated in his home state of Maine, an extrovert who dabbled in such things as magic, collecting model railroad locomotives, and, for children, the making of balloon animals. Bucklin had degrees in divinity and law and was both a Methodist clergyman and an expert on wills, trusts, bequests, and other probate matters. He had few peers in the business of deferred-giving (the euphemism fundraisers use to denote donations you promise while you live but are not collected until you die). Hall had worked with Bucklin at another college and finally talked him into joining his staff at Purdue.

Bucklin was an excellent fund-raiser, but when Hansen decided to move into the most ambitious fund drive in university history, it was entrusted instead to a personable, long-time Purdue academician, John S. Day, then dean of the School of Management and the Krannert Graduate School of Management. Day was a graduate of the Harvard business school and came to Purdue in 1955 to teach accounting. He moved through the faculty chairs relatively quickly and became the associate dean of the schools under their founding dean, Emmanuel T. Weiler. After Weiler resigned the deanship to return to teaching, Day became dean.

Day visited Hansen one day to tell him he wished to resign as dean and return to teaching as Weiler had done. "Hang on, John," Hansen told him, "there's another job I want to talk to you about." That job was the vice presidency in development to direct the upcoming fund campaign named "The Plan for the Eighties." Bucklin resigned to enter private consulting for college and university fund-raising and returned to his native Maine.

Hansen regards his single greatest triumph as a president the building of a strong administrative team. And he did—but not without some early instabilities caused by top echelon personnel turnovers. Yet, in a way, these added to the eventual strength and effectiveness of his senior group.

Much was happening as the Hansen administration began to gain its own momentum. A significant development was the approval in 1974–75 by the trustees of a recommendation to give all but the smallest of Purdue's four regional campuses academic autonomy. The reason was simple: the regional campuses should be free to pursue the undergraduate educational objectives most responsive to the needs of the region each served. The campuses were still tied to the West Lafayette campus administration, but each could pursue individual academic goals through the decision-making power granted to each campus's faculty governing body.

Enrollments continued to increase; a new demand for engineering quickly reversed what could have been a downward trend. The fall enrollment reached 27,466, which included a 16 percent increase in freshman engineers. The same year the university awarded 6,597 degrees.

Purdue had already developed an international reputation; it had enrolled students from other parts of the world since the late 1890s under President Smart. It had joined several consortiums to aid the development of universities in Brazil, Taiwan, India, and Afghanistan. That reputation grew under Hansen, who travelled extensively on behalf of the university to China, Taiwan, and Venezuela. Meanwhile, Nancy Hansen made it her personal project to travel throughout Indiana as a sort of goodwill ambassador to the county home economics clubs—to say, in effect, "Purdue likes what you are doing."

●   ●   ●

Building construction and renovations reached record proportions in Hansen's administration. In 1974, work began on the four-story A.A. Potter Engineering Center, the engineering research center which had been the central goal of the 1969 Centennial Fund campaign. Even then, the $3.8 million in gifts from that campaign required an additional infusion of $2.3 million from the Lilly Endowment Fund. When completed, it was the crown jewel in the university's engineering complex—though hidden from general view by other buildings.

There were many administrative changes. At the retirement of C. H. Lawshe, the Regional Campus Administration he had so carefully fashioned was discarded, and G. Walter Bergren, the affable engineer who had worked under Lawshe for many years, was promoted to administrative dean for the regional campuses. Lawshe had done his work well, and Hansen knew it; he always came away from the regional campuses impressed by what he had learned.

Another significant change in 1974 was the reorganization of the offices of the Dean of Men and Dean of Women into a single unit known as the Office of the Dean of Students. Bryan Clemens, an assistant dean of men under O. D. Roberts, served as acting dean of men in 1971–72 after Roberts's retirement. Clemens was appointed to the post in his own right in 1972 and resigned to enter the ministry in 1974 when the office was reorganized under a dean of students rather than two deans. M. Beverley Stone was dean of women at the time and had been through the campus "wars" of the late 1960s. Caring and sensitive, Dean Stone was also a tough administrator. When the reorganization occurred, she, too, contemplated resignation; her colleagues persuaded her to stay on and to apply for the new post of dean of students. She did, although she had fought even the concept of a dean of students because, as she said, ninety-nine times out of a hundred where it happened at other schools, men were appointed deans of students.

So highly respected and loved by students, staff, and the administration was she that her appointment as Purdue's first dean of students seemed almost a certainty—except to her. When she was tapped for it, no one was, as she now contends, "as astounded as I was."

After she was appointed in 1968 as dean of women, she came to dread meeting Earl L. Butz on the campus. Then dean of agriculture, Butz would invariably say to her, eyes twinkling but in mock solemnity, "The reason for all of this student unrest is the new dean of women. We never had these problems when Dean Schleman was here," he would say. "There were plenty of times," Dean Stone added, "when I thought perhaps he was right."

She had followed her mentor, Helen B. Schleman, into the job. Schleman came to Purdue in the mid-thirties at the behest of Dean of Women Dorothy C. Stratton, who had succeeded Carolyn Shoemaker at her death in 1933. Miss Schleman was the director of the first women's residence hall (Duhme Hall), in what became the Windsor Halls complex, and entered military service to serve under Dean Stratton in the Coast Guard in World War II. Dean Schleman returned to the campus in 1947 when President Hovde appointed her as dean of women, succeeding Clare A. Coolidge, who had been acting dean since 1942. Dean Schleman served through the 1950s and 1960s until her retirement in 1968.

Dean of Students Stone served so capably that at her retirement in 1980 there was little question that one of her close and equally capable assistants, Barbara I. Cook, would be appointed.

She was—and served until 1987 when she was succeeded by another link in a heritage chain, Betty M. Nelson.

The undefined religious and spiritual needs of the student body were met by at least twenty-seven student religious foundations which over many years sprang up on the periphery of the West Lafayette campus. All have spent prodigious sums for facilities and personnel who devote full-time work to the religious needs of Purdue students. Most work closely with the Dean of Students Office, and it has been speculated that the religious foundations and churches do more personal counseling with students than is done by university agencies.

In 1975, the character of the student body was changing within the traditionally male-dominated schools, such as engineering and agriculture. Women's enrollments in engineering increased fivefold, in agriculture fourfold, and in industrial management threefold.

Encouraged by Hansen's more aggressive policy of opening Purdue's opportunities to blacks and minorities, engineering enrollment in 1974–75 reflected a fourfold increase to 120 black students and 20 students with Spanish surnames.

Hansen also set out to implement the requirements of the federal Title IX rules which required colleges and universities to provide funding for women's intercollegiate athletics on the same basis as men's athletics. Purdue got its Title IX program off the ground with seven intercollegiate women's sports the first year, four of them fully funded.

The academic year of 1974–75 had other proud landmarks. It paused to pay tribute to President Emeritus Frederick L. Hovde by conferring on him his twentieth and last honorary degree. He was pleased, of course, but deeply moved when, simultaneously, the board of trustees renamed the Executive Building the Frederick L. Hovde Hall of Administration to honor him for Purdue's illustrious years under his presidency.

The year 1974–75 was also the year Professors Edwin T. Mertz, biochemist, and Oliver E. Nelson, Jr., plant geneticist, were honored throughout the state and nation as co-discoverers of high lysine (high protein) corn, a remarkable breakthrough with the potential of providing a new source of protein to the world's hungry, especially in Third World nations.

Deanships changed across the university (see Appendix), and Hansen worked to insure that the various schools remained relevant. The School of Home Economics was renamed the School of Consumer and Family Sciences; the Department of Nuclear Engineering was given school status; the School of Industrial

Management was changed simply to the School of Management, reflecting the school's broadening curriculum.

Despite gains, austerity continued to be the university's watchword. At a time when enrollments in engineering should have been expanded, in engineering and science they were capped in spite of an overall 5.3 percent increase in enrollment. The austerity with which Purdue had to manage its operating funds was in sharp contrast to a widening construction program at West Lafayette as well as the regional campuses which were showing sharp enrollment increases.

In 1975, construction included a new $1.6 million Nursing and Allied Health Sciences Building adjacent to the relatively new Pharmacy Building. The new nursing building culminated the work of Professor Helen R. Johnson, an Indiana University School of Nursing faculty member employed in 1962 by C. H. Lawshe to begin Purdue's first nursing program, a two-year associate degree program. Johnson, one of the hardest-working members of the Purdue staff, also put into place similar nursing programs at each of the regional campuses and worked tirelessly to obtain foundation grants to support nursing education at Purdue. Purdue hoped its program would help meet a shortage of registered nurses, especially in Indiana, in the face of a reduction in the numbers of hospital nursing school programs.

Nursing at Purdue grew rapidly, moving to various cramped and inconvenient quarters all over the campus. Professor Johnson, working quietly and at times seemingly unnoticed, went about the business of applying for a substantial federal grant for a new building. When the grant was approved, her stock rose considerably. Eventually the Department of Nursing, originally a department of the School of Technology, became the School of Nursing under V. E. Tyler, who became dean of the Schools of Pharmacy, Nursing, and Health Sciences. Professor Johnson remained as head of the nursing school. The school developed a four-year baccalaureate program in nursing and in the late 1970s dropped the two-year associate degree program.

In 1976–77, Purdue was once again forced to cap enrollment in engineering for out-of-state students, thereby raising the ire of some out-of-state parents who also happened to be alumni. Management and forestry enrollments also had to be limited in 1976–77.

Despite that sore point, Hansen could look to widespread activity in graduate research. Across the campus, promising work continued in genetics and in the improvement of the protein content of corn and sorghum. Studies were pursued in the neurochemical basis for alcoholism; others worked in the regeneration of tissue electrically. Renewable resources engineering seemed to make much progress in the development of usable vehicular fuel from such cellulose material as corn stalks. Agricultural scientists teamed with engineers on several interdisciplinary projects. Food science research produced some remarkable new concepts. Research in the war on cancer involved more than sixty different units and groups across the Purdue system.

The residence halls bulged as enrollments soared.

Other activities across the campus seemed to reflect the optimistic tone of the late 1970s, marked by the successes of Purdue's intercollegiate athletics. Not having tasted the heady experience of a postseason bowl appearance since it won the Rose Bowl at Pasadena in 1967, the football team had winning seasons in 1978, 1979, and 1980, which carried them to three successive victories in the Peach Bowl, the Bluebonnet Bowl, and the Liberty Bowl.

Similarly in basketball, the teams were impressive with winning seasons and appearances in both the National Invitational and National Collegiate Athletic Association (NCAA) tournaments.

In retrospect, Hansen could tussle with the problems of gain and knew, on the positive side, that they were far more desirable than the problems of loss. In 1977–78, the energy problem seemed ubiquitous and demanded much attention at Purdue, not only from the standpoint of research in coal, petroleum, and reusable materials but also in the saving of the university's own costly energy. Hansen once replied to an interviewer that Purdue "is not in the energy [research] business because we want to be, but because we were asked to be."

From an energy standpoint, 1977–78 was frustrating, made more so by one of the coldest Indiana winters on record and by a long and debilitating coal strike. The energy pinch was felt everywhere on the campus. Although it was a cold winter, Hansen found it heartwarming that most of the best energy-saving ideas came from students—such as the one which suggested taking a shower with a friend to save hot water. Hansen took some solace in the fact that while the energy crunch was taken with a great deal of humor it was also met with a seriousness reflected in the fact that the university saved substantial amounts during the period. But in the end, it took its toll, and Hansen was a victim of one of those terrible-timing coincidences totally out of his control. He, Haas, and Ford made a decision in March of 1978 to extend the normal one-week spring break an additional week and then extend the spring semester one week in May to make up for the lost class days. Their reason was to stretch the university's dwindling coal supply.

Students accepted that idea with great enthusiasm, and many made plans for the extended vacation period. But before spring break week, the coal strike ended, and the extended vacation was cancelled. The Hansens' telephone rang incessantly for several days, most of the callers loosening streams of invectives at the man in charge, who really was not at fault. At a Purdue home basketball game in March, Hansen took the floor at halftime to explain the reasons for the change and was met with vociferous booing.

His son Paul, a student, came home one night to complain, "How could my own father do this to me?"

Though Hansen worked overtime to be as sensitive as possible to student concerns, it was tough work, evidenced by the continuing "battle" over residence hall visitation hours in which students of both sexes could visit friends in their dormitory rooms. The old "in loco parentis" rule—the university acts in place of the parents—had long been struck down, viewed by the young as an anachronism, by college administrators as largely unworkable in an era of liberal mores, and by parents as an absolute necessity. For Hansen and his staff, it was a terrible vise that squeezed relentlessly. The idea of student rights: Do they exist inherently? Or do they exist only contractually? Fate handed Hansen several tough and unpopular decisions to make.

Two such decisions were whether to approve the Gay Liberation Front and the Communist Youth Brigade as recognized student groups. Great furor was created by Hansen's decision to approve both, but it was a furor that died as quickly as it flared. The Communist Youth Brigade met with fourteen attending the first—and last—meeting.

"I took a lot of heat for those decisions," Hansen recalls, "but one cannot forget what a university stands for. If you destroy the right of free expression, regardless of how repugnant that expression may be, you have destroyed the university. Those of us who are in positions of university leadership cannot ever forget that we are stewards of a public trust."

●   ●   ●

The building program of the Hansen administration grew in intensity in 1978–79, and dollar-wise outdid the phenomenal and feverish building programs of both the Hovde and Elliott years. Under construction in 1977 was the Psychological Sciences Building, intended to replace Peirce Hall (built in 1904 as the Physics

Building, later served as the Biology Annex, later still as Stanley Coulter Annex, and finally Peirce Hall, named for Martin Peirce, an original member of the board of trustees and its first treasurer).

The Indiana General Assembly in 1978–79 provided almost unprecedented funds—$38.1 million in bonding authority (repaid through student fees) and appropriations to add a new Undergraduate Library, a three-level underground facility between Stewart Center and the State Street right-of-way ($9.3 million); an Agricultural and Research Building, built with outright appropriations ($8.4 million); an Intercollegiate Athletic Building, needed to take space pressure off other athletic facilities created by the growth in women's intercollegiate athletics ($4.5 million); and additions to the Recreational Gymnasium originally built in the late 1950s ($3.9 million).

Later, because of the success of the Plan for the Eighties, the new $8.5 million Life Sciences Research Building was constructed with gift funds. The Plan for the Eighties opened in 1980 and closed officially on May 1, 1982. The campaign originally sought $34.2 million. It ended with nearly $10 million more and was immediately termed the most successful fund drive in the university's history. Funds from the campaign produced not only the Life Sciences Research Center—a large part of which involves cancer research—but also funds for microprocessor laboratories for the School of Technology and for the Computer-Integrated Design Manufacturing and Automation Center (CIDMAC). CIDMAC was the brainchild of faculty in both engineering and management, a consortium that involved not only the Purdue schools but corporate industrial sponsors. The common ground of both is research into computer-aided design and manufacturing processes, industrial robotics, production planning and scheduling, automatic inspections, management, and marketing.

Also a recipient of the Plan for the Eighties funds was the Coal Research Center, established in 1979 to tackle the problems of coal gasification and synthetic fuels. Two gifts also were made to establish three new endowed professorial chairs. Overall, nearly every school at Purdue benefitted from the drive.

Meanwhile, building continued, and the Indiana General Assembly approved additional bonding authority to build the new Technology Building, since named Maurice G. Knoy Hall of Technology for the Purdue alumnus and Lafayette industrialist who devoted much of his time and money for the university's benefit. Knoy served a long tenure on the Purdue board of trustees and was its president during much of that period. The $14.8 million structure was built on the site of the former Michael Golden building. The Michael Golden Laboratories attached to it were not only saved but totally renovated beyond the wildest imaginings of the fiery Irish mechanics professor of the late 1800s and early 1900s who put the fear of God and practical mechanics in every engineering student who stepped across the threshold of his classroom.

Purdue University in 1980 and 1981 was a diverse and busy place. A new Department of Building Construction and Contracting was established in the School of Technology, and the General Assembly authorized the establishment of construction engineering and management within the School of Civil Engineering.

Medical research in the School of Science reached major proportions. The work of Michael E. Rossman in the basic structure of viruses was watched with interest throughout the world scientific community.

Herbert C. Brown became a Nobel laureate in 1979 as a co-winner for his research in boron chemistry, the first Purdue faculty member in the seventy-eight years of the Nobel prizes to be so honored.

Brown was the son of Jewish emigrants from Russia who moved first to London, where he was born in 1912, thence to Chicago, where the family name, Brovarnik, was anglicized to Brown. He showed such promise as a student that his mother relieved him of the chore of running his late father's hardware store so he could study chemistry, first at now-defunct Crane Junior College. Later, he studied chemistry privately with a former Crane instructor, entered Wright Junior College, and eventually studied at the University of Chicago, where he received the Ph.D. in 1938.

After college, he began to teach and do research at Wayne University (now Wayne State University) and in 1947 came to Purdue as a professor of chemistry. Twelve years later he was named R. B. Wetherill Professor of Chemistry, and the Nobel award was the culmination of a series of national awards and honors for his work in hydroboration chemistry.

Student fees went up again in 1980 for the fourth year in a row as the university's worst enemy, inflation, continued its blight. In construction alone, dollar value had always been the measure of building programs. In 1979–80, the dollar value of all construction under way at West Lafayette and the regional campuses was more than $45 million—but the square footage of all of the projects was far less than in former years.

Renovation of the Mechanical Engineering Building cost $2.5 million. A new Business and Industry Development Center, located west of the Krannert Building and built largely with gift funds, housed management research and development. It provided seminar facilities for management personnel returning to the university for "updating" their skills. Twenty projects to make the university's buildings more accessible to the physically handicapped were under way.

The close of the 1980–81 fiscal year was also the end of Hansen's decade as president, an occasion he chose to summarize in the president's annual report: "It has been at once a proudly exciting experience and a humbling one. I now realize how keen the perception of a venerated American educator was when he observed some years ago that at an institution of higher education, no one is likely to receive more education than the president. . . . Purdue is a very special place that transcends the ordinary."

As of June 30, 1981, research and teaching were vibrant, seeming not to show the effects of funding problems. Budgeting for research alone neared $80 million per year. The building program moved ahead; the campus seemed to be one large pile of gravel after another. New buildings worth more than $50 million were going up either at West Lafayette or the regional campuses, together with varied rehabilitation, renovation, and expansion projects. University Libraries approached 1.7 million volumes.

For 1980–81, the state appropriation was $97.2 million for Purdue—a far cry from the $4,500 the Indiana legislature had appropriated to run the university in 1880–81. Not only was the early appropriation a pittance, the legislature also detailed how every penny was to be spent. The lesson here is that while the amounts change and needs change, the struggle for the dollars a university needs has not changed. The state university is never state-supported, merely state-assisted. Struggle without end. Amen.

• • •

On November 12, 1981, Hansen informed the board of trustees that he would resign as president as soon as it found his replacement. There was no substantive reason for his leaving Purdue, except that he was tired.

"From our own personal standpoint, Nancy and I feel that the complete and total commitment that the presidency requires has left us little time to pursue other aspects of our private lives. This we now desire. It is wise [therefore] to now seek a new team that will take up where we leave off," Hansen wrote in his resignation letter.

Rumors had floated about the community for several months that Hansen might step down. A Lafayette *Journal and Courier* news story of June 30 attempted to confirm the fact that Hansen was a candidate for the chancellorship of the Texas A&M system. As it turned out, the newspaper's story was right on target.

Hansen told the board that he would remain until his successor was named or until June 30, 1982, whichever came first. Following Hansen's announcement, the selection machinery involving faculty, students, alumni, and adminstrators was put into place.

Hansen had not resigned, however, without some parting shots. He had seen the university through some tough times— financial austerity at a time of unprecedented growth in enrollment; sociological changes in attitude and mores, reflected among students as much as in the population generally, changes that ended forever the concept of in loco parentis (at least in the universities); the advent of rapidly moving technology which strained the university's resources merely to keep up.

At Hansen's final budget meeting with the trustees in June, the president read a prepared statement concerning not the budget itself but the long-run implications of financial and educational trends and their effect on the nation's supply of trained scientific and technical manpower. It was not an unusual tact for Hansen who worked throughout his eleven years to persuade the university to base today's decisions on their implications for tomorrow.

He said, in part:

> It is no overstatement to say that we are rapidly reaching a state of crisis. The demand for engineers, scientists, technologists, computer specialists, etc., already far outruns the supply. Every indication is that this demand will continue to increase, while the supply is decreasing.
>
> Here at Purdue, we have had to curtail enrollment in many of these areas on each of our campuses due to lack of resources, even though there are job opportunities for each of our graduates. Other universities around the nation face the same problem. Society is crying for men and women with these types of training, yet we are unable to admit qualified students because we do not have the resources—the faculty, the supplies and equipment, the laboratories—to handle them. We already have classes which are too large; we are often using obsolete equipment, and our teaching loads are so high that faculty are finding industry more attractive than the university.
>
> And the future appears no brighter. I frankly do not know where the faculty of 1990 or 2000 will come from. Because of the very attractive offers business and industry make to students

with bachelor's degrees, we cannot attract our better students to take the long, hard, low-paying road to a Ph.D. Why struggle for four or five years at a subsistence level, in order to take a job in a university at little if any more than you can now command with a bachelor's degree? The market is working very effectively. It is directing our best minds away from academic careers.

Beyond this, the market is also directing students who are good in mathematics and science away from high school teaching, to the extent that I have no idea who will teach these subjects in our high schools in the years ahead. There are so many attractive offers to a young man or woman with mathematical ability that he or she would be economically irrational to become a high school teacher.

My concern about all of this is not just a concern about Purdue University. Purdue is not an end in itself. As a state university, its reason for existence is to serve Indiana and the nation by providing educational opportunity for students and by discovering new knowledge. My concern is: How will Indiana and our nation meet the trained manpower needs of the future if we cannot offer educational opportunity to qualified students now, and if we cannot attract an adequate number of bright men and women into education to be our future professors and teachers?

This is particularly serious at a time when many of our most pressing national problems—energy, inflation, environmental concerns, health, and perhaps most important of all, the productivity increase necessary to regain our competitive position in the world economy—depend upon exactly the type of men and women who graduate from Purdue.

Inflation, of course, has been the main cause of our problem, compounded by a slumping state and national economy. Prices on the average have more than doubled in the past decade, and the costs of many of the items we require in the university have increased even more. Reduced state revenue has resulted in lower appropriations than otherwise would have been the case. And, at Purdue, enrollments have continued to grow because we have the types of programs which students want to study, due to the job opportunities available to our graduates.

Unfortunately, the Indiana Commission for Higher Education has adopted a wholly unrealistic formula for recommending funding for enrollment increases so that we have been receiving in state appropriations only about 15 percent to 20 percent of the average net cost for each additional student. . . .

I can honestly report to you that I believe no university in the nation is better managed than Purdue. We are getting the maximum out of each dollar entrusted to us. Yet I also must report that, because of all the steps we have taken to compensate for the decline in real dollars per student, we are not able to offer our students as high quality educational opportunity as we did a decade ago. We have slipped because there is a limit to the miracles we can perform.

I am most concerned, however, that we will slip much further in the next few years if the trends in financial support I have outlined are not revised. If there ever was any fat in Purdue's budget, it disappeared long ago. Any further reduction in real support per student can only result in a serious curtailment of the quality and quantity of opportunity we can offer. . . .

•   •   •

In a newspaper interview after he announced his intention to resign, Hansen called the "great erosion of personal life" the biggest drawback to serving as president of a large and complex scientific institution such as Purdue. "I've seen this same thing in my colleagues," Hansen reflected. "Somewhere along the line you say, 'Enough is enough'."

Hansen paid tribute to the university staff at all levels and told his interviewer that "it's due to them that we have been able to go as far as we have on our limited funds." He paused a moment, then added, "If I have pain at this moment, it's because I see so much potential in Purdue. We are properly positioned to take great strides in the next five to ten years."

Hansen also warned that while industries will be a great source of funding in coming years, "it's a careful line to walk. Industries must realize that we cannot survive or produce the quality of student they want without their help. But the danger always is that you must not let the tail wag the dog. The independence of the university must be preserved at all costs. You must watch it—really watch it."

Hansen won praise from all over the university community— much of it from the deans who served under him. President Emeritus Hovde, his predecessor, praised him for "great leadership" and said his leaving was a "sad thing," but he added, "I'm happy he's doing what he wants to be doing."

Hovde, who had more experience at the job than any other president, reflected on some other aspects of the Purdue presidency: "The job is always very difficult. With the money crunch, it's worse than it's been for some time."

Perhaps the most accurate assessment of Hansen's leaving came from George W. McNelly, dean of the School of Technology: "We're fortunate to have had him for ten years. We want the best for him. Everybody loves him."

•   •   •

The process of selecting Hansen's successor was well under way when the announcement was made in College Station, Texas, that Hansen—who had said "enough is enough" about college presidencies—was appointed chancellor of the Texas A&M system, a job that required that he oversee a statewide, 43,000-student conglomerate that included Texas A&M University at Galveston. He also supervised several other state agencies, including the state agricultural experiment station and extension service and the state engineering experiment station and extension service.

The Hansens were in the job about four years but found the cultural differences between Texas and their beloved Midwest so distracting that in 1986 he retired, and the couple returned to Indiana, settling in Zionsville, near Indianapolis. In 1987, he was named director of research for the Hudson Institute, an Indianapolis-based "think tank" once headed by Herman Kahn.

Meanwhile, the trustees had reached no conclusion about Hansen's successor, and the search continued. But in June 1982, the trustees had no trouble deciding on an acting president—John W. Hicks, who had served as executive assistant to two presidents since 1955. Perhaps no other man in Purdue history was as well suited or well trained for a college presidency as John Hicks. But he said, "I'm too old and too undignified." Yet a great many of the policies which had far-reaching implications for the university missions were fashioned and authored by Hicks. Beyond that, he was an extremely popular individual at Purdue among all he met. Eventually that included almost everyone on the payroll.

Hick's roots in Purdue went back thirty-six years when he came to Purdue from Massachusetts as a graduate student and instructor in agricultural economics. The trustees' choice of Hicks as acting president was as wise as it was logical. Not only was he one of the best-known and best-liked persons at Purdue, he had amply demonstrated an ability to get things done by deftly combining intelligence and an easygoing charm with a fierce and contagious loyalty to the university—not to mention an awesome knowledge of the ways of the university and its people. His liberal sense of humor and ability to laugh sharpened his perspective. Beyond such personal appeal, having served more than thirty years as the university's chief liaison (i.e., lobbyist) to the Indiana General Assembly, Hicks became a virtual walking encyclopedia on the Indiana legislature and legislators. He became so highly respected in the corridors of the statehouse that legislators more often than not sought him out for advice and counsel on pending bills, especially those affecting education.

Despite such savvy and personal appeal, Hicks did not fight the university's funding wars without developing an administrative toughness and ability to be a firm, no-nonsense leader.

Hicks was then sixty. He knew that his retirement was nearing and that his year as acting president, by necessity, would be, that of custodian. In jest, at the news conference at which Steven C. Beering's appointment was announced, Hicks quipped, "Now I can quit being president and get back to running the university."

Hicks's year as president was eventful despite the "custodial" label it was given. The university's new supercomputer, a CDC Cyber 205, gave Purdue computing power beyond anything available to most United States colleges and universities. It was instrumental in several breakthroughs, including new knowledge of the virus, a project directed by Michael Rossman, Purdue's genius in biochemistry and biological sciences. Hicks was also in on the formation of the Corporation for Science and Technology, based in Indianapolis. He could take credit for encouraging the establishment of a Business and Industrial Development Center at Purdue. He ceremonially opened the second phase of the Purdue Research Park, a university-oriented project of the Purdue Research Foundation aimed at bringing the expertise of academia and business-industry into a closer relationship, a development that began in 1961.

Hicks became acutely aware that Purdue could make an important and direct contribution toward reinforcing Indiana's economy which, at the moment, was undergoing the transition from a smokestack, hands-on economy to a highly technological and diverse "heads on" society.

Purdue's logical role, Hicks decided, was to buttress the economy through education of a new breed of highly trained industrial worker and thus, almost without infusion of new funds, began the Statewide Technology Program. Hicks put the program in place in 1982–83, but his successor moved ahead in an aggressive fashion. The program upgrades skills of workers for a changing, highly technical workplace that has raced past them.

As acting president, Hicks steered a steady course and made the transition for the new president much easier. In April 1983, in his last official appearance before the faculty at the required spring faculty convocation, Hicks gave the president's "state of the campus" talk, including his own assessment that the climate in Indiana was excellent for academic freedom, free of political influence and restrictions that would hinder Purdue's functions. He praised the trustees for their work and their management of

Purdue while "leaving academic matters completely in the hands of the faculty and the president."

He talked of the loyalty of the alumni body and the excellent relationship which he believed existed between the Greater Lafayette community and the university. But he admitted to disappointment in the Indiana Commission for Higher Education, established by the legislature in 1971, for making recommendations regarding appropriations and new degree programs.

He admitted that he hoped for a "more rational distribution of appropriations among campuses and perhaps also help to convince the legislature that a higher level of investment in higher education would be in the best interests of the people of the state. Unfortunately, the commission has not moved in either of these directions. As a result I have taken a rather hard line with the commission and I am not currently one of their favorites."

Hicks's speech also discussed the university internally, reporting on the "reasonably good shape" of the university's physical facilities and plant, adding that he believed faculty morale was "reasonably good—certainly I have never been more aware of the dedication of our faculty, academic administrators, our business and other administrators, and our professional, service, and clerical personnel."

Hicks closed on a personal note: "Finally, let me thank all of you for the kindness and consideration you have extended to me and my beloved wife, Swiftie, during my 'brief but colorful' career as your acting president. Let me tell you an interesting statistic. I will have spent 46 percent of my own life, and one-quarter of the life of Purdue University, in the president's office, as either executive assistant to the president or as acting president.

"You must forgive me if I seem to have a vested interest in Purdue."

•   •   •

On February 4, 1983, the board of trustees called a special session to make official their selection of Steven C. Beering, dean of the Indiana University School of Medicine and director of the IU Medical Center, as the ninth president of Purdue University in its 114-year history. The vote was unanimous; quite possibly the trustees had picked the best university presidential candidate on the national scene at the time.

At a news conference and picture-taking session immediately following the board meeting, Beering was formally introduced. With his wife, Jane, at his side, he proclaimed, "I accept the challenge and welcome the opportunity."

As chairman of the Indiana Medical Education Board, Beering had become acquainted with several Purdue administrators in the course of developing first-year medical school sites throughout Indiana, one of the most important at Purdue. Two who came to know and admire him were Presidents Hovde and Hansen.

Late in his presidency, Hovde first became aware of Beering's capabilities. He considered him a first-class candidate for the job. In a chat with Board President Donald S. Powers at the halftime of a Purdue basketball game shortly before he was last hospitalized, Hovde, the revered president emeritus, told Powers so. He jabbed his finger at Powers for emphasis. "If Purdue doesn't get Beering from IU," he smiled, "then you aren't doing your job."

Steven Claus Beering was born in Berlin, Germany, and reared in Hamburg. At a time when children should have been in school or engaged in other normal youth activities, young Steven Beering and his peers spent their time in shelters, wondering whether they would survive the relentless Allied aerial bombing in World War II.

Beering's family in 1948 moved to Pittsburgh, Pennsylvania, where he attended Taylor Allerdice, one of Pittsburgh's leading high schools. He graduated summa cum laude from the University of Pittsburgh in 1954 with a bachelor's degree in liberal arts and a Phi Beta Kappa key.

He received his medical degree from Pitt's School of Medicine in 1958 and served his internship at Walter Reed Hospital in Washington, D.C. His residency was in internal medicine and endocrinology (the physiology of the ductless glands) with the United States Air Force at San Antonio, Texas. Eventually, he became director of the education-in-medicine section of the Air Force's Wilford Hall Medical Center there. He was chief of the center's internal medicine section and a lieutenant colonel when he joined the faculty of the Indiana University School of Medicine at Indianapolis in 1969.

Beering was named dean of the school and director of the IU Medical Center in 1974 and served in those difficult positions until Purdue beckoned him for its presidency. He is the second medical doctor to be appointed as Purdue president. The first president, Richard Owen, also held an M.D. degree (although he was not a practioner) when he was elected as Purdue's president in 1871.

•   •   •

Fred Hovde lay gravely ill in the intensive care unit of Home Hospital in Lafayette when Beering, shortly after he was appointed president, made a brief bedside visit. Intensive care units were not new to Beering; he had worked in them countless times. This was different. This was emotional. This was two Purdue presidents, one who had given his life to it, the other about to embark on the same adventure. Beering had come to have high regard for the beloved former president. Now Hovde was mortally ill; he seemed to know that he had not long to live. He had been hospitalized several times before for respiratory ailments, the toll of years of chain-smoking. A 1978 stroke left him partially paralyzed.

Beering and Hovde chatted quietly, nearly in whispers. After a few moments, noting Hovde's weakened and tired condition, Beering said his goodbye. "I think," Hovde whispered in response, "I can die peacefully now—knowing that Purdue is still in good hands."

Afterword

Bob Topping's history of Purdue through its first eight presidents is charged with the excitement and the sense of destiny that have characterized the university from the beginning.

When I became the ninth chief executive in 1983, I was deeply impressed with the institution's administrative efficiency and awed by its vast potential. Purdue students are bright and highly motivated. Faculty are committed to teaching excellence and research leadership. Alumni are loyal and excited about the university's future.

It is the future that I wish to address in this afterword. As I write, Purdue is undergoing enormous growth. We are engaged in one of the largest building projects in our history, and the campuses are transforming before our eyes. But buildings and other physical facilities are merely the outward manifestations of far deeper changes.

The Class of 1950 is raising funds to build a state-of-the-art lecture hall; the Class of 1948 has made a decision to build a bell tower, which will become a centerpiece of the West Lafayette campus; the Class of 1939 is committed to building a retreat center, to include an interfaith chapel, in a wooded glade in Horticulture Park. Never before have Purdue classes sought such ambitious challenges. Our alumni are poised to support and influence the university's growth at whole new levels.

As we assess our needs for the coming fiscal year, a top priority is funding for a new classroom-office building. The building will help us adjust to enrollments which are at record levels, despite a decline in the national pool of people in the traditional college-age groups. More specifically, though, the building will accommodate a huge growth in the humanities disciplines. Enrollment in these programs now equals that of the engineering schools.

This demographic shift in Purdue's student body is only one of the fundamental changes that have occurred in recent years; and the university, as a dynamic enterprise, must respond to all of them. It has been argued that Purdue should limit the pursuit of excellence to the fields in which it has been outstanding throughout its history—that it will dilute its quality by trying to achieve national stature in too many disciplines. I disagree with that position.

In fact, we have no choice. From the instant a program is installed as a major field of study, the university has an obligation to make that program worthy of a Purdue degree. Our students choose Purdue because of the quality associated with its name. The philosophy major has the same right to fulfill his or her dreams as the aspiring engineer. The management graduate will carry Purdue's name into the working world just as proudly as the chemist. Rather than limiting us, our tradition of excellence in some fields can inspire us to greatness in every endeavor.

As we chart our course for the twenty-first century, we must aim high. Many of the children born as this book comes off the presses in 1988 will be graduating from Purdue in the year 2010. In those twenty-two years, this university has the potential to become one of the handful of educational insitutions universally recognized as having major impacts on world thinking. When people speak of Harvard, Oxford, Cambridge, the University of Paris, Purdue's name should be included.

It is within our power to achieve that status if we begin by dreaming big, if we persevere by working hard, and if we self-lessly remember that the fruits of our efforts are to be enjoyed not by us but by future generations.

Contrary to the ivory-tower image perpetuated in folklore, a great university must be very much a part of the world. Our business is to confront the problems that beset humankind at every level. This can be as simple and direct as an extension agent helping a farmer improve his crop yield, and it can be as complex and arcane as grappling with issues that can affect the survival of the planet.

Futurists have identified six problems with which the world must deal in the next century. These include the nuclear arms race, the growing gap between the rich and poor, overpopulation, the environment, public morality, and education. Each of those problems has enormous implications, and none of them will be solved without assistance from the great research universities. Purdue will be a part of meeting the challenge. The prospect is frightening but tremendously exciting. Because this university can contribute, it must participate.

To take on global issues, however, is not enough. We must also tend to the daily business of making Purdue an ever-improving institution. In building an agenda for a better Purdue, we find that it also is an agenda for a better America and a better world. As I look at the decades ahead, here are some of the vital issues with which I believe the university must deal:

Enrollment.   The number of students on the West Lafayette campus should remain in the 32,000 to 34,000 range, regardless of national trends. All of the regional campuses should continue orderly growth to meet the needs of their individual communities. The demographics of the

main campus enrollment will change somewhat as individual
schools respond to the job market and we recruit a larger
number of exceptional students and minority students. The
Graduate School enrollment of slightly more than 5,000
students currently is the smallest in the Big Ten. We must
increase this number substantially for two reasons: first, there
is a correlation between graduate education and the quality
of research; second, our universities will face a serious faculty
shortage unless more Americans pursue the advanced degrees
necessary for academic careers.

Internationalism.   We can no longer think of America
as a monolithic nation. The world's economies, cultures, and
languages will become more and more interdependent. Purdue
will respond to this change in a number of ways. The educations our students receive must better prepare them for lives
and careers in a multinational environment; the university's
Pacific Rim Initiative is a beginning step in this direction.
Purdue also must help the state of Indiana and the United
States compete in the business climate of the future. Our
development of new knowledge through research, the transfer of that knowledge to the working economy, and the education of our students all must keep up with a very fast-paced
world.

Financial support.   Purdue's financial support comes
from four primary sources. Three of them must increase and
the fourth must remain stable. The first three are:

- *State funding.*   State support for higher education has
  dropped significantly in real dollars since the early
  1970s. The state government is growing more aware of
  the value of investing in Purdue, and the university will
  continue to seek a level of funding that will allow it to
  maximize its service.
- *Private funding.*   Gifts from alumni, corporations, and
  foundations are of increasing importance. Although private support is enthusiastic and growing, Purdue is not
  yet at the gift level of many comparable universities; that
  fact must change in the near future. The gifts of alumni
  and friends are the real difference between adequacy
  and greatness for a university.
- *Research funding.*   Corporations, foundations, and the
  federal government are the primary sources for this funding, which is a true measure of a university's excellence.
  Research contracts are awarded competitively: when one
  of our faculty members or research centers is awarded

a grant, it is because the funding agency believes Purdue is the best institution to solve the problem. I am exceptionally proud that our research funding has nearly doubled to the $100 million level, putting Purdue in the top echelon of universities that do not have medical schools. This growth must continue.

The fourth source of funds is student fees. Assuming a stable enrollment, fees should also remain at about the same level with adjustments for inflation.

Education technology.   The electronics revolution with the accompanying development of computer, satellite, and video technology has revolutionized education. The walls of the university are much less important than they once were. Although the traditional on-campus education will remain at the center of our efforts, there are virtually no barriers to delivering courses anywhere in the world; and Purdue is in the vanguard of the utilization of this capability. The timing is fortuitous, because one of the great challenges of the twenty-first century will be adult education. The need to keep up with changing technology on the job and the growing recognition that education is a lifetime—rather than a once-in-a-lifetime—experience mean that the older student increasingly will be an off-campus consumer of higher education.

Reaching downward.   A growing concern on campus is that many students are enrolling in college without the basic skills they need to be successful. If high schools and grade schools are not properly preparing our children for future challenges, we must accept some of the responsibility. We must be certain that we communicate to educators what we expect, and, if necessary, we should develop programs in cooperation with the school systems to ensure that students come to college with the academic backgrounds they need to survive.

As you can see from the foregoing sampler, there is no shortage of jobs for Purdue. The future—bristling with challenges and bright with opportunity—awaits us, and we are eager to greet it. This book of our history is but a short pause for reflection. On this last page, we cannot write, ''The End.'' Instead, let us state, ''To Be Continued.''

Steven C. Beering
President
Purdue University

Appendix

I. CHRONOLOGY OF PURDUE UNIVERSITY PRESIDENTS

Richard Owen (1810–90)* August 13, 1872–March 10, 1874. [0]†

John S. Hougham (1821–94), acting, (unofficial) March 11, 1874–June 11, 1874

Abraham C. Shortridge (1833–1919) June 12, 1874–November 5, 1875. [65]

John S. Hougham, acting, November 6, 1875–April 30, 1876

Emerson E. White (1829–1902) May 1, 1876–August 22, 1883.[150]

James H. Smart (1841–1900) August 23, 1883–February 21, 1900. [231]

Winthrop E. Stone, acting, February 22, 1900–June 30, 1900

Winthrop E. Stone (1862–1921) July 1, 1900–August 4, 1921. [1,012]

Henry W. Marshall (1865–1951), acting, August 4, 1921–August 31, 1922

Edward C. Elliott (1874–1960) September 1, 1922–June 30, 1945. [3,360]

Andrey A. Potter (1882–1979), acting, July 1, 1945–December 31, 1945

Frederick L. Hovde (1908–83) January 1, 1946–June 30, 1971. [11,472]

Arthur G. Hansen (1925–) July 1, 1971–June 30, 1982. [35,864‡]

John W. Hicks (1921–), acting, July 1, 1982–June 30, 1983

Steven C. Beering (1932–) July 1, 1983–. [47,729‡]

---

* (   ) Birth and death years
† [   ] First fall enrollment after taking office
‡ Includes all campuses

II. BOARD OF TRUSTEES PRESIDENTS

1865–67	Oliver Perry Morton*
1867–73	Conrad Baker*
1873–75	Thomas A. Hendricks*
1875–77	John Randolph Coffroth
1877–79	Mahlon Dickerson Manson
1879–81	John Sutherland
1881–88	Joseph E. Ratliff
1888–99	Charles Benedict Stuart
1899–1907	William Vaughn Stuart
1907–16	Addison C. Harris
1916–23	Joseph Doty Oliver
1923–27	Henry Wright Marshall
1927–43	David Edward Ross
1943–44	James William Noel
1944–46	John A. Hillenbrand
1946–50	Allison Ellsworth Stuart
1950–65	William A. Hanley
1965–68	J. Ralph Thompson
1968–79	Maurice G. Knoy
1979–81	Robert E. Heine
1981–	Donald S. Powers

* Governor of Indiana and president ex officio of the board

III. PURDUE VICE PRESIDENTS (to 1987)

Frederick N. Andrews (Hovde, Hansen)* for research and
    dean of the Graduate School
Struther Arnott (Hansen, Beering) for research and dean of
    the Graduate School
Donald R. Brown (Hansen, Beering) for academic services†
Leonard W. Bucklin (Hansen) for advancement(development)
Kenneth P. Burns (Hansen, Beering) for physical facilities†
Paul F. Chenea (Hovde) for academic affairs
John S. Day (Hansen) for development
Michael J. Ferin (Beering) for development
William J. Fischang (Hansen, Beering) for student services
Frederick R. Ford (Hansen, Beering) executive vice president
    and treasurer†
Lytle J. Freehafer (Hovde, Hansen) and treasurer
Ronald L. Fruitt (Beering) for housing and food services†
Richard E. Grace (Beering) for student services†
Robert A. Greenkorn (Beering) for research†
Felix Haas (Hansen, Beering) executive vice president and
    provost
George A. Hawkins (Hovde, Hansen) for academic affairs
John W. Hicks (Beering) senior vice president
Frank Hockema (Elliott, Hovde) and executive dean
John M. Huie (Beering) for state relations†
Charles H. Lawshe (Hovde, Hansen) for regional campus
    administration
Howard S. Lyon (Beering) for business services†
Donald R. Mallett (Hovde, Hansen) and executive dean for
    student services
Robert L. Ringel (Beering) and dean of the Graduate School†
John C. Smalley (Hansen) for housing and food services
R. B. Stewart (Hovde) and treasurer
Winthrop E. Stone (Smart)
Varro E. Tyler (Beering) executive vice president for aca-
    demic affairs
Walter W. Wade (Hansen) for physical facilities
Charles B. Wise (Hansen, Beering) for business services and
    assistant treasurer
Charles B. Wise (Beering) for development†
Ernest C. Young (Hovde) for research and dean of the
    Graduate School

* (   ) Denotes president(s) served under.
† Denotes incumbent as of July 1, 1987.
Note: The previous listing does not include persons who have served as
vice presidents of the Purdue Research Foundation.

IV. DEANS OF PURDUE UNIVERSITY (listed chronologically)

Agriculture
John H. Skinner
Harry J. Reed
Earl L. Butz
Richard L. Kohls
Bernard L. Liska
Robert L. Thompson

Consumer and Family Sciences (Home Economics)
Ivy Frances Harner (head)
Henrietta Calvin (head)
Mary L. Matthews
Beulah V. Gillaspie
Gladys Vail
Eva L. Goble
Norma H. Compton
Donald W. Felker

Continuing Education
Charles H. Lawshe
Earl L. Butz
Donald R. Brown

Engineering
William F. M. Goss
Charles H. Benjamin
Andrey A. Potter
George A. Hawkins
Richard E. Grosh
John C. Hancock
Henry T. Yang

Graduate School
R. G. Dukes
Ernest C. Young
Frederick N. Andrews
Struther Arnott
Robert L. Ringel

Humanities, Social Science, and Education
Marbury B. Ogle
Robert L. Ringel
David A. Caputo

Medicine (1905–7)

Henry Jameson, M.D.

Management

E. M. Weiler
John S. Day
Keith V. Smith
Ronald E. Frank

Pharmacy and Pharmacal Sciences

R. W. Warder
Arthur L. Green
Charles B. Jordan
Glenn L. Jenkins
Varro E. Tyler (also dean of School of Nursing and School of Health Sciences)
Charles O. Rutledge (also dean of School of Nursing and School of Health Sciences)

Regional Campuses (Administrative Dean for)

G. Walter Bergren

Science

Stanley Coulter
R. B. Moore
Howard E. Enders
W. L. Ayres
Felix Haas
Allan H. Clark
Kenneth L. Kliewer

Technology

Charles H. Lawshe
George W. McNelly
Don K. Gentry

Veterinary Medicine

Leslie M. Hutchings
Erskine V. Morse
Jack J. Stockton
Hugh B. Lewis

Deans of Men, Women, Students

DEANS OF WOMEN

Carolyn E. Shoemaker
Dorothy C. Stratton
Clare Coolidge (acting)
Helen B. Schleman
M. Beverley Stone

DEANS OF MEN

Stanley Coulter
Martin L. Fisher
Fred I. Goldsmith
George E. Davis
Donald R. Mallett
O. D. Roberts
Bryan Clemens

DEANS OF STUDENTS

M. Beverley Stone
Barbara I. Cook
Betty M. Nelson

V. DEANS, DIRECTORS, AND/OR CHANCELLORS, REGIONALCAMPUSES

Calumet

Harold Short
Thaddeus Lutes
Millard Gyte
Carl H. Elliott
Richard J. Combs

Fort Wayne

Conwell Poling
Richard M. Bateman
Robert L. Ewigleben
D. Richard Smith
Roger J. Manges
Donald Schwartz
Joseph P. Guisti
Thomas P. Wallace

Purdue North Central
Ralph Waterhouse
Robert F. Schwarz
John Tucker
Dale W. Alspaugh

Indianapolis (IUPUI)
Alton W. Collins
Clifford Larsen
Jack M. Ryder

Note: Purdue and Indiana universities consolidated their Indianapolis campuses under IU management in 1969; the first chancellor of IUPUI was Maynard Hine, who had been dean of the IU School of Dentistry.

VI. REGIONAL CAMPUSES, SCHOOLS, FOUNDING DATES, DEANS

Calumet
GENERAL STUDIES (1969)

Carl H. Elliott (interim)
Jose Gonzales
Alan Gross
Alfred D. Sander
Samuel Paravanian
Saul Lerner

Note: Sander, Paravanian, and Lerner served as acting deans. Lerner is incumbent.

LIBERAL ARTS AND SCIENCES (1985)

Carol B. Gartner

PROFESSIONAL STUDIES (1985)

C. A. Stevens

Fort Wayne
ARTS AND LETTERS (1986)

Dwight F. Henderson
Julius J. Smulkstys

ENGINEERING, TECHNOLOGY, AND NURSING (1977)
John F. Dalphin
Warren W. Worthley

SCIENCE AND HUMANITIES (1976)
Elmer E. Anderson
James Bundschuh

The Indiana University-Purdue Campus at Fort Wayne underwent a realignment of the various academic units. Effective August 1, 1987, divisions and directors were as follows:

ARTS AND SCIENCES
Julius J. Smulkstys (acting)

BUSINESS AND MANAGEMENT
George W. M. Bullion

FINE AND PERFORMING ARTS
James D. Ator (acting)

EDUCATION
Marjorie E. Sowers

HEALTH SCIENCES ADMINISTRATION
Peter T. Zonakis

ENGINEERING AND TECHNOLOGY
Warren W. Worthley

Indianapolis (IUPUI)

ENGINEERING AND TECHNOLOGY (1972)
R. Bruce Renda*

SCIENCE (1972)
William E. Nevill
Marshall C. Yovits*

*Incumbent

VII. UNIVERSITY LIBRARIANS

Faculty Assignees (1874–77)
Jesse H. Blair (student)
Eulora J. Miller
Moses C. Stevens
Richard W. Swan
Elizabeth Day Swan
Blanche L. Miller, acting, (1903–4)
William M. Hepburn
John Moriarty
Joseph M. Dagnese

VIII. FOUNDING DATES OF THE SCHOOLS,
WEST LAFAYETTE

Agriculture 1874
Consumer and Family Sciences 1905 (as Department of
    Home Economics), 1926 (as School of Home Economics),
    1976 (as School of Consumer and Family Sciences)
Engineering (first degree awarded 1878)
    Aeronautics and Astronautics 1945
    Chemical 1911
    Civil Engineering 1887
    Electrical Engineering 1888
    Industrial Engineering 1961
    Materials Engineering (Metallurgical) 1959
    Mechanical Engineering 1882
    Nuclear Engineering 1975 (established as department 1957)
Health Sciences 1979
Humanities, Social Science, and Education 1963
Management 1958
Nursing 1963
Pharmacy and Pharmacal Sciences 1884
Science 1907
Technology 1964
Veterinary Medicine 1957
Graduate School 1929

IX. SIGNIFICANT DATES IN PURDUE HISTORY

- Signing of the Morrill Act (land grant) by President
  Lincoln—July 2, 1862.
- Indiana General Assembly passage of bill
  establishing Purdue University in Tippecanoe
  County—May 6, 1869 (founding date).

- Groundbreaking, first building, by Martin L. Peirce— August 9, 1871.
- First day of classes—September 16, 1874.
- Women students first admitted—Fall semester, 1875.
- John Purdue's death—5 P.M., September 12, 1876.
- First telephone installed on the campus—September 4, 1879.
- University band first established—1886.
- Agricultural Experiment Station founded with Hatch Act funds—1887.
- Colors old gold and black adopted—October 29, 1887.
- First intercollegiate football game—October 29, 1887.
- First honorary degrees awarded to Alembert Winthrop Brayton, honorary doctor of science, and John Newell Hurty, honorary doctor of pharmacy—1888.
- "Boilermakers" nickname adopted for athletic teams—1889.
- Heavilon Hall dedicated—January 19, 1894.
- Heavilon Hall destroyed by explosion and fire—January 23, 1894.
- Big Ten Conference established under leadership of President James H. Smart—January 11, 1895.
- Second Heavilon Hall built and occupied—1896.
- First Ph.D. awarded to Daniel McDougal—1897 (agriculture).
- Deaths of Purdue presidents while in office: James H. Smart—February 21, 1900. Winthrop E. Stone—July 17, 1921.
- First intercollegiate basketball game—1897 (men); 1975 (women).
- Purdue Agricultural Alumni Association organized—1902.
- Football team train wreck, Indianapolis—October 31, 1903.
- Purdue Alumni Association formed—1912.
- "Hail Purdue" copyrighted—1913. (Words written in 1912 by James Morrison, '15, and music by Edward J. Wotawa, '12, shortly thereafter. Song first called "Purdue War Song.")
- Engineering Experiment Station founded—1917.
- Purdue Radio Station WBAA licensed as the first radio station in Indiana—1922.

- University's third power and heating plant (North Power Plant) completed with 250-foot smokestack—1924. (Smokestack lowered by 11 feet in the mid-1960s and by 16 feet more in 1984. As of 1987, it was 223.38 feet from ground level.)
- Purdue Memorial Union opened—1924 (dedication in 1929).
- Purdue University Airport established—1930.
- Purdue Research Foundation incorporated—December 30, 1930.
- Purdue Musical Organizations established—1932.
- Amelia Earhart and Lillian Gilbreth join staff as visiting consultants—1935.
- Dedication of Hall of Music—May 3–4, 1940 (named for President Emeritus Edward C. Elliott—January 1958).
- Bleachers collapse at Purdue-Wisconsin basketball game—February 24, 1947.
- Purdue defeats University of Southern California in Rose Bowl—January 1, 1967.
- Centennial Year observance—1969.
- Students occupy Purdue Memorial Union in ''lounge-in''—Gala Week, May 1969.
- Arrest of 221 Purdue Memorial Union ''lounge-in'' protesters; occupation by students of Hovde Hall of Administration and their dispersal by Indiana State Police—May 6, 1969.
- Black Cultural Center established—June 6, 1969 (dedicated December 4, 1970).
- President's Council organized—1972.
- Statewide Technology established—1982–83.
- Visit by President Ronald Reagan to the West Lafayette Campus—April 9, 1987.

X. FIRST MALE AND FEMALE GRADUATES

John Bradford Harper, Indianapolis, B.S., chemistry—1875.
Eulora J. Miller, Lafayette, B.S., major unknown—1878.

XI. PURDUE UNIVERSITY PROFILE, 1987

Enrollment (fall, all campuses): 51,835.
Physical plant value: $585 million.
Operating budgets (all campuses): $563.4 million.
Number of staff and faculty (full and parttime): 12,800.
Living alumni (fall, 1987): 229,166.

Bibliography

In addition to the material listed, I used sundry articles and clippings from the *Purdue Exponent,* the Lafayette *Journal and Courier,* the *Purdue Alumnus, Perspective,* and the annual reports of the presidents.

BOOKS AND BOOK-LENGTH MANUSCRIPTS

Albjerg, Victor Lincoln. *Richard Owen: Scotland 1810, Indiana 1880.* Lafayette, Indiana: Archives of Purdue, 1946.

Ankenbruck, John. *The Creation Years.* (Indiana University-Purdue University at Fort Wayne). Fort Wayne, Indiana: Indiana University-Purdue University Foundation at Fort Wayne, 1983.

Beard, Reed. *The Battle of Tippecanoe.* Lafayette, Indiana: Tippecanoe Publishing Company, 1889.

Bennett, Joseph L. *Boilermaker Music Makers: Al Stewart and the Purdue Musical Organizations.* West Lafayette, Indiana: Purdue University, 1986.

Burrin, Frank K. *Edward C. Elliott, Educator.* Lafayette, Indiana: Purdue University Studies, 1970.

Collins, Bob. *Boilermakers: A History of Purdue Football.* Lafayette, Indiana: Haywood Printing Company, 1976.

Coulter, John G. *The Dean.* [Stanley Coulter]. West Lafayette, Indiana: Purdue Alumni Association, 1940.

Dehart, Richard P. *Past and Present of Tippecanoe County.* Indianapolis: B. F. Brown and Company, 1909.

Eckles, Robert E. *The Dean.* [A. A. Potter]. West Lafayette, Indiana: Purdue University, 1974.

————. "History of Services to Indiana: The Purdue School of Agriculture, 1874–1974." West Lafayette, Indiana: unpublished manuscript.

————. *Purdue Pharmacy: The First Century.* West Lafayette, Indiana: Purdue University, 1979.

Fatout, Paul. *Indiana Canals.* West Lafayette, Indiana: Purdue University Press, 1972.

Freehafer, Ruth W. *R. B. Stewart and Purdue University.* West Lafayette, Indiana: Purdue University, 1983.

Hand, Helen, and Thomas R. Johnston. *The Trustees and the Officers of Purdue University, 1865–1940.* Lafayette, Indiana: Archives of Purdue, 1940.

Hawkins, Barbara M., and the Tippecanoe County Medical Society. "Men and Women of Medicine in Tippecanoe County, Indiana, and Their Societies, 1825–1976." Lafayette, Indiana: unpublished manuscript on file at Tippecanoe County Historical Association.

Hayman, Allen, ed. *Commemorative Book of Tippecanoe County, 1826–1976.* Lafayette, Indiana: Greater Lafayette Chamber of Commerce, 1976.

Hepburn, William M., and Louis M. Sears. *Purdue University: Fifty Years of Progress.* Indianapolis, Indiana: Hollenbeck Press, 1925.

Kelly, Fred C. *David Ross: Modern Pioneer.* New York: Alfred A. Knopf, 1946.

Knoll, H. B. *The Story of Purdue Engineering.* West Lafayette, Indiana: Purdue University Studies, 1963.

Kriebel, Robert C. *150 Years of Lafayette Newspapers.* Lafayette, Indiana: Tippecanoe County Historical Association, 1981.

Mayberry, Susannah. *My Amiable Uncle: Recollections about Booth Tarkington.* West Lafayette, Indiana: Purdue University Press, 1983.

Munro, George W. "The New Purdue: Sketches of Hitching-Rack Days." West Lafayette, Indiana: unpublished manuscript, 1946.

————. "John Purdue and Purdue University: A Study of the Relations between Them from Its Organization to His Death." West Lafayette, Indiana: unpublished manuscript, 1946.

Parker, William B. *The Life and Public Services of Justin Smith Morrill.* Boston and New York: Houghton Mifflin Company, 1924. (Reprint, New York: DaCapo Press, 1971.)

Smith, William Henry. *The History of the State of Indiana.* Indianapolis: publisher unknown, 1897.

Stoke, Harold W. *The American College President.* New York: Harper, 1959.

Tobin, Terence, ed. *Letters of George Ade.* West Lafayette, Indiana: Purdue University Studies, 1973.

Topping, Robert W. *The Hovde Years.* West Lafayette, Indiana: Purdue University, 1980.

Wallace, Robert B., Jr. *Dress Her in White and Gold: A Biography of Georgia Tech* (revised edition). Atlanta: The Georgia Tech Foundation, Inc., 1969.

Webb, Cecil S. *Historical Growth of the Schools of Lafayette, Indiana.* Lafayette, Indiana: Lafayette School Corporation, 1972.

Wells, Herman B. *Being Lucky.* Bloomington, Indiana: Indiana University Press, 1980.

Wiley, Harvey W. *An Autobiography.* Indianapolis: Bobbs-Merrill Company, 1930.

Yost, John J. *Quasqui Collection.* Kentland, Indiana: Bartlett Press, 1985.

OTHER SOURCES

Boilermaker Media Guide (1982, 1987). Published annually by the Office of Sports Information, Purdue University.

Brown, Mary Wallace. "Reminiscences." *Purdue Exponent,* October 29, October 31, 1916.

"The Building of a Red Brick Campus: The Growth of Purdue as Recalled by Walter Scholer [1890–1972]." Transcribed from audio tape and published in booklet form by the Tippecanoe County Historical Association, Lafayette, Indiana, in 1983.

Cooke, Sarah. "Letters of Jacob Sickler (1848–1852)" Part 2. *Weatenotes* (newsletter of the Tippecanoe County Historical Association, Lafayette, Indiana), vol. 12, no. 2 (April 1983).

Cousins, Norman. "The Promise of a University." Speech to National Assembly, Council for the Advancement and Support of Education. Reprinted *CASE Currents* (Washington, D.C.), September 1979, pp 6–10.

Davis, Edward H. "Birthday of John Purdue." Prepared for the 105th anniversary of the founder's birthday, October 31, 1907. Manuscript in Purdue Libraries Special Collections. Also printed in the *Purdue Exponent,* October 31, 1907.

Dunn, Oliver C. "A Brief History of the Purdue University Libraries—1874–1971." Unpublished manuscript, 1973, in Purdue University Libraries.

Hicks, John W. "A Brief History of Public Higher Education in Indiana." Unpublished manuscript, 1984, at Purdue University.

Holmstedt, Raleigh W. "The Indiana Conference of Higher Education—1945–1965." Bulletin of the School of Education, Indiana University, Bloomington, vol. 43, no. 1 (1967).

Hutchins, Robert M. "A Letter to the Reader." Introduction to Greek Books Series (Santa Barbara, California), September 1963.

"John Purdue," *Debris* (Purdue University yearbook), 1900, pp. 19–22.

"Mechanical Engineering at Purdue, 1882–1982—One Hundred Years of Progress." Brochure published by the Purdue University School of Engineering, 1982.

Munro, George W. "John Purdue." *The Purdue Alumnus,* vol. 41, no. 2 (November 1953), pp. 2–3, 21.

Obituary notices (John Purdue), Lafayette *Journal,* Indianapolis *Daily Sentinel,* and Indianapolis *Daily News,* all dated September 13, 1876.

Purdue Athletics: "A Century of Excellence," Manual published by John Purdue Club and Athletic Public Relations Office, Purdue University, 1987.

"Purdue—Yesterday and Today." Published 1949 by Purdue University observing seventy-fifth year of classes.

Schmidt, Charles V. "When Fraternities Survived at Purdue." *Indianapolis Star Magazine,* May 2, 1976, pp. 44–45.

Smart, James H. "An Educational Outlook." Inaugural address to Indiana State Teachers Association as incoming president, December 30, 1873. Pamphlet in Purdue University Libraries, Special Collections.

————— . "Concerning Agriculture in Purdue University." Bulletin issued in 1891. Pamphlet in Purdue University Libraries, Special Collections.

————— . "Remarks of President J. H. Smart of Purdue University." Speech to the State Board of Agriculture at Indianapolis, January 1884. Pamphlet in Purdue University Libraries, Special Collections.

————— . "Technical Education." *The Inland Educator,* vol. 2, no. 4 (May 1896). Text of speech before the Lehigh University Club banquet, Chicago, Illinois, January 4, 1896. Pamphlet in Purdue University Libraries, Special Collections.

Themmesh, The Rev. Hilary. "Education Is about Civilization; Lose Sight of That and You Lose Sight of Humanity." "Point of View," *The Chronicle of Higher Education,* June 20, 1984, p. 64.

Wallace, Ella. "Faults Fail to Tarnish 'Greatness' of John Purdue." Reprinted from 1897 in Lafayette *Journal and Courier,* May 31, 1981.

White, Emerson E. "The Education of Labor." Address for the State Agricultural Society of Indiana, Indianapolis, January 8, 1878. Pamphlet in Purdue University Libraries, Special Collections.

————— . "Inaugural Address" (July 16, 1876). Printed in 1876 by order of the Purdue University Board of Trustees. Pamphlet in Purdue University Libraries, Special Collections.

Index

399